SUCCESSION

SEASON FOUR

T0323164

SUCCESSION
SEASON FOUR

The Complete Scripts

faber

First published in 2023
by Faber and Faber Limited
The Bindery, 51 Hatton Garden
London EC1N 8HN

Typeset by Brighton Gray
Printed and bound at CPI Books Ltd, Croydon CR0 44Y

A CIP record for this book
is available from the British Library

978-0-571-37977-4

6 8 10 9 7 5

Contents

S U C C E S S I O N
SEASON FOUR

Introduction

When *Succession* was commissioned by HBO I had previously managed to produce a grand total of one hour of filmed television drama as a solo writer. Even that was under the supervision of Charlie Brooker, within the tonal world he had created for his *Black Mirror* anthology. But after my second solo hour was complete – the *Succession* pilot – I rather suddenly found myself alone as the showrunner, final authority and decider on a hundred-million-dollar-plus enterprise. The step up in terms of responsibility was vertiginous. I bought a book called *The TV Showrunner's Roadmap*, but was too intimidated and too busy to ever open it.*

But of all the challenges and responsibilities of the years running the show, the question that weighed by far the heaviest was deciding when to draw it to a close.

It was back when we were still writing the third season that I started sketching out options. Even though the motor in the room was still running hot and we still had ideas – lots and lots of ideas – and even though all the complicated ways people can be still felt inexhaustible, nevertheless the big plot engine, the brutal materialist plumbing which ran under the show, was looking to me like it would eventually start to lose pressure.

Out in the world, legacy media's battle with tech was not a fair fight, it was a rout. The particular generational tussles that were the background to the show were ending the way all generational fights do, as Redstone passed away, Murdoch faded, Prince Philip and then Queen Elizabeth died. The swashbuckling dealmakers of the end of the last century, it seemed to me, had given way to the Thiel generation of Elon, Daniel Ek and Zuckerberg. The action had moved on and we needed to get out of legacy media almost as fast as Rupert had.

---

* I still sometimes fear someone from Business Affairs at HBO is going to call up and say, 'You urgently need to send through all the forms, the B-47Ps by end of day,' or 'Sorry but we don't seem to have all the receipts for the film stock you used?' and I'll have to admit I've done it all wrong and hand back my salary.

So once season three was complete and aired, in December 2021, I got my fellow executive-producer–writers together. Lucy, Tony, Jon and Will joined me at my office in Brixton to look at the alternative future season shapes I'd written up on the walls: one final season of ten episodes, or two of six or eight episodes. My sense was that we should do one last full-fat season rather than stretch it out. But I was wary of saying goodbye too fast to all the relationships and opportunities, of leaving creative money on the table, regretting all the subplots that would go unwritten, the jokes left untold.

We went round the room at the end of the day, this little committee on whether to whack the show. Will, the cold-hearted killer, voted over Zoom for just one more season. Jon thought two more. He had always imagined that five seasons was the right shape. Tony said that what he wanted for us, for himself, was to keep making the show, but in his heart he thought the creatively wise thing might be to end. Lucy, I think, put the question to bed: we could, if we wanted, keep going with a show that became increasingly rangy and fun – a climbing plant grown leggy but still throwing off beautiful blooms now and then. But the ten-episode season was the *muscular* way to go out.

The shape of the final season from then never really altered in its essentials: Logan to die early, a shock, as death so often comes in life; a blast from the captive bolt pistol, experienced as a shockwave by his children while some or all of them were at a wedding. The deal with GoJo had to go through. That was the case in the world, so it had to be the case for us. In terms of the particulars of who might end up as CEO, since season two the idea of Tom winning out had started to glitter in the distance. Not only did the kids lack application, but also, crucially, they were arriving to this particular party at the wrong time. In the fifties and sixties, Murdoch could inherit and grow and thrive. Now if you weren't a media founder, it felt more plausible for an amenable man like Tom to rise gently like a bubble of air in the tank. A corporate fusion of Kenneth Widmerpool and Joseph Stalin.

Notwithstanding this route map, all through the writing and shooting of the final season, with some gentle encouragement from Casey Bloys at HBO, I tried to keep the 'multiple future season' version of the show alive. Almost so that the show itself didn't know it was ending – to keep things open, to allow other possibilities. Partly this was for creative reasons, so that the ending didn't become freeze-dried and pre-packaged. But also because once we pulled the lever definitively, in a pure business sense, the metal gears of LA business, agents and managers would engage and crush all other possible futures out of existence.

But I never had a serious wobble. No other way of going forward felt persuasive. Even when I made the long walk from the season four room in Victoria, hot and queasy past the pelicans in St James's Park, up to the Ivy restaurant to meet Brian Cox to tell him what I thought happened at Connor's wedding. Even then – sad though I was, nervous, feeling a little like a man with a loaded revolver rather than a MacBook bumping at my damp shirt from my backpack, even then – I always had a feeling that this was just right. Whatever people made of the end of the show, we'd thought about it hard, and this was simply how this story *had* to go.

Of course, knowing that the arc of the season is essentially right doesn't mean that the writing goes easily. No, there are still many days when you stare at the index cards which were supposed to spell out the spine of the episode and they no longer connect. You start to feel you can't really remember what a story is. What is it even that people like about a TV show? About anything? What is true? And you can find yourself googling 'what is a story?', 'what things do people do?', 'what is interesting?'

What's so terrifying about writing a show is that, before each draft gets to the level it must, it is always totally possible that it will be a disaster. Indeed, it is only the certain knowledge of the terrible inadequacy of each episode that motivates all the work on the many drafts necessary to save it. And that grinding fear lasts for months, for years. The fear you'll forget the heart of the show, that you'll misplace it, get distracted by some shiny thing, get pulled off the true path by some seductive byway. I can barely describe before the show is written, before it is right, how empty and lacking and wrong it feels. How many days and weeks in Williamsburg and Long Island City there were fearing that this episode, *this* was the one where we lose control, run out of energy and let the whole enterprise be spoilt because of exhaustion or inattention.

And in amongst it, just occasionally, you feel you get it right and the words make a spell. I remember just a couple of times being emotional as I wrote or rewrote. Once in Logan's death episode, which came in a tumble, the long middle section barely revised after its first draft, when Shiv calls her dying or dead father 'Daddy' – and then once in season two, rewriting the scene where Kendall tells Shiv he doesn't know what he would be for if his dad didn't need him.

What I recall most about that Kendall–Shiv scene, though, is not the writing, but how odd it was seeing the brilliant way it was executed on set. Sarah and me and Jeremy had a debate about who should first offer the hug. The actual human acting moment was all about execution, debate, discussion, looking at the angles with Georgia Pritchett and directors Bob Pulcini and Shari Springer Berman. How odd that at Christmas in Brixton it could make me cry, but on set up on the thirty-third floor of World Trade Center 7, it had already happened and all the extraordinary talent and engagement of the actors was focused on landing the fish, making payment on a cheque already written.

After wrestling through all this, the decision to publish the shooting scripts made me feel a little vulnerable. Not because I don't think they're of high enough quality. But because although I think they're basically good and we did many drafts to get them right, the final draft of the show isn't the script. It's the version we air. My fellow writers and I always wrote and rewrote scripts with the knowledge that we could in safety try something a little more greyed-out and subtle, or a little odder, or a little more vivid and 'red', as Lucy Prebble would say in the room; knowing that if the execution on celluloid left something too opaque or too vivid we had a safety net. That we could dance closer to the precipice with the assurance that the final *final* edit was yet to come.

It's a great freedom. Without the power American TV gives a showrunner the temptation can be to write in a closed-off, invulnerable way with every scene sleek and sealed – less prone to misexecution or misinterpretation. And that's a shame. Because I do think the cracks are where the light gets in – the bits of a show that elbow out at odd angles, the bones that stick in your throat.

A friend who loved watching Darcey Bussell, the principal dancer at the Royal Ballet in the 2000s, explained to me once that what made her so compelling wasn't that she executed her performances perfectly. It was that she also drew you in with the fear that she might be on the verge of falling. That's what keeps your guts coiled tight watching a performance, I think, that degree of vulnerability that comes from being on the edge of something. It's like the good poem that 'rides on its own melting'.

What I always hoped for in the shows in the end was that sense of something you couldn't look away from. Episodes that both demand the viewers' full attention and were worthy of it. And that quality comes from the careful plotting in the room, and then careful writing and rewriting. But it also comes from what we choose to leave out.

Because there's a paradox about the core of a TV show. Especially one that lives somewhere in the world of the satirical. If you don't have anything you want to say, there's a danger the show will never live. But at the same time, if you do have something to say, there's a danger that if you ever state it, it will kill the whole endeavour, so it lies flat and dead, like a propaganda leaflet dropped in the street. I think what you have to do is to trust that if you set things up right and hold the tone and create the universe correctly, you can step back from the mechanism, let it run, and say, as in Walter Benjamin's useful but disingenuous declaration: 'I have nothing to say, only things to show.'

An ancillary benefit of keeping yourself out of the show is that what you thought you were transmitting is not necessarily what people will receive. And that's a good thing. People are hungry, especially right now perhaps, for things that are other than what they seem – characters and situations that are allowed to be multiple. We all have an impulse to want to pull the mask off the baddie and have something simple revealed – base truths and clear explanations. But we all have another impulse too and that first reducing, simplifying impulse will likely never wholly satisfy because it offends our deep sense of what the world is really like.

Taking a hard look at the world as it is, that would be my definition of satire, I think. This might be a less lofty ambition than an older version where satire functioned – or was imagined to function – in a sort of dialectic relationship with power. The idea that things happened in the public-political arena, and were then critiqued and mocked, and that interaction provided a release valve or even pointed in the direction of an alternative. I'm not sure that was ever how it actually worked. But even the idea of that relationship feels falsely soothing now that the powerful and the satirists are all seeking attention in the same ring of the circus. Which doesn't mean that the annual article, 'Is satire dead?', is ever going to be more fresh. That article will forever be boring and wrong. But it does mean the satirical approach needs to come in at a different angle. It probably always does, every generation. Comforting the afflicted feels relatively straightforward. But afflicting the comforted? That seems like maybe it will go better if you avoid announcing your intention too clearly at the door.

So here they are. The final season of scripts. I went in not really knowing what a showrunner is. As we finish, I'm still not entirely sure. I think of myself as essentially a writer. But a writer empowered to protect the scripts through the rooms where they are conceived and written and rewritten, performed, captured and edited. From the insubstantial spider crawl down the centre of a page in Final Draft, to that digital flicker that can be summoned from nowhere and disappear to nowhere. Shepherding the show out of one dream state into another through the unbelievably real mess of production – of a thousand early mornings, scrambled eggs, stubbed toes, and fraught discussions under the hot lights of what the hell we were thinking any of this meant.

The shape of the season may have been set from early but getting there was eighteen months of work – from the first writer meetings to the last day in the edit, playing with the sequence of the final shots. You won't find the end of the show, as it went to air, written in these scripts. That we found on the day. I didn't know when we started the day we'd end it looking out to the water and Ellis Island and the Statue of Liberty beyond. In fact, I was worried, shooting into the bitter cold sundown, that the statue's inclusion was too direct a symbol. Mark Mylod reassured me that on a TV screen it would be what it is – a little nub in the distance. But I knew that just as we'd started the show on the endless ride from Battery to holy Bronx with the Beastie Boys trying to lyrically span New York, this little green breast of grass was the place to end. On that tip of New York once partitioned off for safety by Wall Street, where securities and enslaved people were traded, and from where the city first started to grow fat.

Jesse Armstrong
May 2023

Note on the Text

This book contains the scripts as they stood when we started to film each episode. Reading them, you'll discover that they are quite often a little different from what made it to screen. These departures occurred for one of several reasons: a choice we had to make on what to lose in the edit; a new line myself and my fellow writers offered on set; or a bit of improvisation or extemporisation by an actor.

You'll also find a few footnotes scattered through the following pages. I've tried to limit the footnoting to those spots where the reason for a change might not be self-explanatory. Where they occur, I've sometimes also included a little flavour of the research that informed the show. Any errors, failure of memory or omissions are entirely mine.

Jesse Armstrong
March 2023

SUCCESSION

SEASON FOUR

SUCCESSION

SEASON FOUR

Executive Producers	Jesse Armstrong
	Adam McKay
	Frank Rich
	Will Ferrell
	Kevin Messick
	Jane Tranter
	Mark Mylod
	Tony Roche
	Jon Brown
	Lucy Prebble
	Will Tracy
	Scott Ferguson
Writers	Jesse Armstrong
	Jon Brown
	Tony Roche
	Lucy Prebble
	Will Tracy
	Georgia Pritchett
	Ted Cohen
	Susan Soon He Stanton
	Francesca Gardiner
	Will Arbery
	Miriam Battye
	Jamie Carragher
	Alice Birch
	Lucy Kirkwood
	Callie Hersheway
	Nathan Elston
Directors	Mark Mylod
	Becky Martin
	Lorene Scafaria
	Andrij Parekh
	Shari Springer Berman
	Robert Pulcini
Co-Executive Producer	Dara Schnapper
Produced by	Gabrielle Mahon

Associate Producers	Callie Hersheway
	Nathan Elston
	Maeve Cullinane
	Naomi Ranz-Schleifer
Writers Assistants	Siobhan James-Elliott
	Ali Reilly
Script Coordinator	Terry McGrath
First Assistant Directors	Christo Morse
	John Silvestri
	Michelle Flevotomas
Directors of Photography	Patrick Capone, ASC
	Katelin Arizmendi
Editors	Ken Eluto, ACE
	Jane Rizzo, ACE
	Bill Henry, ACE
	Venya Bruk
	Ellen Tam
Composer	Nicholas Britell
Production Designer	Stephen H. Carter
Costume Designer	Michelle Matland
Casting Director	Avy Kaufman, CSA
Original Casting by	Francine Maisler, CSA
Script Supervisors	Lisa Molinaro
	Holly Unterberger
Gaffer	Ken Shibata
Key Grip	Brendon Malone
Property Master	Monica Jacobs
Set Decorator	George DeTitta Jr.
Supervising Sound Editor & Re-Recording Mixer	Nicholas Renbeck
Re-Recording Mixer	Andy Kris
Music Editors	John Finklea
	Todd Kasow
Production Sound Mixer	Ken Ishii
Hair Dept Head	Angel DeAngelis
Make-Up Dept Head	Nuria Sitja
Location Manager	Paul Eskenazi

Episode One
THE MUNSTERS

Written by Jesse Armstrong
Directed by Mark Mylod

Original air date 26 March 2023

Cast

LOGAN ROY	Brian Cox
KENDALL ROY	Jeremy Strong
GREG HIRSCH	Nicholas Braun
SHIV ROY	Sarah Snook
ROMAN ROY	Kieran Culkin
CONNOR ROY	Alan Ruck
TOM WAMBSGANS	Matthew Macfadyen
FRANK VERNON	Peter Friedman
KARL MULLER	David Rasche
GERRI KELLMAN	J. Smith-Cameron
WILLA FERREYRA	Justine Lupe
COLIN STILES	Scott Nicholson
KERRY CASTELLABATE	Zoë Winters
NAN PIERCE	Cherry Jones
NAOMI PIERCE	Annabelle Dexter-Jones
CYD PEACH	Jeannie Berlin
JESS JORDAN	Juliana Canfield
RAY	Patch Darragh
CYRUS TELLIS	Kevin Changaris
BRIDGET	Francesca Root-Dodson
SERVER	Gabriella Kessler
DESIGNER	Richard Jin
CELIA	Schuyler Girion
BUN PIERCE	Robert David Grant
PIERCE LAWYERS	Kate Butler
	AJ Tannen

EXT./INT. SHIV'S CAR – LA – DAY

LA 12 P.M.

Shiv's car makes it through LA and up to Roman's house. She's driving.

> JIMÉNEZ STAFFER
> (*on phone*)
> It won't just be liaison – you'd have policy input.

> SHIV
> Well thank you. No, it is interesting.

> JIMÉNEZ STAFFER
> You can basically write your own brief.

> SHIV
> Well that's very nice of you to say and I'm flattered, but I guess is it a real role?

> JIMÉNEZ STAFFER
> Can I just ask if you have other offers?

> SHIV
> I'm not playing hard to get!

Silence on the other end.

Shiv has pulled up – watches Kendall arrive with Jess and another assistant.

> Look, I am not uninterested in helping a Democratic president. But, you, we've got to win first, right? And obviously there's the 'Nate and Gil' of it all. But the White House would be intriguing. So talk to me—

She listens as Kendall wraps knuckles on her hood and waves – she is being furtive. Secret moves. Motions: In in five.

INT. ROMAN'S LA HOUSE — DAY

Kendall walks through the big house. Maybe past staff.

> KENDALL
> (*sing-song*)
> Oh, Romey?! Where are you? I can smell you, I can smell your little ratty body, bro! Where are you, Rome, I need to start a business with you, brother!

He arrives. Roman is on a couch, feet up on his coffee table. Their banker, Tellis, and maybe an assistant and Roman's assistant too. An array of pastries and smoothies set up for a morning of meetings.

Remotely, a team of graphic designers and brand consultants are sharing their screen onto a big screen in Roman's living room. The creatives are visible on a sidebar.

> ROMAN
> Um, no. Next.
> (*to Kendall*)
> Right, fuckchops?

Kendall regards the logo. Not right.

> KENDALL
> Right. How we looking?

Roman makes a face or gesture to Kendall: Not good.

> ROMAN
> Exciting.

> KENDALL
> (*projecting for the people on Zoom*)
> Hey, guys!

The images are for a logo for a new media brand: 'The Hundred' (Substack meets MasterClass meets The Economist meets The New Yorker). Roman looks at a proposed logo and considers for a beat.

> KENDALL
> (*cont'd*)
> Um, no. Nope?

Kendall looks at Tellis, Tellis agrees.

ROMAN

Hard no.

KENDALL
(*to the designer*)
You guys got the brief yeah? And the notes?

DESIGNER
(*on screen*)
Oh sure. These are just initial thoughts.

Kendall and Roman make faces to one another.

ROMAN

But go on. I do like them. We do.

The team on screen moves on to the next logo.

It's just they're kind of shitty.

The team tries not to react. Kendall smiles at Roman indulgently. Kendall regards the new one—

KENDALL

Not to be rude, because objectively they're high level. But in terms of what we need, for our new venture? They're shitty.

ROMAN

I mean we can be honest here?

DESIGNER

Absolutely.

Designer moves on to next design. Kendall and Roman hate it.

ROMAN

No.
(*then*)
I feel like we said 'iconic' but you're leaning ironic.

Kendall makes a face at Tellis re Roman's comment.

What?

KENDALL

What 'what', I agree, fucking paper-ego man.

They are pretty comfortable with one another.

ROMAN

Well don't patronize me, bitch.

KENDALL

Well, you're the bitch. Because you eat dog food and get hard to dog porno.

ROMAN

Whereas you can only get hard looking in the mirror.

Kendall smiles.

It's true.

(*to Tellis, the TV*)

I hear he got holes drilled in his full-length mirror and his butler stuffs it with kiwis so he can fuck himself awake.

Kendall laughs. They are in the zone where this stuff is affection, not attack. Shiv arrives.

SHIV

Hey. T? I think the money is arriving?

Tellis heads out. Maybe Kendall throws an orange at him as he goes, which he catches.

And, Rome, your security is being weird with them – they seem very stupid and probably racist.

ROMAN

Cool. You look tired and your face is giving me a headache.

Maybe they kiss.

SHIV

I like this place. If I were a wildfire, I'd have first dibs on this fucker.

ROMAN

(*hidden suspicion*)

So, where have you been?

SHIV

(*little lie*)

Traffic. And a call. Business. For this. Good contact.

As the designer breaks in to wrap up, Roman hears him and, wanting it to be all done, closes the laptop on him as he talks and Roman talks over him—

DESIGNER

Look this is great feedback, we'll do some work on your favorites and put together some other ideas plus revisit the 'Centipuss' idea and—

ROMAN

Great, amazing, fantastic, guys. Love it, look forward to it. Great to see you thanks so much goodbye forever.

Kendall looks at Shiv.

KENDALL

Oh 'traffic'. Right.

Shiv picks up an atmosphere.

SHIV

What?

KENDALL

Nothing.

SHIV
(*innocent*)

What?

KENDALL

Shivvy, are you snaking?

ROMAN

We hear you're talking with the Jiménez transition team?

She looks at them both.

SHIV

Well, no.

ROMAN

Oh, no? No? It's no, so that's lies from our friend who told us? They're lying to us?

Shiv thinks . . . and decides to come clean.

> SHIV
>
> I mean I have talked to them. I've been helping them out a little bit as you know.

> ROMAN
>
> So, you *are* talking?

> SHIV
>
> I returned a call. They want to talk about talking.

The boys look at each other like: What?

> What? They haven't won the election, they might not. Maybe Dad won't sell, maybe you two will bail, it's a 'maybe maybe maybe' situation.

> ROMAN
>
> Well obviously Dad is going to sell. We're looking at fucking logos here, I've drafted a resignation statement from Waystar? Yeah?

Shiv pauses, then—

> SHIV
>
> Well, it's just a big step, okay? Can't we keep some options?

> KENDALL
>
> We're two days out from Dad selling. I've smoked horse, Shiv.

> ROMAN
> (*aside*)
>
> Scared of needles, not a real junkie.

> KENDALL
>
> Opiates are nice. Really fucking nice. I need something super-fucking absorbing in my life and if it isn't going to be this, let me know, right? Because I've been flying round the country having serious fucking conversations with serious people, expending serious personal capital on getting big fucking names on board.

> SHIV
>
> Well, me too. Me too.

Roman looks at Shiv—

> ROMAN
>
> Do you think it's too small-scale?

14

SHIV

No. No, I don't. Do you?

ROMAN

No! My only thing with The Hundred is, is it literally too good. Like why hasn't anyone else done it?

SHIV

No sure. I'm in. I am in. I am.

INT. LOGAN'S APARTMENT – DAY

NEW YORK 3:15 P.M.

Logan walks through his birthday party, with Kerry. Surveying the food and drink, the staff and guests arriving.

Connor, Willa, Frank, Karl, Gerri, Ray, Cyd, a number of other friends and acquaintances.

Not all the people he would want. A random harvest.

Logan has a glass in hand but he's making himself unavailable. Smiles. Nods a little but he's unsettled.

He gets to a position where he can survey the scene, Kerry approaches.

KERRY

Okay, Loge?

LOGAN
(*looking around*)
Munsters. Meet the fucking Munsters.

Kerry and Logan see Greg arrive with his date, Bridget. She is excited to be there, carrying a larger bag than other people, maybe branded with a luxury name.

And who the fuck is this now?

As Logan looks at his watch, hides out a little, Kerry goes off to greet Greg and Bridget.

KERRY

Welcome! Welcome, Greg and—?

GREG

Hey, Kerry! Bridget. Bridget, Kerry is Logan's—

KERRY

Friend, assistant and advisor.

GREG

Friend, assistant and advisor.

KERRY

Greg, let me and you grab Bridget a drink. Excuse us, Bridget!

Kerry leads him away.

. . . and who is this, Greg?

GREG

My date?

KERRY

Uh-huh, right but who *is* she?

GREG

I brought a date. That's okay right?

KERRY

What's her name.

He's going to say 'Bridget'.

What's her full name?

GREG

Um—

KERRY

Is she from the apps, Greg?

GREG

I really like her. I might have fallen for her.

KERRY

How many previous dates have you had?

GREG

Um, Kerry, I'm not sure this is appropriate?

They find a private zone or turn in to face each other as they get a little more real.

KERRY

We're not a fucking Shake Shack, Greg? This isn't a pre-fuck party. It's a birthday party.

GREG

I am a cousin. I get a plus-one. I'm like an, an honorary kid.

KERRY

Oh, you're an honorary kid?

GREG

Marcia once said I was always welcome to—

KERRY

Marcia's not here. She's in Milan, shopping, forever. I hear you and Tom have a chart on your wall?

GREG
(true)

That's preposterous.

KERRY

You do know we're in the middle of a very hotly contested election, your uncle is on the brink of a very large sale. And scoping out a very sensitive acquisition. Are you certain she's not gonna leak details right before the board meeting? Do you know she's not a hostile corporate asset?

They look over at Bridget.

INT. ROMAN'S LA HOUSE – DAY

Tellis comes back in.

TELLIS

Okay. They're five out.

SHIV

And this is— Who is this – the flakey money, Nabby and the J-Fund?

Tellis maybe doesn't love that characterization but nods and spills out what's on his mind, he's concerned—

> TELLIS

And so are you gonna pitch dry, or run the deck with me before I bring them in?

> ROMAN

Oooh, we get to run the deck with you? Like we're at Cyrus Tellis' business school?

Tellis smiles – indulgent.

> SHIV

This is informal today, right?

> TELLIS

Sure. I mean, you're a great package with huge credibility. You can just draw them shapes in the sand. I can fill it all in.

> KENDALL
> (*translating*)

He thinks we're milk-fed veal and he's gonna have to run the hard yards.

Tellis smiles. Correct. The kids look at one another.

> SHIV

Okay, fine. Let's dry-run it.

Shiv gets a call. Cancels.

> ROMAN
> (*to Tellis*)

Bankerman, you got a fuckboi we can fire some blanks into?

INT. LOGAN'S APARTMENT – DAY

Connor joins a group where Willa is talking with Greg and Bridget. He is chewing his lip, looking at a text.

> WILLA

You okay, Con?

> CONNOR
> (*after a beat*)

Oh yeah. Just polling. Yeah. Ten days out and – yeah.

> GREG

What are you at now?

CONNOR

Solid. Still holding.

WILLA

One percent.

CONNOR
(*then, re phone*)
It's just, the fear is, in these last days, it could get squeezed.

GREG

What, *down*? The one percent could get squeezed down?

CONNOR
(*to Willa*)
They're saying I could need to get aggressive in certain media markets because both sides will be trying to squeeze my percent.

WILLA

Well that's greedy, when they've got all the other percents?

CONNOR

I know.
(*beat*)
But then it's awfully spendy to get aggressive.

BRIDGET

Like how much?

It's a lot.

CONNOR

Like another hundred mil.

GREG

One *hundred* million?

BRIDGET

Wow. And what do you get for that? Could you win?

Willa chuckles, she knows a thing or two now. Connor looks more concerned.

WILLA

Oh good lord no!

CONNOR

No. No no. That's not going to move the needle. No, the hope is that would maintain my percent?

BRIDGET

Okay? And for your percent you get— I mean you don't *get* anything?

WILLA
(*has heard this many times*)
He gets a place in the conversation.

GREG

No of course. Well that's great.

CONNOR

It is just kind of a lot, right, Will?

He's concerned.

WILLA

A hundred million? Well, yeah. But if you spent it – you'd still be – like, rich?

CONNOR

Oh sure. Sure. Yeah. Nevertheless, like minus, one hundred million?

He thinks. Makes a thinking noise.

Hmm.

Willa and Connor look at each other 'thinking' about whether Connor should spend the extra money? Willa would kind of like him maybe not to – so maybe she makes that kind of face.

WILLA

Hmm? I—
(*then*)
I guess if you didn't spend it, you would kind of – have it? So. There is that?

CONNOR

Hmm.

Greg and especially Bridget join in with the 'thinking' faces, considering the issue. Maybe making a few 'thinky' noises. Connor can feel the way Willa is leaning.

(*defends his position*)
The thing is. I just *do* like my percent. 'One.' 'One percent.' It's that psychological 'one'. 'One.' You know? You can build on one. 'Ooh, there goes Mr One.' Looking out for Number One.

INT. ROMAN'S LA HOUSE – DAY

Tellis leads in his assistant, Celia.

They straighten up and check their notes. Maybe get a presentation pitch document of PowerPoint slides up.

SHIV
Hey! So, we're looking for investment partners for a revolutionary new media brand that will redefine news for the twenty-first century.

ROMAN
It's an indispensable, bespoke, information hub.

Shiv gets a call. Looks at the caller ID. Tom. Cancels.

KENDALL
The hundred greatest experts, best writers, top minds, in every field, from Israel–Palestine to new restaurants. One-stop info shop, available exclusively to our subscribers.

Kendall gets an update on his phone. That's weird. A social media update – someone is posting from his dad's party – including, in the background, Anne Pierce – one of the cousins. Wheels spin.

ROMAN
Every actionable piece of information in the world, on tap, provided in hourly updates across curated verticals in all meaningful areas of: news, finance, sex, food, sports. Inside-inside-inside baseball shit.

KENDALL
A trusted hub in a decentralized information market. Farm-to-table trackable, traceable high-calorie info snacks.

Tom calls again. Shiv stands with her phone.

> SHIV

Listen. I am so sorry. I need to just— Is that okay?

The boys look slightly surprised, but her manner suggests she has to do this – they carry on. But we go with Shiv moving through the house into various rooms and zones.

Hello?

Intercut with:

INT. NEW YORK – THE MARK HOTEL – BAR – DAY

Tom is leaving a hotel bar which feels date-y and cozy.

> TOM
> (*into phone*)

Hey.

> SHIV
> (*on phone*)

Hey?

> TOM

Hey how are you?

Unreadable and normal, except something has been sucked out—

> SHIV

I'm good, how are you, what is it?

Tom says hi to someone he half-knows.

> TOM

Um. Yeah, just a heads-up. And to say hi. And, just to let you know um, I've just had a little drink with Naomi Pierce—

Shiv reacts. She gets to a spot where she can glimpse an entourage of six or seven investors, advisors and bankers.

and, I'm just – leaving the Mark and, just in case, of anything, I wanted to inform you—

> SHIV

You're 'informing' me?

TOM

I wanted to perform the ask, out of due deference. In case of photos or it getting talked about so—

SHIV

Sorry, you're asking me, or informing me?

He looks like: C'mon, let's not do a lot of bullshit—

TOM

Shiv? It's not a thing.

SHIV

So then why are you letting me know?

TOM

Because – it's not business but it is – it is—

SHIV
(*interrupting*)

You know what, it's fine. You're dating my brother's ex.

TOM

Shiv. No, it's social, but it's not, you know, sexual – it's nothing I need to tell you about.

SHIV

And yet you are telling me?

TOM

Look. I bumped into Marlinda and she got her little beak in of course. And I told her it wasn't business because she asked and— Look, the headline is, it's nothing to worry about.

SHIV
(*interrupting*)

Tom, seriously, knock yourself out. Nail her in the coat check. The kid from St Paul has really made it!

TOM

I just thought, under what we agreed, this was something worth discussing—

> SHIV
> (*interrupting*)
> You don't discuss something that's already happening. 'Hey,
> Shiv, me and Naomi are at the Pierre and I'm inside her and
> I was checking how you would feel about me ejaculating?'

He breathes.

> TOM
> Whatever. Fine. And look, I saw the calendar update that you're
> back in the city tonight?

> SHIV
> So what's going on? Why are you meeting with her?

> TOM
> Take care, Shiv.

*Phone down. Shiv thinks and wanders back through the house,
putting it together. Returns as her brothers refine their pitch.*

> ROMAN
> It's clickbait, but for smart people.

> KENDALL
> We have the ethos of a non-profit. But a path to crazy margins.
> (*seeing her shaken*)
> You okay?

> SHIV
> Sure.

> TELLIS
> Okay, this is great, should I go get them?

*Roman can see Shiv's all flustered and uptight and distracted. Drinks
from a bottle, can't settle.*

> ROMAN
> Shiv?

> SHIV
> Great. Let's do this.

> KENDALL
> Yeah?

24

SHIV

Yeah.
(*then, can't hold it in*)
It's fine but apparently, Tom's out with Naomi Pierce?
(*to Kendall*)
Did you know this?

KENDALL

No. Why? Like – what?

SHIV

I don't know. Are you and her, where are you at with her?

KENDALL

Where? Oh, man, I dunno. Emotional hog roast. Carnival of mind-fuck.

SHIV

Okay, well, now she's fucking Tom apparently, so?

TELLIS

Um? Can I—?

SHIV

It's fine.
(*then*)
I'm actually fine. He's not, I don't think. They were just meeting, apparently. Let's do this.

ROMAN

Yeah?

Roman looks at Shiv and Kendall. Shiv screwing and unscrewing a bottle top.

You know what, T, can they give us two?

TELLIS
(*no*)
I mean, it's fine, but they had a long flight, so—

ROMAN
(*interrupting*)
Tell them they can shove their petrodollars up their human rights record – we need to talk to our sister, okay?

25

KENDALL

It's fine. They love it. Get Jess to find them a journalist to burn with cigarettes while they wait.

Tellis motions: Keep it down with the 'jokes' – while smiling along and heading out to placate the waiting investors—

Shiv, is it a date? You okay?

SHIV

He says no. But at the Mark, and worried about phones and gossip? I dunno. I guess – it's— It probably isn't [a date] . . . Honestly? Right. Naomi? *Pierce.* Dad?

ROMAN

You think? What?

They all process.

KENDALL

From my team, I got sent— Anne Pierce has been tagged on some girl's Insta at Dad's?

ROMAN

Board meeting day after tomorrow?
(*thinks*)
He sells up, but with ATN spun off?

SHIV

What, so Naomi, Anne Pierce?

KENDALL

What, he's lining up a Pierce acquisition, to add to his little fucking ATN rump?

They think.

SHIV

I guess? You think?

ROMAN

Or it's a brain-fuck? Dad twisting our turnips and playing the fuck trombone?

KENDALL

Set Tom and Nay up to torture us?

They consider, it's possible.

SHIV

Yeah – doesn't feel, I mean he's a sociopath but – I don't think he'd be a good torturer – not cos he doesn't have the stomach, he just doesn't have the patience.

They laugh. Their dad would be a bad torturer. Kendall is calling Naomi.

KENDALL

Nay-Nay, call me.

ROMAN
(*shouting*)

Hey, Telly?!

Tellis is coming back.

TELLIS

Yeah?

ROMAN

Um, one query – Pierce/PGN – what's the vibezz? Are they in play?

TELLIS

Well they've always been open to offers and the sell contingent on the trust is itchy I believe.
(*then*)
Should I have Nabby come through?

Kendall looks at Shiv and Roman, all thinking. Decides—

KENDALL

Um, just five more please?

INT. LOGAN'S APARTMENT – DAY

Tom arrives. Comes to report to Logan. Past Bridget, whom he clocks. Logan looks at Tom queryingly—

TOM

All good I think.

LOGAN

We gonna square this away?

> TOM

We've got the structure and landing zone, Naomi thinks Nan's lost all interest in the business. The left is going after them now.

> LOGAN

They eat their own. Savages.

> TOM

The cousins want out. Maybe a last push on price. Bit of a tummy tickle on culture. But yeah, Naomi's flown out to reassure.

> LOGAN

Uh-huh.

Logan is pleased. Good work. Gives him a nod. A pat. Tom glows.

> TOM

So this is it, ah? You landed the plane! Forty-eight hours and out? Congratulations, Loge!

Logan doesn't like that. He doesn't know why but wants to put Tom back in his box. Looks over at Cyd.

> LOGAN

Cyd's trying to screw you out. Spreading poison.

> TOM

Oh I know The Peach.

> LOGAN

She's a monster. She'll be feeding you broken glass before we close the deal.

> TOM

Oh I'll fuck her out.

He gives a thumbs up across the party to Cyd. Logan nods. A fun game.

> LOGAN

Heard from the rats?

> TOM

From Shiv?

Tom looks blank. A passive no.

LOGAN

Good.

(then)

And you seen Greg's piece?

TOM

Kerry told me about her bag!

They both chuckle. And look at Bridget who is eating a canapé (everyone else declining). Good-feeling established, Tom has a follow-up.

One thing has been on my mind though, sir.

LOGAN

Uh-huh?

TOM

Yes. Um. Well what with one thing and another, and I'm sure we'll iron it all out but, the rocky old road of life, and the wife part of that – can be a difficult part of it, as you know?

Logan looks at him.

Not to comment, just to say. I just wanted to get your take, on, hopefully it won't come to this but if there is just too much – emotional shrapnel – in the end, what would your view be, not that you necessarily have one, but what could happen, were a marriage, such as mine, and even in fact – mine; if that were to, to falter, to the point of failure?

LOGAN

If you and Shiv bust up?

TOM

Right, I wondered if you as a, a, real – emotional, rock to me, I wondered how such a situation would be viewed?

LOGAN

You'll figure it out.

TOM

Right.

Not really what he needed.

But I guess. We've had this experiment, the trial separation and whatever happens—

(*looks at him*)

we'll, always be good – right?

LOGAN

If we're good, we're good.

Hm. Tom thinks.

TOM

Uh-huh? And—

Tom thinks, wants to clarify, but Logan has had enough.

LOGAN

Kerry! Where's the grub? Tom's going off his fucking nut here!

INT. ROMAN'S LA HOUSE – DAY

Roman, Kendall and Shiv, on phones, sharing stories and images. Passing their phones and iPads to one another. Thinking. Tellis appears. Roman looks at the other two.

ROMAN

Another ten?

TELLIS

Sure . . . Just, we are now potentially approaching the city limits of Rude Town?

Shiv is seeing a whole new future flash before her, looks at Kendall who can see it too. Roman sees it too.

SHIV

We should discuss, right?

KENDALL

It is actually cute. He's selling the fleet but kept his little ATN dinghy so he can wear the captain's hat and go after his white whale.

SHIV

(*to Tellis*)

Can we get— Can they come back tomorrow? Because—

(*decides*)

Roman's not feeling well.

ROMAN

Oh *I'm* not feeling well?

SHIV

Or me?

ROMAN

No fine.

(*to Tellis*)

Tell them I'm – whatever – sudden onset violent diarrhea. I'm sitting on the bathroom floor shooting rusty water through the eye of a needle. Huge apologies.

Not great, but Tellis eats it and heads out with a sigh.

So, you two are thinking we should be buying Pierce?

Kendall and Shiv look at one another. They kind of do, just a bit afraid of going there and all it entails.

Because that's obviously what you're thinking and just to say: it's quite the fucking pivot.

KENDALL

Right. What about The Hundred?

SHIV

I guess maybe, 'fuck The Hundred'?

ROMAN

'Fuck The Hundred'? Shiv, after Dubai you were high as shit on it. It was basically your idea!

SHIV

I do like it. I do. Could we do both?

ROMAN

Right, launch a high-visibility execution-dependent disruptor news brand while also performing CPR on the fucking – corpse of a legacy media conglomerate?

KENDALL

(*disingenuous*)

Should we ask Tellis?

ROMAN

Oh yeah, 'Hey Tellis would you prefer five million in fees from a funding round or thirty-five million from an acquisition?'

KENDALL

Sure. But—

ROMAN

I thought we were going for The Hundred? Small. New. Fast on our feet?

SHIV

Sure, but there was always the thing of – is it a bit college-town fucking bookstore?

KENDALL
(to Roman)
Are you scared of fighting Dad?

ROMAN

No! Ken, it's just fucking – old. You've spent the last three months fucking hustling us contributors and backers and—

KENDALL

I don't have a view. All I would say is it's worth the conversation. It's our wheelhouse. It's a Daimler that's been in the barn for twenty years, clear the chicken shit off that thing, fucking maybe?

ROMAN

Can we even afford it?

SHIV

What's it at now? Halved – more to what, eight or nine bil? After the sale we'll have two to three bil. That's our nut.

KENDALL

We partner up? With our name, these fucks here or some other pieces of shit? Our experience? Shiv the yummy dummy Demmy; my profile as a fearless fighter of the good fight; you as the dirty little fucker pushing the filth buttons? Yeah, I think new-gen Roys, we have a song to sing.

SHIV

And as a business it's a lot better than the made-up company of dreams we were ready to pitch.

ROMAN

But you loved it!

SHIV

I do love it. It's very exciting. It's just kinda bullshit.
(*then*)
Seriously, Rome, I want to do something. There's a seminal
election on. It's fucking 1933. I wouldn't mind having a say?

KENDALL
(*calling*)

Oh Telly Bear!

Tellis comes back.

SHIV

If we wanted to put something together to buy Pierce, could you
swing that?

Tellis doesn't blink. Huge switch. But big money.

TELLIS

Um. What seven to nine bil? You guys are, what, one bil liquid
plus five percent of the holding, which you have the right to
liquidate if Waystar is sold, as I recall?

SHIV

Oh he recalls?

TELLIS

So, yeah, consortium, some debt. Once Waystar–GoJo goes
through? Yeah I could get into that.

KENDALL

Fucking dollar signs in Bugs Bunny's eyes.

SHIV

Who do we call? Do we call Naomi? Do we call Nan?
(*to Tellis*)
Who are their bankers, T? You wanna makes some calls?

Tellis is on it right away.

KENDALL

Rome, it makes sense. Start an empire with an established
brand? At least to rule it out?

On Roman, he shrugs an assent.

INT. LOGAN'S APARTMENT – LATE AFTERNOON

Tom is unsettled from his conversation with Logan. Greg is suddenly on his shoulder with a slap.

> GREG

Disgustibus!

> TOM

So I hear you've made an enormous faux pas and everyone's laughing up their sleeves about your date?

> GREG

What? Why?

> TOM

Why? Because she brought a ludicrously capacious bag.

> GREG

What, it's— [What do you mean?]

> TOM

What's she got in there? 'Flat shoes for the subway'? Her lunch pail? It's monstrous, Greg. Gargantuan. You could take it camping, or slide it across the floor after a bank job.

> GREG

Well, whatever. She's another tick on the chart.
> *(looks around)*
> The Disgusting Brothers!

> TOM

Don't call us that.
> *(quietly, looking around)*
> It was *heavily* ironized, Greg.

> GREG

I'm kidding, I really like her.

> TOM
> *(looks over at Bridget)*
> She used the display towels in the guest bathroom and now they're sopping, she's going around gabbling about herself and

posting to social media. Asking people personal questions and wolfing down canapés like a famished warthog.

GREG

People are overreacting. She brought a normal sort of handbag.

TOM

You're a laughing stock in polite society. You've taken a dump on the dining table. You'll never go to the opera again.

Bridget returns to Greg and Tom. Shaken.

BRIDGET

Maybe we should go?

GREG

Are you okay? What happened?

BRIDGET

Nothing, I just asked Logan for a selfie.

GREG
(*oh fuck*)

You asked Logan for a selfie?

BRIDGET

Yeah? I said congrats on the big deal. I was really friendly.

TOM

Uh-huh, I bet, and what did he say?

They look over at Logan.

BRIDGET

He – growled at me.

GREG

Sorry he *growled* at you?

BRIDGET

Yeah he kind of growled.

TOM

He bit Karl once. Right, Karl?

Karl and Frank are nearby in merry mood.

KARL

It was a nuzzle really. He was horsing around.

As Frank and Karl return to their private chat (excluding Bridget and Greg and Tom), Gerri approaches them—

GERRI

Howdy! So, how are the cowboys?! Looking forward to riding off into the sunset?

KARL

When you've eaten your share of meat from the floor, there comes a time for living high off the hog!

FRANK

Just comparing the size of our accelerated vested benefits. Cash severance payments!

KARL

That's right, Frank baby, talk dirty to me.

GERRI

You two old bastards. The cats who got the cream?

FRANK

Board all good to wave it through?

GERRI

Oh I think so, it's in the bag. What you gonna do with the windfall?

FRANK

Well I think I've got at least one really nasty divorce left in me.

KARL

Boards, Gerri, boards. I'm gonna be all over the Middle East, taking an *extremely* relaxed view of accounting practices and being the trustworthy face of cluster bombs. Can't tempt you?

GERRI

Oh I think I might have one more campaign. Cyd, you planning on sticking or getting out?

Cyd is talking to a friend.

CYD

Me? Oh I'm needed. I need to support Tom.

The others look, like: Yeah?

Yeah. Great asset. But not well liked. Nasty piece of work they say. 'Little handsy.' It's baseless scuttlebutt. I don't buy it.

INT. ROMAN'S LA HOUSE – DAY

Tellis returns, ending a call. He has a headline and some subtext to report.

> TELLIS
>
> I'm in touch with their bankers. Nan thinks she is honor-bound to another buyer.

> SHIV
>
> Did she say no?

> TELLIS
>
> No. But they're close to agreeing the outlines of a deal. There's not a ton of interest and managing the family is a nightmare so they're looking for a preferred bidder to run a bilateral.

> SHIV
>
> Uh-huh?

> TELLIS
>
> She wants to lock in her preferred bidder tonight. So she didn't think it could work, but she did say perhaps she could speak to you, Shiv?

Shiv and Kendall raise eyebrows.

> SHIV
>
> Should I call? Should I at least check in at Grey Gardens. Mano-a-Nano. See if there's anything at all there?

INT. LOGAN'S APARTMENT – LATE AFTERNOON

On Kerry and Logan, Logan looking around the party. He looks unhappy. Kerry clocks it.

> KERRY
>
> You good? Nice ah?

> LOGAN
>
> Uh-huh. Little piggies. Stuffing their faces. Why is everyone so fucking happy?

KERRY

Logan, are you okay?

LOGAN

I've got done a huge fucking deal at exactly the right time. I've got ATN plus Pierce, I've got the election. I've got plenty on my plate.

KERRY

Sure.

LOGAN
(*looks around*)
I thought there might be a churchman?

KERRY

I'm sorry?

LOGAN

I thought a cardinal was mentioned. Bit of fucking class. What about Jeryd?

KERRY

Mencken? I think, he hopes to but – realistically. But he hopes to. Gillian's here though?

LOGAN

Whoop-de-doop.

KERRY

You want me to get Gillian, hear their numbers?

He shrugs.

Want me to be in touch with the kids?

LOGAN

When's she calling?

KERRY

Nan? I think she just wants to talk to her whole gang.

LOGAN

Uh-huh. Well listen I'm fucked if I'm going to wait like a cunt for that old crone.

He wanders off around the party. Dissatisfied.

Looks at people. He's lost in a reverie. Disappointed. No kids. No Mencken. No wife. He sees Colin, and gives him a nod.

INT. ROMAN'S LA HOUSE – DAY

Shiv returns from the phone.

>   SHIV

So. Um, yeah. It is Dad.

That lands.

> Complicated woman. Um, it was like: 'No, no, my mind is made up, I've given my word, I'm honor-bound.' But also, how soon can we be there?

>   ROMAN

Oh, *fuck* her.

>   KENDALL

What do you think?

>   SHIV

I think she hates Dad, but she – maybe wonders if we're, fake fruit, display only. I don't know?

>   ROMAN

Listen, should we just tell her to fuck off? Not go back to the mat with Dad and just – you know, back into that fucking room?

Kendall and Shiv look at one another.

>   KENDALL

Shall we cards on the table? Because I do like Pierce.

>   SHIV

Agreed.

>   ROMAN

Oh for fuck's sake.

>   SHIV

It makes sense, Rome. We want to do something together. We know news, entertainment. It's off the shelf, it's got progressive roots, it's— Yeah. Tom Wambsgans' ATN versus our PGN?

KENDALL

Fucking 'Battle Hymn of the Republic'. It's weighty. There's a wealthy audience in the alienated center.

SHIV

Chance to make amends. And get rich . . . er.

ROMAN

And so until now you were just stringing us along?

Roman looks at Kendall for support.

SHIV

No. The other shit felt good. But yeah I like this. Besides, everything might fall apart—
(*re Kendall*)
he might kill a guy and get high, you might get your dick stuck in an AI jerk machine. I have to look after myself because no one else fucking will, okay?

ROMAN

Alright, Molto Agitato, you wanna fly there? Like Nan Pierce's little Windsor Dog Show bitch?

KENDALL

It's just a check-out?

Roman looks at them.

ROMAN

Well we're not getting on a plane without an NDA so we can see everything under that cronky old fucking hood.
(*then*)
Look. I'm worried. I am.
(*to Kendall*)
You wanna fuck Dad.
(*to Shiv*)
You wanna fuck Tom.
(*then*)
I'm the only one who wants to set up a business as a business, that doesn't wanna fuck anyone.

KENDALL

This acquisition would be nothing to do with Dad, that's completely unrelated.

Roman looks at Kendall.

ROMAN

Yeah. I don't believe you.

SHIV

Honestly, I wouldn't be doing this to get back at Dad . . . but it doesn't bother me if it hurts him.
(*to Roman*)
I think you're scared of this because you don't want the conflict.

Roman thinks – anything to that? Kendall looks serious.

KENDALL

Being rational, Rome, try to put out of your mind the personal concerns, the tittle-tattle, and instead focus on how fucking funny it will be if we screw Dad over his decades-long obsession?

Roman smiles, Shiv smiles.

ROMAN

Please. Guys. Really?

SHIV

Seriously, Rome, we're not raising a banner saying 'Fuck you Dad', it's a banner saying: 'We're doing our own thing, we're happy.'

ROMAN

But can't we do that, but, like, without a banner for Dad?

Kendall considers.

KENDALL

Uh-huh. Sure.
(*then, dry as a bone*)
But then how would Dad know that we're happy?

They all smile. Lots of layers. Roman is tempted.

EXT. CENTRAL PARK – DUSK

Logan walks. Another security guy ahead. Colin ten or so paces back.

INT. DINER – NIGHT

Logan is seated opposite Colin. Other guys discreetly outside. Looks at the menu.

> LOGAN
>
> Can't eat a fucking thing here. What you having?

> COLIN
>
> Tuna melt.

> LOGAN
>
> Uh-huh.
> (*as he studies the menu*)
> You're a good guy.

> COLIN
>
> Thank you, sir.

Logan looks at his phone. Nothing.

> LOGAN
>
> You're my pal.

> COLIN
>
> Thank you.

> LOGAN
>
> You're my best pal.

> COLIN
>
> Thank you.

> LOGAN
>
> I mean what are people?

> COLIN
>
> Right.

He seems to be really asking—

> LOGAN
>
> What are people?

> COLIN
>
> Um . . . like—?

> LOGAN

They're economic units. I'm a hundred feet tall. These people are pygmies. But together they form a market.

> COLIN

Okay. Right.

> LOGAN

What is a person? It has values and aims. But it operates in a market. The marriage market, the job market, the market of ideas, et cetera.

> COLIN
>
> *(so your point is . . .?)*

Uh-huh? So, everything is a market?

> LOGAN

Everything I try, people turn against me.
> *(tries to get things straight)*

A person is a person, but what is—
> *(then)*

Is this the place where the cheesecake is good?

> COLIN

I don't know.

> LOGAN

Nothing tastes like it used to, does it? Nothing's the same as it was, is it?

Colin nods.

Do you think they put something in things?

> COLIN

Yeah, I think so.

> LOGAN

I had a burger the other day that tasted so—

> COLIN

It was good?

> LOGAN

It was fine. I dunno.
> *(then)*

Do you think there's anything after all this? Afterwards?

COLIN

I don't know.

LOGAN

I don't think so. I think this is it, right?

COLIN

Maybe. My dad is very religious but I don't know. I hope so.

LOGAN

Uh-huh. Being realistic though?

COLIN

I don't know.

LOGAN

That's right. We don't know. We can't know.
(*then*)
But I've got my suspicions. I've got my fucking suspicions.

EXT. SOUTH CALIFORNIA — PRIVATE AIRPORT TERMINAL —
DAY

The gang waits for their private plane. Jess has been negotiating for them, tough gig, emerges.

JESS

Okay. I think I've done it. I've got you ahead of the line and we've got you a plane.

ROMAN

Uh-huh, well it took long enough. What is it, a fucking goose with a saddle?

Jess bites her lip. Assholes.

JESS

It was quite short notice so.

KENDALL

Thanks, J.

Roman is given a cappuccino, it has a laser-printed version of his face on it.

ROMAN

What the— Sorry, is this me?

> JESS

Um, it's a selficcino?

> ROMAN

Well it's weird. Where did they get the photo?

> SERVER

It's a service we offer. The selficcino. No one else offers it. Some of our clients like to Instagram it?

> ROMAN

Yeah well it makes me want to join ISIS, okay? Stop it. Jess?

Jess explains, smooths over the assholery and directs the kids out.

Incoming call. Shiv looks at her phone.

> SHIV

New mom calling.

> ROMAN

You gonna?

> SHIV

Oh yeah. Be great to catch up.

She cancels. Roman's phone goes.

Intercut with:

INT. LOGAN'S APARTMENT – NIGHT

Kerry in a quiet spot in the party and apartment.

> ROMAN

Well hello, Kerry. And how are you doing?

> KERRY

Can you hear me? The, line is—

> ROMAN

Yeah we're – in transit and—

> SHIV

Tell her you'd be able to hear her better if she took Dad's cock out of her mouth.

45

KERRY

What's that?

ROMAN

Um, that was my sister saying that I'd hear you better if you took Dad's cock out of your mouth?

KERRY

So my question was, would you consider giving him a call?

ROMAN
(for the group)
Would we consider at least a call?

SHIV

Is he apologizing?

KENDALL

Did he ask?

ROMAN

Did Dad ask?

KERRY

Um, he – he— I know he would love to hear from you.

SHIV

Maybe, maybe a hello, if he was to apologize. *Maybe.*

ROMAN

Look if he was to call, we could see.

Shiv mocks: Kissy-kissy.

KERRY

I think it's going to be a lot to get him to call? Just knowing him—

ROMAN
(interrupting)
Oh we actually know him quite well, Kerry. I mean we've never licked his big omelette nipples but—

KERRY

I could ask him to text the request for a call?

ROMAN

I am going to need to hear that voice I'm afraid, Kerry?

Karl comes over to Kerry—

                              KARL
Problem. He's not picking up for me, will he pick up from you?

EXT. SOUTHERN CALIFORNIA AIRPORT – DAY

The kids' plane takes off.

INT. DINER – NIGHT

Logan gets a call.

                              LOGAN
Hey.
                        (*listens, then*)
Okay, let's go.

EXT. NORTHERN CALIFORNIA AIRPORT – DAY

The kids land in their private jet.

Exit to car.

INT. LOGAN'S APARTMENT – NIGHT

Connor approaches Willa.

                             CONNOR
So listen, you know the wedding? I've been thinking.

                             WILLA
Oh, okay, like?

                             CONNOR
Don't worry! No wobbles! 'Keen as mustard'!

                             WILLA
Oh, good. Right?

                             CONNOR
No, just a question. We're only going to do this once. So, are
we thinking big enough? Should we actually – get shot out of a
freakin' cannon or something?!

She looks at him.

> WILLA
> Um, I think I'd rather not get shot out of a cannon on my
> wedding day.

> CONNOR
> Sure but is the boat special enough? Like, brainstorming, what
> if we got married under the Statue of Liberty with a brass
> band? Get a rapper or Major League ball player to lure out the
> paparazzi? Woody Allen playing the old licorice stick?

She makes a face.

> I don't know. Jet packs. Confetti guns, razor wire. Man fights.
> Goodie bags, hoopla and razzmatazz!

> WILLA
> 'Man fights', Con, you sound unhinged. What is this?

> CONNOR
> (*leveling*)
> It's just something that was floated. Weaponizing the wedding.

> WILLA
> Turning my wedding into – a weapon?

> CONNOR
> See if I can get myself inserted into the news cycle, that's a huge
> saving. Instead of paid media.

> WILLA
> Wow. Right. It's just. The wedding. I mean, I have always, it's
> dumb, but quite wanted a – nice – wedding. And Woody Allen
> and goodie bags and – what – journalists?

> CONNOR
> A hundred mil is a lot of cheese, Willa.

> WILLA
> Sure, but I'd have this weird corndog wedding.

> CONNOR
> No sure. Sure.

> WILLA
> Yeah? Con?

CONNOR

I'm scared, Will. I've spent so much fucking money and it's a little bit scary.

WILLA

Con. It's okay?

CONNOR

I've spent so much. And if I got under one percent I feel like I'll be a laughing stock. Would you consider it. Just a bit of hoopla. For the final push?

WILLA

Well. I guess. If I loved you – I should say yes. And if I didn't love you, I shouldn't be getting married to you – so.

CONNOR

Thank you, Wilton. Thank you so much.

WILLA

Can we just not have jugglers. Or the – the hippies with the sticks and strings?

Greg and Bridget are returning from upstairs. Tom is looking at his phone.

GREG

Hey hey hey!!

Bridget heads off to grab a drink. Tom thinks—

TOM

Kerry says she knows where he is and he's coming back.
(*looks at Greg*)
What are you smiling for?

GREG
(*with a twinkle*)

Oh, nothing!

Greg is smiling. Tom stares: Tell me.

(*sing-song*)
Disgusting Brothers! On motherfucking tour!

Tom looks nonplussed.

We did it.

> TOM
>
> What do you mean you 'did it'?

> GREG
>
> She's a firecracker, man, she's crunchy peanut butter.

> TOM
>
> You did it. Are you serious? Where?

> GREG
>
> We were looking for the armory slash cigar humidor. But we ended up in a guest room and – bingo bango hit that bongo!

> TOM
>
> You did it? Oh, Greg.

> GREG
>
> Disgustibus Maximus!

He goes for a high five. But Tom doesn't reciprocate.

> Don't leave me hanging, brother.

> TOM
>
> Greg, you are fucked.

Greg looks at him: What?

> Logan – he's camera-ed up the wazoo. CCTV. He's bristling.

> GREG
>
> Which room?

> TOM
>
> Every room. You know that.

> GREG
>
> Well no, I evidently did not know that.

Logan and Colin are arriving back.

Greg and Tom look over at a house manager whispering in Logan's ear.

> Are you serious?

TOM

Of course I'm serious. He watches back every night with a
Scotch. Seeing if anyone's stolen a butter knife. He's gonna gut
you like a fucking rainbow trout!

GREG

Oh, man. Fuck. Really?

TOM

What did you do? Were the lights on? Did you actually do it?

Greg looks like: Kind of.

Precisely what did you do?

GREG
(*after a beat*)
Well, I guess we put our hands down each other's pants and had
a bit of a – rummage.

TOM

And did you rummage to fruition?

GREG

Is it important?

TOM

It could be.

GREG

Um, can I not say?
(*then*)
I mean it will look bad. It will.

TOM

You've accidentally made him a sex tape, Greg. You need to tell
him.

GREG

Uh. Well, no. No.

TOM

Well you either tell him or wait for him to watch it by a
crackling fire, drinking an old fashioned, watching your little
white bottom do its revolting business like a nodding donkey in
the California desert.

Then from Logan—

> LOGAN
>
> Okay! C'mon, party's over. Rival bid. Gerri. Tom. Frank. Karl. Study! Let's flush it out!

They all start to head up. Greg starts to apologize to Bridget – he'll be back. Tom thinks. Rival bidders. Hm?

EXT./INT. CAR – PIERCE VINEYARD – DAY

Their car arrives on the property.

> ROMAN
>
> How's your vineyard, Shiv?

> SHIV
>
> Yeah great. I guess.

She looks at them. Prickled.

> What? I'm busy, sure I'd like to fly over on weekends to float around wearing a straw hat surrounded by the toddlers they keep for me in cold storage, but you know, been busy.

They look at her.

> The Hundred. And – saving democracy. Hosting fundraisers.

As they pull up outside the house, Naomi is there to collect them.

> ROMAN
>
> Uh-huh. Brave. Fighting through all the chiffon, eating all that chicken breast. Fucking Che Guevara.

As they get out, Shiv and Roman watch Kendall, who, with a look for their assent, walks ahead for first contact.

> NAOMI
>
> Hey.

They regard one another. A lot passes between their eyes.

> KENDALL
>
> Hey.

Quite a lot to say, are they going to get into it? But there is a pressing matter.

NAOMI

So, um, she's having a little wobble.

KENDALL

Nan. Like what?

NAOMI

She's not sure it feels right to meet you guys. She feels terrible.

KENDALL

So – what do we do?

NAOMI

Yeah she might be getting a headache. She wondered if you could give her five to see how it develops?

KENDALL

Okay well great. Let's see how the headache develops?

INT. LOGAN'S APARTMENT – STAIRS – NIGHT

Logan is ahead, heading up with Kerry. Followed by Karl, Frank, Gerri. Tom and Greg grab a word. Kerry takes a call.

GREG

Okay. I'm going to tell him. I'll tell him. I will.

TOM

You should.

GREG

I will.

INT. LOGAN'S APARTMENT – LIBRARY – NIGHT

As they make it into the room, Greg watches Logan settle, braces.

Kerry gives the phone to Logan. He's talking to his banker.

LOGAN

Who's crawling out of the woodwork? Ah? Who is it?

As they arrive, Frank gets a text. Karl can sense it's not good, he knows Frank's face so well.

KARL

What?

                    FRANK
                  (*quietly*)
It's the kids. The kids are with the Pierces.

                    KARL
They're the rival bidders? Oh flibbertigibbet. How did they pick
up the scent?

Tom thinks he knows.

                    TOM
                  (*defensive*)
A million ways. Everyone knows they're looking for suitors.

Gerri joins, keeping an eye on a distracted Logan settling.

                    GERRI
Could they put the money together? Could Logan not stop
them?

                    KARL
If Waystar is sold, they have the right to liquidate their five
percents.

                    FRANK
You should probably tell him?

                    KARL
                (*doesn't want to*)
I'm very focussed on the GoJo deal. This is really a side issue.

                    GERRI
You're such a trusted advisor—

                    KARL
I'm getting out though, Ger?

                    GERRI
                (*no fucking way*)
I don't know what the news is and it's beyond my purview and
I am walking away.

She goes for a drink. Karl sighs, gets up. As he goes—

                    FRANK
                  (*quietly*)
Beware the blood sugar!

Greg has finally plucked up courage and is ready to talk to Logan.

GREG

Um, sir?

But then Karl approaches with a bowl of nuts.

LOGAN

What?

KARL

Cashew?

Logan eyes him, knows what this nut offer heralds—

LOGAN

What? What's the issue?

KARL

The rival bidder. It's probably the kids.

LOGAN

Uh-huh.

KARL

I don't think you have anything to concern you. You're the solid option.

Logan gets up.

LOGAN

Uh-huh?

(*then*)

Call your wife, Tom. Call your fucking wife and tell them they need to get their own fucking idea. It's pathetic. Tell her she's never had a single fucking idea in her whole fucking life!

Greg is still there.

What?!

GREG

It can wait.

LOGAN

What? What else now? Ah?

GREG

Can I – can I at least do it privately?

Logan looks at him. Greg shuffles away, pleading eyes.

EXT. PIERCE VINEYARD – DAY

The kids wait outside, looking at one another. Naomi gets a text message.

> NAOMI
> Um, she's feeling a little better. If you like, she'll see you?

> ROMAN
> Oh, we get to talk to an old lady about newspapers now?
> Amazing! Thank you *so* much.

Naomi leads off, Kendall by her side.*

> KENDALL
> And are we gonna talk or just fuck it?

> NAOMI
> Um? Yeah. 'Sorry.'

Kendall nods.

> I tried to explain I guess?

> KENDALL
> Sure, thanks for all the voicenotes.

> NAOMI
> Hey c'mon. What about the letter?

> KENDALL
> It felt like a legal disclaimer, Nay.
> *(kinda joking)*
> Jess boiled down the headlines. 'Tough time'. 'Out of control'.
> 'Emotional black hole', et cetera.

> NAOMI
> I just found – things – a bit much.

> KENDALL
> 'Things'? Things like, me and my personality – my very essence?

---

* We had to cut this glimpse of how Naomi and Kendall's relationship developed for time.

It's on the edge of being intimate or just rude. But he smiles, walks the line.

NAOMI

Kendall, I liked you – a very great deal. I – very – like you. But it was quite— It didn't feel very safe. But I've been doing a lot of work. I've made a few breakthroughs.

KENDALL

Sure. Me too.

NAOMI

But I have!

KENDALL

Me too.

(*then*)

In fact, the good thing about me now is that I'm a fully realized individual.

NAOMI

Yeah. Well, me too.

They smile, at one another. He actually is better – cleaner than in a long while. Her too and they can smell that off each other. They arrive.

A main dining room, where the cousins are gathered, and some anterooms and sitting rooms. They go to greet Nan.

INT. LOGAN'S APARTMENT – LIBRARY – NIGHT

Greg returning to Tom. Colin is with Logan. Logan giving instructions. Tom is busy. Greg wants to speak, Tom makes him wait while he finishes a text.

TOM

How'd it go?

GREG

Yeah, he says he finds me disgusting and despicable. But he kind of smiled?

TOM

Yeah? What did you say?

> GREG

I— Yeah, I said— She was, a bit 'wild' and quite, eager and –
maybe she'd had a bit of the old, wacky-tobaccy or worse, and,
yeah, I'd gone along with it against my better judgment, sorry –
and maybe she's a bit of – a bit of a—

> TOM

A drug-addled cock-mangler? You blamed it all on her? How
gallant.

Colin approaches.

> COLIN

So, she's gonna have to leave, okay?

> GREG

Um, that seems a little— Really?

> COLIN

Do you have an issue with that?

> GREG

Well, no, look. I am fond of her. But. Colin, in the end, we must
each of us do as we see fit.

> COLIN

She posted to social media so I'm gonna have to ask to go
through her phone. You wanna come explain?

Greg thinks.

> GREG

You know what? I think it is best if you just do what you have
to do.

Colin looks at him.

I don't wanna know what happens in Guantanamo. You go, do
your ways, and God be willing!

*Colin looks at Greg, not impressed. Then, as Colin heads out, Greg
has some final words of wisdom, keeping his voice down—*

Be gentle if you can, be forceful if you must!

INT. PIERCE VINEYARD – DAY

Nan is there with the cousins, advisors. The kids walk in with Naomi.

NAN

Hello, welcome. Apologies for the kerfuffle. I have an appalling migraine but I can manage. How are you all, more importantly?

SHIV

Great. Good to see you. Lovely place.

NAN

Hmm. It would seem they shred hundred-dollar notes for fertilizer. Now. How are you faring in terms of your father?

ROMAN

We're fine. It's a complicated private situation.

SHIV

Whereby we all hate him.

Roman shifts. Nan laughs.

NAN

Well, look, as you probably know, we're talking with our bankers. And we have a whole number of very interesting proposals to consider.

Everyone knows this isn't the case.

And I think it's all wrapped up. So I wanted to say thank you for coming, but I think it's just a little bit too late. We have a preferred bidder. So, I hope I haven't inconvenienced you?

ROMAN

Okay, well, lovely trip, great to see you guys!

NAN

I am sorry. Can I offer you some bottles?

Some of the very good, expensively packaged red wine from the vineyard is around.

It might as well be jars of jam to me. But the connoisseurs seem to like it. I fear I have peasant tastes.

KENDALL

You don't want to just hear the offer?

                                NAN

I got a taste for *hypermarché vin ordinaire* when I was nineteen
and I've never been able to shake it. I like my wine thin and
vinegary.

                                NAOMI

Like your men.

                                NAN

Ha! No, but I really fear it's a trip made in vain. The other offer
is just too—

                                KENDALL

Listen long story short – Nan, you called this right before – Logan
wants to take your company and fuck it. He loathes you and
he wants to take your properties and roll them in the dirt. We
wouldn't do that.

Little shiver at the curse. How will it play?

                                NAN

Well. Naomi and I have received certain undertakings, and put
in place various measures, so.

                                SHIV

He's lying.

                                KENDALL

He only looks forward. He's a machine for the completion of
aims.

                                SHIV

After this election we all, the country, could be in a bad place,
I could, we would, maintain your values.

Now the nub of things—

                                NAN

Well that's all good and well. But obviously, with one thing and
another, we have a responsibility to get the best deal possible for
my family and other shareholders.

                                SHIV

We're confident we could be competitive.

NAN

Just because. Jamie's divorce. Anne's disaster in Maine. This place. How's your financing? Not that I understand it all.

Roman really can't stomach the bullshit. But his siblings won't meet his eye-rolls.

KENDALL

It's robust. Tellis and our team can talk to your people.

NAN

And in terms of your futures—?

SHIV

We have our resignation letters written. The GoJo deal signs in forty-eight hours.

NAN

Nevertheless, you'd still be married to the head of ATN. That's a bit messy?

SHIV

Well, I'm going to be getting a divorce. So.

NAN

Okay. I'm sorry to hear that.

Maybe this is news to the bros. But Roman covers.

ROMAN

Don't worry, she doesn't care, she isn't really a human being.

NAN

Listen, this is all very confusing.
(*then*)
And I don't want to talk numbers.
(*she does*)
It's not about the numbers.

Roman contains a sigh. It now very much is.

KENDALL

Totally. Shall we just say our number though? See if you understand that?

Nan acts a little flustered.

NAN

Oh! I don't like this, it makes me feel like I'm in the middle of a
bidding war! It's horrible, people saying different numbers—
(*very carefully chosen figures*)
eight, nine. What's next?

ROMAN

Sure, confusing. What comes after nine? There must be some
planet brain out there who can figure it out. Whither Hawking?

Nan smiles. She and Roman have one another's numbers.

NAN

Listen, would you mind if we all just had a brief chat? Thank
you.

The kids start to withdraw.

INT. LOGAN'S APARTMENT — LIBRARY — NIGHT

*Greg smiles at Logan. Logan smiles sarcastically back. Tom
approaches Logan, off the phone.*

TOM

Um, Nan's apparently 'thinking' and she wondered if she could
just ask for your indulgence?

LOGAN

Is it the kids? What does she want?

TOM

They say it's not a money question. Is that okay? Just to hold on
one minute before she talks to you?

LOGAN

Well, what can I fucking say?

Tom goes off to talk to Nan.

Logan in a bad mood, looks around. Karl, Frank, Gerri huddled.

Uh-huh. No one makes jokes anymore do they? Karl, you got
any jokes?

KARL

What's that?

LOGAN
(*slowly and menacingly*)
I was saying: this is a bit dry, Karl, have you got any jokes?

KARL
Um. Let me think. Let me think.

LOGAN
Fucking dry as dust. Do an Englishman, an Irishman and a Scotsman.

KARL
I think you know them all.

LOGAN
Uh-huh.
(*then*)
Come on. Let's have some fun?
(*then*)
Why don't you roast me? Ah? Give me a fucking drubbing.

No one is keen.

Frank. Start. Be funny.

FRANK
Not really my thing, chief.

LOGAN
You don't think I can take it?

FRANK
It's not my style.
(*then*)
I mean I can— The thing about Logan Roy is, the thing about Logan is – he's a tough old nut. He's a toughie.

LOGAN
Uh-huh.

FRANK
You can be a mean guy, you can be mean. Usually you have your reasons, but nevertheless.

LOGAN
Fucking Sid Caesar here. Karl?

KARL

You're careful with the old pocketbook. Few moths flew out last time you picked up a check, ah?

Logan nods – that's the kind of thing.

LOGAN

Tom?

He's on hold in a corner.

TOM

Roast you, sir?

LOGAN

Greg?

Greg has been thinking.

GREG

You're mean. You're a mean old man.

Logan looks at him.

You're a mean old bastard. And you scare the life out of folks, and this is scary right here now, so I can't even think of anything to say . . .

LOGAN

Who wants to smell Greg's finger? Ah? Guess the scent and win a buck. Come on, roast me!

Greg flashes.

GREG

Where are your kids? Where's all your kids, Uncle Logan?

LOGAN

Where's your dad, ah? Sucking cock at the county fair?

Greg looks injured, but smiles.

FRANK

'A hit. A very palpable hit.'

LOGAN

Come on, Karl. Call me a dumb old queer.

KARL

I don't want to.

LOGAN

Why you so fat, Karl? Ah?

Karl has been hit enough and also, golden parachute is coming, so, if the old bastard really wants it, then—

KARL

Because every time I fuck your wife she gives me a cookie?

LOGAN

Hehehe. Exactly. Gerri?
                    (*he hasn't forgotten*)
Got sent anything funny lately, Gerri? Ah?

GERRI

All a bit horrible for me thanks, Logan.

LOGAN

I'm not being horrible, I'm being fun! Fucking Munsters. At least I'm not being boring.

Karl and Frank smile politely.

I don't know why you're smiling, fucking golden parachutes.
                    (*then*)
Where's your wife, Tom?

TOM

Not here right now, Loge.

LOGAN

Uh-huh.

Someone comes on the line with Tom.

TOM

Okay.
                    (*listens, then reports*)
She'd like to get it figured out, in theory at least tonight, the uncertainty isn't good. She'd like to get our best foot forward on an indicative price tonight?

INT. PIERCE VINEYARD — ANTEROOM — DAY

Shiv and Roman and Kendall in a private but connected anteroom. They speak into Shiv's speakerphone—

> SHIV
>
> Hey, Tellis?
>
> (*on phone*)
> Nan is looking to get an indicative offer tonight?

INT. LOGAN'S APARTMENT — LIBRARY — NIGHT

Tom to Logan—

> TOM
>
> No reason to play nice, should I tell her to fuck off?

> LOGAN
>
> Uh-huh.

> TOM
>
> Loge . . .?

> LOGAN
>
> I'm thinking.

Long beat. Logan gets up.

> Is she talking to them?

> TOM
>
> I think so.

> LOGAN
>
> Okay. Okay. Hold on.
>
> (*then*)
> Kerry. I might need input.

Karl and Gerri and Frank huddle with Logan.

> KARL
>
> It doesn't mean anything, you can adjust. Loge?

INT. PIERCE VINEYARD — ANTEROOM — DAY

Shiv with the boys.

SHIV

Tellis, are you there?

TELLIS
(*on speakerphone*)

Hey.

SHIV

We're starting at eight? We're going to go in and say eight, yeah?

ROMAN

But if we're going for this, let's not be hard-asses, let her know we can see upside if she can help us prove it out.

Shiv and Kendall look at him – so he is interested?

INT. LOGAN'S APARTMENT – LIBRARY – NIGHT

TOM
(*to Logan*)

What number do you want me in at? You wanna talk direct?

LOGAN

She doesn't like me. They like you. Tell her, what?

Banker is on speakerphone.

We anchor at seven?

BANKER
(*on speakerphone*)

Not a problem.

LOGAN

Yeah?
(*to Kerry*)

Not too insulting?

KERRY

It's fine. It's insulting. But it's not like you're wasting relationship capital. She hates you.

LOGAN
(*to Tom*)

Let's do six – but like you're kidding around.

TOM

But seven is what we soft-floated?

LOGAN

Six. Find something we lost conviction on. Just to fucking let her know we're not Terry Turnip Truck over here.

TOM

Okay?

(then, off mute)

Hi. Hi, Nan?!

INT. PIERCE VINEYARD – DAY

Shiv heads in. Nan is listening to the phone.

NAN

(into phone)

Thank you.

She hands the phone off, muted.

SHIV

Hi, yeah we're looking at, I think we're very relaxed about the eight billion landing spot.

NAN

This is disgusting. But thank you.

INT. LOGAN'S APARTMENT – LIBRARY – NIGHT

Tom and Logan et al.

TOM

Yeah, they didn't love it.

LOGAN

What are they up to, you think?

TOM

I don't know.

LOGAN

I don't want to lose this, Tommy.

TOM

Okay, you wanna just jump right up, what to?

INT. PIERCE VINEYARD — ANTEROOM — DAY

Shiv with her brothers, assessing. Looking through to the family in the other room.

                         SHIV

They like eight.

Naomi comes in.

                         NAOMI

She appreciates eight.

                         ROMAN

Oh she appreciates?

                         NAOMI

But she wonders if there's a little more upside?

The kids smile, Naomi smiles as she withdraws.

Tellis on the phone.

                         KENDALL

Can we go there, T? Eight-five?

                         TELLIS
                    (*on speakerphone*)

Well I don't have the precise composition of our consortium and obviously DD but we know the asset and I think we can get there.

                         ROMAN
                    (*into phone*)

You fucking jerking off to your yacht catalogue there, T?

The brothers nod to Shiv who goes out to Naomi.

                         TELLIS

This is exciting.

                         KENDALL

Thanks, T, good insight.

                         ROMAN

He's going to bill us two hundred mil for that strategy advice. Thanks, T.

There's a call to Shiv's phone. She answers.

                              SHIV
Hello? Tom?
                        (*to brothers*)
He wants a discussion?

                            ROMAN
Fucking Tom's on this for Dad?

                             TOM
                     (*on speakerphone*)
Hi, Shiv?

                           KENDALL
                         (*shouting*)
Hey, Tom!

                            ROMAN
                         (*shouting*)
Fuck you, man mountain!

Intercut with:

INT. LOGAN'S APARTMENT – LIBRARY – NIGHT
                             TOM
Hi. Yeah, look, we are just wondering if, we're getting played a
little here, and since this is all indicative—

                             SHIV
What did he go up to, Tom?

                             TOM
Well I can't tell you that.

                             SHIV
Oh come on. You can tell me. Did he go to nine? He didn't go to
nine did he?

                             TOM
We were just wondering if all things being equal, the asset has a
price and it would be crazy for us to add an emotional premium
here so – should we open a back door on this?

                             SHIV
What's Dad's ceiling?

Beat.

> TOM

Well, what's your ceiling?

> ROMAN

Go first, Tommy. Build the trust, bro.

> TOM

His ceiling is— I don't know, I mean this is what he told me, Shiv, so I can't— Shiv, can we talk?

> SHIV

Our ceiling is twelve.

> TOM

Fuck off.

> SHIV

Yup.

> TOM

Okay. Well, fine. Ours too.

End of call. Shiv looks at her brothers.

> SHIV

I think he'll go to nine, nine-five. So I think we need to be at nine-five. I think, Tellis, right?

> KENDALL

I wonder if we don't nickel-and-dime it and we just go to ten?

INT. LOGAN'S APARTMENT – LIBRARY – NIGHT

> TOM
> (*reporting*)

Hi. I think nine is good. I think we're good on nine – they're scared and bluffing. I think you're good?

INT. PIERCE VINEYARD – ANTEROOM – DAY

Shiv with brothers and Tellis on speakerphone.

> ROMAN

So we think Dad's around eight-five, nine, so we're nine-five to top them out? But ten to show we're really serious? So, the half-bil extra is just – that's just an extra half-bil?

> KENDALL

It ends the conversation.

> ROMAN

That's a pretty penny for a conversation-ender? Can't we just fart?

> SHIV

It rounds it out.

> ROMAN

Oh it rounds it out, it does that, it makes it *extremely* divisible. You do know what half a billion dollars is? Five hundred million dollars?

> KENDALL

Tellis?

> ROMAN

A million is a thousand thousands. You do know that. So this is five hundred times one thousand, thousand dollars of actual money you could spend on fucking – snowmobiles and sushi.

> TELLIS
> (*on speakerphone*)

It's getting toppy but be great to be the preferred bidder here.

> ROMAN

Sure but is it worth it?

Beat. Then—

> TELLIS

It's worth what the top bidder will pay, I guess?

> ROMAN

Man, I wish I went to Harvard Business School like you, T. Did they crochet that onto your ballsack?

> SHIV

Ten?

> KENDALL

Ten.

They look at him.

> ROMAN

Ten. Fuck you. Ten.
> > (*then*)

But I get to run granny porn on PGN, midnight to two.

INT. PIERCE VINEYARD – DAY

They all go in.

> SHIV

Hi. Nan? Yeah, look, we love the company and the heritage and we'd love to make an indicative bid we think values the company and ends the conversation and closes this out. On an indicative handshake, we'd like to take Pierce into the next stage of its evolution with a bid of ten billion dollars.

INT. LOGAN'S APARTMENT – LIBRARY – NIGHT

Tom ends call. With trepidation, reports.

> TOM

They're not accepting another bid.

> LOGAN

Excuse me?

> TOM

They say they've received a conversation-ending offer.

> LOGAN

Tell them I'm willing to go up.

> TOM

She says they're content.

> LOGAN

That's bullshit.

> TOM

I get the impression it's upwards of nine-five.

LOGAN

Fucking geniuses. Ten?

TOM

I got a ten feeling.

LOGAN

Fucking morons.

EXT. CAR – PIERCE VINEYARD – DUSK

Shiv and Kendall and Roman.

KENDALL

Want to open some champagne?

ROMAN

I am going to fly to LA, retire to my bedroom and pull myself off quite painfully hard.

Shiv's phone goes.

Intercut with:

INT. LOGAN'S APARTMENT – LIBRARY – NIGHT

Logan watches Tom.

TOM

Hi. I'm sorry. I'm sorry, Shiv. Can you speakerphone me, Shiv?

She does.

SHIV

Hello?

TOM

Hi. Sorry. I have your dad? He has a message?

The kids look at one another – should they end the call?

LOGAN

Congratulations on saying the biggest number, you fucking morons.

The kids look at one another. Painful, but a bit funny. Will they respond? They make faces but Shiv puts her finger to her lips and they all stay silent through a bit of static. Then they hear Tom end the call and Kendall and Shiv giggle and laugh until Roman does too and they might even play-fight a little.

EXT. NEW YORK – SHIV AND TOM'S APARTMENT – NIGHT

Shiv returns to her apartment.

INT. SHIV AND TOM'S APARTMENT – NIGHT

Shiv comes into the apartment. She gets a glass of water. Mondale barks.

After a while, Tom comes through.

> TOM
>
> Hey.

> SHIV
>
> Sorry, did I wake you?

> TOM
>
> I thought, you were hoteling?

> SHIV
>
> Yeah, I need wardrobe access actually. Sorry.

Probably not true.

> TOM
>
> Oh, okay, I thought you took your favorites?

> SHIV
>
> Uh-huh, I don't want to be restricted to my favorites.

> TOM
>
> Do you want to talk?

Long beat.

> SHIV
>
> I hear you and Greg call yourselves the Disgusting Brothers now?

> TOM
> Right.

> SHIV
> That's pretty cool?

Tom looks at her: I'm not getting into this.

> Do you have a logo?
> (*waits*)
> Do you do 'The Rules', is Greg your 'wingman'?

> TOM
> We sometimes grab a drink, Shiv.

INT. SHIV AND TOM'S APARTMENT – BEDROOM – NIGHT

Shiv goes through to their bedroom.

> SHIV
> That's so cool. And I hear you date models now?

Tom follows.

> TOM
> Right. Well, we both agreed we could – have a look around
> while we had a think and—

> SHIV
> You look good. Ripped.

> TOM
> Right. Thank you.

> SHIV
> Did you get 'buff' for the models, Tom?

He's not about to answer that.

> Do you get them back here and do positions? Do you do all the
> positions with models now, Tom?

But Tom isn't going to get shamed without a fight—

> TOM
> Do you really want to get into a full accounting of all the pain
> in our marriage? Because if you do, I can do that.

That hits a bit. She changes tone.

> SHIV

How's Mondale?

> TOM

Mondale's fine. Don't worry about Mondale.
> *(re the barking)*
I guess he doesn't recognize your scent any longer.

> SHIV

Uh-huh. Well, I think – things have become quite complicated.
I wonder if there's even a way through this?

> TOM

Right.

> SHIV

I wonder if we've run out of road?

> TOM

I mean, we haven't— We were going to have a big talk.

About Italy, his betrayal.

> SHIV

I wonder if we might want to make it official?

> TOM

But do you want to talk?

She shrugs. Doesn't want to say no, but can't hear it all.

There's some things I wouldn't mind saying and explaining?

> SHIV

I don't want to rake up a lot of bullshit for no profit.

> TOM

Because I feel I . . .

> SHIV

No, Tom. Okay? I don't know if it's good for me to hear all –
that.

She looks at him.

I think it might be – I think it might be time for me and you to
move on.

> TOM

Uh-huh.

They look at one another. The end?

That makes me sad.

> SHIV

Sure.

> TOM

And you don't want to talk about what – happened?

> SHIV

Tom, I think we can talk things to death but actually, we both just made some mistakes and I don't think a lot of crying and bullshit is going to help, so if you're good I think we can just make quite an adult split here and walk away with our heads held high and say, good luck. Yeah?

He could dive in, but it won't be much fun . . .

> TOM

Well. Okay.

Beat. She sits on the bed.

He sits next to her. No more words.

We could see if I can make love to you?

> SHIV

Would you like to?

He shrugs – he'd give it a shot? But the atmosphere is not that.

I don't think so, Tom.

> TOM

Should I go? Are you going to go?

> SHIV

I'm tired. But you can stay there if you like.

> TOM

Okay.

She lies looking at the ceiling. Beat.

This is it, huh?

He holds her hand. She lets him.

> SHIV
>
> I guess. We gave it a go.

INT. ROMAN'S LA HOUSE – NIGHT

Roman is walking the house recording birthday messages for his dad.

Hits record on a voice message.

> ROMAN
> (*robot voice*)
> Happ-y birth-day. Fuck, you. From Ro-man.

Delete.

> Hey Dad. This is not me and it's not a message but fuck you and happy birthday. I love you. Fuck you. You're the best. Kissy kiss.

Delete. Can't get it right.

INT. LOGAN'S APARTMENT – STUDY – NIGHT

Logan can't sleep. He has a glass of water and some salted almonds that he eats one by one as he watches ATN. Middle-of-the-night programming. He's in open shirt and loosened pants, not made it to bed.

He makes a call. It rings quite a few times.

> CYD
> (*waking; on speakerphone*)
> Hello. Logan?

Big gap. Is he going to speak?

> Hi, Logan?

> LOGAN
> I just watched the top of the hour and it's bullshit. Jiménez got a sound bite that ran fifteen fucking seconds. And who the fuck is this lunk? People watch at night, you know? I watch at night.*

---

* By the time we shot this scene we had written the piece of news Logan was watching so were able to tailor his lines specifically to the images.

CYD

Okay. Sure. I get it. What's the issue?

LOGAN

Are you losing it, Cyd, ah? Are you fucking losing it?

Long gap.

Episode Two
REHEARSAL

Written by
Tony Roche & Susan Soon He Stanton
Directed by Becky Martin

Original air date 2 April 2023

Cast

LOGAN ROY	Brian Cox
KENDALL ROY	Jeremy Strong
GREG HIRSCH	Nicholas Braun
SHIV ROY	Sarah Snook
ROMAN ROY	Kieran Culkin
CONNOR ROY	Alan Ruck
TOM WAMBSGANS	Matthew Macfadyen
GERRI KELLMAN	J. Smith-Cameron
WILLA FERREYRA	Justine Lupe
KAROLINA NOVOTNEY	Dagmara Dominczyk
HUGO BAKER	Fisher Stevens
COLIN STILES	Scott Nicholson
KERRY CASTELLABATE	Zoë Winters
LUKAS MATSSON	Alexander Skarsgård
CYD PEACH	Jeannie Berlin
JESS JORDAN	Juliana Canfield
STEWY HOSSEINI	Arian Moayed
SANDI	Hope Davis
JENNIFER	Sydney Lemmon
CYRUS TELLIS	Kevin Changaris
SYLVIA FERREYRA	Cynthia Mace
CINDY	Elizabeth Greer
SARA	Sarah Lyddan
CANDICE	Polly Lee
PRODUCER	Jonathan Randell Silver
SARAH	Katie Lee Hill
SECURITY	Thamer Jendoubi
SHAW	Kate Arrington
DANIEL JIMÉNEZ	Elliot Villar
CRAIG HAMILTON	David Briggs
JOHN PORTIS	Iain Page
JUNIOR PRODUCER	Ian Lowe
KARAOKE SINGER	Gianna Rapp
NATO EXPERT	James Michael Reilly
CATHLEEN CARMICHAEL	Kelly Nash

EXT. LOGAN'S APARTMENT – DAY

Logan comes out with Kerry (checking her phone). Walking to the car.

> KERRY
>
> So. Everything – I think everything nailed on for tomorrow. How you feeling?

> LOGAN
> (*mixed feelings*)
> How am I feeling? Fucking great!

Kerry smiles: Of course! Fine! But Logan grumbles at her.

> Why do people keep asking how I'm feeling?!
> (*then*)
> I'm selling. My decision. Feeling great.
> (*displacement anger*)
> And yes. Yes we axe that chopper. They can fucking walk.

> KERRY
>
> Right. Right you are.

At the car.

> Hey.

> COLIN
>
> Office?

> KERRY
>
> ATN.

Change of routine.

> COLIN
>
> Oh, okay? And call ahead to set it?

Logan shakes his head.

> Surprise visit?

Logan gets in. Looking forward to his plan—

> LOGAN
> Happy Christmas, you clock-watching fucks.

INT. UPSTATE NEW YORK RESORT – CONFERENCE ROOM – DAY

A rented conference room at a nice resort upstate (there's a table with lots of expensive fruits cut and arranged and high-end treats), where Kendall, Shiv and Roman are having a creative retreat to brainstorm their Pierce vision.

They are maybe on a bit of a break from a morning of meetings and discussion. There might be two areas, one where the kids are together, doing some reviewing . . .

Tellis (banker) and Candice (media consultant) are looking at materials. Jess and other assistants nearby.

Roman and Shiv are watching PGN coverage on an iPad – hooked up to a big screen. Shiv gets a text.

> SHIV
> Connor. Again. 'Have we left yet?' Eyeballs emoji. Fingers crossed emoji. Helicopter emoji.

> ROMAN
> *So* many olds. They're running a silver mine over there. Where are the hotties?

> SHIV
> This needs the living shit kicked out of it.

Kendall looks at segmentation studies of PGN programming.

> KENDALL
> A show about politics called *Inside Baseball*? How fucking confusing is that?

Roman remains mesmerized by the boring PGN footage.

> ROMAN
> Bloodlust! God our PGN will crush this peanut brittle.

> TELLIS
> Not quite yours yet?

ROMAN

Creative retreat, Telly. Blue-sky. No bad ideas, except yours.

KENDALL

(*looking at studies*)

Wednesdays, dookie . . . Sundays, *massive* stinky dog dookie . . .

SHIV

Gotta say the upside is huge if they broaden out and stop over-indexing to wine moms.

KENDALL

And not to get ahead of ourselves, but I do think we're uniquely positioned to ride the macros without also making the American shit-slope more slippery, right? Yay ratings, yay democracy?

Roman's distracted by the PGN on his tablet.

ROMAN

Sorry – I just can't seem to tear my eyes away from the bald man talking about NATO.

KENDALL

So, my floaty kinda semi-pitch would be: hardcore, international news. Jess, would you watch that?

JESS

I mean. If it was on . . . sure.

KENDALL

Like, maybe a focus on Africa. Every day, just: what is happening in Africa. A show for each part: the Maghreb; sub-Saharan, east; sub-Saharan, west; South Africa. I would watch that.

ROMAN

You would not watch that.

SHIV

It does sound a bit like *Homework: The Show*?

Kendall smiles.

KENDALL

Point is: global reach. A network that teaches you how to watch it.

> ROMAN
> Or? Shove all your farm report, melatonin news-hour info dumps into daytime and primetime, we go full *Clockwork Orange—*
> *(pulls eyelids open wide)*
> this is the world, feast your peepers on its horrible delights!

> SHIV
> Sounds kinda Dad?

> ROMAN
> Dad occasionally had some success running a news network, Siobhan?

Shiv gets a call.

> SHIV
> *(as she retreats)*
> Yeah until he took on these motherfuckers. Daddy-fuckers.

EXT. UPSTATE RESORT – GROUNDS – DAY

Shiv walks outside the room to a portico area. She's on the phone with her assistant, Sarah.

> ASSISTANT
> *(on phone)*
> Yeah, so unfortunately Gretchen Yung is conflicted out.

> SHIV
> *(surprised)*
> Oh yeah? With Tom? He went with Gretchen? Okay, who's second position?

> ASSISTANT
> Crowley.

> SHIV
> *('let's go with him')*
> Okay, sure.

> ASSISTANT
> I contacted his office. He's also conflicted out.

Shiv stops. Starts to see what's happening.

> SHIV

Uh-huh. And Kohlmeyer, and Bulloch, and Camden—?

> ASSISTANT

Yeah. Conflicted out. It's weird.

This is somewhat humiliating to Shiv.

> SHIV

Uh-huh, sure. Thank you.

Shiv hangs up. The anger rises in her face. She briefly does something weird – presses her fingers into her arm hard like she might break the skin. Does a weird shudder like she's remembered the most embarrassing thing in the world to herself? Shakes her head out?

INT./EXT. TOM'S CAR – DAY

Tom is walking and talking with his junior assistant, Sara.

> TOM

And what is the status, have we tied up all five now?

> SARA

Yup.

> TOM

And those are all Mr Roy's office gave us right?

A nod from Sara.

Good. That's great.

Tom starts to get into his car as he gets a call.

Intercut with:

INT. ATN – BULLPEN – DAY

Greg is watching from a vantage point.

> GREG

Hey, Tom. So Logan's in.

> TOM

Logan's in. Upstairs? In the sales meeting?

GREG

On the floor, Tom.

TOM

He's on the *floor*? What's he doing?

GREG

Um, kinda – moseying. Terrifyingly moseying. Like a warden on death row.

A big open-plan office, full of producers, APs, production teams, runners, working on their news desks/shows/segments.

Logan is strolling.

TOM

Okay. Hold on. Hold steady. I'm coming in!
(*to the driver*)
Let's halt please, Sergio.
(*to Sara as he exits*)
Cancel my afternoon, Sara. And follow me at your discretion.

Tom halts the driver, climbs out of the car and, with as much dignity as he can muster, runs back towards work.

INT. UPSTATE RESORT – CONFERENCE ROOM – DAY

Shiv re-enters the room. Hiding her roiling resentment.

She can't keep focussed.

KENDALL

Or it's ecology-focussed? But visceral and spooky.

ROMAN

Yeah. An environmental show but not all doom and gloom?

KENDALL

It kinda is, Rome?

He looks at Shiv to share a smile about Roman but she's distracted. But Roman notices the patronizing look.

ROMAN

Not all of it? Sharks?

KENDALL

Sharks?

(*then*)

So, *Shark Week*. You're pitching *Shark Week*?

Roman notices Shiv's distraction.

ROMAN

All good?

SHIV

Yeah, yeah. Where are we, uh?

KENDALL

Candice was trying to ground us but we're staying poco loco and thinking we bring in some hot-shit brand guru like Glenn Boeckner to walk us through positioning and also tell us why Candice sucks.

Kendall winks at Candice: Kidding. Shiv gets up and goes back, as she goes, thinking—

Well this has been great. Hasn't this been great?

SHIV

Sure, three-hour commute and I can still hear a highway and smell an incinerator.

ROMAN

Dad would shit. There's fruit on the table I don't know, and I know my fucking fruit.

KENDALL

Yeah well there's no actual need to work in a fucking strip-lit thyroid bunker sweating it with heart-attack men. Doesn't prove anything. Does it?

SHIV

Candice. Shall, I actually call Gary? Not even a soft pitch just 'Hiya?'

Shiv's already on her way.

CANDICE

Um, sure, Gary's super-talented. I mean. It's early, it's very early—

(after her)
but if that's your instinct?

KENDALL
(after Shiv)
She's saying no. Shiv, she's saying you'll look mad and desperate.

Shiv looks at him.

Why not? I trust you.

After she goes, Roman waits a beat, then—

ROMAN
Shall we watch it again? As a treat?

EXT. UPSTATE RESORT — GROUNDS — DAY

Shiv makes a call and paces impatiently while she waits.

SHIV
Hey, Tom. So all the top attorneys are conflicted out. Did Dad
teach you that? Nice move. Does he want to marry you now?

Intercut with:

INT. ATN — HALLWAY — DAY

Tom is heading upstairs to his office at quite a pace.

TOM
Well I don't know what you mean?

SHIV
Uh-huh? So you've met or retained every useable divorce lawyer
in New York to fuck me?

TOM
Is that what's happened? Shiv, I don't know. Maybe Sara, by
mistake—

SHIV
You think I don't recognize my own dad's playbook? Fuck you,
Tom.

> TOM

I didn't intend this to be aggressive, Shiv. But, I've seen what, your – family can do in these situations and I want it to be amicable. I'm sure we can figure it out?

> SHIV

Uh-huh. Sure, Tom. Well, listen, if you're going to be my dad's little bitch boy, how about you deliver this message to him, bitch boy? Tell him to fuck off and stay out of my life?

Shiv hangs up angrily.

Tom shakes off the unpleasant call and arrives to join Greg at a point where they can monitor Logan.

> TOM

So, what's happened?

> GREG

He's just kinda walking around. But with the slight sense he might kill someone.
> *(then)*
It's like *Jaws*. If everyone in *Jaws* worked for Jaws.

They watch as Logan walks around. Everyone who clocks Logan tenses. It ripples around the room.

As they watch, Tom and Greg chat, commentate—

He did one big shout. He doesn't like the countdown-to-election chyrons. He hates the new font. Too small. Too 'ingratiating'.

We're aware of Logan, circling.

What is this, do you think?

As he strolls, people don't know whether or not to look at him. A little like the Angel of Death has shown up and is taking a walk.

> TOM

Probably here to issue on-the-spot cash bonuses.
> *(then)*
The future starts now, Greg. Once the board rubber stamps, regulators nod the deal through, four, five months, Waystar's gone. This is home.

People feeling Logan's chilly gaze over their shoulders, stiffening slightly, but trying not to react, while co-workers surreptitiously sneak furtive, fearful glances. The little things they say to one another, work queries feeling clipped and unnatural under his gaze.

> GREG
>
> So he'll be in all the time? In person?

> TOM
>
> Yep. Just hanging around like the threat of nuclear war.

Eventually Logan settles behind a junior producer who is typing. They see him coming, try to keep going, but they're nervous. Logan standing right behind them.

His breathing feels loud. The junior producer doesn't know whether to look or not. Tries to keep on typing. Making a lot of mistakes, correcting on screen in the email he's writing.

> TOM
> (cont'd)
>
> He says he's spent too long looking at the cost of pumping sewage tanks on cruise ships in Port-au-Prince.
> (then)
> You might wanna get a shoeshine, Greg. Tits and teeth!

He spots Cyd, who's seen Logan is in and is coming down the stairs.

Okay. Here we go!

Tom heads down to greet Logan and head off Cyd.

Sir! Mr Boss Man!

Logan references the person he's been watching.

> LOGAN
>
> One email? Fucking Stakhanovites in here. Don't exhaust yourself will you?

Tom tries to redirect Logan's attention.

> TOM
>
> How you like your election refit?

LOGAN

Pretty fucking penny. It's a fucking aircraft hangar. What's the air-con bill?

TOM

Cyd loved the sense of space. It's certainly interesting.

LOGAN

Where is she?

TOM

Cyd? Oh well, doesn't stay late when the opera's in town! Cyd!

She ignores Tom and addresses Logan.

CYD

Boss. Didn't see you. I was busy.
(*like it's a joke:*)
But I see my social secretary has been looking after you! He's always lounging around!

They smile at each other, but it's a death match.

LOGAN

So, you two looked at the tape?

Trouble!

TOM

Hm?

LOGAN

Have you watched Kerry's tape? What did you think?

Kerry is in view ahead but out of earshot.

TOM

Of Kerry? What did I think of her audition? As an anchor?

LOGAN

Yes?

Agony. A beat as Logan looks at them both. They look ahead to Kerry waiting, looking at her phone. Cyd calculates, best to pass the buck, looks away.

TOM

Well did you— What did you think, Loge?

LOGAN
Oh no no no no, kiddo. You go first.

TOM
Well. I think I liked it more than Cyd did?

Logan considers this weasely answer.

LOGAN
Smart. Nice.

Cyd makes a calculation.

CYD
I mean I did like it.

LOGAN
Oh? You did?

They think they see what he wants to hear.

TOM
Oh sure. She's got something.

CYD
She really does.

TOM
Are you thinking we give her a slot?

Logan looks like: Don't ask me. But might be a good idea.

Because I personally think that is an interesting idea? Loge?
Right?

Logan looks at him. Nice dance.

LOGAN
Oh I'm keeping out! She's my assistant. It would be very
unprofessional for me to get involved. Whatever you two
geniuses think.

Tom nods: Got it.

Right. I wanna talk to them, little speech?

CYD
Loge, listen, I'll call building services. Do it properly, we'll knock
you up a little stage here?

He looks at her skeptically.

INT. UPSTATE RESORT – CONFERENCE ROOM – DAY

The siblings watch Kerry's ATN audition tape on a laptop. Roman and Kendall watch eagerly. They are on a break.

Shiv has placed another call. She can see her brothers watching.

> ROMAN
> Man. Dad was a god. Tomorrow he's selling the empire to a 4chan Swede and dishing out jobs for BJs.

> KENDALL
> She's just aggressively serviceable. But like an inch off is a thousand miles.

Shiv moves outside but can still see and watch her brothers mocking the tape, doing impressions, maybe doing obscene things towards the screen as they watch.

EXT. UPSTATE RESORT – OUTSIDE CONFERENCE ROOM – DAY

Shiv looks inside. She connects—

> SHIV
> Hey, Sandi! I was going to set something but I thought I'd just try you? Because it's kind of urgent.

> SANDI
> *(on phone)*
> No problem. Is it about your older brother's wedding because I was such a regretful 'no'.

> SHIV
> Ha, no, just thinking back on our chat and your pitch . . . I feel like I was maybe a little hasty.

> SANDI
> Okay?

> SHIV
> In fact. I actually, wonder if— First time for everything! If I was just – wrong.

97

> SANDI

Uh-huh. And, do your siblings feel the same or still no?

> SHIV

Well, I actually haven't talked to them about it yet. But I'm going to bounce it around. See if I can't persuade them. Because I really think there's upside there.

> SANDI

I mean obviously I agree. But the board meet is tomorrow, Shiv?

> SHIV

Well, look, can – I just put you on alert in case there's room for a discussion here, and just to say, this is a live issue for me. Maybe we don't just wave this through. Maybe it pisses off my dad but maybe that's okay? I'll circle back if that's okay, Sandi?

Shiv hangs up. Maybe a brief pause, then she heads back in.

INT. UPSTATE RESORT – CONFERENCE ROOM – DAY

> ROMAN

That voice! Vocal-fry Goebbels. What the fuck is that?

As Jess lingers, trying to find an appropriate moment.

> JESS

Um, guys – we have transpo on the tarmac to get you back in time for Connor's rehearsal? He's messaging me direct, which is—

> (*weird/aggressive*)

helpful.

But Kendall can't stop . . .

> KENDALL

This is – this is special. Who leaked us this, Justin? Because he puts her on air, this is easily packaged as symptomatic of total loss of judgment and control, right?

INT. ATN – BULLPEN – DAY

Logan has had assistants build a stage from a platform of copier-paper boxes. Cyd looks at it skeptically.

> CYD

I'd really prefer something a little more stable.

> LOGAN

No need for a song and dance. Cheap and cheerful.

> CYD

This is an insurance risk.

> LOGAN

Uh-huh. Who am I gonna sue? Myself.
> (*to Tom*)
You wanna do an intro? Sprinkle some sugar?

> TOM

Of course?

Tom climbs up. Clears his throat. Sees Cyd watching him, with a couple of assistants.

Hey, guys? Just to say hi, tough few weeks it's been. Election in view now. Appreciate you all. Cyd. My partner in crime!

Mask-smile from Cyd.

But from my POV. Keep cranking.
> (*for Logan's benefit*)
We're doing great. Up three percent in the demo week-over-week.

> LOGAN
> (*sarcastic*)

Oooooh.

> TOM

But we can do more.
> (*bumped, tries to keep on*)
Fifteen percent year-on-year. So. Great work. And my pleasure to have the big man here to give us some support! Sir?

Claps. Tom steps down. Logan gets up, takes Tom's hand to steady. Tom is nervous.

Can I get you at least a— No, made it! There we go.

Tom is struck by the fact they are now at the same height.

Oooh. I could give you a kiss!

But regrets it, takes a step back.

> LOGAN

Evening, all! So. Fifteen percent up. Year-on-year? It's a shame
we're up forty on costs. Still I guess it evens out. Does it?
> (*looking at a guy*)

Is fifteen equal to forty, pal?

> PRODUCER

Um. Um—

> LOGAN

Is fifteen equal to forty?

> PRODUCER

No.

> LOGAN

No. Good. Good head for numbers.

Tom laughs heartily.

Alright. Look. You're good folks. You're the best or you
wouldn't be here, alright? But you've got to buckle down for
me. Waystar, I can't say too much yet but . . . I'll be spending
a lot more time with you guys. Because I love it in here. Ah?
I fucking love it. So. I don't want to know about three percent
week-over-week, I want to know if we're killing the opposition.
I want to be cutting their throats. Our rivals, should be checking
in. Up back of their 'chauffeured cars' – cos they can't believe
what we did! So fucking spicy! So true! The stuff everyone
knows but no one says, cos they're too fucking lily-livered,
ah? They can't fucking believe we said it! They're fucking jam
smears on the highway. Alright?
> (*looks around*)

So. Anyone who heard I was getting out, shove the bunting up
your ass. This isn't the end. I'm gonna build something better.
Something lighter, faster, meaner, wilder, and it's all gonna
happen from in here. With you lot. We're fucking pirates!
Alright?

He steps down to applause. Performance is over.

Tom slaps him on the back.

Sugar and spice.

EXT. HELICOPTER PAD/SMALL HELIPORT – DAY

The kids exit their car. And head towards a helicopter or a small terminal or portakabin.

> KENDALL
> And who are you most excited about never having to see again, once GoJo closes?

> ROMAN
> (*immediately*)
> Hugo – no question. Absolutely.

Kendall takes a large inhale. Shiv checks her phone. She's expecting an update. Nothing.

They reach Jess, who is ahead with Cindy, the operating manager for the heliport.

> JESS
> Um, so apparently there's a problem. Your dad's tightening up on use of choppers.

> ROMAN
> Excuse me?

> JESS
> 'New policy' apparently.

> SHIV
> You're serious?

Cindy comes over.

> CINDY
> Hi, I'm so sorry, I don't know what this is, but apparently I'm not authorized to let you take off. The company sent word.

> SHIV
> We are the company. Our dad's the—

KENDALL
(*to Shiv and Roman*)
Guys? He's fucking us. He knows we're out here making moves
and he's scared.

ROMAN
We're good. We'll just jump in and figure it out—

CINDY
I'm really sorry, I can't let you board. You're not authorized.

Kendall is wryly amused.

KENDALL
Oh this is good. Hats off.

ROMAN
We have to be somewhere and if we don't take that chopper—
I will set aside several hundred thousand dollars, and I will
dedicate it to destroying your life.

CINDY
I can't speak to that.

ROMAN
Oh you can't speak to that?

KENDALL
Dude. Relax. It's just theater.

The helicopter starts to take off.

ROMAN
What's it doing?

CINDY
It's going back to the city.

KENDALL
So pathetic.

Kendall's laissez-faire attitude only provokes Roman further.

ROMAN
It's fucking nuts. We're going to be late. Connor's gonna shit.
It'll be guilt trip to the moon. Do we call. Maybe this is a
mistake?

KENDALL

Yeah sure. It's a mistake, Rome.

Roman and Shiv fractious – but beatific Kendall maybe films the chopper as it leaves.

Clumsy old Daddy. Always getting it wrong. Bye-bye birdy. There goes Daddy. A chopper full of fuckery.

SHIV

Well I guess we're taking the car?

They start heading back towards the car.

ROMAN

Oh great, what? Getting stuck in traffic with all the fucking, traffic fucks.

KENDALL

You know I was talking to my guy and in Buddhism your greatest tormentor can also be your most perceptive teacher?

ROMAN

Uh-huh. Hey, Buddha, nice Versaces.

Ding. Message for Shiv – she reads it, parses it, adjusts.

KENDALL

Con?

SHIV

(re her phone)

Um, no, okay, so this is interesting? Sandi and Stewy want to meet? Call or meet. Prefer the meet?

KENDALL

Uh-huh?

SHIV

They're asking if we'll be back in the city in the next one to two.

ROMAN

Sandy? The brain in a jar with a dildo attached?

SHIV

Daughter Sandi.

> KENDALL

For what?

> SHIV

They want to do it in person.

> ROMAN

Tonight? Nah. It's the board again. Right? Stewy's been saying Sandy thinks there's more juice in the Swede, are they flying that again?

Shiv gets a second message.

> SHIV

They're offering to come to us?

Shiv looks to Kendall and Roman: Thoughts?

> ROMAN

Well they can't— We'll be at the rehearsal dinner. So, no, right? I don't want it to get all hokey.

> SHIV

Do we string them along on the board vote? Then hit them with our Pierce pitch? We could do with partners.

Kendall gestures: Why not? Shiv looks to Roman.

> ROMAN

Late for Connor's rehearsal? Even later. Nah, I think it's just fuckery.

> SHIV

Pretty fucking standard for a board to ask for more?

> ROMAN

Oh come on. It's done. Dad's lots of things, but no one ever accused him of being soft on a deal. It's fuckery.

> KENDALL

It's bullshit, Shiv. We're done. Yeah? We've moved on.

Shiv looks at them. Thinks. Messages back something else. We might clock. Kendall gets in the car.

ROMAN

I agree with the fucking hippy here. Alright, two-hour commute! Woo! Let's get into it. See the unhappy couple! Get this shit show on the shit road.

INT. ATN — HALLWAY — DAY

Logan and Kerry are walking the corridor. With Karolina.

LOGAN

I don't like the silence. Give it a last buzz round alright? Kerry, can you get Frank, Karl on the independents, let's triple-lock this.

INT. ATN — CONFERENCE ROOM — DAY

As Logan and Karolina head into a conference room, Kerry heads off.

Hugo is there with Gerri. Hugo is sniggering at something he and Gerri are watching, a little fearful, reluctant.

HUGO

Hey!

Hugo slams his laptop shut.

KAROLINA

Hi. We had a gap so we thought we'd pull this forward, okay?

GERRI

Okay!

Weird atmosphere.

LOGAN

What's going on?

HUGO

I'm sorry? Just some prep. For post-board meet. The signing of the deal. Seems like Matsson would love to do an actual photo op and I guess it's just, is that what you want or—

Logan is staring at him as he talks until he cuts Hugo off.

LOGAN

Uh-huh. And what the fuck were you laughing at?

> HUGO

What? Gerri was, we were chatting and it was amusing, that—

> LOGAN

Okay. Fine. What are the options? I don't know if I want to shake his hand, he's been a fucking prick about the spin-off.

Panic.

> HUGO

Karolina, can you do the option deck?

> KAROLINA

Well you're ready to go in?

> HUGO

Uh-huh. But – could you?

She senses something. Opportunity to torture. Hugo gives nothing, avoids eye contact.

> KAROLINA

Is yours not working?

> HUGO

Nope.

> KAROLINA

Give it a go?

> LOGAN

It seemed to be working, give it a go.

Hugo swallows. He plugs in a cable and connects his laptop to a big screen. Opens it. After unlocking the home screen, there is Kerry's tape. He quickly closes the window and there's a pitch deck for options on how to handle the GoJo–Waystar deal.

> HUGO

Yeah great stuff.

> KAROLINA

Okay? Shall we get into this?!

Logan eyes Hugo, who tries to look away. It's obvious what was going on. Logan is hurt but it will come out later.

> LOGAN

Nah. I don't want to be standing around like fucking set dressing.

> GERRI

I mean, the only thing is, everyone's saying the timing, the deal you've done. You don't want your moment in the sun?

> LOGAN

You working for him already? I'm not fucking gone yet, am I? Ah? You getting your Viking hat on early?
> (*looks around*)
Nah this is bullshit. Hugo, we might need someone to go and suck off an independent director, put your fucking lipstick on.

And he's off.

Gerri and Hugo look at one another.

EXT. NEW YORK – HIGH-END VENUE – NIGHT

Car pulls up. Kendall, Roman and Shiv get out.

Shiv's looking around.

> SHIV

I mean do we even go now? Is it kind of worse to go?

Roman and Kendall look – they have to go.

> ROMAN

I mean I love the idea of not going. But I think we have to drink at least a couple of Martini Passive-Agressos to make up, no?

A pair of security people approach diffidently.

> SECURITY

Hi? Um, hi, we wondered if we could beg your attention?

They look over.

Sandi and Stewy waiting in a car – maybe Stewy out of the door waving.

> STEWY

Hey? Wanna ride? JFK, flat fare. I make good price!

They head over to greet them.

> ROMAN

Hey? What the fuck?

A look between Shiv and Sandi.

> SHIV

What is this? We're kinda pushed.

> ROMAN

Well more than— What is this, an ambush?

> STEWY

We just wanted to do five in person, right, Sandi?

> SHIV
> *(feigning surprise)*

Okay, right, not very convenient but do we want to go somewhere?

> SANDI

We have a suite booked across the way with some materials and we can do it all in—

> KENDALL
> *(interrupting)*

Well no. We do not want to go somewhere, we want to go and see our brother. Shiv? What the fuck?

Sandi gives him the pitch—

> SANDI

We're prepared to vote 'no' on the GoJo deal at the Waystar board meeting tomorrow. We want you to join us in pushing for a higher price. We think there's more money to be squeezed from the Swede and we think you're rushing this for emotional reasons.

> ROMAN

I don't think so. Okay – see you!

> SHIV

Let's at least—

> STEWY

The premium looks weak on market comparables. Look at last week's—

> KENDALL

Different deal. Not relevant.

> SANDI

We want your dad to ask for more, but he's stopped engaging, palmed us off with Karl. He can get the deal through without us but if we get you guys on our side, we can force him back into the ring for one last round.

The kids 'think'.

> SHIV

Well I guess, in one way, 'board pushes back on price'. What's the big deal?

Roman looks skeptical.

> KENDALL

We'd have to weigh that against the risk of blowing everything up.

> STEWY

We see that.

> ROMAN

Look, I think our position might be that we're done cornholing our dad.

> SANDI

It just feels like your old man got hot for this. Can't we cool him off?

> KENDALL

Stew?

> STEWY

Honestly. Look. There is some risk. But it's small. And yes, I've been persuaded by my associates that this is the play. There's money, for all of us, if we ask nicely. If we push too hard, danger but yeah. It's there.

> SANDI

My dad is clear. He wants to vote 'no'.

> STEWY

Amazing what you can get a guy to say when you control his feeding tube.

Sandi reacts – too much.

I'm kidding. He's doing great.

Maybe he makes a face behind her back. Like he's ill, sucking in his cheeks and shaking.

> SANDI

Us plus you guys. That's it. He's outvoted. This doesn't get through the board. Send him back to the table. It doesn't need to go nuclear.

> STEWY

It's just one more squeeze of the toothpaste tube. It goes two ways: Logan grovels, nets another bil. Or, Matsson plays hardball. The well's dry. No harm, no foul. We only asked.

The siblings take a beat. Are they sticking to their plan?

> SHIV

Can we think?

> SANDI

Board meeting first thing? Be great to know in the next hour or two?

> ROMAN

Sure. So either we vote 'yes' tomorrow and we all make billions of dollars. Or sign up for your cool shit and get Dad to disinherit us entirely? Hm, it's a toughie, but we'll weigh it up.

Roman and Kendall head off, leaving Shiv to have last words with Sandi.

INT. HIGH-END VENUE – LOBBY – NIGHT

As Kendall and Roman head in, Willa is heading out with a few girlfriends—

> WILLA

Oh, hey? Oh so you're here now huh?

ROMAN

Yeah sorry. Willa? You okay?

Jennifer from Willa's play is in Willa's gang. She walks past Kendall.

A million years ago.

JENNIFER

Hey.

KENDALL

Hey.

Kendall wants to say something.

Um. Yeah, hey. Sorry.

JENNIFER

Sure. See you around.

And she goes. But some of Kendall's Buddhist facade has been rocked.

Over with Willa and Roman—

WILLA

Yeah I am – I'm just. I'm just going for a little drink.

ROMAN

Is it over?

WILLA

The rehearsal? Um no. No. But I think, they can take it from here. I'm not vital from here?

ROMAN

The bride is normally, I guess, is generally considered one of the first team at the old wedding?

WILLA

Hahahaha! Yeah right. I should go. And have a think. I'm in a bit of a fuzz. Everything feels very vivid today doesn't it?

She seems distracted, a little odd. Her friends wait, wanting her to come with them. Shiv joins.

SHIV

Uh-huh, all okay?

> WILLA

Uh-huh. Yeah. Sure. I mean you can't be jumping for joy the whole time can you?

> ROMAN

Um, no. I guess?

> WILLA

No it's exciting. Just a little worried. But yeah. And I am just wondering, a little about the venue? Have we rushed it on the venue? It smelled quite old and sort of – sweet. *The boat. And my speech.* Do you think they put something on their carpets? Do you think they get a lot of seasickness?

> ROMAN

Um. I don't know?

> WILLA

No. Nor me. It's fine. Maybe – I don't think it matters.
> *(to her friend)*
Francis! It doesn't matter!
> *(then)*
But the bathrooms, the water pressure? The flow is *so* weak. But. All in all. Good! Look, I should go!

Her pals, theater friends and young folks, sweep her off. They're full of weird energy.

> ROMAN

Oh, man.

> SHIV

Do we even go up?

They look at her like: A little callous?

> ROMAN

I think it seems like we should?

> SHIV

I mean we have a lot to discuss?

> ROMAN

That bullshit?

> SHIV

Few weeks' pain, might just set us up? I mean I do think we overpromised on Pierce.

The brothers start going up.

> ROMAN

It's a Sandy mind-game. Fuck 'em.

INT. REHEARSAL DINNER – NIGHT

They arrive. Find Connor – he might be alone with a bottle of red. He might have an unpredictable edge.

> CONNOR

Okay. *Here* they are.

> KENDALL

We're so sorry, man.

> SHIV

Yeah, Dad screwed us.

Connor looks at them.

> CONNOR

Sure. Look at you. The Rebel Alliance. How is it out there in the hills? Supply lines okay? Got enough to eat?

> ROMAN

You okay, man?

Connor drinks, hard.

> CONNOR

So this is it, huh? The battle royale. Me and Dad on one side, you guys on the other!
> *(machine-gun noise and action)*
Me Crips! You Bloods!

> ROMAN

We saw Willa?

> CONNOR

I think it's all fine. I think it will . . .

> (*then*)

Willa stood up to do her speech and said, 'I can't do this' and went to the bathroom for forty minutes with her so-called friends.

ROMAN

Nah, come on, Con, you're good. Throw her another ten K? Snowmobile and some teeth-whitening vouchers? I'm kidding.

Willa's mom, Sylvia, passes.

SYLVIA

You alright there, Connor? I think it's fine. I think it's nerves. I'm calling!

Sylvia tries to connect on phone.

CONNOR
(*big smile*)

Thanks, Mrs F!

SHIV

Sounds like it's all good?

CONNOR
(*but the real story*)

I've been putting her up at the Surrey. Breakfast, lunch and dinner on room service. I mean. You might like to see the city, visit a Starbucks? But god forbid it doesn't go on that tab?!

Sylvia approaches.

Any luck, Sylvia?

Shiv looks at her brothers, they huddle as Connor drinks.

SHIV

So, do we regroup at my place?

ROMAN

Shiv, he looks pretty rough?

SHIV

Sure, and I'm sorry Dad fucked us and we're late but we need to decide what we're doing fast?

KENDALL

Well I think we know, right?

SHIV

Well do we though? They made some pretty compelling
arguments?

ROMAN

Sandi's a greedy little bitch, she's got her hand up the ass of the
carcass of her dad, Stewy's come along for the ride. It's a packet
of horseshit.

SHIV

What if I want to talk it through?

KENDALL

I think we rise above it, Shiv, right? It's annoying. But like, float
out baby, we float out. The deal, is the deal. The world likes it,
the market likes it. The board likes it, the independents—

SHIV

Maybe Dad's not on it like he used to be? Maybe he's
underplayed his hand and the board's all hand-fucking-picked
Japanese plastic cats, waving it through.

Connor gets up, looking at his phone, drinking.

CONNOR

Incommunicado. I just really hope she's okay.
(*cracking slightly*)
Whaddya say, a little bit of karaoke?

The three don't like the sound of it much. Look at each other.

ROMAN

Would it be possible to do anything other than that in the entire
universe also including mainlining ratshit?

CONNOR

She's partying, so I can party?

ROMAN

I mean we can do one drink though? Yeah? Little bachelor
party?

SHIV

I really think we three— We just have quite a lot to— We're
kind of in the middle of something?

>   CONNOR
> Oh sure! Everyone's busy.

>   KENDALL
> Let's give him a drink, sis?

>   CONNOR
> But – not your usual stupid places. Somewhere – real and fun.
> Away from the fancy dans. A real bar with chicks – and guys
> who work with their hands and grease and sweat from their
> hands and have blood in their hair.

Shiv looks pleadingly . . .

>   ROMAN
> I don't like these guys. They sound like a medical experiment
> gone wrong.

INT. ATN – KITCHEN – NIGHT

Greg and Tom are waiting.

>   GREG
> He said it was a big problem.

>   TOM
> Is it election-related? Because he was talking about doing drastic
> things with the decision desk . . .

>   GREG
> I dunno he just said – he just said—

Logan arrives.

>   TOM
> Hi, Loge. So what's up?

Logan is uncomfortable.

>   LOGAN
> It's – all this pizza.

There are some boxes on top of a bin.

>   TOM
> Uh-huh? Okay?

> LOGAN

Uh-huh. Why am I looking at all this pizza? Is this place out of control, Tom? No more fresh pies, right? They're sending out for fresh pies and this is three or four here that are perfectly good and it could go in the microwave.

> TOM

Uh-huh. Good.

> GREG

Right. Noted. It tends to – lose a certain, there's a sog factor, but I'll note that, shall I, Tom?

Logan thinks. Privacy needed.

> LOGAN

Greg, fuck off.

Greg retreats.

Look, it's not the pizza, it's the culture.
> *(then)*
I've been thinking. About Kerry.

> TOM

Uh-huh. Very excited. We'll get into it. She's a natural.

Logan looks at him, makes a bit of a face. Tom tries to read.

Amazing. She's – she's got 'it' you know?

> LOGAN

You think she's the finished article?

Tom's searching Logan for clues – has he changed his mind?

> TOM

Oh, well, finished article, no. But you wouldn't expect her to be.

> LOGAN

No?

> TOM

No, she needs a little time.
> *(looks at him)*
Maybe quite a bit of time?

                    LOGAN
Interesting.

                    TOM
I do, yes. She's raw. We should probably start her out of the way.
Under the radar. I mean, yeah.
                    (*looking*)
She has a lot to learn. A lot and yeah, it can be damaging to put
talent out there too early.

                    LOGAN
That's smart. You're smart. Let her down gently, yeah?

                    TOM
                    (*shit*)
Of course. No problem, sir.

Logan nods.

                    LOGAN
I'm not involved. Okay? I'm nowhere near this. I know nothing.

                    TOM
Sure. Understood.

Logan exits. Nightmare for Tom.

INT. BAR — NIGHT

*Kendall, Roman, Shiv and Connor head in. Everyone takes in their
surroundings as they approach the bar.*

                    CONNOR
Ah, America! I've missed you!

                    KENDALL
What's everyone having?

                    ROMAN
Do you think they know the recipe for a vodka tonic?

                    SHIV
Do I dare the house red? No, I think, a club soda. But a sealed
bottle—
                    (*aside*)
Nothing from that tainted nozzle.

KENDALL

Con?

CONNOR

I'll just have whatever a regular Joe would have. Just a Belgian weissbier? Not Hoegaarden ideally.

Kendall attracts the bartender.

SHIV

Did you see the 'Heard on the Street' bit? On what they think the Waystar price will come out at? Sandi shared.

Con is looking at his phone, checking Willa's whereabouts.

ROMAN

Hey, Con? You with us?

CONNOR

Oh sure.
                    (*explaining*)
Just Willa – I have her location shared?

Shiv looks at him.

I think it's just a factory setting.

SHIV

Sure.

CONNOR

Anyway, I'm reassured – she's definitely not on her way to Cuba.

KENDALL

Well her phone isn't.

CONNOR

She's stopped moving. Guess she's found a spot she likes?

ROMAN

Sure. On another guy's dick.
                    (*off Connor's look*)
Sorry. Too soon.

CONNOR

Can we not— [do the dark jokes?] I'm feeling a little . . . I have certain anxieties? Hm? I want to have a good time. I was imagining this place would be like – a little more. I thought it would be more – *Top Gun*-ny – winos and Bukowski, wise-apples, goodfellas, hookers and like the guys from *Cheers*. I wanna have fun . . .

The others wince.

> KENDALL
> We can monitor her dot together – get it up on the big screen?

> CONNOR
> Ugh. She's— Why so long at— Her dot is in an aquarium supply retailer, that doesn't make sense? A dry cleaners? What's going on?

Kendall has an incoming FaceTime. He heads out.

EXT. BAR – NIGHT

> KENDALL
> Lukas? What's up, brother?

> MATSSON
> *(on FaceTime)*
> What's up? Well. First off, I can't fucking sleep. Do you sleep good?

We might see a screen behind him, a video game paused.

> KENDALL
> Er, well, honestly, no.

> MATSSON
> No. I never met someone I respect who sleeps good. Yeah, 'Turn off the unit.' I fucking wish.

What the fuck? But Kendall rolls with it.

> KENDALL
> Oh yeah. One eye open, bro.

> MATSSON
> Second, I shouldn't be talking to you about this, my team say, but I am because – blah. But I've got a read-out that the activists hustling on the price are targeting you to sign up for their little scheisse party?

> KENDALL

Uh-huh. Well I can't give you a play-by-play. But I think you can take your nap.

Matsson thinks. The reassurance, for some reason, doesn't work. In fact, it unsettles Matsson.

> MATSSON

Yeah? Because I know you tried to screw this deal with your dad. And I know he hates you now. So. You're out of options, okay, bro. I hear you're going around offering old ladies suitcases full of money. Well if you want to have a full suitcase anytime soon, don't push me. Okay?

> KENDALL

Okay, dude, I hear you, man.

> MATSSON

He's going to sell. But if he pushes me again it won't be me he sells to is the actual situation.

Kendall says nothing. Matsson feels he might've come on too strong. Maybe he is riding a THC or booze wave.

This isn't aggressive. When I am direct I'm told it can code aggressive. It's late here and I thought, 'What is the issue?' So forgive me. I've switched to edibles but – I like you. I thought some clarity, before any nukes get launched? Am I wrong?

> KENDALL

Nah, brother. I got you. It's good. Let's keep the door open.

> MATSSON

Thank you. The deal's taken forever. It's boring. Your dad is grumpy. But that's cool. Sixty-nine waves of enemies, plus the boss. I can grind. But not this. I'm over it. We're not paying more. So don't push us or I'm out. Yeah?

But might that work for Kendall? Matsson frustrated that he's not giving anything back. He's tired, bored, out of patience.

> KENDALL

Loud and clear. Loud and clear.

> MATSSON

Okay. I appreciate this.

(to his room)
That wasn't rude. I was polite!
(then)
Thanks, K-Roy. I'll be able to sleep now.

Kendall maybe blows him a kiss. End of call. Thinks.

Deal falls apart . . . No other buyers?

He goes and bums a cigarette from a couple smoking outside.

Sends a message to Stewy: 'Send me the detail on the comparables.'

INT. ATN — SMALL CONFERENCE ROOM — NIGHT

Tom and Greg are sitting. They finish watching Kerry's tape.

> TOM
>
> This is an incredibly delicate piece of diplomacy. This is Israel–Palestine, Greg, but harder and much more important.

> GREG
>
> She's not gonna be happy.

> TOM
>
> But I think there's a way through.

> GREG
>
> Uh-huh.

> TOM
>
> You tell her?

> GREG
>
> Um, interesting. I mean I don't like it.

> TOM
>
> You're a little frustrated. You want next-level tasks?

> GREG
>
> Yeah but – like not telling our boss's girlfriend she can't be on TV?

> TOM
>
> Honestly, I think it tracks. I'll give you the playbook.

(*sells Greg*)

So, what you do is you say, like, you say, you know it's hard, being a *cousin*, and you've seen what's happened to the kids. How it can go wrong, get muddled?

GREG

Uh-huh.

TOM

She's good, not too good, keep Logan and me out of it, but the focus group had thoughts?

GREG

Okay?

TOM

So yeah. Does she really want to like get handed it on a silver platter, the resentments, the accusations. You make it her idea, to cool things? Maybe she should think about doing it herself, from local?

GREG

Okay. Okay? I mean, yeah. But if she's like, 'Fuck you, Greg, I wanna be on TV tomorrow, ATN.'

TOM

Then fine. Back away to a position of safety and I'll march in and mop up the rage.

INT. BAR — NIGHT

Shiv is talking with the manager, who has asked a server to move a family so the kids can have a secluded table. Kendall arrives back.

KENDALL

Hey. What's up?

ROMAN

We're eating. Right here in Billy Ray Cyrus's Kentucky Fried Shit Shack?

CONNOR

It looks like they have some hearty fare!

Connor crosses to get some menus.

ROMAN

And what was that?

KENDALL
(*covering*)

Stewy.

ROMAN

Oh fuck. What now?

KENDALL

Guys, can I show you something?

Kendall offers his phone. It shows various comparables, charts, etc.

Shiv has a bite – she lights up.

ROMAN

Oooh 'wings'. I wonder from which particular creature they snipped these 'wings'? You think a mammal?

KENDALL

On the comparables. Intriguing, no?

SHIV

Makes you think – what if he's not on it like he used to be? Pushed around by Matsson, pushed around by Kerry – giving shows to his girlfriend? Maybe she's leading him around by his cock? Maybe he's gone full Xanadu. Lions walking around the kitchen. He's growing his toenails long and shouting at shadows.

Connor looks at his phone.

CONNOR

Oh fuck. She's in the East River. She's in the fucking—
(*then*)
No! She's on the bridge! She's on her way to . . . Williamsburg?

KENDALL
(*scrolls*)

Rome? Look. I think Matsson has deliberately lowballed the synergies.

SHIV

Exactly!

CONNOR

What is this?

SHIV

It's not really for you, Con?

CONNOR

Oh, high-level family business I wouldn't understand?

The server approaches.

SERVER

So have you had enough time to look at the menu?

ROMAN

Oh my god yes. It's quite the compendium of delights! I think
I'll be ordering off-chef.

SERVER

Off-menu? You want to substitute?

SHIV

Yes I want to substitute everything you have for someplace else?
Is that okay?

ROMAN

We'll get back to you, we're gonna order off-restaurant.

Roman pulls out his phone to look at a menu. Puts it on the table.

SHIV

And not to be dicks, Con, and we'll be right, right back – but is
it cool if we just do a break-out chat – just for like two?

Roman calculates.

ROMAN

Why don't we fold Con in?

SHIV

Well, he's not on the board?

ROMAN

But he has a share. If the deal collapses, he'll lose his payout?

CONNOR
(*suddenly quite interested*)

Excuse me?

ROMAN

Shiv wants to get us mixed up in some drug deal to screw the vote tomorrow.

SHIV

Delay, just a small delay, everyone wants the deal.

KENDALL

And look. I think I agree?

ROMAN

Oh what the fuck now?

KENDALL

Just looking at the numbers. It's compelling.

ROMAN

Really?

KENDALL

I'm at equanimity with Dad, this is a business decision.

CONNOR

You're gonna force Dad to grovel? Oh, man. How long will a renegotiation take?

ROMAN

Exactly. Maybe *forever*.

SHIV

I really think we should discuss this in private and then fill Con in? Because, Con, you don't have a say here, dude, in a – in a technical—

CONNOR

Oh really? Well, I disagree. I need that money. Lukas is very unpredictable.

KENDALL

Nah. He's on the hook. He needs scale and who else can he buy?

SHIV

It's a play. More money is more money. That's all there is to it.

Roman's phone is there on the table.

Ding. Message from – Dad.

They all look.

KENDALL

Er, Roman?

SHIV

Dad's – messaging you?
(*then*)
Why is Dad messaging you, Rome?

Roman picking up phone. Playing dumb.

ROMAN

I don't know. Ask him.

Watching Roman.

KENDALL

Uh-huh? You not going to read it?

ROMAN

I dunno. Sure.

Roman unlocks his phone and takes a beat to read the message.

It's just a check-in.

SHIV

Mm, a check-in. Classic Dad. Always checking in. What the
fuck, Rome, is this part of an ongoing conversation?

ROMAN

No. Look – I guess he's got voting fears. He's got the vibrations.

Kendall and Shiv look at one another.

KENDALL

Can we see?

ROMAN

My phone? No! Look, I said one happy birthday, I said sorry we
missed it. This is – now an unprovoked check-in.

SHIV

Wait – so you texted him initially?

KENDALL

He's using you as malware, Rome, he's spying on us because he's
heard about the Stewy meet.

> SHIV

We're not communicating with Dad. We had rules.

> KENDALL

No contact, dude? He'll get his fucking screwdriver in?

> SHIV

I've blocked him. You sending one text is basically being in bed with him. That text is a portal to hell.

> ROMAN

Drama queen.

> KENDALL

We don't talk to him until he apologizes.

> ROMAN

So, never?

Shiv and Kendall look at one another.

Fuck you, looky-lookies.

> SHIV

You know I'm sorry but I think I might need to see your phone.

> ROMAN

Show us your phone. World's biggest WhatsApp group for sharing shots of your snatch. Fuck you. No.

> KENDALL

We have to trust each other for this to work?

> ROMAN

Are you fucking serious? Oh my god you're serious. My god.

> KENDALL

It's just – why you holding out? We need to be a three-legged table here.

Roman feels he needs to offer something to mend the alliance.

> ROMAN

Fine, fucking bullshit.
> (slides it over)

It's mostly dick pics I sent him anyway. He kind of got a taste for them.

They scroll and read.

SHIV

Hm . . .

KENDALL

Okay . . .

SHIV

Well . . . this is – three messages total?

KENDALL

Bit warm?

ROMAN

Why? What did I say?

KENDALL

'Take care.'

ROMAN

He's our dad, what do you want me to say, 'Happy birthday hope you fall down the stairs, shithead'?

They hand the phone back.

SHIV

Well look. I do feel weird about this betrayal.

ROMAN

Fuck you 'betrayal'. 'Happy birthday take care'?

KENDALL

Me too.

ROMAN

Fucking family guilt trip, European vacation.

CONNOR

Hey it's hard, it's been hard on everyone.

SHIV

You know he advised Tom on divorce? Dad trick – he's spoken to every pitbull in Manhattan and tied them up. Can you believe it? I've gotten Mommed.

This sharing is relatively new. Shiv looks around. Roman is reminded of this side of his dad.

KENDALL

Unbelievable. I mean, except that it's – totally believable.

ROMAN

I'm sure there's maybe one more horrible motherfucker lawyer left in the United States, if you really look?
(*then*)
But I'm sorry.

KENDALL

I feel like, we need to stick together and we should push back and you should come with us and put the squeeze on.

ROMAN

But we want to do Pierce, we wanna get out?

KENDALL

Exactly, with just a *bit* more money.

ROMAN

But Matsson won't go up in price. I know. I spoke to him earlier.

KENDALL

You spoke to him?

ROMAN

Yeah, he's secretive. But we're tight.

KENDALL

Oh yeah? You got a special thing going on? Is he your snow bro, Ro?

ROMAN

Look, he thinks I'm fucking cool and he tells me everything. And he told me, this is his ceiling.

KENDALL

Oh is that what he said? Oh well if that's what he said, it must be true?

ROMAN

Seriously. I think he might walk.

SHIV

Oh might he? And he could ever— Could he, could he consider, saying a – not. The thing that, isn't. A – lie?

> KENDALL

I mean why would he say that?

> SHIV

It's negotiating one-oh-one. Did they not teach you that when you did management training?

> ROMAN

He sounded like he meant it.

> SHIV

That's negotiating one-oh-two.

> KENDALL

'How much is carpet?'

> SHIV

'One-twenty dinar.'

> KENDALL

'No no no, too much, too too much, I walk away now!'

Roman shakes his head.

> CONNOR

Pretty basic stuff, Rome.

That was fun. But a bit mean.

> SHIV

I get it, conflict is not nice. But we overpromised on Pierce. This gives us the cash to make it right.

> ROMAN

I don't give a shit about conflict, I'm in constant fucking conflict.

> SHIV

Is this about Dad for you? You've still got 'Dad feelings'.

> ROMAN

If anyone's got Dad feelings it's you. Poking Satan with a – fork. I'm fucking genuine about us three.

> SHIV

Me too, that's why we're not texting Satan.

ROMAN

Fine. Fine. Just spare me the fucking talking to, okay? Stop fucking ganging up on me like you're Lennon and McCartney and I'm George. I'm John. You're Ringo. You're Yoko.
(*re Connor*)
And he's the drummer from Wings.

KENDALL

Honestly, I think going with Sandy and Stewy is the right thing for us to do, this group.

It's what they have to say. And maybe they believe it.

It's just a move. A delay. A couple of weeks. He'll get it. It's what Dad would do in his prime.

ROMAN

It's just a move?

KENDALL

Absolutely. Totally, Rome. It's just a play.

They look at Roman. Maybe Connor starts to moan, seeing what's coming

ROMAN

Then I guess, so long as it's a play I'm in.

CONNOR

God fucking dammit. You've ruined it all. You've fucking ruined it all!

KENDALL

C'mon, Con. It's okay. What do you want to do?

CONNOR

What do I want? I wanted to get married tomorrow. I wanted to be with my family tonight. And my dad tomorrow. I wanted to get my fucking money out. And I wanted to sing one fucking song at karaoke because I've seen it in films but no one will ever go.

They look at each other. They shrug and relent: Okay sure. As they get up to go, Connor starts typing out a message (to Logan).

INT. ATN – HALLWAY – NIGHT

Greg catches up to Kerry.

> GREG
>
> Hey! Kerry? Could I possibly please grab you for just five minutes please at all?

> KERRY
>
> Why not. You've already grabbed every other woman in Manhattan.

He ushers her into—

INT. ATN – SMALL CONFERENCE ROOM – NIGHT

Greg is making out he's nervous, but he has a certain amount of control.

> GREG
>
> So, look. Kerry, I wondered if I could trouble you for one quick minute? I hope I'm not getting above my station but it's the whole tape thing and the TV thing?

> KERRY
>
> I'm not sure I want to talk about that with you.

> GREG
>
> No fair enough. But just as a – a friend, I wondered if I could, on the down-low, give you a heads-up on what the murmurs are and say, you know, how careful I have had to be about – my particular position as a family member and how people chatter so unpleasantly about accusations of legs-up and unfair – things and—

> KERRY
>
> What is this?

> GREG
>
> Just are we, you, in danger of rushing things a bit and could that long term actually harm your—

> KERRY
>
> Tom doesn't think I'm ready and he's sent you to—?

GREG

No. Not at all. He thinks you're great. I mean, there are some little doubts, from the focus group but—

KERRY

They focus-grouped me?

GREG

But what I'm saying is, big picture, like how Kendall and Shiv have – have an entitlement problem?

KERRY

What did they say? The focus group?

GREG

Well, headlines: great, but just maybe not fully there, a few criticisms, so my thought is—

KERRY

Such as?

Thinking fast—

GREG

Minor shit. Like nothing. Great package – maybe, your arms, looked a little un-TV?

KERRY

My arms?

GREG

Not a biggie. Fixable, with a few years. But on TV. Not in life. It can happen. That they shoot weird. It's the camera. And it's fine. Let's not dwell.

KERRY

In what way do my arms look weird?

GREG

Well not weird no, I don't want to get into it. They said they don't hang right or some shit.

KERRY

Who was in this focus group, Greg? Just you? Is it Tom? Logan?

GREG

Noooo no no no. No this is real feedback.

> KERRY

Uh-huh and can I see it?

> GREG

No.

> KERRY

Because—?

> GREG

It's private?

> KERRY

Well it's not. What if I want to see it? What if Logan does?

> GREG

Well, no sorry, it's confidential.

> KERRY

From the CEO?
> (*looks at him*)
> Thanks, Greg. Must've taken a lot of bravery, to put yourself in such an incredibly vulnerable position.

Kerry walks out, hard to read. Greg looks anxious.

INT. ATN – CONFERENCE ROOM – NIGHT

Logan is looking at his phone, stewing. Gerri is there.

Kerry comes in. Looks at him. He looks at her.

She's piecing it together. A new distance.

> KERRY

Hey.

> LOGAN

Hey.

An atmosphere. Kerry looks to Gerri for an explanation.

> KERRY

Okay?

> GERRI

The kids. Sandy and Stewy. They have the numbers.

> KERRY

What do you do? Do you want me to call? Do you want me to ream them out for you?

Logan doesn't hate it. It's a little puzzle he has to figure out.

> LOGAN

Nah. Delicate. Delicate. This is— They've got some juice here. They have some fucking juice.

INT. KARAOKE BAR – NIGHT

The kids, looking ambivalent, head in. They've called ahead, and an employee, whom Shiv greets, is waiting to smooth the way.

INT. KARAOKE BAR – HALLWAY – NIGHT

The kids are led by the employee, past various doors. As they pass one, someone comes out – we can see inside. A bridal party is singing 'Wonderwall' by Oasis.

> ROMAN

Boooo! Booo. Bad. Bad singing. Your wedding is doomed!

INT. KARAOKE BAR – PRIVATE ROOM – NIGHT

The kids are shown into their room.

> CONNOR

Okay.

He looks around.

So now what happens?

> SHIV

Now someone has to humiliate themselves in the Shame Palace.

Connor starts looking at the songs on the selection.

> CONNOR

Do you think they have 'Desperado' by The Eagles?

> ROMAN

I would imagine that's a yes. Longest night of my life.

Connor checks his phone, sees Willa has turned off location tracking.

CONNOR

Oh shit, she's gone dark. Why's she gone dark? Is this it? Is she going off with some buck and they'll just— You know?

KENDALL

Take it easy. Maybe her phone just died?

Sounds like that might be the reason.

SHIV

You know what? Maybe she's not right for you? Have you thought about that? This could be good. You'll meet someone else.

Roman looks at Kendall.

KENDALL

You're not doing better than Willa.

ROMAN

I would agree. Don't listen to Shiv, Con. Do not let Willa go.

Then Connor gets a text—

CONNOR

Okay so Dad's on his way.

KENDALL

What?

CONNOR

He wants us to go down to the car?

SHIV

What the fuck—?

KENDALL

How does he know we're here and how do you know he's coming?

CONNOR

Well. I told him it's the night of a thousand wobbles over here and he needs to talk to you. My life isn't full of secrets like some people. I am an open box which I have been told is one of my lovable qualities. I share things. And I want my father at my wedding.

                              SHIV
      You mean you want the money?

                            CONNOR
      Well, no, Shiv, that was not my primary consideration.

                             ROMAN
      What do we do? Should we leave? Will he come in? He won't
      come in?

                            KENDALL
      Relax. This too shall pass, bro.

                             ROMAN
      What happens if I kill a Buddhist? Do I get reincarnated as a
      fucking Buddhist?

EXT. KARAOKE BAR – NIGHT

Logan's car pulls up.

INT. LOGAN'S CAR – NIGHT

*Colin and Kerry are in the car. Logan stares at his glowing phone for
a moment. A little hesitant.*

INT. KARAOKE BAR – PRIVATE ROOM – NIGHT

Connor is singing 'Famous Blue Raincoat' by Leonard Cohen.

                            CONNOR
                       (singing/speaking)
         'It's four in the morning, the end of December
         I'm writing you now just to see if you're better
         New York is cold . . .'

                             ROMAN
                             (over)
      This is some Guantanamo-level shit. What is this? Con. I think
      I want 'Desperado'? Please?

*Roman's phone rings. It's Dad. He shows the others. Maybe Connor
tries to go on, or slowly peters out . . .*

      Okay, I don't know why he's calling me?

> CONNOR
>
> Really he should be calling me?

> KENDALL
>
> Don't answer it, Rome.

> ROMAN
>
> I'm not!

They're all staring at the phone like a bomb in the middle of things. Eventually, Shiv dives in to reject the call.

> Hey! You could've just let it ring out?

> SHIV
>
> Oh no! Naughty Shiv! I hope he's not mad. Oh wait, he's always mad.

INT. LOGAN'S CAR – NIGHT

Logan turns to Colin and Kerry anxiously.

> LOGAN
>
> How do these places work?

INT. KARAOKE BAR – PRIVATE ROOM – NIGHT

Lighting changes for no effect. Roman looks a bit sick, but alive. Kendall's looking thoughtful. Connor's cycling through song options. Roman nervously toys with props. Tension.

> KENDALL
>
> Do you think he'll come?

> ROMAN
>
> I don't think he'd come?

Colin enters, followed by Kerry. Bump for Kendall but he recovers. Colin checks out the room.

> KENDALL
>
> Oww shit! It's the fucking underlings.

> KERRY
>
> Guys, he's waiting. Name a place, we'll all go together.

> SHIV
>
> Sorry. We've got a lot to get through. Packed program of sad bangers.

> KENDALL
>
> 'All Out of Love'.

> SHIV
>
> 'Love Don't Live Here Anymore'.

> ROMAN
>
> 'My Dad's a Media Mogul and a Terrible Scary Bastard'. It's an album track.

> KERRY
>
> He has something specific to say.

Shiv shakes her head as Colin investigates the props in a bucket – inflatables and wigs.

> You shouldn't make him do this. Come down here.

> ROMAN
>
> Says the woman who's been making him jizz into a cup so she can create a monstrous Frankenbaby.

> KENDALL
>
> We're not making him do anything.

> SHIV
>
> We don't want to see him. Our position's clear.

Kerry leaves with Colin.

> ROMAN
>
> He's not going to come, right?

Kendall shrugs.

> KENDALL
>
> Whatever. Sometimes you just have to put your face in the buzzsaw to remind yourself you're alive.

INT. KARAOKE BAR – HALLWAY – NIGHT

Logan is led down the hallway by Colin and Kerry. Doesn't like being here. Feels out of his element. He stops near the door. Takes a beat.

INT. KARAOKE BAR – PRIVATE ROOM – NIGHT

The kids are waiting. Maybe Connor's singing quietly 'Africa' by Toto.

ROMAN

Too late to jump out a window? Hari-karaoke?

Then Colin opens the door and Logan appears in the doorway.

LOGAN

Hey.

He waits but he doesn't get anything back. Roman smiles.

CONNOR

Hey, Pop.

LOGAN

Okay, listen, let's go somewhere. The lights. I could have a seizure.

SHIV

We're not going anywhere.

LOGAN

Fine. Very well.

He enters, and Kerry follows him in.

SHIV

We won't be needing you, Kerry.

ROMAN

Yeah, this is family fuck-fuck.

He gets into a position, helped by Kerry, where he can have some authority.

LOGAN

So let's get this figured out. Then I can let you get back to your fun.

KENDALL

Might have been a wasted trip? Want to give us a quick blast of 'New York, New York' and fuck off?

LOGAN

Well I've got something to say.

> SHIV

Reasons we should vote through the sale. No surprises there. Unless you sing it to the tune of 'Girl from Ipanema'?

> LOGAN

Look. It's not . . . Leaving that, aside. I wanted to say I guess. I wanted you there, a bit – at my party.

This is a surprise.

> KENDALL

Holy shit, did Dad just say a feeling?

> LOGAN

It could maybe have been nice.

> KENDALL

Oh fuck! Now it's all coming out! Mr Melodrama over here. It's like a fucking telenovela.

> CONNOR

Come on, guys? He's trying something.

> LOGAN

You knew I wanted Pierce. From way back. So losing out on— That was not a good feeling.

> SHIV

No shit. We practically had to walk back from Albany. So can we cut the shit, it's obvious why you're here.

> KERRY

Your father wanted to address the personal stuff and not just launch into the business.

This was evidently Kerry's idea and Logan's practically sweating with it.

> SHIV

The thing is, Dad – this isn't personal. This is a business decision. It's about the money.

He eyes her – doesn't believe it.

> LOGAN

Look, you're smart to ask for more money. You are. But Matsson won't go there. You've been outside this. I've got to a good deal. And you get enough to do what you want. I'll do ATN, you'll do Pierce. It'll be a fresh start for us. It'll make things better. And it's right there. All you need to do is vote 'yes' and support the deal.

Nothing from the kids.

KERRY

You know what he's offering? You can separate the business and the personal. You can reset your dynamic as a family.

SHIV

Oh super, like it used to be?! Maybe we can all go on a summer vacay? Drive down Route 1 in an RV, singing showtunes?

ROMAN

It's maybe more complicated than that.

SHIV

I guess you're still in the honeymoon period? Getting your own show on TV?

They see something in Kerry's look or body language. She looks down.

ROMAN

Oh? You're not gonna be on TV?

SHIV

Oh has he fucked you on that?

KENDALL

That will happen. The fucking. But congrats on losing your betrayal cherry!

LOGAN

Enough. I thought you'd be interested in an apology but that's enough.

SHIV

Wait, what, apology? We missed that?!

KENDALL

Er didn't hear that, Dad. Want us to get the words up on the screen for you to follow along?

LOGAN

Look, I don't do apologies. But – you know. If it matters to you.
Sorry.

Silence. This is huge. But also nothing.

SHIV

I'm sorry, there's nothing you could say to me now that I would
ever believe.

That's cold. Is it true? A tough thing to hear.

KENDALL

This deal push could be worth a hundred mil to us, Dad, how
many apols do we get for that?

KERRY

To be clear—

ROMAN

What are you apologizing for, Dad?

CONNOR

Cos if apologies are going, Pop—

SHIV

Not now, Con. What are you sorry for?

LOGAN

Well, I'm sorry about the helicopter for a start.

SHIV

Guys, he's sorry about the helicopter from today. Well I guess
that's the big one, right?

ROMAN

Are we actually doing this, Dad? Cos. I think. You know.
Seriously what fucked all this was . . . when . . . with Mom and
Italy and . . .

Roman is drawn to try and make this work.

LOGAN

Yes okay, I guess I'm— I've got certain – thoughts about—
                    (*tries to get it straight*)
Look, out of the best of intentions, I got the structure of – the
holding company, the ownership structure of the family trust –

has meant there's been a lack of clarity, so maybe you got certain impressions? But I saw it differently so . . .

Beat.

> SHIV
>
> Amazing! Are you sure you're not having that seizure.

> CONNOR
>
> I mean, he is trying? You said what you wanted was an apology?

> LOGAN
>
> You blew up over a by-law. But maybe that's on me.

> SHIV
>
> Anything else?

> KENDALL
>
> Ignoring Connor his whole life?

> CONNOR
>
> Bit strong?

> KENDALL
>
> Hitting Rome when he was a kid?

> ROMAN
>
> Well, no.
> (*then, aside*)
> Everyone hit me. I'm annoying.

> KENDALL
>
> Having Connor's mom locked up?

> CONNOR
>
> Can we not do a whole show trial here?

> SHIV
>
> How about advising Tom on my divorce? That's above and beyond, that took effort.

> LOGAN
>
> Tom asked my advice. He spoke to someone I recommended. You weren't around. If you'd been around I would've given you the same advice. I can't help you if you won't see me.

He's had enough of being the beating post. Gets up.

> Look, bottom line, if we ask for more, Matsson walks. I know it.

It sounds certain. It always does.

> SHIV
>
> You don't know that! You don't know him!! You don't know everything. Saying it doesn't make it true! Everyone just agrees with you and believes you so it becomes true and then you can say, 'See, what I said was right,' but that is not how it is!? You're a human fucking gaslight!

Logan soaks it up.

> LOGAN
>
> Fine. I've actually— And I didn't want to tell you like this. But. The truth is. I have something.

They somehow can sense what's coming—

> CONNOR
>
> Dad, what?

> LOGAN
>
> A growth. They did tests. And it's cancer.*

They look at him.

> CONNOR
>
> Oh Jesus, Dad.

> KENDALL
>
> Is this for real?

> SHIV
>
> When was this?

> LOGAN
>
> Now, I don't want to talk about it.

> ROMAN
>
> What kind of—? One of the bad ones?

> CONNOR
>
> They're all kind of bad, Rome?

---

* This extraordinary gambit felt like it might have been the heart of the scene on the page, but the rest of the scene played so powerfully it felt like a stratagem too far in the cold light of the edit. (It was also a dynamic I tried in the Murdoch script which was a forerunner and cousin to the development of the show.)

> LOGAN

I'm not getting into it. But that is one of the reasons I want this done.

The kids start to get a little tiny bit suspicious.

> SHIV

This is for real? You're not bullshitting us?

> LOGAN

Oh that's nice, that's charming.
> *(then)*
I've had fucking cancer.

> KENDALL

'Had'? When.

> SHIV

Since when?

> LOGAN

I've got it. I've had it. I'll be okay. But I want to move.

Then. Beat. It doesn't sound quite right.

> KENDALL

Can we talk to your doctor?

Logan looks at him.

> LOGAN

You want me to bend over so you can prod my fucking prostate? I'm fine. I've been under the knife? Not that you care.

> ROMAN

What is this, Dad?

He pauses, searching for a name. Kerry comes in, helpful—

> KERRY

Basal cell carcinoma.

Maybe Logan looks at her like: You shouldn't have said.

> SHIV

Uh-huh, so you've had some moles removed? Big fucking whoop.

> LOGAN
> (*maybe*)
> Oh, I'm sorry my cancer isn't big enough for you.

> SHIV
> Tom's dad had one. He had it removed in his lunch hour.
> They're nothing.

Logan shrugs.

> LOGAN
> It was an issue. I'm okay now. But it makes you think?

Roman looks relieved but sick. Shiv's disgusted.

> KENDALL
> Classy.

> ROMAN
> So you actually don't have cancer?

This has taken Roman to a place of shock and disgust.

> LOGAN
> It was a scare.

> SHIV
> What a piece of shit.

> CONNOR
> Dad, you had me worried there.

> LOGAN
> I'm trying to get us back together. You kids need to realize.

> SHIV
> By lying about cancer? Best Dad Ever.

> ROMAN
> I feel like I might be getting cancer now?

> LOGAN
> We need this deal. The world likes it. It makes sense. But deals
> fall apart every day. Because pricks like Matsson get pissed off
> or snubbed. This is fucking real.

Shiv looks at Kendall.

>   SHIV
> Yeah I think I can speak for all of us, can I? When I say—

Kendall nods. Roman says nothing.

> go ask him for more money.

>   LOGAN
> But why?

>   KENDALL
> It's just good business sense. Got to make our own pile.

>   LOGAN
> Oh come on.

>   SHIV
> 'It's what my gut is telling me and I've just got to listen to my
> gut. It's all I've got to go on.'

Logan's bustling out, humiliated.

>   LOGAN
> You're fucking dopes. You're not serious figures to me. I love
> you, but you're not serious fucking people.

He and Kerry leave. It's another blow for Connor.

>   CONNOR
> Well this has been fun.

EXT. KARAOKE BAR – NIGHT

*Outside some guy is collecting soda cans to cash in for their recycling
value. Logan turns to Kerry—*

>   LOGAN
> Look at this prick. They should get up here – some cunt doing
> the tin cans for his supper. Take a sip of that medicine.

He's in a world of his own.

> This city. The rats are getting fat like skunks, they hardly
> fucking care to run. I don't know—

Then, focussed again. He looks at Kerry.

Meeting's off. I need to see Matsson. It'll be me, you, Tom, Frank, Karl. No Gerri.

INT. KARAOKE BAR — PRIVATE ROOM — NIGHT

Shiv and Kendall are a little shaken, but exhilarated.

Shiv takes a sip of champagne.

> SHIV
>
> So how was it for you? Fucking Dad?

> KENDALL
>
> Amazing. Just over too soon.

Roman looks a bit concerned.

> SHIV
>
> Fake cancer was pretty special.

> ROMAN
>
> Nuts.
> *(aside)*
> We should check that out though.

> KENDALL
>
> How you going to vote 'no'? I might bring one of those Alpine horns and do a: 'Noooooooooooooo!'

> SHIV
>
> I'm not even going. I'm gonna fart down the phone.

Roman still doesn't love the braying, doesn't join.

> KENDALL
>
> Kidding, Rome. Kidding, man!

Roman feels like it really was about fucking Dad. Doesn't want to be part of this gang anymore.

> ROMAN
>
> Yeah, uh-huh. Cool.

> SHIV
>
> He's gonna cancel though isn't he?

> KENDALL
>
> Yeah. Shame.

Connor's had enough.

> CONNOR

Okay, I'm going home.

> SHIV
> (*off his look*)

I'm sure she'll be in touch.

> CONNOR

You know what? It's fine.

Surprising.

> KENDALL

Yeah?

> CONNOR

Yeah. The good thing about having a family who doesn't love you, is you learn to stop needing it.

> SHIV

Con, come on. That's not—

> CONNOR

Sometimes I think you think I don't know it. But I know it. And you know what? I'm a cactus in the desert. I persist. You're all chasing around after Dad, saying, 'Ooh please love me. I need love, I need attention.'

> SHIV

I think that's the opposite of what just hap—

> CONNOR
> (*interrupting*)

You're needy love sponges. But I'm a plant that grows on rocks and lives off insects that die inside of me.

> SHIV

Jesus Christ.

> CONNOR

If Willa doesn't come back it's fine. Cos I don't need love. It's like a superpower. And if she comes back and she doesn't love me that's okay too. Cos I don't need it.

The siblings look at him. Unsure what to say. He leaves.

INT. KENDALL'S CAR – NIGHT

Kendall has a serene air of Buddhist calm. But then he can't help breaking into a smile as he thinks about what just happened.

INT. SHIV'S CAR – NIGHT

Shiv thinks about texting Tom. But it's not an option.

INT. CONNOR'S CAR – NIGHT

Connor stares at the location tracking on his phone. Still no sign of Willa. Then suddenly she reappears. Relief floods over him.

He leans forward to his driver—

> CONNOR
> Location services enabled!

INT. CONNOR'S HOTEL SUITE – NIGHT

Willa's in bed. Connor comes in. He lies behind her. He takes her hand. She lets him. He smiles a sad smile at her. And she smiles one back. It's not quite clear where they're at.

INT. LOGAN'S APARTMENT – STUDY – NIGHT

Logan and Tom, holding whiskies, with Kerry.

> KERRY
> It wasn't even my idea.

> TOM
> Oh no I'm sure.

> KERRY
> It was him who said. It was a joke. So it was just a little rude what Greg said, you know?

> LOGAN
> Not good. Defiled my home. Indelicate with Kerry?

> TOM
> You want me to do anything?

> LOGAN

I just don't want to see him so much. Okay? In the freezer.

> TOM

Of course. And, Kerry, you'd be such a great fit. Like ATN Citizens or something, to start?

> LOGAN

Well that's interesting, Tom.

> KERRY
> (*no but yes*)

It's really so fine.

The kindness makes Kerry want to get away fast to go and welcome Roman in who is arriving . . .

Okay, I'm gonna prep us for Sweden.

Kerry shows Roman in and heads off next door.

Roman enters.

> ROMAN

Hey, Dad. And looky looky here. Twin Cities Tessie. Thought I smelled dairy.

Logan hands a drink to Roman, who looks uncomfortable.

So yeah, just felt that got weird and there was a lot going on.

> LOGAN

Oh, we know what they're like.

Maybe a wink. A bit of connection.

I've pushed the board meeting. I want you to come see Matsson with me. I could use your help.

> ROMAN
> (*feigned indifference*)

Oh yeah? I mean, it's the wedding. Con's wedding?

Logan makes a face: No biggie.

But – feels, yeah, let's see—

Logan nods for Tom to head out.

> TOM

Let me refresh the glasses!

Tom moves into another room. Just Logan and Roman.

> LOGAN

ATN's getting leaner. Cyd thinks she knows it all. She's on eight digits. Her sushi bill could fund a news chopper. There's a Night of the Long Knives coming. I need a fire-breather. A ruthless fuck who'll do whatever it takes?

> ROMAN

What about Tommy Two-Tits?

> LOGAN

Sure. He's got a face. Tom's the meat locker.

> ROMAN

Uh. Sure. I didn't come to – to you know—

> LOGAN

Son, every time you say what's true they'll roll their eyes.

> ROMAN
> *(re the alliance)*

Maybe I should go?

> LOGAN

You're not Pierce. Perimenopausal professors and pollution of the Ganges? You're ATN. I can't do it all again from scratch.

That lands for Roman. He thinks.

You're afraid you get left with nothing?

> ROMAN

Nah. No.

He is.

> LOGAN

What you're doing right now is how you get left with nothing.

> ROMAN

Uh-huh.

> LOGAN

Smart people know what they are.

> ROMAN

You really want me? At ATN?

> LOGAN

More, Romulus. I need you.

> ROMAN

Well, it sounds good. Can I think about it? But it does.

> LOGAN

Tom? Roman might help me when I have a question, yeah?

> TOM

Look forward to working with you.

Tom offers a hand and Roman shakes, a little unsure.

> LOGAN

In fact why don't we put the news on? Have a drink, make some notes. Dissect the frog!

Logan is happy to have people around. He goes to turn on ATN.

Let's fucking get into it!

They all watch ATN together, drinking.

Episode Three

CONNOR'S WEDDING

Written by Jesse Armstrong
Directed by Mark Mylod

Original air date 9 April 2023

Cast

LOGAN ROY	Brian Cox
KENDALL ROY	Jeremy Strong
GREG HIRSCH	Nicholas Braun
SHIV ROY	Sarah Snook
ROMAN ROY	Kieran Culkin
CONNOR ROY	Alan Ruck
TOM WAMBSGANS	Matthew Macfadyen
FRANK VERNON	Peter Friedman
KARL MULLER	David Rasche
GERRI KELLMAN	J. Smith-Cameron
WILLA FERREYRA	Justine Lupe
KAROLINA NOVOTNEY	Dagmara Dominczyk
HUGO BAKER	Fisher Stevens
COLIN STILES	Scott Nicholson
JESS JORDAN	Juliana Canfield
KERRY CASTELLABATE	Zoë Winters
SYLVIA FERREYRA	Cynthia Mace
OLIVIA	Nadia Brown
BETH	Jamie Chung
FLIGHT ATTENDANT	Sanam Laila Hashemi
JULIE	Paula Jon DeRose
JOURNALISTS	Andrea Prestinario
	Laura Sudduth
	Alan Kelly
MARTYN	Jim Newman
PILOT	Tom White
CELEBRANT	Katie Fabel

INT./EXT. NEW YORK – ROMAN'S CAR – DAY

Friday afternoon. Roman is in his wedding gear. His phone goes.

> ROMAN

Oh, hey, Pop?

Intercut with:

INT. LOGAN'S CAR – DAY

Logan is in the back of his car with Kerry.

At a certain point he will arrive at the airport.

> LOGAN

Hey so, son, I was thinking, we could hold for you? You wanna come see the Swede. Get inside this?
> *(relishing a little)*
It could get fucking brutal.

> ROMAN

Oh? Okay. Um. Yeah. Yeah. Yeah? Um—

> LOGAN

C'mon. He likes you, you'll keep it – light.

> ROMAN

Just only thing is. Con's wedding?

> LOGAN

It'll be okay.

> ROMAN

Are you gonna make it at all?

> LOGAN
> *(no)*

Mmmmh.

(then)

But let him know will you? Let him know I'll call when I have a minute. If I get one.

He probably won't.

Send him my best. Then you could be over in twenty?

Roman looks around.

> ROMAN

It's his wedding day, Dad. I don't want him to shit his bag. You know?

> LOGAN

Uh-huh. We got him some Napoleon thing sent.

He checks with Kerry that the gift was sent.

He'll be okay.

> KERRY
> *(whispers)*

Napoleon and Josephine letters.

> ROMAN

Right.

(then)

But also, I guess. The sort of shift in things with— I haven't actually told Ken and Shiv yet, that I might not be following through on our plans and—

> LOGAN

You should.

> ROMAN

Uh-huh. I will.

(then)

Maybe not today.

> LOGAN

Well maybe today. I need you. And I wouldn't be fucking going if it wasn't for you.

> ROMAN

Right.

> LOGAN

Cross the Rubicon, Romulus.

> ROMAN

Yeah. No, sure.

Logan feels the wobble and wants to test him.

> LOGAN

And listen. One thing and another, you know what's happening. The clear-out? Cyd?

> ROMAN

Uh-huh?

> LOGAN

I'm feeling now more and more. I'm uncomfortable with Gerri. How she handled things. On the DOJ number, on the spin-off.

> ROMAN

Oh yeah?

> LOGAN

Yeah. I think we want to let her go.

> ROMAN

Oh right. Right. Okay. Well, let's discuss?

> LOGAN

So will you give her the heads-up?

> ROMAN

Me?

> LOGAN

Yeah. Be nicer coming from you.
> (*then*)
> I know you were close.

At a certain point, Roman arrives at the wedding and exits the car.

> ROMAN

Dad?

> LOGAN

I mean, you are with me? You weren't fucking me around?

> ROMAN

Well. Sure. Yeah. Okay. Yeah?

> LOGAN
>
> We'll make it tidy afterwards. Just give her the word today? We don't need the mess. Thank you.

On Roman. Something feels off. He's less comfortable with this than he used to be. He hangs up. He's arrived at the wedding and takes in the scene.

EXT. DOCK – DAY

A yacht is ready for a wedding party. Dockside, last preparations are being made. Beth (party planner) and Julie (party planner assistant) converse.

The boat is all ready for a party. But a bit of election razzmatazz has been added, some reds, whites and blues, bunting, maybe a jazz band on the dockside.

Not such a great day ahead now.

EXT. DOCK – ARRIVALS – DAY

Guests are arriving. A mixture – Connor's friends from New York and New Mexico; a smattering of celebrities; wealthy pals; folks the PR team invited to try to get the press interested; friends from Willa's home city, friends of her mom and dad, Willa's New York friends – theater friends and actors.

There is also a little gang of 'embedded' friendly journalists and photographers being corralled by a small political communications team.

Greg, on his phone, is surveying the scene—

> GREG
>
> Just checking he definitely doesn't want me coming with you guys?

Intercut with:

EXT. TETERBORO AIRPORT – DAY

Tom is at the airfield waiting for Logan.

> TOM

Correct.

> GREG

And do you think I should speak direct to him – or to Kerry to apologize?

> TOM

You're in the bad books. Just keep your head down.

> GREG

I have a little list of nice things to say about Kerry.

> TOM

Well that sounds creepy. No, look. It's not your fault, but he finds you visually aggravating right now.

> GREG

Visually aggravating?

> TOM

You have too many molecules, occupying too much space.

> GREG

But, you have all the support you need, for Sweden?

> TOM

I have like five people Gregging for me.

> GREG

'Gregging'?

> TOM

Roped in a couple of mini-Gregs from the pig pen. Greglets.

> GREG

Well don't turn me into a word, Tom. I'm a guy. Who are all these 'Gregs' anyway?

Greg passes Willa.

They exchange smiles but we stay with Willa as she talks to her mom, Sylvia.

> WILLA

The boat leaves in thirty and there's canapés and champagne till Ellis Island where there's something more substantial after the ceremony?

Sylvia looks around at the dock and the boat, all decked out.

> SYLVIA
> Look at the boat, Willa? It's like you're a princess in a film!

> WILLA
> Thank you. I guess all in all it wasn't maybe, what we –
> expected but . . .

> SYLVIA
> He'll look after you.

> WILLA
> He will. He will.

Connor comes over, shielding his eyes from Willa.

> CONNOR
> I'm not looking, I'm not looking, no bad luck!

Willa makes off, shielding her eyes.

> WILLA
> I'll go, I'm going!

Willa moves off to talk to theater friends.

> SYLVIA
> It's all so lovely, Connor!
> (*looks around*)
> Look at all the young people!

> CONNOR
> You seen the freak in the monocle?

> SYLVIA
> I know! Keep *him* out of the photos!

They chuckle.

> CONNOR
> I heard a few of them moaning about 'the rich'.

> SYLVIA
> But they don't seem to mind the taste of your champagne!

> CONNOR
> Mr Scrooge just happened to be a huge wealth creator. They
> don't mention that in Mr Dickens' books do they?

SYLVIA

No they do not. Very convenient!
(*then*)
And your father?

CONNOR

Hoping for a glimpse. But he is very busy.

SYLVIA

I bet. I'm sorry.

CONNOR

These things happen. It was my brothers' and sister's fault but—

SYLVIA

Oh, Connor.

CONNOR

Yeah he was gonna be my best guy but— Yeah got my sibs instead. No, he's not gonna make the ceremony but he should make a pop-in before we leave. He's aiming to make a 'hello' – which is cool.

He looks at his watch, looks to the dock arrivals area for a car pulling up as—

EXT. TETERBORO AIRPORT – TARMAC – DAY

Logan is arriving. Tom waits. Opens his car door, mock courteous.

Karolina and Colin are there, hanging back.

TOM

Hail, Loganus Maximus! Slayer of Vikings!

As Logan gets out.

LOGAN

Uh-huh. What you got me on Matsson?

TOM

Playing hardball. But everyone says he still wants the deal.

They head towards the jet.

Might make us weave a little bit. Still some grumbles about the ATN carve-out.

LOGAN

Well that's not on the table.

TOM

Right. He's gonna play tough but if there was no more upside he wouldn't be making the time.

They walk towards the plane.

LOGAN

Uh-huh.
(*then*)
And listen, I think today's the day. I'll talk to Cyd.

TOM

Oh yeah? Time to—

He mimes holding a scalp and shooting someone.

LOGAN

Uh-huh. And Gerri. Will you check – when he's done it?
(*looks for Karolina*)
Karolina. Gerri's getting the push.

KAROLINA

Oh okay . . . ?

Logan clocks a bit of regret somewhere.

LOGAN

What?

KAROLINA

Nothing.

LOGAN

So we'll tell her today, swing the legals in, but we can start letting it seep – hang cruises around her neck?

KAROLINA
(*accommodates the news fast*)
Sort of incompetence or worse?

Logan nods to Tom. He's inside it.

TOM

I think the idea would be how she took her eye off the ball?

>   LOGAN
> Clean out the stalls. Strategic refocus. Bit more fucking
> aggressive!

>   TOM
> Got it. You push Cyd, Roman knifes Gerri. All in a day's work!

INT. ROY PRIVATE JET — DAY

On the plane, Karl and Frank say hello.

Tom makes a call.

EXT. DOCK — WEDDING TENTS — DAY

*Gerri gets out of a car, or arrives at the wedding tents with her date,
Martyn. Roman is watching. Shiv approaches him.*

>   SHIV
> Hey. What you heard about Matsson, is the deal going to be
> okay?

Roman is distracted.

> You okay?

>   ROMAN
>   (*testy*)
> Yes I am. Why?

>   SHIV
> I dunno fuck you I'm only asking.

>   ROMAN
> I'm fine, Shiv.
>   (*then*)
> Let's just enjoy the freak show.

Roman's phone goes. He angles away as Shiv moves off.

>   TOM
>   (*on phone*)
> Hey, you done it?

Roman looks at Gerri.

Intercut with:

INT. WAYSTAR JET – DAY

Tom on the phone as people settle for take-off.

> TOM
> Your dad wants to know, have you done it yet?

> ROMAN
> No. Jesus Christ, Tom. I just spoke to him. She's not here yet.

Roman looks over to Gerri.

> TOM
> But you are going to do it?

> ROMAN
> Yes I am going to do it.

> TOM
> Once you give her the knife we need to notify HR, outside counsel? So let us know.
> > *(then)*
> And have you told Shiv?

Roman looks at Shiv.

> ROMAN
> I'll let you know, okay? Back off, inflatable dicky-dick?

> TOM
> We just need to know for the choreography so –

Roman puts his phone down.

He watches Gerri as she approaches with Martyn. Martyn greets someone he knows.

> ROMAN
> Hey, Ger. How you doing?
> > *(feeling guilty)*
> You look – well.

Suspiciously straightforward? What's coming next?

> GERRI
> Thank you? And?

> ROMAN

And nothing. You look, healthy.

Roman is uncomfortable.

> GERRI

No jokes about Martyn or something disgusting about – dicks or – vaginas?

> ROMAN

I was being nice. Can a guy not be nice anymore? Happy whatever. Happy Whoremas.

He avoids her eye.

> GERRI

What?

> ROMAN

What what?

Roman trying to straight-bat it. Gerri angles them so their talk is private.

> GERRI

Why are you not looking at me?

He looks at her hard.

> ROMAN

What? I'll stare right in your stupid face if that's what you so desperately desire.

> GERRI

What is it?

> ROMAN

Nothing. You just make me go weird, as you know and fully intend.

Roman can't quite do it.

Look, let's talk. Later. In thirty. Once we set sail?

Odd.

> GERRI

What's going on, Roman?

> ROMAN
>
> I just need to talk with you and we should do it later. It'll be better, because—

She looks at him and he withers.

> No doubt you can tell from looking at me, it's not great. But my dad said it, so— It's a message, really.

She looks at him. Bad vibrations. Sniffs it all out.

> GERRI
>
> Is this why I'm not going to Europe? What the *fuck*?

> ROMAN
>
> Look, it's not official, and, it's a heads-up from me, but yeah, they're gonna stuff your mouth with gold, and it's all good and maybe we can talk him down but yeah as an early warning and I didn't intend to get into this – but yeah.

He makes a 'you're getting killed' noise.

> GERRI
>
> Why?

> ROMAN
>
> He's unhappy about how long it took you to settle with the DOJ.

> GERRI
>
> Bullshit.

> ROMAN
>
> And the number – the fine. Too big.

Also bullshit.

> GERRI
>
> I danced us through a fucking thunderstorm without us getting wet.

> ROMAN
>
> I guess you've lost his confidence.

> GERRI
>
> Since when? Since you sent me repeated images of your genitalia?

> ROMAN

No, don't be so stupid and reductive.

> GERRI

He can't fire you, so he's firing me?

He looks at her.

> ROMAN

Oh fuck off, Gerri, don't moan. You're not a moaner.

> GERRI

And you're going back in?

Roman looks around.

> ROMAN
> (*maybe*)

No.
> (*yes*)

I don't know. Gerri, don't be weird.

Gerri thinks.

This will all be totally fine.
> (*then, looking at her*)

It's nothing, so shut up.

Gerri is looking around.

I'm doing you a courtesy by letting you know. You can go legal but we'll stuff your mouth with so much fucking gold and that's just how it's going to go. You wrote the playbook, Gerri.

Gerri is recalibrating but Roman is completely excluded from the ambit of her considerations. He's dead to her.

> GERRI

Okay. Well. Fine. That's – fine.

He looks at her.

> ROMAN

I am, on a 'human level', obviously sad so—

Gerri looks around, maybe gives him a nothing smile. Roman tries to be human. Wants a reaction.

I am sorry. And off the record, Ger. I do perhaps owe you the opportunity to throw your shit at the wall?

> GERRI

I'm good.

He looks at her.

Maybe a steam whistle blows to summon people aboard, and an announcement is made.

> BETH
> (*over PA*)

We'll shortly be boarding all guests. Starting with red-invite family and friends. Welcome aboard.

> GERRI

This is fine. It's nothing at all. Thanks for the consideration.

Gerri walks off. Not prepared to give him anything. But she is walking off, maybe if we see her face it's recomposing itself after the moment of surprise.

He watches her walk off – up onto the boat, where Willa is ready to welcome people.

By her side, Connor is distracted, talking to a catering person and Beth about the wedding cake.

> CONNOR

I am saying we can have it for display, obviously, but I do not want it served, okay? I don't want to see the internal – qualities! Thank you!

Connor moves away – upstairs to discuss further.

We see some wedding guests getting greeted – heading onto the ship. Greg, Shiv amongst the first to go up. A little time passes.

EXT. DOCK – DAY

On shore. Waiting for Kendall, Roman has made a call—

> ROMAN

Dad. Can you call me back? That was— It was horrible. With Gerri. So. I'm just— I dunno if— Don't listen to this if you don't want to but I'm, I'm not totally okay with . . . Are you being kinda shitty with me? Cos your son's getting married and you can't just – fucking keep expecting me to bend over for you being cunty. I'm just asking. Yeah so that's the question. Are you a cunt? Give me a buzz!

Even if disguised with lightness, that's the most anger he's ever expressed to his father. He's scared but freed. Then, Roman gets hit like he's fifteen from behind.

KENDALL

'Kidneys!'

Kendall chops him from behind in his midriff, roughly where his kidneys are. Something from childhood.

Hey. Can we go?

ROMAN

Uh-huh. I think we have a head start on all the – face-people.

They head aboard.

INT. WEDDING YACHT – DAY

Kendall and Roman greet Willa – welcoming the first guests aboard.

KENDALL

Congratulations. How's the groom?

Connor is distracted from the welcome line. Going upstairs with the catering people—

WILLA

Um, worried about you guys and his dad. And the embedded press. But fixating on the cake. He says it's 'looney cake'? What is that?

KENDALL

Um, I believe, when they told Connor his mom was getting you know taken into, to—

ROMAN

—the funny farm—

> KENDALL

—into mental health care they gave him cake. Dad and whoever, to calm him down. Dab of sugar, bite of cake. He was eating Victoria sponge for a week straight.

> WILLA

Oh. Right. 'Looney cake'.

> ROMAN

And um, Willa – I'm looking forward to saying 'hi' to everyone, and mixing it up and whatnot. But is there also an area that is – if we don't wanna get Roy-ed by the Big Gulps?

> WILLA

On floor two there's an area.

> ROMAN

Thank you. I mean I wanna meet everyone and get into it all about their jobs and children and everything but – you know?

> WILLA

Oh sure, sure. Julie?

> JULIE

Right this way.

Julie leads them up.

> KENDALL
> (*as they head off*)

Unbelievable. Can you believe this guy?

They head up towards the family-only area.

So what are you hearing? Is he coming by?

Shiv is ahead of them, already onboard. Kendall gives her a kiss on the cheek. They all walk up together.

> ROMAN

Me? No idea. I don't know.

> SHIV

I hear Stockholm. Gone, or going.

> KENDALL
> (*interesting*)

Oh? Okay? Matsson wouldn't fix it with him on a phoner? He's flying over?

They pass Greg talking to a female journalist, Olivia.

> ROMAN

Don't talk to him, he's a filthy pornographer.

> GREG

Ha! Oh, hey, guys? Guys? Could I chat to you later? About – about—
> (*re Pierce*)

everything that's going on for you?

> KENDALL

Get your nose out of our trough, Greggy!

And they walk on. We stay with Greg for a beat.

> GREG

We're always kidding around.
> (*then*)

So how long have you been covering Connor's campaign?

> OLIVIA

Oh. From the start. Since before he fired the first running mate.

> GREG

Interesting! 'Journalism'. Taking quotes and kicking asses!

> OLIVIA

Huh.

> GREG

I'll tell you one thing, that's a fact. My uncle Logan is a – smart, kind, wise old frickin' genius. You can quote me.

> OLIVIA

Huh. Okay?

> GREG

I mean really. Quote me. Shall I repeat it? Cos that could be a good little nugget, to report, right? Little human-interest story. 'Nephew adores uncle'?

Back with the kids as they head through the party, following Julie—

SHIV

You think Matsson's gonna tell Dad to fuck off?

KENDALL

He'll improve the offer is what will happen.
(*to Roman*)
Dad's gotta go fucking lingonberry picking with Matsson. We're puppet-mastering the old bastard!

Shiv's phone goes – Tom. She cancels.

SHIV

What do we do if it falls apart, Ken? What's the latest from Nan and Naomi? You in touch with Naomi—

KENDALL

He'll land it. And we'll pocket that sweet bonus loot.

Shiv's phone goes. Tom again. She cancels.

Connor is there on the upper floor with Beth. As they pass by—

CONNOR

Hey, so listen the idea is, Dad will pop by and be dockside and you guys are up here and I think that's just cleanest?

SHIV

Okay? You think he might drop by?

CONNOR

Spoke to Kerry and he's hoping!

He walks off – fingers crossed. They continue.

SHIV

Should we tell him? Someone should tell him.

They look at one another. It's gonna be Shiv.

Really?

KENDALL

He likes you.

Shiv heads off back to catch Connor and give him the bad news.

Roman and Kendall reach the special Roy bit – discreetly VIP, separated off. Maybe one or two donors are in there already by the bar.

ROMAN

She's a good person. She's like a decent human being.

KENDALL

Fucking bossy boots.
(*motioning spooning it up*)
'Umm, drama! Is there some for me?'

Roman smiles. His phone goes – Tom. He's expecting something about Gerri, so is on the defensive—

ROMAN

Hello, fucky sucky brigade, how can I help you?

We hear in Roman's ear—

TOM
(*on phone*)
Hi, Roman your dad's very sick. He's very very sick.

ROMAN

What?

Kendall sees right away the change in Roman's tone.

KENDALL

What? Okay?

ROMAN
(*to Ken*)

Dad's sick.
(*to Tom*)
How sick? What is it? Hello? Tom, what's happening, what's going on?

KENDALL
(*to Roman*)
Who's there? What's going on, what is it? Is he okay?

Roman puts Tom on speaker.

If they are exposed in the room they huddle to a corner.

Intercut with:

INT. WAYSTAR JET – DAY

Tom is in the back of the plane. Up front we can't see exactly everything but there's activity. Logan is out of sight being treated. Possibly a crew member runs through with something from the back to the front.

TOM

We don't know. He's – he's had a very serious— I don't know. It's very, very bad. It seems very bad. I'm sorry to call like this.

KENDALL

Who's with him, what's going on? What happened?

TOM

He had an issue, he was short of— I wasn't there – but he was short of breath and then he went to the bathroom. He was gone, he was gone but, someone heard something and then he was, we were concerned and they went in there.

KENDALL

You broke in?

TOM

They have a key, and they got in and he's non-responsive.

KENDALL

Oh fuck. What, is he – [talking, can he talk?]

TOM

They're doing chest compressions.

ROMAN
(physical blow)

Oh fuck.

KENDALL

Has his heart stopped?

TOM

I don't know. No. I don't know.

ROMAN

And the – the – machine, the— You have a—

> KENDALL
> (*to Roman*)

Well not unless his heart has stopped. What's going on, Tom?
Who's in charge?

Karl might say something to Tom in the background.

> TOM

Is Shiv there?

> KENDALL

What is going on – *right now*, Tom?

> TOM

He might – Karl says he is breathing, maybe.

> KENDALL

Who is medically competent there?

> TOM

They're trained. The people are— The attendant is trained.

Karl chips in—

> KARL

The captain has been in touch – he's in touch – they, the cabin
staff, are receiving medical advice from their service. They have
a service.

> ROMAN

Who is that, what is that?

> KENDALL

Can we be looped in on that?

*Frank comes through from the front, speaks off, a bit inaudible to the
kids—*

> FRANK
> (*muffled*)

They should speak to him.

> KENDALL

What's that?

Frank might brief Tom as he talks.

> TOM

Frank thinks you should speak to your dad. I can hold the phone. I can hold the phone near him if you like.

> ROMAN

Why does Frank think that?

> TOM
> (*tiny beat*)

I guess, in case, it's a chance to— In case it's a last chance.

> ROMAN

What the fuck do you mean, Tom?

Frank is there, now speaks over Roman's phone—

> FRANK

He's not in good shape, Roman. He's not in good shape, they're doing chest compressions.

> ROMAN

Well should they be?

> FRANK

They're getting good advice, they're good people. But I think you should talk to him. I'm not sure he's breathing.

> ROMAN

Are you serious, Frank, fuck me.

> FRANK

I think it's very grave, Roman.

> KENDALL

We *just* heard he was breathing. You shouldn't do CPR to someone whose heart is going, Frank, what the fuck is going on?

> ROMAN

Can you even breathe without – heart— Can you?

There is commotion in the background, phone being passed, off speaker.

> TOM

I'm taking you to him and to put you by his ear. He'll be able to hear you.

(correcting)
If he can hear, he'll be able to hear you.

Roman and Kendall look at one another: This can't be happening, can it?

You might want to get—?

ROMAN

We'll get Shiv.

But he doesn't move, it's happening too quick.

Tom gets through to the front. Maybe we don't see too much of Logan. Tight on the phone tucked into a pillow by his ear.

Further down his body there is medical activity. In the distance, Kerry and the airplane staff. One on the phone to their medical service, getting advice.

TOM
(more distant)
Okay, you're by his ear. You're by his ear now.

ROMAN
(projected a bit)
Can he hear, is he okay? Is he okay?

TOM
(leaning in)
He's not okay, Rome, he's not. But you're by his ear.

Tom is further away. His voice small from the phone—

(muffled)
You're by his ear.

KENDALL

Can he hear?
(projecting)
Can he hear?

TOM
(projecting)
The phone is— I don't know. It's— You can speak into his ear.

Silence.

> KENDALL

Can he hear? Does he know?

Kendall and Roman look at one another. Roman is holding the phone. Kendall motions: You go. Roman takes the phone off speaker. Turns for a tiny bit of privacy. Takes a few steps away from Kendall. So he can talk privately, pacing towards a corner—

> ROMAN

Hey, Dad. Um. I hope you're okay. You're okay. You'll be okay, alright? You're a monster. You're a, you're a fucking Trojan. You're going to win this okay? I – I don't know. You're good. You're a good dad. You're a good dad. You did a good job.

That's where he gets to. It feels strange with no responses. Roman turns to Kendall.

I don't know what the fuck I'm doing. I can't do this.

Roman hands the phone to Kendall.

> KENDALL
> (*to Roman*)

Am I by his ear?

> (*to phone*)

Dad? Are you awake?

> (*projecting*)

Am I still by his ear?

Roman shrugs, off in a world of his own.

> TOM
> (*projecting*)

You're by his ear. If he can hear, he can hear you.

> KENDALL

Okay.

Kendall turns for privacy – talks into Roman's phone.

Dad?

> (*then*)

I love you, Dad. I love you. Okay? It's okay. I love you. It's okay. You fucking— I don't know. I can't forgive you. But it's okay. And I love you.

But it doesn't feel adequate. He needs time or room, he thought he'd know what to say but he didn't think it would feel like this—

                    (*projecting*)
    Can he hear me?

Tom picks up the phone, noise.

                    TOM
    Is Shiv there?

Kendall turns to Roman.

                    KENDALL
    I didn't know what to say.

                    ROMAN
    I don't fucking know.

                    TOM
              (*on speakerphone*)
    Is Shiv there? He's not here I don't think.

Kendall looks at Roman. Roman wants the phone. Will Kendall get Shiv?

Kendall shrugs, he doesn't know. He heads out.

We stay with Kendall as he heads towards Shiv. Down the stairs and through the main party floor. He cuts through the crowd. Maybe some people smile at him and, on autopilot, he smiles them off, not giving the chance for interaction.

Eventually gets to Shiv. Talking to someone.

He takes her wrist gently but firmly—

                    KENDALL
    Shiv, Shivvy honey . . . I'm sorry.

Right away in his look, his manner, she sees . . . maybe not all of it, but much of it – a fear, the worst fear suddenly crystalized.

                    SHIV
    . . . Mum?

Kendall tries to be gentle but tell her the news fast so they can get back to Dad, whispering to her as they go—

> KENDALL

Dad's in trouble.

> SHIV

What? What's happened?

> KENDALL

He's on the plane. He got sick, they're doing chest compressions.

He leads her through the crowd.

> SHIV

What, Ken?

As they go Kendall might remember to tell some or all of this to Shiv.

> KENDALL

I don't know everything. He's with Tom and Frank and Karl and they're on the line to doctors, I don't know, he was in the bathroom and he had trouble breathing and they're doing chest compressions and he was still breathing. But it's looking very bad.

They reach Roman back in the private room.

He's on the phone. Talking to his dad again as Shiv and Kendall arrive.

> ROMAN
> (into phone)

It's okay. You're a good guy. You're a good guy.

Roman sees Shiv. His hand over phone.

> (reporting)

They think he's gone now.

> SHIV

What do you mean?

> ROMAN

They think Dad died.

And Shiv right away lets out a cry/scream of agony. Sharp and immediate and from somewhere beyond reason or regret.

Kendall goes to hug her – she can't quite take it yet.

SHIV

No. It's too much. It's too soon.

She wobbles. Roman maybe steadies.

I can't have that, it's too soon.

ROMAN

I'm sorry.

And she folds into Kendall or Roman or both a little. Kendall takes the phone.

KENDALL
(into phone)

Hey. Can she do it, can Shiv speak to him? I'll put her on.

ROMAN
(to Shiv)

He's been putting us by Dad's ear, to speak.

TOM

I'm putting you by his ear, Shiv.

SHIV
(to brothers)

Can he hear?
(to phone)

Is he still hearing?

TOM

I don't know? I'm putting you there.
(muffled, projected)
You can go now. You're talking to him now.

She takes the phone.

SHIV

Um. Hello, Dad?

The brothers motion. Turns away to be private, they back off as she starts—

I um, you're gonna be okay. And – um—

Then turns to her brothers in despair—

I don't know if he's dead. Is he fucking dead?

>   ROMAN
> I don't know.

>   SHIV
>   (*projecting*)
> Tom, is he alive? Tom!

Scratching noises as Tom picks up the phone.

> Is he even alive?

>   TOM
> I don't know, Shiv.

>   SHIV
> Are you just being nice? Has he gone?

>   TOM
>   (*yes*)
> I don't know. He— We don't know.

>   SHIV
> Oh Jesus.

>   TOM
> I'm gonna put you back there. Okay?

>   ROMAN
> Go private. Just speak. It's weird, but speak. You never know?

Shiv shuffles away, talks into the phone.

>   SHIV
> I don't know. Dad?

What does she feel? She doesn't know, so just lets go.

> Don't go. Dad. Don't go, Daddy. I love you. Don't go please.
> Not now. I love you, Daddy. You fucking, I don't know. Oh god.
> Dad. There's no excuses for – for— But I love you. I do. You
> fucking— I don't know. I do love you. It's okay, Daddy, it's okay.
> I love you.

Static, dead air from the phone.

Beat.

The phone gets picked up.

TOM

Do you want to stay on?

Shiv hands the phone to Roman. She's drained.

ROMAN
(*into phone*)
What's happening? What precisely is happening now?

He puts it on speaker.

TOM
(*on speakerphone*)
Um, we're all here, I'm heading into the back. He's up front on the – on the floor, and they're doing chest compressions. And we're in the back.

ROMAN
(*bit of hope*)
Okay, so they're still doing the chest compressions?

TOM

Yeah. They are. But not because— [he's necessarily alive.]
(*then*)
I think they have to. I think they have to keep doing that?

ROMAN

Yeah well do— Who is their medical people. Who the fuck are these people? Who are they? Tom?

TOM

Um—
(*to Karl, Frank*)
Who are their medical people they're on with?
(*calling through to the plane staff*)
Who are your medical people?

STEWARDESS
(*from off*)

MD Live.

TOM
(*muddled*)

I think it's MD Line.

> STEWARDESS
> (*correcting in the distance*)

MD Live.

> TOM

'MD Live'?

> ROMAN

Okay. And they're what, in contact? Direct, another line?

> TOM

They're in contact and the plane people are lovely, they're good people. I think he's— I think they made him very comfortable.

> SHIV

But— [he's gone?]

> KENDALL

But is he okay? Is he okay at all?

Tom has to tell the truth.

> TOM

He's not okay. No. He's not.

> SHIV

Has he gone, Tom?

> TOM

I mean his— They say his heart has stopped and his breathing has stopped. For a while maybe.

> ROMAN

But that doesn't mean he's dead? Medically, right.

A tiny beat – where people think it kind of does?

> TOM

I don't know. They're still doing chest compressions.

The horror, the happening-ness of it all hits Shiv, she looks around, can't believe it.

> SHIV

Oh Jesus fucking Christ.

> ROMAN

Do those fucking clowns know what they're doing though, Tom? Are they hurting him?

TOM

They're good people. They're doing their best.

ROMAN

When are you gonna land? Are you turned around? Are you coming back?

TOM

I don't— I think yes, yes we're coming to— We're heading back I think.

Kendall butts in—

KENDALL

Can you put me through to the flight deck. Can I speak with the pilot please? I'll call Frank's phone and he can take me through to the flight deck, okay?

He dials, Jess first.

TOM

Frank, Ken's going to call your phone to be taken through to the pilot.

Meanwhile Kendall is on his phone to Jess.

KENDALL

Jess. I need a few things, my dad's dying, I'm just gonna do facts okay, I need my doctor and—
(*to Shiv*)
Do they have his doctor?

SHIV
(*to Tom on Roman's phone*)
Do you have his doctor on the line?

TOM
(*to Karl*)
Is that his doctor you have?

Off, Karl says no, they have the medical service on a phone.

No, we have their service, their medical service, which they have, and we had – we had Karl's guy listening and— No we couldn't get— [hold of Logan's doctor.]

Shiv calls to Kendall who is on the line to Jess.

> SHIV

They couldn't get his doctor.

> KENDALL
> (*to Jess*)

And Dad's doctor – Doctor fucking – Judith get that lazy
bastard and get him and get the best heart doctor in the world
and the best airplane-medicine expert in the world and get
them conferenced in and waiting and send a conference call
number to me and to Tom and to Karl's phone and any or all of
those we will take, but I would like that in the next minute/two
minutes please, Jess. Okay?

*Kendall makes another call. He walks to somewhere private. As he
goes—*

We need to tell Con. Let's get Con?

*He heads out and through a door marked 'Crew Only'. Out in the
fresh air there is a rope and guests one way, he needs air and heads
up a deck, as he calls Frank. Frank has walked through to or by the
cockpit.*

> FRANK

Hey, Ken?

> KENDALL

Can I speak with the pilot, Frank? Are you with the pilot?

> FRANK

Um, the pilot says he can't talk to you, Ken.

> KENDALL

Yes he can.

> FRANK

He's flying the plane, son.

*That word vibrates, maybe wrong, maybe right. But Kendall rides it,
is bursting with the desire to do things.*

> KENDALL

What's happening? I need— What's— Where's the information?

> FRANK

We're coming back in to land at Teterboro.

KENDALL

Uh-huh. Okay. Well fucking, tell them to, tell them to do it, do it *right*. Okay?

FRANK

I will.

(*then*)

I'm sorry, Ken.

KENDALL

Uh-huh.

(*it sinks in*)

Has he gone, Frank? I mean basically, has he— [gone?]

FRANK

I don't know. He got very short of breath and he was hurting and then very fast, I don't know, I don't want to bullshit you, Ken. I think he went. I think he's gone.

KENDALL

Okay. Thank you, Frank. Thank you.

Kendall ends that call.

He is out on a bit of deck. He can see the city skyline and the confluence of the Hudson and the East River and the Atlantic beyond—

And something creeps over him – the feeling he's at the sharp tip of the city, and America and history and . . .

A mixture of things. But one thing – a certain weight lifting from him. Awful, but liberating, to still be alive. The worst thing has happened and the world maintains around him. The world is solid and still but within it, for him, gravity and all the laws of being are suspended. He feels he could float off like something insubstantial, a wraith or maybe a super-being.

And he walks back down and into the private area.

ROMAN

What did Frank say?

KENDALL

Have you got Tom?

The phone is right there. On speakerphone, nothing coming out.

ROMAN

Tom's open but there's nothing to say. They're, doing – they're still doing it.

KENDALL

Yeah, um, I don't know, Karl, they'll land in, I don't know what he said?

ROMAN

Tom said like forty minutes.

KENDALL

Right. No, that's right.

ROMAN

Right.

KENDALL

He said he got short of breath.

ROMAN

He got short of breath?

KENDALL

Yeah and— But yeah, I don't know, Frank thinks he's gone.

Beat.

SHIV

Why didn't you come get me?

KENDALL

I did, Shiv. We did.

SHIV

How long was it happening before— I was right out there.

KENDALL

I'm sorry, we did but— I wasn't thinking. I'm sorry. I didn't—

ROMAN

There was like no time, Shiv.

SHIV

Sure. No, it's okay.

(*then*)

But you got to say things?

KENDALL

We don't know if he could hear.

SHIV

Tom just said Kerry spoke to him quite a bit?

KENDALL

Right. Well. I don't know.

SHIV

It's okay. I don't mind. I just. I'm sad I guess.

Little smiles. They are sad. Then a thought Roman's had—

ROMAN

What was he— [doing?] Was he *on* his phone. Do we know if he checked his messages?

Nothing. Seems like just another disconnected thought. Then Roman picks up the phone.

(*projecting*)

Is anything happening?

TOM

No. Nothing. Nothing good is happening. They have to keep doing the chest compressions. For twenty-five minutes is the idea apparently. In case.

ROMAN

Oh Jesus.

He looks a little broken.

KENDALL

You okay, Rome? We're okay.

ROMAN

I don't know. I don't know if I said – good things?

KENDALL

To him?

ROMAN

Yeah I don't know what I said?
                    (*can Kendall remember?*)
What did I say?

> KENDALL

You said good things. You said good stuff. It was good. You did good.

> ROMAN

Uh-huh. Did I say I loved him?

> KENDALL

I think so. Yeah.

> ROMAN

This is so fucking—
> *(then)*
Tom, can you put the phone back with him maybe? Or I don't know. I don't— Shall we just leave it open here?

> TOM

I'll tell you if anything happens.

From an area behind the private area, a door swings as someone brings stuff through from a 'backstage' storage room and we hear Connor shouting something about the cake.

> ROMAN

Oh fuck. We should tell Con. We should get Connor?

They look at one another. Who will go? Shiv into the phone.

> SHIV

Nothing's happening, right? You'll tell us if *anything* happens.

> TOM
> *(from phone)*

Of course.

Kendall gets up. Roman is flooded with relief and gratitude. He couldn't face telling Connor right now. Drained.

> ROMAN

Can you, Ken? I don't think I can. I could, but— [I'd be really grateful.]

> KENDALL

It's okay.

> SHIV

You want me to?

> ROMAN

I mean do we definitely tell him?

Little beat. They can see him, maybe the door's propped open.

> SHIV

Oh I think so. Yeah?

> ROMAN

Sure. I mean, just to be nice, would it be, better to, like there's nothing he can *do*?

A moment where maybe they think – could they not tell him?

> SHIV

We've got to tell him. Too weird.

> ROMAN

Too weird, too weird. No, go.

Shiv goes with Kendall.

Roman sits there. He looks at the phone buzzing with static. He can't believe it. So blank. The room, everything is unbearable.

He looks at the phone. Looks at the walls. Looks out at people on the harbor. Everything strange and fresh.

Outside, Shiv and Kendall head through together, maybe as they go into Willa's dressing room their hands touch and their fingers intertwine.

They walk through to Connor, who is near Julie.

> SHIV

Hey, Con?

> CONNOR

Hey hey! Fucking cake *nightmare*.

> KENDALL

Con. It's very serious. Come here.

> CONNOR

What is it?

They try to lead him away, but he wants to be near the preparations—

> SHIV

We should do this privately.

> CONNOR

What is it?

> KENDALL

This is private, Con . . .

> CONNOR

What is it? Is this important?

> KENDALL

It's very, very serious.

> CONNOR

What?

> SHIV

I'm— Let's just get you to—

> CONNOR

Is it Dad?

Shiv and Kendall look at one another.

Is he okay?

> KENDALL

I'm sorry, Con, let's just get you here . . .

They try to wait until they get him private. But Connor can feel the bad vibrations.

> CONNOR

What is it? Is he sick? What is it?

> SHIV

Dad's on an airplane to Sweden, but they're coming back and we think he died. They think he's dead.

> CONNOR

Well is he?

> KENDALL

Everyone says he is, we don't know. They're still doing heart compressions.

CONNOR

Oh, man . . .

It just comes out, a blurt—

He never even liked me.

KENDALL

Hey, Con?

CONNOR

Sorry, I don't know what I mean. He did. He did. But I never got the chance to make him proud of me. He's dead? Oh Jesus.

They support him.

SHIV

Come on. Roman is on the phone to the plane and— [you can try to talk to him if you like.]

CONNOR

Oh, man.

Roman comes to them.

ROMAN

Hey, Con. I'm sorry.

SHIV
(*to Roman*)

Anything?

ROMAN

There. People. People came. I couldn't speak to—

In the private room we might see some donors, Ravenhead perhaps. Beth follows behind.

SHIV

Look – let's get private okay? Let's get this private.

Connor knows a place, he leads, walking from Willa's dressing room to VIP Room #2.

CONNOR

So, like? What happened?

SHIV

We don't know – Rome?

> KENDALL
>
> Um, he was on the plane and—

> ROMAN
>
> I said, 'Hello fucky sucky brigade,' and he was in the bathroom.

> SHIV
>
> He was in the bathroom?

> ROMAN
>
> Yeah, I don't know, he was in trouble and—

> CONNOR
>
> But what was it, what is it?

> ROMAN
>
> We don't, I mean we don't actually know, like we don't *know* he's gone.

> KENDALL
>
> He's apparently not breathing and not— His heart has stopped.

A couple of people try to say hi as the kids pass and head up to the private area behind the bridge.

INT. WEDDING YACHT – PRIVATE AREA BEHIND BRIDGE – DAY

Connor leads them in.

> ROMAN
>
> I think we just need to get him back, we need to get him back and find out, like what is going on, it may be, fucking, those goons, it may be, you know. We don't actually know anything really. Fucking Tom.

> SHIV
>
> He was in the airplane toilet? Can we get this straight please what actually happened?

> ROMAN
>
> We need to get some proper doctors in there.

> KENDALL
>
> Sure.

(*then*)
I mean, he has gone, he has died I think, Rome, so?

ROMAN
Yeah well we don't know that – so?

KENDALL
Sure, I get it, but like, they will know, they will know.

Roman shrugs: Maybe.

SHIV
I think, Roman, you do have to accept . . .

ROMAN
I'm not saying anything, all I am saying is we don't actually know.

SHIV
Right, but you sound delusional, because they said he's [dead]—

ROMAN
Oh what I'm fucking *outvoted*?

SHIV
Rome? C'mon. He's – you know – they know he's – dead.

ROMAN
Well there's no need to keep saying it, is there? Till we know? Ah? What's the point in keeping on saying it? All I'm saying, I'm not being crazy I am saying a fact. We don't know and until we do it's not a very nice thing to say, is it?

Shiv shrugs, it's okay, cuts him some slack.

INT. WAYSTAR JET – DAY

In the back. Tom, Karl, Karolina.

Through beyond, Kerry is with Logan and the stewardess, who we might sense is still doing chest compressions.

Karolina is writing a list on a piece of paper.

Frank comes in—

> FRANK
> (*re the chest compressions*)
> They have to keep doing them until they're exhausted or thirty minutes of nothing.
> (*then*)
> Or – he comes back.

Doesn't feel likely. Karl looks at his watch.

> KARL
> Okay. Well. Jeez Louise.

They all look at one another.

> FRANK
> How long was he in there before we got them to go in?

> KARL
> The bathroom? Oh. Not long, because, you heard the bang, right, Tom?

Karolina writing.

> TOM
> Me? I think you heard the bang? Or no, they did, because by the time we were going back there they had the special key thing?

> KARL
> Not a key, there's a latch.

> TOM
> Right? Oh okay? But I mean, it wasn't long he was in there, right?

> KARL
> No. I mean he was, his breathing was odd before but—

> TOM
> Yeah? His breathing was odd?

It wasn't meant that way but just very vaguely Karl senses this could be used against him.

> KARL
> We all noticed he was breathing heavy?

Frank and Tom. Frank is a stand-up guy—

FRANK

Sure. Look, it's okay. We did the right thing. They did the right thing.

KARL

I might have a little stiffener. Just— Gents? Karolina?

TOM

(*should we?*)

Um?

KARL

Let's drink to him.

No stewardess. Karl goes to the drinks.

TOM

Well. I guess we're off the clock?

Weird atmosphere.

KARL

He died with his boots on.

Frank reaches for a laptop.

FRANK

Karolina, I'm just gonna put down notes – my version, while it's fresh.

KARL

How do you mean, your version?

KAROLINA

It might be smart for us to start putting together a little timeline?

Maybe Tom puts down a drink he's taken.

Then. I, um, and I have been drawing up, in case we should need, a little contact list?

KARL

My god, they're still pumping on him in there, Karolina?

KAROLINA

I'm not happy about it, Karl. I want to be respectful. I am being respectful. But this is going to be quite a complex—

(what is it?)
situation – to handle and so: if we get a miracle, we get a
miracle and god bless us all. But if we don't, I need to prepare?
That's all.

FRANK

Uh-huh. Well, sure. Go ahead.

Checks her list.

KAROLINA

So I guess we call Matsson and let him know?
(looks at them)
We have to at least let him know we're, he's, delayed.

KARL

Oh he's heavily fucking delayed.

KAROLINA

Then, not necessarily this order but: um. The board. Gerri, the
president. Frank, you and Simon, will hit the board? Unless
should we handle Sandi, Sandy, Stewy differently?

Frank shrugs.

Then: we need to figure out a plan for major shareholders.
Josh A and the Ulsterman? From there on maybe I handle? Also
Marcia. Personal we can leave to the kids? Their mom.
(considers)
Frank, do I need to get into that?

Frank thinks, then resents thinking.

FRANK

Um?
(then)
Let's just take five and drink a toast shall we? At least until
he's – you know, actually— [dead?]

Then Kerry comes through.

KARL

Hey, you okay?

*Kerry is in shock and not really in control of her reactions. It comes
out as being almost giggly in her response—*

> KERRY

It's fucking nuts. Isn't it crazy?

> FRANK

It is. It is. We're all in shock—

She looks around, trying to get a grip on what's happened, and in amongst her responses is an odd smile.

> KERRY

Wow.
> *(looks around, then)*
So fucking, weird. Jesus. Are you guys okay?

People nod.

> FRANK

We're good. Thank you.

Kerry stands there but a force field is growing between her and the others. They're all aware of it.

> KAROLINA

If it's okay, Kerry, in a moment we could do with this space for coordinating a response, if we need to? Is that okay?

> KERRY

Uh-huh? Do you want me to . . . [help]?

> KAROLINA

That's kind but you're in shock. We can make you comfortable in there or whatever you need?

> KERRY

Do you want me as part of that, of the response and the – whatever?

But that's not going to happen. Her status was all via Logan and it has drained mostly away.

> FRANK

That would be great, Kerry. You rest up – in there and let us get our ducks in a row and we'll get your input?

It's like Kerry's deflating. As she heads back out—

> KERRY

Of course. I'll be right there.

After she's gone – Tom raises his eyebrows. His expression says: She was acting a little weird, no?

> KAROLINA
>
> Think she's just freaking out, Tom.

> TOM
>
> No, I'm sure. I am.

Karolina rips out a page—

> KAROLINA
>
> Okay. I've got a list of names if we wanna divide as soon as we get the – the—
> *(looking for the word)*
> the— Not the 'all clear'. The word. Once the thirty minutes are up?

She hands Tom the sheet. He looks.

> TOM
>
> Some of these are [small potatoes]— Can we get Kerry to do some?

> KARL
>
> Chuckles the Clown? I think not.

Frank takes the sheet, looks at it with Karl.

Tom looks into space for a beat.

> TOM
>
> Fuck. He's gone. He's really gone? What a shitty way to go.

> KARL
>
> Uh-huh.

Tom goes towards the back of the plane, or a private area. Getting his phone out.

> KAROLINA
>
> Who you calling there, Tom?

> TOM
> *(fuck you)*
> Oh just *The Daily Planet* to get my five bucks for the tip-off. C'mon?

Karl and Frank watch Tom go. Then—

                    KARL

You get the feeling there are two dead men on this plane?

                    FRANK

Don't. Karl.

Tom gets private. Makes a call.

                    TOM

Hey, Greg?

Intercut with:

INT./EXT. WEDDING YACHT — DAY

Greg is talking to the journalist, Olivia.

                    GREG

Hey, Tom!

                    TOM

I might need you to go into the office?

                    GREG

Um, it's a wedding day, Tom? Why?

                    TOM

Why? Because Logan's dead. I might need you in there as my eyes and ears.

                    GREG

Uncle Logan? Really. What? How?

                    TOM

Stick to Cyd like a limpet. Delete my J drive and delete it from the trash. I might need you calling around with my narrative. Sing my song. Merry Christmas, Greg.

                    GREG

Tom? What? What do you mean?

                    TOM

He's passed away. You've lucked out. What's at the bottom of your stocking, Greg, huh? An old guy who hated you.

                    GREG

Tom? Man! Easy. Holy cow. He just— He just—?

> TOM

Yes. So get your party hat off. Stop celebrating, you piece of shit.

> GREG

I'm not! Are you okay? Jesus.

> TOM

I'm sorry. I'm not okay. I'm sad. I am. I'm sorry. But fuck. I don't know. It was pretty grim, man.

> GREG

I'm sorry.

> TOM

I lost my protector. They're gonna change the locks on me. Watch Hugo. I was the right-hand man. Okay? This is total lockdown. This leaks, it's stock-price rodeo. And a slit throat for the big mouth. But people should know I was with him. Okay?

End of call. Greg's world flips on its axis. The world turned upside down. He looks at Olivia, the journalist.

Olivia smiles.

> OLIVIA

Everything alright?

> GREG

Uh-huh.

He looks freaked.

Yeah fine.

> OLIVIA

So do you think your uncle's going to make it?

> GREG

What? Do I? I— Um. Yeah. I I I I don't know. It's kinda rude to be nosy.
> (*sad, flailing, covering*)
Wanna dance?

> OLIVIA

Well? What, there's no music?

> GREG

No. I'm sorry. You were only asking.

(then)
You don't need music to dance, Olivia.

Just then, Hugo is arriving, bustling onto the yacht.

Greg and Hugo scoping each other out. What do they each know?

Hey, Hugo.

*Hugo angles Greg private with a minimum-required-civility smile for Olivia.**

> HUGO
>
> You heard?

> GREG
>
> I've heard. Have you heard?

> HUGO
>
> I've heard.

> GREG
>
> Great and this is Olivia, a *journalist*.

> HUGO
>
> Oh, pleased to meet you. May I borrow the prime rib?

Hugo leads him away.

I might need you to lock down your mom and Ewan for me?
I need positive statements lined up . . .

> GREG
>
> Sure. I mean, I could be busy. Because I have other duties to—

> HUGO
>
> No. This first. Okay?

Greg hesitates.

Look, kid, there's two ways this goes when this breaks:
'Lamentations! An irascible genius has passed and lucky were those
who drank at the well of his wisdom!' Yay! Your rep is bolstered!

> GREG
>
> Uh-huh?

---

* This moment between Hugo and Greg felt a little tonally awry once we looked
at it in the edit.

HUGO

Or: 'Celebrations, a hate-monger, sex pest has been toppled and anyone who worked with him is toxic.' Boo! Your rep is tarnished.

GREG

Right. Uh-huh.

(then)

And— I mean, are you okay?

HUGO

Sure, training kicks in! Lock down your side of the family okay? I'm gonna try to get a peek at the *Times* obit.

GREG

But let them know, we grieve together. Hirsch and Roy. Let no man put asunder—

Hugo heads off, perhaps a little indecently energized.

INT. WAYSTAR JET – DAY

Tom returns to the others from his call.

The gang has been putting together a sort of framework of what the hell happened—

FRANK

Hey, Tom, last words? What were his last words?

TOM

Um.

(then, chancing it)

Was it 'Fire Cyd'?

Wan smiles.

KARL

Seriously? For Karolina and the kids and – for history. You know?

FRANK

Honestly wasn't it when you asked, 'You okay?' and he went to the bathroom and he said—

> TOM

He said he – he was going to lay some cable or what's that disgusting thing, 'hatch a brown trout'?

Karolina isn't going to write that down.

> KAROLINA

C'mon, that's not his wisdom for the ages, is it?

Frank has ended his call. A little concerned.

> FRANK

Okay. So, I've spoken with Gerri and for the statement. We think, it goes: the board announces the news, and expects to provide additional information in due course?

> TOM

Uh-huh? And in terms of leadership?

> FRANK

Well, Simon's on a flight from Singapore, Sandy's in the hospital – I think we have to wait to get the full board on the phone to agree. In like the next twelve hours. Eighteen max?

What isn't he saying?

> KARL

Might be nice to have an interim. Right? What do we have on emergency planning . . .

> FRANK

Well, Simon and I have been pushing Logan – on this point, and we are actually getting our crisis documents redrafted to include leadership planning so—

> TOM

And in the draft?

This is what he didn't really want to get into.

> FRANK

In the draft, well, in the draft it posits, I believe, COO – or COOs in our case, move to CEO in the interim.

> KARL

Uh-huh. Kendall and Roman?

They all consider this.

Right.

                    TOM
Uh-huh.

                    FRANK
But that's all complicated and it's a draft. And they're so shaken
up? I think we wait for the board and just remind the world of
the—
                    (*motions them*)
experience here on the bench?

They all consider.

                    TOM
I mean if it's a matter of hours?

                    KAROLINA
I mean that's kind.

                    KARL
I think that sounds wise. I do. No need to get it all tangled.

INT. WEDDING YACHT – PRIVATE AREA BEHIND BRIDGE –
DAY

Hugo enters.

                    HUGO
Hey, guys?

                    SHIV
How did you . . . You heard already?

                    HUGO
Indeed. Sorry for your loss.

                    ROMAN
Yeah we don't know shit. They're still working on him.

                    HUGO
Right. Absolutely.

Fingers crossed.

                    ROMAN
Anything could be happening. Could be a fucking hoax.

Shiv and Kendall exchange a glance.

It could. What if it's a drill? What if it's all a big test? Ah?

SHIV

If it was a drill I'd say: hats off to the planning department.

ROMAN

It just does not feel very likely to me that he is dead?

Kendall gets a call.

KENDALL

Hey, Tom?
                    (*listens*)
Fine. Okay. Thank you.
                    (*to the room*)
They've stopped the CPR.

ROMAN

I don't know if they should though?

SHIV

Maybe they do eventually, leave him, alone?

KENDALL
(*into phone*)

Is he covered?

ROMAN

Should they cover him actually in case— [he needs to breathe or something?]

KENDALL

Hugo – Karolina wants you?

Kendall gives Hugo the phone.

HUGO

Hey, K. Yeah all good. Under the circumstances.

Hugo listens, the kids are very aware but then . . .

The boat perhaps starts to leave the dock.

SHIV

What the fuck— Are we going?

ROMAN

I think we're going.

HUGO
(*listens*)
Uh-huh. Okay. Okay. Sure. Well I'll ask, we'll discuss. Sure. I get
it, no, okay, well let's stay in contact.

Phone down. He's a bit troubled.

KENDALL

Hugo, can you find out what the fuck's going on? Where are we
going?

HUGO

Sure, sure and – just – last words we're saying were— Breathing
was heavy but we think it was – 'Nothing stops the deal.'

They look at him. Yeah? Fine.

I think maybe not the last *last* thing but – yeah, and I, for your
information, they're starting to draft the statement.

KENDALL

How do you mean?

HUGO

Karolina and Frank and Karl and Tom are putting something
together for when we're ready to release the news.

The kids feel a bolt of electricity. They are highly sensitive.

SHIV

They're on the statement?

KENDALL

Who asked them to? That feels – that feels—
(*looks to siblings*)
Right?

*Roman makes a call, Shiv and Kendall tacitly agreeing he should do
so.*

Hey, Hugo, fuck off and find out what the fuck's going on with
this boat, yeah? We wanna go back.

Meanwhile—

> ROMAN
> (*connects*)

Hey, guys.

> (*puts phone on the table*)

You're on speakerphone.

> SHIV

Hey there. Hey gang, listen, what's going on with this statement?

Intercut with:

INT. WAYSTAR JET — DAY

Frank and Karl and Tom and Karolina are there.

The men look at Karolina.

> KAROLINA

Hey. Um, yeah – just starting to put the bones together for when we want to announce this – and—

> (*then*)

Sorry for your loss.

> SHIV

Uh-huh, well it feels fucking presumptuous.

On the plane – silence. Maybe faces at one another: Get a load of these kids! So hair-trigger and annoying.

The men look at Karolina. She looks like: Fuck you, I tried. Then—

> FRANK

Well, sorry that's how it seemed. But you know regardless of our personal feeling of loss, in terms of the business position—

> KARL

This is a material event.

> ROMAN

Oh it's a *material event*?

Karl looks pained, he was only trying to help.

> FRANK

We just need to put something together from the board to reassure the market.

> SHIV
> Oh, the *market?* Will nobody think of the poor market!

Frank is out of patience.

> FRANK
> I don't know what to say, Shiv. I'm trying to do my job. He's
> like twelve feet away and I knew him for forty years. We're not
> pulling anything here.

Karl acts the good pal to Frank and helps out—

> KARL
> Since you guys were estranged we thought you might want us to
> be the hub on this— [to make it easier.]

> KENDALL
> We're not estranged. We weren't estranged.

On the plane, the faces say: Really?

> KARL
> No I simply meant—

> KENDALL
> We've all had communications with him.

*Roman and Shiv look at Kendall. See the angles and tacitly agree to
this characterization.*

> We've been tight. Some road bumps but tight. We had a family –
> function with him last night.

*Shiv and Roman won't meet Kendall's eye. This mischaracterization is
useful to them too but they'd rather not admit they are complicit.*

> So 'estranged' is a strong word and not accurate.

> FRANK
> Fine. All good. We've got it.

> KARL
> Look. Let's stay close. Best to you guys.

> FRANK
> Good strength, friends.

*End of call. We stay on the plane. A beat of silence. Will they call the
kids on their bullshit?*

TOM

Going through a lot.

But the question has been raised by this more political call.

INT. WEDDING YACHT – PRIVATE AREA BEHIND BRIDGE –
DAY

Hugo brings Gerri in.

GERRI

Hey, how are you all doing?

HUGO

I briefed her.

GERRI

I'm really sorry. I'm very sorry.

She suddenly realizes a little more is required.

He was a— He was – an important man in all our lives. But
especially yours.

ROMAN

I'm welling up.

Roman has trouble with how or when to look at Gerri.

GERRI

I mean he was a lot more but – yeah [now is not the time to]—

ROMAN

He might not be dead. I mean he might be but all the
information we have is from some fucking – corporate bozos
and some airplane sluts. They probably tried to resuscitate him
by blowing up his dick.
(*off the looks no one is giving him*)
No doctor has actually seen him.
(*challenging the room*)
I know what is likely but I am actually not being crazy. Mad shit
happens. It's fucking five, three percent possible. That is all I am
saying so don't look at me like I'm five fucking years old.

SHIV

It's true.

KENDALL

And, Gerri, in terms of the breathing space, until we have to say anything, we have a bit of time to think, right. Until they land?

GERRI

Are you thinking can we hold this information till the markets close?

He hadn't really been. Too much for the kids right now. They are in their own worlds.

Because, obviously this will be— It is a significant private thing—

ROMAN

Oh, pretty significant. For him, we're talking top ten right?

They're still not really meeting one another's eyes.

GERRI

But it's also a big thing, in terms of public, the company and the world?

KENDALL

I honestly don't know how much I can get into this. How long till they land?

HUGO

I'll check.

SHIV

We can't think, Gerri. Can we keep it up there for an extra beat while we— Until we can— I don't know. I'm not ready to— So we have a minute?

ROMAN

I think we should get him down.

SHIV

I have a headache.

Hugo sees the chance to cement himself with this family group—

HUGO

I think it's good for you guys to stay across this. Because, Karolina's great, the best. But her like – her communications excellence, can sometimes – out of an abundance of good intentions – get out ahead of the wider corporate strategy.

ROMAN

Hugo. Easy. She's doing her best.

HUGO

You want me to ask if they can circle?

Gerri looks at him like: C'mon, we're the grown-ups. Her phone goes.

GERRI

Karolina?

She steps out onto the deck.

SHIV

No. No. We can't get them to stay up there until markets open on Monday. Can you get me an Advil, Hugo? I don't fucking know. At least, Hugo, can we get back to fucking land, we want to go to him, yeah?

Hugo heads out. The kids watch them go.

KENDALL

Look, this is very surreal. And, not to big-brother it but, just for our own sakes to say: everything we say and do today is going in the memoirs, the bios, it's going in the fucking Congressional Record, it's coming up at board meetings, it's going in SEC filings, it's – like— We tell them to circle for half an hour so we can get our heads straight and then some fucking rumor starts, we get crucified for being cold-hearted or I don't even know. Grassy knoll. We are highly liable to misinterpretation. What we do today will always be what we did the day our father died. So, let's grieve and whatever but – not do anything that restricts our future freedom of movement.

They look at him.

Is that cold? Am I being cold? I'm not. I'm broken-hearted. But – you know? I'm thinking of all of us.

ROMAN

No, it's okay, it's sensible.

Roman appreciates it. But the imp of the perverse in him can't let it lie—

I know you're glad he's dead and you want to grab the crown.

Maybe Kendall finds it funny but also fears the old fights starting up. Shiv smiles, maybe laughs.

> SHIV
>
> You can say it. Joke.

> ROMAN
>
> This is. I keep— FUCK.

He makes a weird long sound. They all sit in the sound.

INT. WEDDING YACHT – DAY

Connor and Willa are in some private special bride-and-groom area.

Beth is with them. She doesn't know what the hell is going on, who is having a wobble.

> BETH
>
> I've spoken to them and while you both decide, on what you want to do, there's no pressure, okay? We have a slot. You take your time and – I'll get out of your hair.

Willa shows her out.

> WILLA
>
> Thank you. I'm sorry about all this. I can explain later.

> BETH
> (*quietly*)
>
> Is it cold feet, honey?

But Connor can hear.

> CONNOR
>
> It might be my cold feet?

> BETH
>
> Oh sure.

(*patronizing smile*)
But can I just say, I hope this isn't above my pay grade but
I've seen this a lot, 'the last-minute gremlins'. And for what it's
worth, you seem like a great couple. And my advice is go for it!

Willa smiles her out. Returns to Connor.

> CONNOR

What you think? It's cancel, yeah?

> WILLA

I think it is cancel?

> CONNOR

What do we tell them?
(*then*)
I mean everyone will assume it's you, backing out and that's fine.
(*thinks*)
Or – or do we – just—
(*then*)
I guess – could – something good come out of something bad?

Quite touching.

> WILLA

Uh-huh?

> CONNOR

Too weird. Right?
(*seems to be forcing the positive case*)
Or is it?

> WILLA

Con, you seem like you kind of want to do it?

> CONNOR

I don't know. I don't.
(*then*)
I guess the truth is, I'm scared if we don't, that – that you'll walk
away. I'm always scared you're gonna walk away. I'm so much
older than you, Willa. And you're young and full of life and
I'm— I don't know. My dad's dead and I feel old.

> WILLA

It's okay.

CONNOR

And I'm sorry – I don't know – that I stole you from the world.

WILLA

Nah. Con, no.

CONNOR

Are you just with me for money, Willa. Really? Basically?

Should she lie? But the gravity of the day has stripped some layers away.

WILLA

Well. There's something about money and safety here, yeah. Yeah there is. But – I, I'm happy. I am.

CONNOR

I don't know if you're getting everything you deserve?

WILLA

It's okay. It's— I know what I'm doing, Con.

CONNOR

You're okay? It's okay?

WILLA

I'm safe. You're kind. It's not everything. But it's okay. I'm not gonna walk.
(*little joke*)
Not today, anyway.

CONNOR

Yeah? You'll stick around. For the big payday.

WILLA

Sure, I'll stick around for the big payday.

They hold hands, tight.

INT. WEDDING YACHT – PRIVATE AREA BEHIND BRIDGE – DAY

Kendall and Roman and Shiv sit in thoughts.

ROMAN

I did say I loved him, didn't I? Did I?

KENDALL

You did.

ROMAN

I feel like I didn't.

(*then*)

I spoke to him twice, right, once, then you went to get Shiv?

Kendall nods, he thinks so.

What was it like when he told you, Shiv?

SHIV

Yeah, um, I thought I knew, when I saw his face, and I actually, thought it was Dad but I said Mom, I said Mom, right?

KENDALL

Yeah you asked if it was Mom.

SHIV

I was thinking was it Dad. I think I sort of— I think I hoped it was Mom. Oh, man, the fucking shit, the *lists*, the fucking – everything. I don't know if I can do it?

ROMAN

We don't have to. We don't have to do anything. Our dad died.

KENDALL

We'll be okay, we'll get people. We'll get a funeral off the rack. We'll do Reagan's with tweaks.

Gerri knocks on whatever is available if there is a door or table, enters.

GERRI

Hey, guys? Karolina.

Gerri hits speakerphone.

I'm putting you on speakerphone with the kids, K?

SHIV

Hey, Karolina?

KAROLINA

(*on speakerphone*)

Yeah, hi. Look I got a call from a reporter who's heard a rumor about Logan's health.

SHIV

Where from?

Intercut with:

INT. WAYSTAR JET – DAY

KAROLINA

I don't know what the source was and I – I said there was
nothing on that, which is— It's not great but—

ROMAN

Oh, man. How?

KAROLINA

I don't know. Plane-to-ground comms. Um, tail number – us
turning, they're tracking, who knows down there? I don't know.
An eavesdrop. I don't know. Kerry? Hugo has a theory.

KENDALL

So can we make it till the markets close?

KAROLINA

Gerri?

GERRI

Till four? I just don't know if we can get there?

TOM

We just do probably need to figure out the choreography?

SHIV

Oh you want to choreograph some steps with my dead father?
That the dance you like, Tom?

Static, everyone avoids her eyes.

I'm sorry.

TOM

It's okay. It's a difficult day.

KAROLINA

So we will need the statement. So you want to do that? Or us?

KARL

Get everyone on the same page.

Is this pre-planned?

GERRI

So, guys, it's tough, for you, I understand. So if you like we can give the word, Frank and Karl and myself and Karolina can handle the immediate, chowder. And if you like we can excuse you from the board meeting on compassionate grounds?

Kids look at one another.

KENDALL

Um-huh, thanks, Gerri.

SHIV

Can you give us five? Before we do anything or speak with Matsson, yeah?

ROMAN

Right.

SHIV

Thanks!

Shiv leans in and disconnects the call.

EXT. WEDDING YACHT – DAY

Hugo with Greg. He is near to Olivia, a little way off. Hugo walks over.

HUGO

Hey, how you doing?

GREG

Um, not good. Sad. Weird and . . . yeah, sad and—

Hugo keeps smiling, looking around.

HUGO

Uh-huh and have you fucking squawked?

GREG

Excuse me?

HUGO

Have you fucking squawked, Chicken Man?

> GREG

Well don't call me Chicken Man – Duck Man.

> HUGO

Cos we've got some leakage?

> GREG

Well I'm tight as a drum. I'm sad!

> HUGO

Sure you are. Did you sell us out for a lay?

He nods to Olivia, who is on the phone.

> GREG

No I'm sad as fuck.

> HUGO

Well me too. He was my boss.

> GREG

Well he was my uncle.

> HUGO

Oh yeah well, we've got leakage and the circle is tight and if it's you trying to get your little pecker oily, you'll be in big trouble. I'm clearing this area.

> GREG

Yeah well it wasn't me. And I don't take kindly to these kind of accusations.
> *(starts to move)*
> I'm like fourth or fifth in line to the crown. So don't forget that.

EXT. WEDDING YACHT – OUTSIDE PRIVATE AREA – DAY

The gang might step out if they need air and it's all clear. Leaving Gerri inside on the phone.

> SHIV

Um. So, I can't do this, really, my head is full of fuzz.

She looks at Roman, Kendall.

I feel sick. I can't . . .

KENDALL

Uh-huh. Rome?

ROMAN

Um. Yeah. Same. Can't think.

KENDALL

Sure. Uh-huh. Do we— Maybe we do let them pilot this, and we just take a day or two out?

They all consider. It feels good.

But . . .

SHIV

Yeah?

ROMAN

Yeah.

KENDALL

Yeah. Yeah?

ROMAN

Yeah?

SHIV

Yeah. Yeah?

KENDALL

I can't think.

The other two kind of want him to say what they all feel too weird about saying. Kendall summons the will—

Okay. But just to say, we give control to Gerri and Frank and Karl and Tom and Karolina up there— I don't know. I don't really want to be the one to have to say things, I feel like you're looking at me, and— Yeah. But.

They look at Kendall.

SHIV

It's okay. We know. It's okay, Ken. I don't think anything of it, you can say.

                    KENDALL

I mean, who knows, maybe we, tomorrow hand them the
crown, probably a good idea. Finish the sale. Great. But, just
should we keep our options open?

                    ROMAN

I just don't know if I can, literally, do anything, or talk to
anyone.

                    SHIV

We need to be across the statement, Rome. It could be all Frank,
Karl, Gerri. And even for overnight I think – whatever the text –
the subtext has got to be – Logan Roy is – you know— But
Roman Roy, Kendall Roy, Shiv Roy are here?

                    ROMAN

We don't want to just let Karolina handle?

                    KENDALL

Just for the statement, Rome. It'll be for the board to decide. But
I think until then, for the markets, we need to be in control.

They look at him.

Us.

                    SHIV

Uh-huh. Just until the board can meet.

                    ROMAN

Uh-huh. Well, I mean, I would, I don't want anything happening
we don't, like approve. So. Yeah. Yeah?

They look at one another. It's kind of agreed.

                    SHIV

Hugo.

                    KENDALL

We'll draft the statement okay?

                    HUGO

Uh-huh? I mean we'll need them to sign off? It will need to
come from Frank or Simon or the board or—

KENDALL

Yeah but we'll draft. It goes: the sad news. Board will meet to discuss leadership.

SHIV

But don't worry—
                    (*points at herself, them*)
President of Domestic, Co-COOs, all the Roys are here. Captaining the ship. Plus the execs. Yeah?

Hugo makes a calculation. Is he going to go with it? Yes.

HUGO

And who'll call Matsson?

A significant role. Roman knows him best. They look at him—

ROMAN

Oh, man, I didn't really want to do anything.

SHIV

Hugo?

ROMAN

The only thing, it's delicate. Oh fuck. Okay. Okay.

He goes back to the little room to make the call.

INT. WEDDING YACHT – PRIVATE AREA BEHIND BRIDGE – DAY

Roman re-enters the private room.

There's Gerri. Doing some texting.

ROMAN

Hey.

GERRI

Hey.

ROMAN

Yeah. Um, I need the room.

GERRI

Of course. Fine.

She gets up.

> ROMAN

I'm pretty sad.

> GERRI

Uh-huh.

> ROMAN

Yeah. I mean I'm actually – right now. I'm totally numb. But yeah, theoretically, you would say, I'm – yeah, sad.

> GERRI

Yeah well. Sorry.

> ROMAN

Yeah. And – I don't know, what happens – about earlier.
> (*then*)
I actually called him back and I called him – a— I said he was a cunt or something.

> GERRI

'Thanks.'

> ROMAN

So. That's nice to know.
> (*then*)
It was like a joke I guess. But. What a fucking mess.

She's not able to give him much, honestly, and she's not about to fake it. Maybe a shrug that says some of that – too much water under the bridge, and—

> GERRI

Yup. Well. Room's all yours.

And she's gone.

He can't quite believe it. Dad gone. Maybe he bangs his head on a piece of ship as he goes.

Trying to feel something. Because right now he's gone a bit numb.

EXT. WEDDING YACHT – OUTSIDE PRIVATE AREA – DAY

Kendall and Shiv. Looking at the sea, the wedding, one another.

They look at wedding guests dancing or drinking. In at Roman on his call.

> KENDALL

Think he'll be okay?

> SHIV

Yeah. Yeah. Yeah?

They look at one another. Communicate certain concerns and feelings and head inside . . .

INT. WEDDING YACHT – PRIVATE AREA BEHIND BRIDGE – DAY

Roman is on the line. Shiv and Kendall come in.

> ROMAN

Good. No still excited. Very excited. Full steam ahead. I think. More to follow, Lukas, more to follow.

He looks at Kendall and Shiv.

Yeah.
> (*winces*)

I'll pass that on to, to him. It is serious. It's serious, but hoping for the best. Hoping for the best. We'll let you know. Thanks, Lukas.

End of call.

Urgh. Didn't feel great. But I guess. We can explain.

> KENDALL

It's fine. And what did you say about the deal?

> ROMAN

Well, just sort of – steady as she goes.

> KENDALL

Uh-huh. Uh-huh. You said full steam ahead?

> ROMAN

Well, we're already full steam ahead so – full steam ahead is steady as she goes?
> (*looks at Kendall*)

What? I didn't even want to fucking call.

> KENDALL

No it's fine.

>   ROMAN
> That's just – a continuation. He just died, Ken. Man. It wasn't a
> move.

>   KENDALL
> No. It's fine, I'm sorry. It's just the day. I'm paranoid. Dad is
> dead and I'm paranoid. Okay? It's all good.

Beat. Silence. Consideration.

>   SHIV
> Okay. Shall we draft this fucking statement?

EXT. HELIPORT – DAY

Either from Ellis Island or Governors Island—

Kendall, Shiv, Roman, Hugo board a helicopter, which takes off.

EXT. TETERBORO AIRPORT – DAY

The Waystar plane lands.

EXT. TETERBORO AIRPORT – TARMAC – DAY

The siblings in their cars wait as Frank, Karl, Tom, Karolina descend.

There are press at the wire.

Hugo greets them on the tarmac.

>   KAROLINA
>   How we getting him off?

>   HUGO
>   Jesus. I dunno. I'll handle.

>   FRANK
>   You saw the edits? On the statement.

Hugo nods.

>   We do feel for market confidence it's important for Karl, myself
>   and Gerri to be mentioned by name.

>   HUGO
>   Uh-huh. And you saw the counter?

                    FRANK
The name order is fine.

                    KAROLINA
Great. I'll get it out – right away.

                    HUGO
And look – we had shutterbugs all around the perimeter and
we're looking at a feeding frenzy if we don't talk. So we're
gonna do some comments from the family. I've primed our
friendlies?

He motions to the terminal – journalists.

                    KAROLINA
Yeah? Who's gonna speak?

                    HUGO
Kendall was pushing but—
                    (*makes a face*)
So the feeling was Shiv or Roman and she's easier on the . . .
sense of things.

Karolina and Old Guard exchange looks.

                    KARL
Moment in the sun, huh?

INT. TETERBORO AIRPORT – DAY

Little press huddle hastily assembled.

Kendall and Roman nearby. Shiv looks at some notes.

Roman and Kendall look at one another.

                    ROMAN
Are we gonna be okay?

                    KENDALL
We'll be okay. You'll be okay.

Then a funny serious joke—

                    ROMAN
Yeah, you're not gonna be okay. You're fucked. You are
completely fucked.

> **KENDALL**
> Well you're fucked. You're totally fucked.

They touch or smile secretly away from the press and cameras.

With a look to her brothers, Shiv gets up.

> **SHIV**
> Hi. Thank you. As you know my father, Logan Roy, was pronounced dead on arrival at Teterboro Airport this afternoon. I'd like to thank the press for their respect at this time. You'll understand I won't be taking questions. But my brothers and I just want to say Logan Roy built a great, American, family company, and as you know, the board will be convening in the next hours to decide on the leadership of the company going forward. This nation has lost a passionate champion, an American titan. And we have lost a beloved father. Thank you.

She moves away. But as she goes—

> **JOURNALIST**
> And in terms of your roles, at the company?

Karolina and Hugo both look like: No not that one. Try to lead her away.

> **SHIV**
> We intend to shepherd it through its future whatever that might be. We'll be there. We'll be in there.

She walks off and gets private as Karolina and Hugo shield.

As she gets private, Tom is there. He gives her a smile. Does she want more?

Yeah, right now she'll take it.

He gives her a hug.

It lasts a while. She is on the verge of losing it. But he holds her. She appreciates it.

INT./EXT. ELLIS ISLAND VENUE – DUSK

In the empty hall. Or outside.

With just a few attendees. Mostly empty. Sylvia. Couple of witnesses.

Connor and Willa get married. He kisses her.

EXT. TETERBORO AIRPORT – DUSK

*Kendall, Roman, Shiv in a desolate spot. They are looking at the
Waystar plane. Attended by an ambulance.*

*Out in the fall dusk. But the rough, noisy stuff of airport life goes on
around them. Trash, workers, sewage-drainage trucks.*

Roman shows Kendall an iPad. Stock prices. A drop in Waystar.

>   ROMAN
> There's Dad.

*Roman is sort of torturing himself. He measures the price fall with
his fingers – the half-inch, inch or so – and holds it up for Kendall's
inspection.*

> You see him?

It's so bleak Kendall smiles or shakes his head.

> We gonna go look?

>   KENDALL
> Do you want to?

>   ROMAN
> I don't know. Should we?

>   SHIV
> You mean, will he be angry if we don't?

*Shiv looks at them. Almost a smile. He's gone. He doesn't get to be
angry anymore.*

She kisses or touches or hugs her brothers. Shiv walks off.

*Shiv walks – maybe a long way towards her car. She doesn't really
want to ride into town alone. But can't show vulnerability. She calls
over, quite a long distance.*

> Tom. Will you go through it again? Is that okay?

*Tom is some way away. Talking to Karolina and Hugo and with some
last remaining press.*

Tom heads towards her.

Next to Kendall, Roman is caught in indecision.

> ROMAN
> I dunno. I think, I think I'm going to see him? Yeah. You coming?

Kendall thinks. What can he bear, what does he want?

> KENDALL
> I'm gonna watch him down.

Roman can't quite believe it but he dives in – we might see his face as he walks out alone towards the plane.

> ROMAN
> Oh, man.

Then we see as Kendall watches Roman on the long walk out across the tarmac.

Stuck between the two – his sister departing and his brother going to Dad.

INT. SHIV'S CAR – DUSK

Inside with Shiv and Tom.

They drive off. After a beat—

Maybe she cries. Sort of from nowhere, or from holding it in.

> TOM
> You okay?

> SHIV
> I'm good.

He offers a hand or a touch. But after that hug she won't allow any more intimacy. Instead gets out—

> You know which side your bread's buttered.

> TOM
> What?

> SHIV
> I said, you – know – which – side your – bread – is – buttered.

                              TOM
Shiv. I was being nice.

                              SHIV
Sure.
                             (*beat*)
Smart move. Nice move.

He can't say anything.

EXT. TETERBORO AIRPORT — DUSK

Kendall watches as, onto a hydraulic lift at the back (or perhaps a stretcher down the back stairs), Logan, in a bag, is removed from the plane.

Episode Four
HONEYMOON STATES

Written by
Jesse Armstrong & Lucy Prebble
Directed by Lorene Scafaria

Original air date 16 April 2023

Cast

KENDALL ROY	Jeremy Strong
MARCIA ROY	Hiam Abbass
GREG HIRSCH	Nicholas Braun
SHIV ROY	Sarah Snook
ROMAN ROY	Kieran Culkin
CONNOR ROY	Alan Ruck
TOM WAMBSGANS	Matthew Macfadyen
FRANK VERNON	Peter Friedman
KARL MULLER	David Rasche
GERRI KELLMAN	J. Smith-Cameron
WILLA FERREYRA	Justine Lupe
KAROLINA NOVOTNEY	Dagmara Dominczyk
HUGO BAKER	Fisher Stevens
COLIN STILES	Scott Nicholson
KERRY CASTELLABATE	Zoë Winters
STEWY HOSSEINI	Arian Moayed
SANDY FURNESS	Larry Pine
SANDI	Hope Davis
MARK RAVENHEAD	Zack Robidas
NAOMI PIERCE	Annabelle Dexter-Jones
CAROLINE COLLINGWOOD	Harriet Walter
MARK ROSENSTOCK	Brian Hotaling
RAY	Patch Darragh
CYD PEACH	Jeannie Berlin
CONGRESSMAN JERYD MENCKEN	Justin Kirk
RON PETKUS	Stephen Root
SYLVIA FERREYRA	Cynthia Mace
OSKAR GUDJOHNSEN	Jóhannes Haukur Jóhannesson
LAUREN PAWSON	Crystal Finn
VANCE	Sean-Michael Wilkinson
PENELOPE	Anne Bates
GRAHAM	Allen Fawcett
PRESS GUY	Michael Broadhurst
SECRET SERVICE AGENT	Tyler Hopkins
DR SHARON HASFORD	Dee Pelletier
CATHLEEN CARMICHAEL	Kelly Nash
DELTA PIKE	Sharla McBride

INT. KENDALL'S APARTMENT – MORNING

Kendall is sitting, looking out at the city. He's woken early. Naomi comes into view, looks at him just looking.*

                    NAOMI
You okay?

                    KENDALL
I think so. I don't know. Um? Yeah. I dunno.

                    NAOMI
You want me to come?

                    KENDALL
That's kind. But I think, too much – too much, spaghetti, yeah?

He means emotional mess but – she's so used to the corporate maneuvers.

                    NAOMI
Jeez. Oh, Ken, man, already it's plans and positions?

                    KENDALL
Nah. Nay. No. No more fucking plans and positions.

An end to plotting? Or an end to prevarication?

INT. ROMAN'S APARTMENT – MORNING

Roman brushes his teeth. On a sound system hooked up around the whole place techno plays, blasting away feelings. But as he brushes his teeth, what does it feel like?

It kind of feels like a . . . day. He's alive. What's really changed?

As he walks out of the bathroom, by voice activation or remote he turns up the music even louder. Maybe he nods to the music a little.

---

* In the edit, a moment of Kendall totally alone felt more eloquent.

INT. SHIV'S PLACE – MORNING

Saturday. Dawn in New York.

Shiv is waking. Alone. A changed world.

She lies diagonally.

Her phone vibrates with a call. She is uninterested until she sees who it is. She answers. Speakerphone feels more appropriate somehow. A voice trying to indicate presence.

SHIV

Hello?

If she sits up – maybe cross-legged with her phone in her lap, speaking into it.

DR HASFORD
(on speakerphone)

Good morning, Siobhan, sorry to bother you today.

SHIV

Oh. No worries, hey, Sharon.

DR HASFORD

I'm really sorry to call today. How are you?

There's more to this question than casual inquiry. Shiv sighs – she has to manage everyone else managing her grief now.

SHIV

Hi. I'm . . . I'm fine I mean I'm, it's . . .

DOCTOR HASFORD

Of course. I wanted to discuss your results and I didn't know but— I thought you would want the chance to be aware if you're up to it?

SHIV

Yes sure.

DOCTOR HASFORD

I won't draw it out. It's a good, result. The journey we went on with the amniocentesis after what the blood tests showed us, everything looks healthy.

SHIV

Okay. Good.

Shiv takes it in.

Was Sharon expecting more? Beat.

DOCTOR HASFORD

Great. And you're still well? No spotting, no bleeding?

SHIV

Um, nope.

DOCTOR HASFORD

Okay, well we tested the cells from the sample and we have no reason to suspect any chromosomal abnormality. Obviously, we can't predict with one-hundred-percent certainty that there will be no further issues—

SHIV

No of course.

DR HASFORD

But in terms of all the results I have for you, there is nothing I think we should be concerned about.

SHIV

Great.

Shiv thinks. Nothing to be concerned about. That's . . . good? A flood of feeling, like relief? Or is it fear?

DOCTOR HASFORD

So Davina will reach out to make an appointment for your twenty-week scan. But I'm thinking of you at this time and if there's anything I can do.

SHIV

Thank you, Sharon, thank you.

Shiv takes charge and ends the call, doesn't want to get into it. Okay. Wow. This is really happening. She feels strangely alone.

She dials another contact.

Intercut with:

INT. CAROLINE'S MANOR – DAY*

Eventually, Caroline answers.

CAROLINE
(this is unusual)

Hello. Siobhan?

SHIV

Hi Mom.

CAROLINE

Hello. Is everything alright?

SHIV

Um? I mean – no further deaths. So.

CAROLINE

Are you okay, darling?

SHIV

Yeah. Yeah it was— Wow.

CAROLINE

It is so awful isn't it? You know Anita, my dear Anita is on her way out?

SHIV

Yeah. Yeah. I'm sorry.

Will she tell her?

Um – so. Yeah.

A silence.

CAROLINE

Are you still there?

SHIV

Yeah.

(then)

Yeah. I don't know why I called.

---

* As with Kendall, it felt more appropriate for Shiv to be alone in this moment.

> CAROLINE

It's nice. It's nice to hear you. Are you okay?

> SHIV

I'm okay, I think. Yeah. There's nothing I can do about it. Listen. Just – hello. And I'll see you at the . . . If you're – coming?

> CAROLINE

Of course I'll see you at the funeral.

Shiv ends the call. Slightly less alone.

INT. ATN – DAY

Tom is in at ATN. Out behind the control room, or leaving an edit with a bunch of screens. Talking to a senior producer, Lauren Pawson.

> TOM

I like it all, Lauren. Let's just keep running the obit package and then panel and just – Logan Logan Logan.

> LAUREN

I mean the only thing is, we are hurting our numbers, a little bit. You know, there is an election on?!

> TOM

Uh-huh. I think honestly, Lauren, fuck the numbers, this is – this is for an audience of three, okay? Between us, that's who this coverage is for.

> LAUREN

And can we just spice it up a bit now. There's a lot of disgusting stuff out there? Gil Eavis liked the – the TikTok of the Congresswoman dancing to 'Celebrate Good Times'? The death parties?

> TOM

Nah, sorry. First forty-eight is strictly Full Stalin. Martial music, artillery volleys fired into housing projects. Honest Abe Elvis Kennedy King Junior has passed. Then we can get into the delicious righteous indignation, okay?

> LAUREN

Mencken, we heard, did you hear, he said off the record, 'I thought he was dead already.'

Tom's phone goes.

> TOM
>
> I can't get into that. I have to get the tone just right okay? Lot of
> risk. Lot of opportunity here. I mean where even is Cyd?

Intercut with:

EXT. STREET – DAY

Greg is on the street.

> GREG
>
> Hey, man. Just checking do you wanna go together, to the
> gathering.

> TOM
>
> Hello. I'm sorry, 'the gathering', what 'gathering'?

> GREG
>
> The gathering? The family are gathering with close friends and
> and – to – you know, to just to be together, a little Scots wake
> to—

> TOM
>
> To plot and connive and anoint? Why didn't you tell me?!

> GREG
>
> I – I thought you knew. Weren't you with Shiv?

> TOM
>
> I hoteled, Greg. I thought today was a down day!

> GREG
>
> A 'down day'?

> TOM
>
> Yeah, set aside for wailing and – firing machine guns in the air.
> Is it invites? Oh, man. Greg. I need to get the fuck over there.
> This wake is going to kill me. Wait for me. Okay. Wait for me.
> (*then*)
> Sara!

INT./EXT. KENDALL'S CAR — DAY

Kendall is driven over, gets out near Logan's apartment.

Past a gaggle of press photographers gathered some way from the entrance.

INT. LOGAN'S BUILDING — LOBBY — DAY

Kendall heads in from his car.

He passes Hugo on the phone. His back angled away from Kendall.

> HUGO
> You know you fucked me. You fucked me in the ass here. What you've done, Juliette, is you've taken a strap-on and fucked me right in my ass? Yeah? Call me. Please.

INT. LOGAN'S APARTMENT — ELEVATOR — DAY

Kendall in the elevator . . . The doors open.

INT. LOGAN'S APARTMENT — FOYER — DAY

And there is . . . Marcia. In black, looking rather radiant.

> KENDALL
> Oh, hello, hi Marcia?

She gives him a little light hug. Not what Kendall was expecting.

> MARCIA
> Condolences. Sorry for your loss.

> KENDALL
> Um. Thank you.
> (*then, is this appropriate?*)
> Likewise.

> MARCIA
> Yes. It was a terrible shock.

> KENDALL
> Uh-huh. Right. And where have you— [come from?] When did you get in?

> MARCIA

We spoke every morning and afternoon, so I came as soon as I heard.

> KENDALL

Okay?

> MARCIA

I rushed. I couldn't sleep another night.

> KENDALL

Okay? I mean.
> *(tries to summon an honest response)*
I honestly, I didn't think you guys were – you know—?

> MARCIA

We were very close. It was complicated but we spoke intimately every evening.

> KENDALL

Right. Okay? Well . . .

Behind him already the elevator bell dings.

> MARCIA

My love, strong Kendall. After everything for you.

Hint of a reference in Marcia's eye as she effortlessly moves on to the next arrivals.

Ah Graham! Janet! Thank you so much!

Old family/business faces—

> GRAHAM

Ken.

> KENDALL

Hey.

Kendall doesn't linger – walks on in as behind him Marcia greets Graham and Janet—

> MARCIA

Thank you. Thank you. If you are sending flowers, to Campbell's. Cards and so on, to Richard. I am so pleased to see you, dear ones.

Maybe Mark Ravenhead, Ray and Cyd and ATN folk are there.

Kendall walks in. Eight or nine people in the middle lounge. They nod respectfully.

MARK

Sorry for your loss.

PENELOPE

So sorry, Kendall.

KENDALL

Thank you, Penny. Thanks.

He sees some of the Old Guard in the dining room. And in the study, Shiv and Roman. He goes on through.

INT. LOGAN'S APARTMENT – STUDY – DAY

KENDALL

Hey.

ROMAN

Hey, man.

They do a hug, Shiv too.

KENDALL

What's up with—?

ROMAN

Marcia? The belle of the ball.

SHIV

Death becomes her.

KENDALL

And, like, where's, you know, Kerry?

ROMAN

In Marcia's trunk. Inside an anaconda. Inside a sarcophagus.

SHIV

I don't think Marcia's seen him for seven weeks, his calendar says.

KENDALL

'Intimate calls' every night, did you get that?

> SHIV

Uh-huh. I might sue her for making me think of Dad doing phone sex.

They kind of expect Roman to say something, instinctively look. But nothing.

Nothing?

> ROMAN

I can do a phone-sex bit if you want. I thought you might not be in the mood?
> (*then, to Ken*)
Yeah, I'm actually fine.

Kendall looks at him: Yeah?

I mean I'm sure it'll crush me eventually. Freight train coming – but today – I'm okay.

> KENDALL

Yeah? I feel knocked out. I don't think I slept.

Shiv assents. Same.

> ROMAN

I wonder if I thought about it so much, one way and another, maybe I've, I don't know – pre-grieved?

> SHIV

Got your homework in early?

> ROMAN

I know he's – gone, I do know that. But I've maybe sad-hacked it, thought it out?

> KENDALL

Okay, dude. Well, congrats.

> ROMAN

I guess I've been paying into a grief bank for years, so, I'm sad – but I'm fine.

> KENDALL

Well good for you.
> (*then*)
I mean, I don't believe you.

SHIV

But listen, Ken, we need to huddle. For some of us it's a sad day, for others – it's coronation demolition derby.

She nods to the Old Guard – what has he missed?

KENDALL

What's the schedule?

SHIV

The board call I think, is – eleven. But you saw, you saw from Hugo the thing about – the by-law, the crisis plan or whatever?
(trying to remain neutral)
They have COO step up?

KENDALL

Right. Or COOs, I guess?

ROMAN

Right.

They look at one another. How does that feel?

SHIV

But that's just draft. So I think their thing will be—

They look through to the other end, the Old Guard.

Well I don't know what their thing will be? But it's just a draft so.

Into her field of vision, Tom and Greg arrive in the wood-paneled middle living room.

Tom looks both ways – the kids one way.

Does Shiv (almost like in Italy) avert her gaze to not meet his eye? Tom looks at the three of them – then through to the Old Guard.

That looks more welcoming . . . He heads through past Cyd and Ray.

RAY

Hey, Tom. How are you doing? Must have been awful.

CYD

Yeah. We heard when *he* died *your* life flashed before your eyes?

Greg looks towards the kids.

INT. LOGAN'S APARTMENT – DINING ROOM – DAY

In the dining room, the Old Guard are gathered. Karl, Gerri, Frank, Karolina joined by Tom—

> TOM
> Hey. How we doing?

Somber.

> FRANK
> Oh, you know?

> GERRI
> So strange to be here. Without him.

> TOM
> Indeed.
> (*then*)
> And. Um, what have I missed?

> GERRI
> Lot of incoming. Lot of incoming. Presidents, prime ministers.

> KARL
> Lot of our business partners are calling to start with 'so sorry' and end with 'is this difficult time a good moment to fuck you on carriage fees or ad spends?'

> FRANK
> Just trying to keep everything stable. Board on the line in – what – an hour to pick a new top dog.

> TOM
> Uh-huh. And, what's your sense, Frank. What are the CEO vibes?

Frank looks around.

> FRANK
> Would anyone care for a – a – a – a, look at the china?

INT. LOGAN'S APARTMENT – STUDY – DAY

The kids peer through and can glimpse the Old Guard slightly surreptitiously heading out of the dining room into the china store.

ROMAN

He was gonna fire half that room. Do people know that? Should we get that out?

Kendall looks not uninterested.

SHIV

We don't want this to look like a shit show. Chaos narratives, fratricide narratives, bad narratives.

Greg comes through to join the kids.

GREG

Hey, guys. Sorry for your loss.

KENDALL

Thank you.

GREG

It's a sad day. It feels like a light has gone out. Just great the family can stay strong and support each other through this?

SHIV

Great.

GREG

I hear some studio talent and creative folks, and such were being in touch and just to say any – like – low-priority shit. I've learned how to handle the ATN talent, so you want me to lighten the load. Saddle me up, guys. Yeah?

Maybe he tries to put his arms around Roman and Kendall if they are close enough together.

GREG

My guys. My lovely guys.

But it doesn't take.

ROMAN

We're not playing Chutes and Ladders, Greg. Our dad just died.

GREG

Dude. No. I'm sad. And just thinking about how things shake down. There's the board meeting and I've spoken to Ewan and I know he'll have a say so—

Roman looks at him.

> ROMAN

You need to find a new mommy, we're not your mommy.

Roman's phone goes.

Um. Matsson. Do I?

They look at one another.

> KENDALL

Let's just— Let's do five and get our ducks in a row. We fucking blurt and he puts it on his socials and suddenly we sold Manhattan for glass beads, okay?

It rings out.

INT. LOGAN'S APARTMENT – CHINA STORE/KITCHEN OFF DINING ROOM – DAY

Frank, Karl, Gerri, Tom and Karolina. A bit crushed in there.

> FRANK

So the aim is – we'd like to make an announcement today stating who will be taking over in the interim, ready for Monday.

> KARL

Right. And here's my position. I wonder if we don't want to take control of the plane here?

> FRANK

Uh-huh. I guess the first thing is the GoJo deal. The board, the shareholders. Everyone is very keen.

> KARL

Exactly. I worry about the kids' commitment to the deal?

> GERRI

If we called around the board, Frank? You'd hold a lot of sway on the interim appointment.

Everyone nods—

> FRANK

They'd like senior management input.

KARL

And if the message we gave was, to be – but that the kids are – are—

TOM

Screw-ups and dipshits.

KARL

Maybe not constitutionally well-equipped at this point to take on the role. I guess the question then would just be who we might favor?

Karolina and Gerri have spoken before—

KAROLINA

Gerri obviously is a safe pair of hands, she's done it recently.

Gerri looks modest.

FRANK

Right. Yes. Although obviously generally speaking, the CFO might be considered the natural interim?

Frank and Karl have spoken too.

KARL

I guess you've already had your tilt at the windmill, Ger?

GERRI

Exactly. I've already done it. Quite successfully—

Does Karl make a 'not that successfully' noise or face?

and this is an interim role. To do the deal. I'd get it done. Buckle you up into your golden parachute, Karl.

KARL

Well don't push me out the plane so fast, Ger! With the old man gone, I wonder I don't have a little left to give?

GERRI

You're halfway out the door.

KARL

My only thought, Gerri, and I don't engage with gossip and innuendo. But it could be hurtful to the company if there were – tittle-tattle?

> KAROLINA

Well if we're speaking frankly, Karl, there's a lot of tattle on your tits.

Karl stares Gerri down.

> GERRI

Look, I think you're a corporate legend. What you did in the nineties, with cable. Huge.

He sees there will be a sting in the tail.

> KARL

Uh-huh. Thank you so much.

> GERRI

But as CFO I don't know if people will think you're broad enough?

> KARL

Logan was souring on you.

> GERRI

Logan's not around anymore.

> KARL

He didn't respect you.

> GERRI

He didn't respect anyone. Except maybe Pinochet, Johnny Weissmuller or Hayek?

Have they fought themselves to a draw? Karolina gets a message, edges out. Acting nonchalant, Tom picks up some food.

> TOM

Ahem. I just wanted to say to this senior group of very respected gray beards, that all I have ever personally asked is the chance to serve?

They look at him.

I mean I'm sick with grief. But . . .

> GERRI

Oh you're sick with grief? You might wanna put that fish taco down. You're getting your melancholy everywhere.

KARL

Breaking news: Head of ATN so bereft, can barely stomach second mimosa.

TOM

Well, very funny but, if that opportunity was to arise, all I'll say is – if there's a ring. My hat's in. Respectfully.

KARL

I suppose I'd just say if we were going to recommend you to the board the question they might ask— Can I frame the question for you, as a friend, so you'd know how to respond?

TOM

Sure.

KARL

I guess the negative case would go: 'You're a clumsy interloper and no one trusts you. The only guy pulling for you is dead and now you're just married to the ex-boss's daughter, and she doesn't even like you and you're fair and squarely fucked.'

TOM

Jesus, Karl.

KARL

That's how the naysayers might frame it.

GERRI

Those darn naysayers.

Silence. Karolina comes in and whispers to Frank.

KAROLINA

Um? Frank? Frank. I think there's something?

INT. LOGAN'S APARTMENT – STUDY – DAY

The kids around the phone.

SHIV

So. We're doing the call together because we're all allied. Floppy floppy, pally pally. We want the deal, we love the deal, new CEO, whoever that might be.
(*coughs, points to herself*)
Joke!

(*then*)
Will be in touch post-board to talk more?

They nod. Roman dials.

> OSKAR
> (*on speakerphone*)
> Hey, Oskar on Lukas's phone?

> ROMAN
> Hey? Oskar? Um. Roman Roy, Lukas called but I was just rounding up my chimpanzee friends because they wanted to say hi too. Is he there?

> OSKAR
> Oh no, he went now he says.

> ROMAN
> Oh right? Can you get him?

Roman does a jerk-off signal.

> OSKAR
> Yeah he was calling last chance unfortunately. Because you know we have this— We're having a company strategy sesh this week.

> KENDALL
> Hey this is Ken, come on, man, we dropped a call because we wanted to all be on, out of respect, can you grab him? It wasn't a power play.

> OSKAR
> Oh sure, man, no, that's cool. No we know, and this isn't from him, he's just on a super-tight schedule now.

> SHIV
> He doesn't want to say hi? Is he still buying the company?

> OSKAR
> Hahaha. Sure, man. Maybe, if you don't squeeze too tight. No. He's excited to speak to you guys. Who'll be leading?

They look at one another.

> SHIV
> We're just huddling on that. We're a pretty fluid group.

Looks from the other two?

KENDALL

But listen, seems like maybe this retreat has come at a good time. You guys get your ducks in a row we do our board – pick our captain, and we can reconfigure in a week or—

Does Matsson – or somebody – say something in the background to Oskar? He sounds like he's relaying a message—

OSKAR

Well we don't want to lose momentum.

KENDALL

Oh. Okay. No. Nor us.

SHIV

You obviously know what happened over here, yesterday.

OSKAR

Oh sure. Yeah. We really feel for you guys. Bad one.

ROMAN

Thank you. Yes. Yes.

OSKAR

But could you guys or whoever, one of the old guys you have be here in like twenty-four to do this?

SHIV

Our father just died, and the election is coming, and— You know how would you feel about a meet in the US or—?

OSKAR

This is the annual retreat. We can't just drop it.

Motherfucker.

SHIV

Fine well, no we see that.

OSKAR

Great. Well, we look forward to talking, to whoever, like tomorrow tomorrow? Yeah.

They look at each other. No way out. After a beat—

> ROMAN

Okay. Okay, man. Great.

End of call.

Okay, well. Jesus fucking Christ.

> SHIV

Cold motherfuckers.

> KENDALL

Go sell the company in Europe. Good way to stop thinking about – pulmonary embolisms?

> SHIV

I feel sick. Do we have to do this?

> KENDALL

Maybe it's not a big deal? Maybe we flip a fucking coin and – boom: me or you or you or Frank, Karl, Gerri leads but we all huddle, grit our teeth, do the deal?

INT. LOGAN'S APARTMENT – FOYER – DAY

Greg has come to talk to Marcia.

> GREG

Sorry for your loss.

Karl and Frank hurry upstairs together.

Marcia watches—

> MARCIA

See how they run!

> GREG

So self-important! All puffed up like, puffins. So humorous.

As Cyd makes her way out, back to vacant ATN.

> CYD
> *(to Greg)*

I'm heading back to ATN. Would you tell Tom I say goodbye in case I never see him again?

Connor and Willa arrive.

> WILLA

Marcia. Sorry for your loss.

> MARCIA

Thank you. And to you, Connor.

> CONNOR

Thank you.

> MARCIA

And congratulations—
> > (*looks at her, with a little edge?*)
Look how far you have come.

> WILLA

Yup. Well, look at us both!

> MARCIA

So sorry about everything. After your wedding – to have to do this?

> CONNOR

Oh we're gonna head off next week. You know we have a little trip planned out. Wisconsin, Minnesota, Michigan, Pennsylvania.

> WILLA

'The Honeymoon States'.

He looks at her. She smiles, it's okay. Willa goes to say hello to someone she knows. Connor wants to mention—

> CONNOR

I'm going to go through but I wanted to say because – these things can happen in a flash, but if and when the time comes for you to consider selling this place, I would be— I am wary of even saying the words, but—

> MARCIA

No need to be ashamed, we are family. I will be looking for between sixty and seventy million dollars.

> CONNOR

Oh right. Okay. Wow.
> > (*then*)
So. Like, sixty-three or—?

                              MARCIA
Done.

                              CONNOR
Done?

                              MARCIA
Done.

She spits on her hand or pretends to and offers it. He does the same.

                              CONNOR
Okay? Yeah? Done. Wow.

Connor and Marcia shake. Him a little freaked.

INT. LOGAN'S APARTMENT – LIBRARY – DAY

Karl arrives upstairs with Frank.

                              FRANK
Karl. Hey. So, listen. In my role as executor I've had passed to
me a rather worrying piece of paper?

He hands it to Karl. Who reads.

                              KARL
Uh-huh.
                         (*takes it in quite fast*)
Okay and . . . who else knows?

                              FRANK
As of now, so far as I know, just you and me.

                              KARL
So, what are you thinking?

                              FRANK
I honestly didn't even want to start thinking till you were here.

                              KARL
You're pre-thinking?

                              FRANK
Correct.

> KARL
> (*then*)
> I mean, could it, might it – go away?

Frank doesn't say anything. Maybe a mere flicker of interest.

> I mean, it might get lost? I hope it doesn't. But what if your
> hand went a little wobbly and the draft took it away and it got
> flushed down a toilet by mistake?

Frank looks like: Could we? It's tough.

> I mean I'm kidding of course.

They look at each other totally straight-faced.

> FRANK
> Oh sure. You're speculating in a comic mode.

> KARL
> In a humorous vein.
> (*then*)
> We're not gonna let the little princes screw things up, right,
> Frank? I want out. I want my fucking package. I'm halfway in
> on a Greek island with my brother-in-law?

Gerri comes in.

> GERRI
> Say, what's up, boys?

*They look at one another. Should they tell her? No way out really.
Karl shrugs: Go ahead.*

> FRANK
> Well, I've actually been handed a piece of paper, Gerri. And it
> has a number of wishes in the event of Logan's death – funeral
> arrangements and so on. Little stuff. Hymns and heirlooms. But
> it also suggests that Kendall is or was his preferred candidate for
> CEO?

A lot to download. But she gets it right away.

> GERRI
> May I?

She takes the paper.

And where was this found?

> FRANK

In his private safe.

And examines—

> GERRI

And this penciled addendum—? Is, what?

> FRANK

We haven't touched it. The underlining, the pencil is his –
undated apparently. Not even shared with his lawyer or myself,
so?

> GERRI

So what are you thinking?

> FRANK

Well, legally, since the family doesn't have full control. Legally, it
doesn't—

> GERRI

Legally, it's up to the board to decide who's next. So this is not
germane—

> FRANK

We were joking about how it could fall in the toilet?

> GERRI

Yes well that's a very funny joke. And all I would add is that,
legally speaking it doesn't have much, if any, value.

> KARL

In that sense, it could be argued, legally speaking, that it is
perhaps already in the lavatory?

Gerri makes a face. Karl tests something out—

It's just because I'm worried about the provenance? In some
ways it raises more questions than it answers.

Frank and Gerri look at one another: No.

> FRANK

Unless of course. Someone else is aware or there's another copy?
> (*then*)
> I think, I think we have to accept it exists.

INT. LOGAN'S APARTMENT – LIVING ROOM – DAY

Connor joins Willa in the living room.

> CONNOR
> Um, so, listen. I think I just bought the apartment?

> WILLA
> Like – while I— What – this apartment? Just then?

> CONNOR
> Yeah. I couldn't see it go to a stranger. Is that okay?

> WILLA
> Um? I don't— Could we have discussed? I mean, Con. It's kind
> of – quite emotionally loaded?

> CONNOR
> Hm, I was hardly ever here. Plus. The location?

> WILLA
> And you don't think. Weird energy? A weird kind of feng shui.
> Like feng shouty?

He considers.

They do say it's not smart to make big decisions right after—

> CONNOR
> Sure but – they also say, it's pretty smart not to pay realtor fees?
> And it's such a bitch to get into these Good Buildings—

He winks.

He sees the siblings and heads through to them in the study.

INT. LOGAN'S APARTMENT – STUDY – DAY

> CONNOR
> Hey, guys. How we faring? Seen the obits?

*Maybe Willa starts going around the room knocking on walls,
considering the space from a new perspective – a potential
resident . . .*

> SHIV
> Oh sure. You like the *Globe* photo?

KENDALL

Where's that from? How many times did Dad laugh?

ROMAN

Only really if he saw a hobo on fire.

Shiv reads.

SHIV

I have to say, Dad sounds amazing. I'd like to have met Dad.

KENDALL

I know. He was a great businessman and a great father to boot.

CONNOR

But you guys doing okay, really?

Shiv has defense shields up.

SHIV

Roman's pre-grieved. He already gave at the office.

ROMAN

To be honest, from where I'm sitting, it's you guys who look
naive. I've been worrying this was going to happen for ages.
(*to Connor*)
How are you?

CONNOR

I have no clue. I'm okay. Ken?

KENDALL

Me?
(*tries to be honest*)
Er, acute grief. Crying. Keening. Couldn't sleep.
(*then*)
I actually managed to, in the middle of the night I tried, I did
one, talk. My therapist recommended someone and I got to him
and he's kind of good. I have his number if you want? It's dumb,
but there are actually things you can do. One important thing
is – is – is, not for now, but is to progress, eventually, to the
integrated grief stage.

They look at him.

And not get stuck in a spiral.

A beat, then – not unkind, but they know each other well—

> SHIV

Sounds like you have the best grief guy?

> KENDALL

I have a great grief guy, fuck you.

> SHIV
> *(ashamed of her curiosity)*

What did he say actually?

> KENDALL

Um, bullet points: helps to talk; get a dog; say their name; you can't get over it, you have to get into it.

> ROMAN

You're going to destroy this.

Smiles. Hugo comes in.

> HUGO

Um, some more hard copies. Obituaries.

He has many papers, national and international.

> ROMAN

The reviews are in.

> SHIV

And they're mostly five stars.

> HUGO

And I think the board will assemble now at one?
> *(looks around the room)*

So, do you want me seeding anything ahead of that? Little chats to the board, little media round? Because I think your friends will be hitting the phones and Karolina can rather hog the old corporate megaphone?

The kids look at one another. Do they have the stomach for it?

> KENDALL

Thanks, Hugo.

> HUGO

And um, Ken. Just to say—

Hugo nods and gets Kendall to walk him to the door.

I, I er, I could have caught myself up in a little bit of something. Nothing. So sorry to trouble.

> KENDALL
>
> What?

> HUGO
>
> I just found out my daughter, she happened to sell a bunch of Waystar stock just before the news about your dad, went – went public.

> KENDALL
>
> Uh-huh?

> HUGO
>
> Total coincidence. But I hope it doesn't come up as an issue?

> KENDALL
>
> Did you speak to her, on the day? What will the phone records say?

> HUGO
>
> I can't recollect.

Kendall looks at him.

> KENDALL
>
> Oh Hugo.

> HUGO
>
> I don't even have a relationship with Juliette is the sad fact. That's the irony, we hardly talk.

Hugo heads out as Kendall edges back. Shiv has been reading and considering.

> SHIV
>
> Oooh, man, the *Courier*? You need a codebook for this one. Ready?
>
> (*reads*)
>
> 'A complicated man'.

> KENDALL
>
> Uh-huh. Threw phones at underlings.

SHIV

Right, 'a sharp reader of the national mood'.

ROMAN

Bit racist.

SHIV
(*then, reads*)
Um, 'very much a man of his era'.

KENDALL

Again racist. Also relaxed about sexual assault.

SHIV

'Business genius'.

They chuckle. At the codewords and their naughty decoding.

ROMAN

Never paid a penny in US tax.

SHIV

'Didn't suffer fools gladly'.

KENDALL

Made underlings honk like pigs for sport.

SHIV

'Widely respected'.

Brothers look blank.

Um, is that – is it – rumored to have a picture of the director of the CIA using a novelty butt plug?

There once was a similar rumor and they are bonded by the memory, they chuckle because Logan would be chuckling.

'Well connected'.

ROMAN

Now that's unfair. I think 'well connected' is generally accepted to be a euphemism for pedophile? And no one ever suggested—?

KENDALL

Fuck a child? He wouldn't even hug, his grandkids.

They are all laughing – not at Logan, with his memory, or that is how it feels.

But then Tom comes in, opens the door.

> TOM
> Um, guys, I think they want to see you in the library?

Shiv and Roman head out. Tom makes eye contact to seek to detain Kendall and grab a word.

> And um. Ken, just to say—
> *(checks he's out of earshot)*
> Lot of water under the bridge. Lot of history but as far as I am concerned. The big man, passing cleaned the slate. And – yeah. I'm sorry for your loss and there's maybe some words I wish I could take back – but I just want you to know I'm here to serve.

> KENDALL
> *(no chance)*
> I like you, Tom. Good luck.

Kendall heads on up. Leaving Tom most un-reassured.

INT. LOGAN'S APARTMENT – LIBRARY – DAY

Roman, Kendall and Shiv enter.

To join Karl and Gerri and Frank.

> FRANK
> Um. Hi. Hello, yeah come in. How you doing?

> KENDALL
> Yeah, hanging in. You guys?

> KARL
> Tough day, tough days, my friends.

> FRANK
> So, listen, I'm one of the executors of your dad's affairs.

Bit of a beat. The arrangement of bodies, the atmosphere prompts Roman to look around and say—

> ROMAN
> Oh shit! It's *Brewster's Millions*! Who's got to marry who? Is Connor the child of an oak tree?

> FRANK

Ha. Well, look. This is not a legal matter, but certain wishes have been discovered and it appears – at a certain point, undated, it was suggested that it was your dad's wish that Kendall take over as CEO.

Everyone looks at each other.

A bolt through Kendall of an old and dangerous drug.

> ROMAN

Uh-huh. From when?

> KARL

It was in the safe between pieces on the Raymada acquisition and the first US Virgin Isles reorganization. So?

> FRANK

It's old. From, as far as we know from four years ago or so.

Roman looks at Shiv.

> KARL

Then there— It looks like there are pencil addendums, from another time?

> GERRI

We don't know its status and we— I mean it holds little legal value, so we wanted to let you know but we wouldn't want it to feel more significant than it should?

> FRANK

Because the family no longer has majority control of Waystar. Any such suggestions are non-binding.

> KENDALL

Sure . . . but effectively—

> FRANK

So while they will of course be taken into account by the board when selecting a new CEO we wouldn't see them as—

> KENDALL

Dad was the founder – and—

>   FRANK
> Of course it is from some time ago and things changed and
> Logan was a man of – different moods. So—

>   ROMAN
> Yeah. Yeah.

>   FRANK
> There's some later additions he made in pencil about artifacts
> that I think, we think from context were maybe added in the last
> eighteen months?

Kendall peers at the paper.

>   KENDALL
> Oh so, he underlined, recently?

Shiv looks.

>   SHIV
> Is it underlined? Or is that crossed out?

>   KENDALL
> Shiv?

>   SHIV
> I'm not saying anything for or against. But as a matter of fact?

>   KENDALL
> Are you serious?

*Kendall's name is typed. But then a pencil line is drawn in such a way
that it goes under a few letters but wavers up to cross through some
others.*

>   ROMAN
> He's torn it to tiny shreds but if you put it together again it
> reads 'Kendall'?

Kendall looks at him.

> Kidding. I'm kidding. Let me see?

Gerri looks.

>   SHIV
> Look, underlined, crossed out. Whatever, it's still the board,
> legally, who are going to choose, right?

> GERRI

Exactly. The market, the shareholders, the board, we all want
the sale to go through. So it's an interim role, to shepherd the
sale through.

> KENDALL

Sure. I mean, anyone could do that? And since he said, I mean
he has said—

> ROMAN

Ken, sure, man, I get it, but, it's old. You tried to send him to jail
like twelve times since then?

> SHIV
> (*apparently somewhat kindly*)

Look, I wonder if what with the, the underlining or crossing
out, the unknown age, right, if the document, isn't essentially, it's
moot. It's impossible to decipher.

Kendall is trying to be cool and not heat things up.

> KENDALL

Well it sure as fucking shit doesn't say Shiv.

They look at one another.

> ROMAN

So, what else does it say?

> FRANK

Music, burial in the city. Catholic. The hymns. You can see.

Roman takes a look.

> KARL

Should we get Greg now? Clear that up?

Karl goes out to get him.

> FRANK

There's a mix of business and personal. A watch for Colin.

> GERRI

It feels quite – a late-night sort of document. It looks honestly
like he drafted it himself and never sent it to his lawyer and just
put it in the safe. More of, in some ways, a selection of musings?

Kendall is stewing.

                              SHIV
Right.

                              GERRI
Some thoughts on the tax position of the artwork in storage.

                              SHIV
He had— What does he have?

                             ROMAN
He has a shit-ton of investment impressionism. He's got three
Gauguin's no one's ever seen for tax reasons.

                              FRANK
I think his suggestion is it might be smart tax-wise to leave them
in the Geneva vault?

*Greg is brought in. Maybe at a certain point Kendall gets up and
takes the paper to look at. People are aware of its location in the
room. It has weight.*

                              SHIV
Fuck it, why not burn them for the insurance?

                              KARL
That would be the dream, financially speaking.

Is he kidding?

                              GREG
Hey. Hey, everyone.

                              FRANK
Yes, um, Greg, in case it comes out, we thought you should be
aware you're on a piece of paper. A side letter. Left by Logan
with some wishes and disbursements.

                              GREG
Oh, okay, in what capacity? In what fashion.

                              FRANK
You're an addendum. It's just. 'Greg – question mark'.

                              GREG
'Greg'. On I'm – on – with all his important wishes?

FRANK

On a note of miscellaneous matters, in pencil, with a question mark.

GREG

Nevertheless?

KENDALL

It was in the personal safe. So.
(*aside to Greg*)
Dad said he wanted me to take over.

GREG

Okay, well, quite telling? So like, with Kendall it's me and – so then maybe the natural conclusion might perhaps be I'd be his number two?

Chuckles all round.

FRANK

Nice try, kid.

ROMAN

He probably wrote it to remember your name.

GREG

He knew my name alright.

ROMAN

He wanted to see less of you. That's probably, like fifty-fifty, '*fire* Greg or kill Greg'?

GREG

I don't see that at all. I don't think so. No. It's significant.

GERRI

It's marginalia. It's a doodle, but we thought we should make you aware.

GREG

Pretty interesting. Rather fascinating.

Tom knocks and enters.

TOM

Hey? Um, Marcia asked me to let you all know, there are some informal— Some words to be—

> FRANK

Okay, well, we have a lot to consider. Shall we reconvene before the board meeting to pool thoughts?

Kendall looks at his siblings – an offer, a request: Can we talk? Maybe he even verbalizes a word?

But Roman and Shiv need time to consider their reactions – they avoid his gaze and head out, maybe together.

Frank is last to go. Kendall looks at him.

> KENDALL

What a fucking waste. It was so stupid. He was old. I should have gone to him.

> FRANK

It's alright, kid. It's okay.

> KENDALL

He made me hate him, and he died. I disappointed him.

> FRANK

No. No, come on. We think these grand – horrors when these things happen. These ice shelves will come at you in the night and they'll take your head off, but that's not true. He was an old bastard and he loved you. He loved you.

> KENDALL

You think?

> FRANK

I think so.

> KENDALL

Is it real, Frank? This?

> FRANK

I dunno.

> KENDALL

My dad wanted me to take over?

> FRANK

Well – sometimes. You know that. He did, sometimes.

Frank gives him a pat on the back.

KENDALL

If I get them in behind me, will you follow?

Frank looks at him.

FRANK

Ken. You've got stuff cooking, you seem so well. Do you really want back in?

INT. LOGAN'S APARTMENT – STAIRS – DAY

Shiv is in thought at the bottom (or maybe top?) of the stairs, talking with Roman.

SHIV

I dunno. It's what he's wanted his whole fucking . . . Part of me is like give the poor orphan the thing he wants. I don't know what's wrong with me.

ROMAN

Hm. Hm. Yeah. And it is interim.

SHIV

Well, so long as it is?

He looks at her. Roman had woken up feeling blank about business stuff – Waystar. But the vibrations Kendall gave off were powerful.

ROMAN

What you thinking? Regulatory issues? If the deal wobbled or—? What?

SHIV

Yeah. Just. No, I mean, it's felt good. Us? Right? And does this feel good? Would that—
                    (*i.e. him*)
feel good?

They look at one another. Tom comes down.

TOM

Hey. How are you doing?

Roman heads to the lounge and dining room (or downstairs) where people are gathering.

                                SHIV
Yeah, you know.
                        (*looks at him*)
You?

                                TOM
Yeah. He wasn't my dad, but, he – he— It's sad.

                                SHIV
Worried you picked the wrong horse? Picked the dead horse?

                                TOM
Don't.

Shiv remains hard.

You'll regret it. Let me show you some kindness?

                                SHIV
My main thing, honestly, I guess has been just slowly coming to
accept that we killed him.

                                TOM
Shiv?

                                SHIV
He died on the plane and he wouldn't have been on the plane
except we made him get on there. So that's just very cool.

                                TOM
It could have happened any time. A million things could have
happened.

                                SHIV
I just don't want to fake myself out. If we'd just said 'yes' to
GoJo he might have been around for twenty more years – to
rock his grandkids to sleep?

                                TOM
As he was evidently so keen to do?

A little smile.

                                SHIV
Sure. Well.
                        (*then*)
I dunno. That's fucked now too.

Does she mean having kids? Too flammable. He looks at her.

I'm angry. My dad died. My mom's a fucking— [disaster.] My husband is – is— And Kerry. Marcia.
                (*then*)
It feels like I'm the only one who actually lost something they wanted here. And it's not coming back. So.

He wants to make contact. Might this work?

> TOM
>
> Siobhan. Do you remember, when we first – knew one another? The first time, in France, when I flew to you, it was that difficult time for you, and I'd sent you all those handwritten notes and then, the first time, you were wearing, that – very fine, silk shirt and I put my arm around you and I was so tentative and I said, I kept asking, 'Do you like this? Do you like this?' And you said, eventually, 'I like it all'?

> SHIV
>
> Uh-huh. That was a while ago now.

> TOM
>
> Not that long?

> SHIV
>
> It was a while back.

INT. LOGAN'S APARTMENT – LIVING ROOM – DAY

And she heads towards the living room (or downstairs), to where Roman hovers in the doorway.

He's watching—

Colin there with his wife and his twelve-year-old son, awkward in casual wear. Jeans and a dark jacket. Talking to his number two, Billy.

> ROMAN
>
> Colin does jeans?

> SHIV
>
> He doesn't know what the fuck to do with himself. Look at his arms.

Kendall has come down the stairs and comes over to join.

> ROMAN
> What happens to Colin now? Does he go do security for
> Hooters?

*Kendall is a little stiff. Looks over to Colin talking to Billy on the
steps of the living room. Kendall wants to talk but needs a way in.*

> KENDALL
> Weird. Like a dog without its person.
> (*then*)
> So listen, guys, what do you think?

*But just then three Secret Service agents and a search dog arrive in the
elevator with one staffer, greeted by a staff member.*

> SHIV
> What the fuck now?

Marcia spots or is alerted and comes past the kids.

> ROMAN
> Hey Marcia, who ordered the beefcake?

> MARCIA
> The Secret Service are conducting a sweep. Jeryd Mencken is en
> route.

Shiv and Roman exchange looks.

> I thought you knew?

> SHIV
> Er, well, I'm not sure about that? I'm not sure I want him here
> today.

> MARCIA
> Well he asked. And he was a friend of your father's, no?

> SHIV
> Well, they spoke. But – no – it was transactional.

*Marcia walks off to talk to the staffer with the Secret Service, who
have moved out into the apartment to scope it out.*

> ROMAN
> Right, not like all his *real friends* from – his men's group and
> choir. His pals from the corner bar.

SHIV

He hardly knew him!

ROMAN

Shiv, we've got all sorts of ghouls here. C'mon.

SHIV

I just don't want to see his smirky little autocratic face.

ROMAN

The guy might be president this time next week?

SHIV

I think I have a veto, my dad just died.

ROMAN

Oh I think I have a counter-veto, cos, weirdly, my dad just died too?

Kendall is kind of the casting vote it feels like. They're both aware their brother hasn't weighed in.

KENDALL

I think on a business level alone we need to have a relationship.

SHIV

Oh, you do? Now you do?

KENDALL

Shall we talk about that. Up there. Because I think I'd like to talk about that?

SHIV

Well I would say. I think what has happened is – is, an opportunity to change some things.

A coded presentation of her case?

ROMAN

Oh what Dad's gone, let's get Big Bird on ATN doing round table?

(*then*)

Do we wanna make the one thing we're left with worse?

SHIV

Should we not at least talk about what we're gonna do with the company for two minutes before we let Mencken up here? And whether our ATN is even gonna be in bed with Mencken. And like a hundred things?

KENDALL

But, realistically?

SHIV

Maybe we're gonna change? Dad's just died, maybe we should do real news?

ROMAN

We can't— You can't do the Emancipation Proclamation in a day.

SHIV

Well you can. I think they did.
(*then*)
Do you turn on ATN, Ken? Rome? Do you watch it? They're hot for civil war. They're laying serious track. It's embarrassing.

ROMAN

It's the circus. 'If there is no God, why do walnuts look like tiny brains?' That was a segment.

SHIV

They're one step from showing fucking road maps to National Guard weapons depots?

KENDALL

Shiv, we're not about to pull the guts from ATN days from the election?

SHIV

I thought you had feelings, Ken? Because I think for the sale, for ATN, we maybe need a moral compass?

They hear the tinkling of glass. They move around into the wood-paneled lounge . . .

INT. LOGAN'S APARTMENT – DINING ROOM – DAY

And they can see that, at the other end from the head of the table, Ron Petkus is addressing the thirty or so people in the apartment. Maybe twenty or so in the dining room. More out beyond, listening from the wood-paneled lounge.

> PETKUS

Friends! Good friends all. This isn't a speech or a eulogy—

The kids watch.

> SHIV

Ugh. I didn't know we were having a kids' entertainer.

> PETKUS

I just wanted to maybe try to gather some of the feelings we're all having and express them.

> ROMAN
> (*whispered*)

Who the fuck made him king of the day?

> PETKUS

When a great man passes, the angels of heaven weep. But when a giant of the Conservative movement passes, a shard of freedom falls also from the shield of Achilles, the titan Atlas tires, to carry his load yet further unsupported. Logan Roy was such a giant. A figure of humility, grace and dignity.

Tom and Greg are in one corner.

> TOM
> (*whispered to Greg*)

Who died fishing his iPhone from a clogged toilet.

> GREG

Really? Oh *man.*

> TOM

So they say. Karl blocked it.

Maybe Tom smiles to Karl on the other side of the room, standing with Frank and Gerri.

> (*nodding*)

He lives off Wonder Bread and steak frites. He hasn't shat for twenty years.

Petkus continues—

> PETKUS

He was a man of wisdom. A man of humility, a man without vanity.

> TOM

A man who wasn't wearing his compression stockings to look hot for Kerry.

> PETKUS

He was a Prometheus, who looked to build for us, a slip road off of that accursed Road to Serfdom. He molded the country like clay in his hands.

Greg tries one.

> GREG

Into the shape of a dick.

Tom looks like: C'mon.

> PETKUS

Made it stronger, more coherent.

Shiv with her brothers.

> SHIV

I'm sorry but I am going to puke.
> (*then to Ken*)
Can't we get rid of these old men telling me who my dad was? Jerking off all over his body? Every man with a mustache and a war crime to his name is in here.

Does Kendall want to gain some advantage with Roman?

> KENDALL

What do you want? Get Maya Angelou over to read a poem.

Petkus continues.

> PETKUS

When I think of LR, I think of a great lion of freedom.

Connor shuffles forward to whisper to his siblings.

> CONNOR

Can you believe this shit? He's trying to make Dad into a neoconservative! He wasn't a neocon, he was a paleolibertarian. He was practically an anarcho-capitalist. Right?

> ROMAN

Dad? Um, if you like Benny Hill and Sinatra is that an anarcho-capitalist?

> CONNOR

They're trying to bodysnatch him. We gotta grab the information beachheads, history is being written, the next forty-eight hours are crucial.

> PETKUS

We may not see his kind grace the earth again. Godspeed to thy place at the Lord's side. For surely soon, Logan Roy will be running rolling news in heaven.

> ROMAN

Worst play on Broadway. Two stars. Check your brain at the door.

Perhaps Ravenhead steps forward to say a few things.

The elevator opens and the kids see Stewy, Sandi and Sandy – in a wheelchair with some medical equipment hooked up – arrive with a carer.

> SHIV

Okay. Incoming.

Shiv backs away to say 'hi' as the speeches go on.

> STEWY

Hey. How you going, guys. So sorry.

> SHIV

Thank you, Stew.

> SANDI

Hey. I'm so sorry.

> SHIV

Thank you.

Roman backs away to join.

> SANDI

My dad was very affected.

They look over to Sandy who has a slightly unreadable look on his face. Is it a smile or a smirk, or the look of someone who is back in a familiar space for an unfamiliar reason? His attendant wheels him through into the wood-paneled lounge. Roman watches him pass.

                    ROMAN
And so, why is he doing that with his face can I ask?

                    SANDI
That's just how his face looks these days.

                    ROMAN
Frozen into a – smile?

                    SANDI
Please. He's sad. He knew your dad for a long time.

                    ROMAN
Uh-huh. Sure.
                    (*then*)
I think he just winked at me.

Sandi says 'hello' to someone else.

Can we put a drape over him? He looks like he might start
dancing.

*Sandy is moved through to a spot where he can hear the ongoing
speech from the head of the dining table. Kendall kneels solicitously.
Sandy was an old friend and rival but, of course . . .*

Roman looks at Shiv. What's Kendall doing?

I guess they were close. Dad and him?

                    SHIV
Plus, still has a board vote?

True. Roman motions to the Old Guard.

                    ROMAN
Sure. But I guess, who do we prefer, one of us or one of them?

It is true. Shiv looks.

The elevator opens again and here is – Kerry.

*Marcia is next to Greg in the doorway between the wood-paneled
lounge and the hallway.*

                    MARCIA
Ugh.

Greg is next to her.

> GREG

Oh dear. Yes. Look who's crawled out of the woodwork.

Kerry looks adrift. A little lost. Marcia looks away at the speeches—

> MARCIA
> (*to Greg*)

I asked her not to do this. What's she doing?

> GREG

She's coming over! Oh god. It's so distasteful.

Kerry arrives. Colin and Marcia make eye contact. This eventuality has been discussed.

> KERRY

Hi.

> MARCIA
> (*coolly*)

Oh, yes. Hello?

> KERRY

I got your message but I want to go— I have some things upstairs of mine I need.

> MARCIA

They're in a bag.
> (*calls over*)

Richard? Maria?

> KERRY

I just need to go up thank you.

> MARCIA

Um, no please. Not upstairs, there are private documents and a variety of private items.
> (*to Colin/Billy*)

I don't want her up all amongst our things thank you.

Kerry tries to go up. She makes a move, Colin steps across her.

> COLIN

Come on. Easy. Easy.

He just lightly touches her arm or something.

> GREG
> (*to Marcia*)
> Don't look, Marcia. It's too unpleasant!

A member of staff brings out a hessian tote bag with some possessions.

Shiv, Roman and Kendall have become aware of the commotion.

> ROMAN
> Hey, you okay.

> KERRY
> Yeah. Yeah. I'm good.

> ROMAN
> I'm sorry. Do I have your private number? Will you send it.

> KERRY
> (*quietly to Roman*)
> We were talking about getting married and he was making arrangements about us. Will you check? He was going to make a note or send his lawyer an email?

> ROMAN
> Uh-huh. Sure.

Kerry is looking in the bag. Within are a number of different thin plastic bags. With bedside things, books, stationery and one with make-up and some jewelry. As she looks at the one with make-up and jewelry and, one-handed, manipulates it from the bottom to look if everything's in there, she fumbles and some make-up and jewelry spill from the bag in the hall.

Kerry scrabbles on the marble floor for half-used lipsticks. Small objects that are hard to pick up.

Colin motions for Billy who is on duty to escort her.

Roman picks up a couple of items, lipsticks.

> KERRY
> I'll send my number.

> ROMAN
> (*quietly to her*)
> I can get it, it's okay. It's okay.

COLIN

There's photographers out front. Billy, take her out the back, yeah?

Kerry maybe starts to cry or looks like she might cry a little at the indignity of it all.

GREG
(to Marcia)

Oh god. Here come the waterworks!

Billy heads out with Kerry, under the stairs towards the door at the back.

Roman retreats to Shiv as they watch—

ROMAN

'Take her out the back, Billy.' Always good to hear.

SHIV

'Take her out the back, Billy, and don't make a mess of my trunk'?

Roman turns to Marcia.

ROMAN

Seems a little tough?

MARCIA

We are calling her a taxi to the subway so she can go home to her little apartment.

Marcia edges towards the dining room where the speeches and comments continue.

Kendall comes back from Sandy to Shiv and Roman. Kidding around to make connection.

KENDALL

What you reckon about all the almond butter and maca root? She got one in the chamber?

Shiv smiles – not there for a joke right now.

ROMAN

Is she carrying Dad's luggage? I don't think so. Nah.

SHIV
(*pointed*)
How's your friend Sandy?

KENDALL
Yeah. I dunno. 'Gurgle, gurgle, Red Sox. Viagra.'

SHIV
Uh-huh.

KENDALL
Shiv. Shall we talk? Yeah? Nothing needs to change too much?
Whatever you're thinking you can say? Yeah?

She looks at him.

SHIV
Uh-huh. Okay. Okay. I know. I'm happy to talk.

Kendall heads off to the living room. Shiv heads to check her phone.

Roman adjusts to watch Ravenhead give a little speech.

*A neat guy, Vance, in business casuals near Roman is watching the
speeches, a little excited to be there, but keeping it respectful.*

VANCE
Hey. Vance.

ROMAN
Hey.

VANCE
So how did you know the great man?

ROMAN
I work with his barber. You?

VANCE
Oh I'm a friend of Ray's and we're—

Now that he's established Roman is not close family—

on our way to golf.
(*then*)
I'm a big fan. Studied a couple of his deal structures. So. Yeah.
Glad to be a part of the day.

> ROMAN

Exactly. Grab a corn dog and enjoy the ride!

Tom sidles up to Roman.

> TOM

Hey, man. How you doing?

Roman looks like: Not too bad.

Yeah, so, listen. Tell me to fuck off if you like but . . . this 'piece of paper' situation?

Roman looks at him.

Yeah I heard and yeah I don't want to speak out of turn but we both know Logan – he only wanted one person to take over. He'd just asked you back in?

Roman looks at Tom. Something reinforced, but not about to let that show.

> ROMAN

Oh, Tommy Wamby. Tightrope Tommy. Riding his fucking subtle-cycle across Niagara Falls?

> TOM

Just here to serve, man. Here to serve.

INT. LOGAN'S APARTMENT – LIVING ROOM – DAY

Kendall walks down into the living room.

> STEWY

Hey, man.

> KENDALL

Hey, dude.

They hug. Some old vibes. It goes on a while.

> STEWY

You okay?

> KENDALL

Nope.

> STEWY

Uh-huh. Fuck.

> KENDALL

Yeah.

> STEWY

That – that old – fucking bastard.

Stewy and Kendall have enough history for this to be kind of comforting.

> KENDALL

I know.

> STEWY

I never thought, man. I thought he'd be like my dad. Ninety-five and he's just started suing his neighbor. What was it, dude?

> KENDALL

Embolism. Pulmonary.

> STEWY

Uh-huh. Because I heard he saw your Pierce business plan and choked laughing.

Kendall smiles. Too much?

> KENDALL

You fucking prick.

Maybe Kendall rests a head on his old friend's shoulder. Just one beat and Stewy pats him and then they're back.

So listen. You gonna do the board call from here.

> STEWY

Uh-huh. Here or car.

> KENDALL

Because there's a piece of paper with me on it. That Dad said it should be me?

> STEWY

Oh. Okay. Wow.

KENDALL

Can you swing in for me? You know me. You know my flaws.
It's short-term.

STEWY

Oh you're really selling me.
(*then*)
I guess, I got my pubes a little singed the last time I went in with
you?

KENDALL

Yeah well that was a different time.

STEWY

What was that though, Ken, in England?

KENDALL

My dad – my dad doesn't have many limits. For my family I had
to back down. There was no card he wouldn't play against me.

STEWY

Your dad was a terrible bastard.

KENDALL

Well. Yeah. I dunno. He – he wanted to look after me. So. He
was a lot of things.

STEWY

My dad's a bastard but. Jesus. Remember? Fucking pop quiz,
capital of Uganda. You got it wrong, he threw a fucking shoe at
your head?

KENDALL

Yup. Good technique. Kampala.

STEWY

The Strap, Punch-Chess?

KENDALL

Yup. Yeah.

STEWY

Dinners for Winners?

KENDALL

(*doesn't immediately recall*)
He had a lot of fun games.

> STEWY

I won and I got to have dinner with your dad. You had to serve us?

> KENDALL

Ah, Dinner for Winners. Yeah. Solid game. Fun game.

> STEWY

But look, straight up, we'd be tempted to encourage and support Gerri. She's done it before.

> KENDALL

My dad had soured. Lot of baggage. Seriously. Kinda gross.

> STEWY

Or Karl.

Kendall makes a face.

Do you like the deal?

> KENDALL

Yes. Yes I do.

> STEWY

Because people know you three tried to stop it in Italy?

> KENDALL

Because we were being cut out – behind our backs. We had no plan B. Look. The deal has to happen. We can't live in a haunted house. I have plans, with the sibs, we'll take news and maybe fuse with Pierce. But it will be a feather in my cap to bring in the deal. Sticking close with you. Yeah? You'd be inside it all with me.

> STEWY

Can you bring it home. I mean, is your head on straight?

> KENDALL

I'm twin-track. I'm dead but I'm alive.

> STEWY

Yeah. 'Dive into work'?

> KENDALL

Dude, I have the best grief guy.

(*then*)
What am I gonna do, sit in the dark and drink Laphroaig?
(*then, seeing a bit of hope*)
Matsson will destroy Karl. He'll probably mort on the plane over. I got this.

STEWY
Uh-huh. And what's in it for me?

KENDALL
I dunno, man, like – maybe do a solid for your oldest pal the day after his dad died. How about that?

Stewy looks at him.

STEWY
I think. I think what you do is you dry it out. It's the deal. It's just the deal and you're best placed for the deal.
(*sees a flicker of excitement*)
But don't fucking drool, man. Okay? Subtract the heat.

KENDALL
Sure. And I got the name, bro. Bit of that old-time religion. The Roy fuck-dust? The market acts all money-money but the market loves a narrative?

Kendall gives Stewy a pat, a smile. And heads through to . . .

INT. LOGAN'S APARTMENT – STUDY – DAY

Connor in the study. Past Willa and her mom, Sylvia, looking at the walls.

WILLA
What you think of the apartment, Mom?

SYLVIA
Very pleasant. Very commodious. Lots of power points.

WILLA
Do you think this is a supporting wall? I think this is load-bearing.

She motions to the wall dividing the study from the living room.

We need to figure out which walls are structural because I'd actually like it to feel bigger.

Kendall reaches Connor and Roman and Shiv. Roman and Shiv clam up a bit. They have been chatting.

CONNOR

Willa's mom? God love her, her plate is groaning.

KENDALL

So listen. I think Stewy would swing behind one of us?

ROMAN

Okay?

(*re Willa's mom*)

Jesus Christ, does she know she can go back?

Kendall is waiting for a response but Shiv plays hard to get.

SHIV

Her boat came in didn't it? This has really turned into the grand tour for her?

KENDALL

I guess the agenda for me is, do we, you know, do we agree to flying to Matsson?

SHIV

You know Connor's moving in?

KENDALL

Okay. What?

In the lounge, the Old Guard and Tom are starting to round themselves up. Kendall is very aware. Shiv and Roman too but pretending to be less so.

CONNOR

Well Marcia gets it but she – she kind of, she sort of sold it to me—

ROMAN

Shall we all move in. Like the Banana Bunch?

KENDALL

We've got like ten till board time?

SHIV

Uh-huh. You speak to Mom yet?

KENDALL

Um. Yeah. No. Swapped messages.

The evasions are getting too much.

Shiv? Shall we?

ROMAN

You know Peter Munion was flying to Spain and tried to fly right here. He wanted to be with us 'at this difficult time'.

CONNOR

He left me a message saying it was 'a rum situation' and 'one in the eye for all of us' and also 'just an awful pain in the bum'?

Sylvia passes.

ROMAN

Can I get you anything else, Mrs Ferreyra?

KENDALL

Shall we get private?

SHIV

You seen this? Hearts – the soccer fans celebrating online. Nasty.

ROMAN

They wanted us to 'shore up the midfield' and Dad was reluctant to spend.

CONNOR

Also because I – believe, is this right, Hearts are – more, for the Protestants and Hibs for the Catholics, I think, right, so – Dad owning Hearts. It's complicated. Is that right, Rome?

ROMAN

Dude, don't ask me. Not only did I not know Hibs were Catholic, I didn't really know I was.*

In the lounge the Old Guard heads upstairs.

Kendall snaps.

* This is a joke I tried to get in a number of places, including season two, episode eight, but it never stuck.

KENDALL

For fuck's sake. Ah? Come on. We've got somewhere. Let's talk about it, yeah? I don't even care what happens? But let's not just give it to fucking Team Viagra because we didn't talk?

Shiv and Roman exchange looks.

SHIV

Con? Do you mind?

She goes to close one set of doors, Roman the other, so they are private.

Then—

KENDALL

So. What do you think? Do you have a problem with me? Because. Yeah. That's fine. But I'd like it to be one of us – and – yeah? Dad said so.

SHIV

Okay. Let's discuss, but stop jonesing, Ken. It's like you're walking round the wake with a fucking hard-on, you know?

That's horrible. But Kendall buttons it.

KENDALL

All I am suggesting is I swing it for us and then we move ahead, us three, Pierce, ATN.

SHIV

Um, yeah. Okay. Good. But I have thoughts.

From his serious look Kendall sniffs a bump.

ROMAN

I guess I do too.

KENDALL

You're not pulling for Ger-Bear?

ROMAN

Nah, I'm done with helping old ladies across the road. I just wonder about – about – about – about—

KENDALL

About me, dude?

                          SHIV

I think it needs to be me too.

                          KENDALL

Uh-huh? Okay?

Looks at Roman – he doesn't look into that but . . .

                          SHIV

We're doing what we do, together.

                          KENDALL

Well that's ultimately how I want it.

                          ROMAN

You know everyone remembers you trying to send him to
prison?

                          KENDALL

That's an asset. Fresh blood. I'm the clean broom.

                          SHIV

His *son* is the clean broom? You were jerking it over a piece of
paper he'd scribbled your name on. There's an argument you're
the worst of both worlds. Different but the same.

                          KENDALL

That plays, Shiv, it does. With the board? Same-old but with a
vibey new banner.

Roman has a pitch.

                          ROMAN

COO is on the draft plan, right? I'm a COO. I know Matsson.
I was very close with Dad. We had a number of communications
you were aware of and some, that honestly, now isn't the time,
but you weren't. And yeah, I just think. We were close and—
Honestly, Ken, it just, it feels better. It doesn't feel good to us –
right, Shiv, right now for it to be just you. So. Them's my words.
I don't know, this whole thing is a big deal but I'm done fucking,
twisting and turning, I'm just gonna say it.

Kendall looks at them. Both. Fighting two is going to be hard.

He makes a calculation.

> KENDALL

Uh-huh. I see that. I see that, bro.

What's his move?

> ROMAN

Yeah?

> KENDALL

Yeah. I mean, Rome. It doesn't have to be just me. I'm down. I'm down. That makes sense.

> SHIV

Uh-huh. And what about me?

> KENDALL

Well. Yeah. Honestly, I just worry it looks like special pleading. It's the COOs? It's in the draft plan. I'm on the piece of paper. It needs to look dry and clean and tough.

> SHIV

Oh and I don't, I look all teary-eyed and mascara-streaked and like I might faint? Fuck you. It's plenty clean enough.

> KENDALL

No. Really. Shiv. It's not. I don't think it works, you actually don't have experience. It starts to look flaky.

> SHIV

I did the Strategic Review.

> KENDALL

That was Daddy make-work. And besides, two is cool but three is – three is –

> ROMAN

Three is a bit wacky?

Has Shiv been fucked by Roman here or is this just his view?

Two is fucking. Three is a weird cuddle puddle and no one gets laid.

She looks at the two of them. Tough – their arguments are strong even if she doesn't know how much she can totally trust . . .

> SHIV

Well I need to wet my beak.

> KENDALL

We'd only be fronting it.

> SHIV

I don't need to be front-facing. It's not ego.

> KENDALL

Really it's the threeby, it's the team.

> ROMAN

You're inside everything. Look. I'm not fucking anyone, this is just to sell and— Yesterday was real, it was real, we're connected. I feel good on this. I feel really good.

She looks at them.

> SHIV

I don't know.
> (*then*)
I'd need to be across everything.

> ROMAN

Everything.

> KENDALL

It's a holding position. It's holding. We'll do the deal. Spin ATN, fold in Pierce, six months, eight months?

> SHIV

Uh-huh. And that's all equal?

> KENDALL

Equal as fuck. To the gram.

> SHIV

Uh-huh. I mean, you fuck me, that's – it's— This is a Dad promise. On yesterday.

> KENDALL

On yesterday.

> ROMAN

Yesterday.

A knock on the door.

                    GERRI
                    (off)

You guys wanna talk?

They head out.

INT. LOGAN'S APARTMENT — FOYER — DAY

Mencken arrives with a pair of aides and some extra Secret Service.*

A shiver of excitement goes through the party and it rearranges itself for him. The big man.

Roman makes it over to greet him.

                   ROMAN

Hey.

                  MENCKEN

Hey. So. Sorry for your loss.

                   ROMAN

Cool. Dry opener.

                  MENCKEN

Hey. Man. This is real. But your call. How about 'Take me to your leader.'

                   ROMAN

Ha. Well. Yeah. Good. I guess that's 'under discussion'. Come on in.

Shiv and Kendall are there.

                  MENCKEN

Sorry for your loss.

Shiv doesn't come forward. Kendall shakes hands.

                 KENDALL

Thank you.

---

* We really wanted to see Mencken this episode to tee him up for later in the season, but in the edit it became clear that though the moment was fun nothing really *happened*. So the brutal logic of the edit determined it had to go.

MENCKEN

Don't worry, Siobhan, no photographers here. You can kiss me
if you want?

(then)

Thanks for hosting me.

SHIV

Thanks for coming. Shitting your whack about what we're
going to do to ATN?

MENCKEN

Paying my respects.

SHIV

I heard this morning you were going around your plane with a
joke – telling people you thought he was dead already?

MENCKEN

I'm here partly to say, I know there's been a remark going
around.

ROMAN

You didn't say that?

MENCKEN

I did say it. I said it to be funny. So. I don't apologize for saying
it, but I apologize for you hearing it.

There's something disarming about his brutal honesty.

ROMAN

Well you keep working that routine.

MENCKEN

I don't think your father would care about the disrespect but
maybe it wasn't funny enough. What did we go with?

PRESS GUY

'A great man has died, a conservative colossus to a generation.'

ROMAN

Oh thanks.

PRESS GUY

'Always vigilant in exposing the encroaching threat of heartless
globalism.'

> SHIV

Professors. Jews.

> MENCKEN

Hey I don't talk about my *own* father like that.

> KENDALL

I'm sure he'd be appreciative.

> SHIV

Actually I think he was mostly pissed you didn't deign to visit on his birthday?

> MENCKEN

Yeah, well I had him in the tank, and I haven't got you in the tank. So here I am! Paying respects.

To them. He's playing it well.

Off by the side Connor approaches one of the agents.

> CONNOR

Hey.
> (*not much response*)
Yeah. How you going? Who's the head honcho here, buddy?

> SECRET SERVICE AGENT

You can talk to me?

> CONNOR

Connor Roy? Presidential candidate. Not a significant candidate apparently though.

> SECRET SERVICE AGENT

Right.

> CONNOR

Yeah I was denied a piece of this action?

> SECRET SERVICE AGENT

Well, that's not my decision.

> CONNOR

But I get death threats. I get 'em alright. But no, doesn't matter apparently? Target practice. Interesting huh? Makes you wonder huh?

> SECRET SERVICE AGENT

Above my pay grade, sir.

> CONNOR

Sure. What is that? That pay grade? How's the pension package?

The agent shrugs.

You sitting pretty on a government pension package? Yeah, the old Secret Service might regret the day they decided Connor Roy didn't need protection?

> SECRET SERVICE AGENT

Right.

> CONNOR

Kroll? Blackwater? Lean and mean. Outsourcing. Just pass that up the chain there? Not too late.

Now in a private spot – Kendall and Roman and Mencken chat.

> MENCKEN

So look. One thing I did just want to say. I want to be treated fairly – in this home stretch and on the night.

> ROMAN

Oh hell yeah. Yeah.

> MENCKEN

You know your decision desk is full of people who call me silly nasty names in private?

> KENDALL

How do you know?

> MENCKEN

How come you don't?

> KENDALL

Uh-huh.

> MENCKEN

Who's King Kong on the night? Because Cyd, I have some concerns about. Can you be a point of contact?

Kendall and Roman exchange a glance.

> KENDALL

Well, we insulate our people.

> MENCKEN

That's nice.

> (*then*)

Look, I knew where I stood with your old man. Where do I stand with you?

> KENDALL

Uh-huh?

> MENCKEN

We were talking about me having someone close to the desk, election night.

> KENDALL

Nah. Nah.

> MENCKEN

Your dad told me, in confidence, over dinner, he was gonna get your editorial team to coordinate with my campaign, for the last week. Are you gonna follow through with that?

> KENDALL

Just you and him was it?

> MENCKEN

That's how he liked it.

> (*then*)

C'mon. We can feed you the scoops and I won't get ambushed and rolled by those fucking abacus-monkey bullshit artists. Yeah?

> ROMAN

Let us talk to some folks.

> MENCKEN

You're gonna welch on a deal? You gonna Jew me?

> KENDALL

Easy, tiger.

> MENCKEN

Fucking kidding! Jesus Christ, man.

Kendall looks at him.

KENDALL

Uh-huh.

MENCKEN

Great to talk. So sorry.

Connor approaches.

CONNOR

Mr Mencken, I presume. My most unworthy adversary!

MENCKEN

Still clinging on to your slice of pie?

CONNOR

Pies can get bigger you know?

MENCKEN

Uh-huh and how will you feel if your nought-point-eight percent
hands it to the other side?

CONNOR

One-point-three percent by my reckoning. And I'll feel like
democracy has won out!

*Kendall and Roman have acted as a team – share a glance as they
head upstairs . . .*

INT. LOGAN'S APARTMENT – LIBRARY – DAY

Kendall and Roman assemble with Shiv, Frank, Karl, Gerri, Stewy.

GERRI

Um? I think – for pre-board? Um, Ken – we were thinking,
maybe – just—?

ROMAN

This is a good group.

FRANK

I'm just not sure it's appropriate for this discussion?

ROMAN

If you're uncomfortable you can leave, Frank. It's a lovely gang
of pals having a chat.

KENDALL

Look. It's simple. COOs are on the draft emergency plan. It looks perverse not to honor that and it looks pointed for it not to be us. Me and Roman step up.

Silence, then—

KARL

I mean when was the last time you spoke to him?

ROMAN

Like forty-eight hours ago?

FRANK

And how did it go?

They all look at one another. Is Shiv on board for the plan? Well, in public—

SHIV

It went okay.

ROMAN

Our dad was tough.

KENDALL

But we spoke frankly.

GERRI

I guess there is the thing, Ken, that – in the public imagination, you are quite closely tied to the idea of him being corrupt? And the company complicit.

Kendall plays it straight.

KENDALL

Uh-huh. Yup, all the better. It makes perfect sense.

KARL

Ken. The DOJ is all wrapped up. And everything you said about Logan amounted to nothing. Your outburst amounted to nothing. You're damaged goods. People call you the Anti-Climax . . . the boy who cried wolfpack . . .

GERRI

Whereas I shepherded through a lot of cultural change.

KENDALL

All because I blew the whistle.

Gerri and Shiv – hm?

FRANK

Gerri has done it before?

ROMAN

I think we all know he had soured on you, Gerri?

GERRI

I don't think there's anything on paper to that effect?

Gerri's aware of the many people in the room who know she was on the verge of getting the push.

But I'm not going to push it.

ROMAN

We're obviously the people to take over from Dad because we were closest to him.

FRANK

I think the board could have concerns?

STEWY

Kendall's on the piece of paper. Logan said it should be Kendall.

FRANK

But when?

STEWY

A few times. You've lost Logan and for his faults, he was the founder. Kendall and Roman – I think a Roy at Royco works. It's not for long.

FRANK

So you can puppet-master them?

STEWY

Who, me?

ROMAN

Yeah right.

FRANK

There will be the renegotiation with Matsson?

> KENDALL

I want to do the deal and get out. We've got our own ideas with ATN refreshed, there's a shape for things for us, we have things cooking.

> ROMAN

We know the board is very excited about the deal and so are we. It's a good deal.

The Old Guard look at one another. Kendall gives him a nod – Stewy heads out.

> FRANK

Okay, look, Simon is keen to have the senior leadership in agreement on this, given the need for immediate progress, so, are we happy to advise him and the board?

They look at one another.

INT. LOGAN'S APARTMENT – LANDING OUTSIDE LIBRARY – DAY

On the landing outside the library. Tom and Greg with Hugo and Karolina; Ray, Mark wait.

> KAROLINA
> (*checking her phone*)
> Getting hit by all the royal families now.

> HUGO

Same.

> KAROLINA

What's the order of priority?

> HUGO

Saudi first, Belgians last?

> GREG

Can you smell it? History is happening.

> TOM

Uh-huh.

Karolina gets a ping of a text.

> KAROLINA

Okay. Okay. It's done. Hugo. It's done. They voted it through.

> TOM

Ken and Rome?

> KAROLINA

Ken and Rome step up from COO. Let's draft. Hugo!

The doors open.

After a beat—

Kendall and Roman head out, to a little applause from the Waystar folk waiting.

Karolina and Hugo approach Kendall and Roman.

They bask. Shiv marches down past through the throng. Not so excited perhaps.

INT. LOGAN'S APARTMENT – FOYER – DAY

Shiv makes it down.

> MARCIA

Everything well?

> SHIV

Oh yes. Yup.

> MARCIA

Good. Good. Company things? All good?

> SHIV

Uh-huh. All great. All good.

Shiv wants to hit out. Put some distance between herself and this interloper.

Listen. Richard and Katy have done everything wonderfully. But shall I get Richard to call and we can get this catered? Let the staff take some downtime?

> MARCIA

Katy and Richard can cope. It's what your father and I paid them for.

> SHIV

Yeah, they're just servants after all, huh?

Marcia looks at her.

> MARCIA

Are you okay? Darling?
> (*smiles*)
It must be very hard for you, all this.

> SHIV

Uh-huh. I'm good. I just need – I need a glass of water. I—

INT. LOGAN'S APARTMENT – LIVING ROOM – DAY

Shiv walks towards the living room.

Ravenhead and Stewy are talking, there are some laughs.

> SHIV

Yeah ha-de-ha. Can you maybe shut the fuck up? This is not a fucking comedy night.

Shiv makes it down the step. She's boiling with feelings. She stumbles, her ankle buckles under her and she's suddenly down. More humiliating than dramatic. Aware of Sandy Furness watching her.

Tom, who has followed her down, joins Stewy and Mark in coming to her aid.

> SHIV
> (*cont'd*)

I'm fine I'm fine I'm fine. I'm fine. I'm fine. Don't fucking touch me!

INT. LOGAN'S APARTMENT – LOGAN'S PRIVATE STUDY – DAY

Karolina, Hugo, Kendall, Roman enter.

The safe is open there. The whole room vibrates for them.

> KAROLINA

So you're running the company. Congratulations!

> ROMAN

Yeah. Thanks. Great day. Great week.

Roman looks at an unfinished Sudoku puzzle. The pencil. Maybe last touched by his dad.

> ROMAN

God. Did you know he did Sudokus?

> KENDALL

Er yeah. Yeah. I guess. I think I did? He did them.

Kendall spots – tucked right into the back of the desk chair – a cardigan or sweater that Logan was wearing and must have slipped down there. He draws Roman's attention to it.

> ROMAN

Oh Jesus Christ.

> KAROLINA

Okay? You okay?

They nod.

Yeah sorry but I'm— We are putting together the statement announcing you and we'll just go through the biographical details we have with your offices and – yeah. Just wanted to check in on comms and PR? We have a lot of material for you on the – on the forthcoming investor presentation. Karl will brief you on that and a number of imminent quite difficult decisions. But yes, Hugo?

Karolina looks like: Go on.

> HUGO

Okay, but I guess what we wanted to say, from a comms point of view and listen this is strictly comms. But – the markets are gonna open on Monday, and there are a number of ways to – to solidify your position.

> KAROLINA

When Logan was alive, we did everything we could to burnish his reputation. Now you're taking over, we need to do everything we can to burnish your reputations.

HUGO

Yeah I guess, there's two ways to go, sort of Operation Embalm
Lenin, Operation Red Square, or there's another way?

KAROLINA

For the first we get together a nice package of photos of you
with your dad. You're a safe pair of hands. Mention the piece of
paper. You're gonna follow what Logan Roy did to the letter.

HUGO

Or, more complex, more fresh start.

KENDALL

Go on.

KAROLINA

Well. Just— This is from a PR perspective? There will be an
issue about your competence and for example if we were to
stress how involved you were previously?

Karolina nods to Hugo: You do the horrible stuff, my deputy.

HUGO

Toughest version, we could say he was losing his focus towards
the end? Or – since say the stroke, that perhaps what looks like
a new and shocking set-up has actually been, behind the scenes,
the case for quite some time?

KAROLINA

It's about reassuringly positioning for change.

ROMAN

It's Operation 'Shit on Dad'.

KAROLINA

No. No!

KENDALL

I think the piece of paper is strong.

Does Roman look tired of that?

ROMAN

Are people gonna buy that Dad was a puppet?

> KAROLINA

It's just an option. I could get a bundle. Boosting your profiles and reminding people maybe of the less appealing things that happened under the old regime?

> HUGO

Logan Roy was a great man. However, the people around him have been making the big decisions, his kids have been – pulling the strings. We could go as far as you like?

Kendall looks at Roman.

I wouldn't but it's our job to say we could go to – Connor's mom. Physical and verbal abuse. The Kerry situation.

> ROMAN

Whoa!

> *(then)*

Yeah. I do have certain feelings of queasiness, about, I guess – shitting on our dad while he's still up at Frank Campbell's?

> KENDALL

Yeah. Right now, I would say, considering our dad has just died, we should maybe not shit on Dad?

> ROMAN

Thanks, Hugo. Karolina. But never bring us this disgusting shit ever again thank you?

> HUGO

Understood!

INT. LOGAN'S APARTMENT – DINING ROOM – DAY

In the dining room. The speechifying is coming to an end when Greg pipes up—

> GREG

Hi. Hi. Um, I wanted just before we all depart, to – dear friends and family and associates, we've lost a great man. A legend. A genius, unquestionably. But also a friend, a mentor, a loyal supporter of new talent. My name is Gregory Hirsch. As many of you know, as well as being Logan's nephew, I'm also a senior executive at ATN. And that's because Logan took a chance on me. He was a great judge of character. He instantly saw my passion for media and communication.

Maybe Greg makes eye contact with various divisional heads.

TV, movies, theme parks and cruises. Publishing. News. Everything he was interested in, in fact.

Maybe he's nodding at some politicos in the room.

He also recognized my love of politics. And how to be part of a thriving organization that pursues excellence. He wasn't always the easiest or most patient of tutors, but my god, I couldn't have learned from anyone better. He taught me how to overcome new challenges, how to adapt to difficult, high-pressure situations and, above all, how to prove myself. I will miss him dearly. As will we all. To my favorite uncle. And in some ways, my best friend. To Logan Roy.

Tom joins Greg.

> TOM
> Nice speech, Greg. I'm surprised you didn't say, 'Proficient in Microsoft Word, clean driving license, can start immediately'.

> GREG
> No. That was – from the heart.

Tom looks like: Sure.

I'm relaxed. I featured prominently in Logan's letter of wishes.

> TOM
> 'S fine. I get it. The big ship's gone down. You're doing some personal brand promotion. But just remember, you try to swim away from me?

Maybe Tom smiles to someone nearby as—

> (*hissing to Greg*)
> I'll grab a leg and drag you down to the cold floor of the fucking Atlantic Ocean just for company, okay?

That sounds spooky. Greg tries to banish the concern by saying 'hi' to some important guests who are starting to filter out.

INT. LOGAN'S APARTMENT – BATHROOM – DAY

Kendall sits on the closed toilet seat. He looks at a photo he's taken on his phone. He enlarges the image of his name underlined. Other parts of the letter.

Eventually he gets up and heads out . . .

INT. LOGAN'S APARTMENT – LOUNGE/STUDY – DAY

Through the lounge.

Most people have filtered out. Staff are tidying. Couple of stragglers. Kendall returns to Hugo, whom he's told to wait for him in the downstairs study.

> KENDALL
>
> So, Hugo. You know the stuff?

> HUGO
>
> What stuff?

> KENDALL
>
> The 'Bad Dad' stuff?

> HUGO
>
> Uh-huh. Yeah?

> KENDALL
>
> It's what he would do. I think he'd want this. For the firm.

> HUGO
>
> Right. Okay.

> KENDALL
>
> So action that. But – soft. No prints.

> HUGO
>
> Right. I mean I don't want to— I'm a little concerned to freelance. Can I get a sign-off? From Karolina and Roman and—

> KENDALL
>
> Nah, pal. Nah. Down-low. You get on it.
> *(with emphasis)*
> Not unless you want me to pull out the strap-on?

Hugo looks at him. Checkmated.

Episode Five
KILL LIST

Written by Jon Brown & Ted Cohen
Directed by Andrij Parekh

Original air date 23 April 2023

Cast

KENDALL ROY	Jeremy Strong
GREG HIRSCH	Nicholas Braun
SHIV ROY	Sarah Snook
ROMAN ROY	Kieran Culkin
CONNOR ROY	Alan Ruck
TOM WAMBSGANS	Matthew Macfadyen
FRANK VERNON	Peter Friedman
KARL MULLER	David Rasche
GERRI KELLMAN	J. Smith-Cameron
WILLA FERREYRA	Justine Lupe
KAROLINA NOVOTNEY	Dagmara Dominczyk
HUGO BAKER	Fisher Stevens
JESS JORDAN	Juliana Canfield
MARK ROSENSTOCK	Brian Hotaling
RAY	Patch Darragh
LUKAS MATSSON	Alexander Skarsgård
OSKAR GUDJOHNSEN	Jóhannes Haukur Jóhannesson
EBBA	Eili Harboe
ANDREAS	Christian Rubeck
RASMUS	Kristofer Kamiyasu
GOJO FACILITATOR	Ellen Bendu
ADVISOR MARLENE	Brynne McManimie
ADVISOR RALPH	Torsten Johnson
REMI	KeiLyn Durrel Jones

DAY ONE

INT. KENDALL'S CAR – MORNING

Kendall rides through the city looking at papers and laptop. Jay-Z's 'Takeover' playing. Phone pinging with updates.

They pull up at the Waystar building.

                    KENDALL
    Thanks, Fikret.

INT. WAYSTAR – EXECUTIVE FLOOR – ROMAN'S OFFICE – MORNING

Roman is working, lots of papers. But looks up from reading to look over to his dad's office.

The moment broken by the arrival of Ralph and Marlene, one other Waystar advisor and a banker.

EXT. WAYSTAR – MORNING

Kendall heads in. Outside – scrolling chyron on the outside of the Waystar building reads: 'America Mourns Logan Roy, American Patriot, Media Titan'.

INT. WAYSTAR – LOBBY – MORNING

Inside there is an 'In Memoriam' image on the video wall.

Kendall heads in. How does he feel? Sad. But maybe less wounded. Iced over. And fucking busy.

Hugo is there to greet him, along with Jess, Remi, three extra assistants.

> HUGO

Just wanted to be on hand to smooth and say – welcome home.

But it doesn't slow Kendall's progress much, he looks to Jess—

> KENDALL

Rome said he's in?

> JESS

Uh-huh. Yup. Five-ish.

Maybe as they head towards the elevators Kendall looks to the assistants.

> KENDALL

And these are?

> HUGO

Additional manpower, for the new role.

> KENDALL

Okay well they can fuck off until I need them. I just want to show my face, check in with the prune-chewers and get to the plane. I'd rather have more time other end, okay? Maybe I get in early and fucking, slip a mickey in Matsson's meatballs?

Jess, Remi, Hugo and one close assistant enter the lift.

INT. WAYSTAR – EXECUTIVE FLOOR – DAY

Kendall arrives, with Jess, Remi, assistant and Hugo.

They enter the bullpen. Hugo makes a clap or cough to get attention – the room becomes aware of Kendall.

People clap him in and also, maybe a Waystar tradition, bang their desks with fists and objects as Kendall progresses through towards Roman's office. Kendall acknowledges, then, as they walk—

> HUGO

Before take-off could be nice to get a shot – you and Roman on the— Candid shot. 'Stepping up', 'CE-bros' is the bad version.

> KENDALL

Shall we maybe not do the bad version?

INT. WAYSTAR – EXECUTIVE FLOOR – ROMAN'S OFFICE – DAY

They get to Roman's office where he is feet-up behind his desk, has three corporate advisors and a banker in there. Kendall, from doorway – people still clapping and banging—

KENDALL
Rome, come get your dopamine topped up.
(*to the room*)
Thanks, all. Sad times. Exciting times.

ROMAN
(*shouts out from inside*)
Thank you. More to follow!

KENDALL
Get any sleep?

They embrace.

ROMAN
Little bit. You get the condolence assistants?

Three or four new assistants are gathered near desks outside Roman's office, looking at phones and without assigned desks.

KENDALL
Uh-huh, what you think? Old Guard, loading us up with human listening devices?

The room smiles. Kendall looks at them.

Look at you fucking chumps! This the Romey A-Team? What's shaking? You camp out overnight?

ROMAN
Ha! I wanted to get in early, just – getting briefed. Should I get Shiv?

Kendall makes a face, that's like: Yeah sure, do we need to? Roman nods to an assistant who goes to call or get her.

KENDALL
So what's bubbling? Don't crush us, we have infinite deal variations loaded, just short-range top lines.

ADVISOR RALPH
Uh – the ransomware situation. Is currently being managed but could blow up?

ADVISOR MARLENE
Studio would like to schedule a call this morning. Red flag.

Kendall looks – Roman knows.

ROMAN
Okaying *Kalispitron* reshoots. Panicky vibes.

ADVISOR MARLENE
Second producer signed off on leave citing mental collapse, overload.

KENDALL
Uh-huh? I mean? We okay it, yeah? We're balls deep already?

ROMAN
Yup. I think gotta keep spending. I will say 'no', a lot, and shout, obviously, initially.

KENDALL
(*to Rome*)
And you got my email on Matsson angles, deal thoughts?

ROMAN
Which, cos you sent several?

KENDALL
(*smile*)
The last one – 'ignore previous emails'.

ROMAN
Yeah.

KENDALL
Yeah?

ROMAN
Yeah. Yeah.

KENDALL
Talk on the plane?

Kendall gets up. Roman nods for Ralph and Marlene and the others to leave them.

ROMAN

Yeah. And is it, it's not *the* plane?

KENDALL

Nah, Gulfstream.

ROMAN

I mean I'm sure I'd be fine but—

KENDALL

I know. I saw his handwriting on some deal materials at three
and it spun me out so – yeah.

*Before Roman can answer they become aware of Frank, Karl and
Gerri approaching . . .*

ROMAN

Okay. Here we go: March of the Emperor Penguins.

*Karl and Gerri enter. Frank gets detained at the door by another
assistant, who's just arrived with a message for him to make a call.*

KARL

Morning, welcome back. Congrats.

KENDALL

Nothing to celebrate, but thank you.

Frank's call distracts the room a bit through the following—

ROMAN

What is this? Coming to re-interview for your jobs?

Maybe a frisson of edge between him and Gerri?

GERRI

No, just a check-in, pre-Norway.

ROMAN

I think we checked in on the board call? And on the follow-up
call and with your thirty-three thousand emails?

KARL

Or anything we can do to be helpful – in terms of dry-running
the negotiation?

KENDALL

Okay. 'We trust you absolutely, now tell us every single word you plan on saying to him.'

KARL

We're not gonna big-foot you guys. Okay? Play it how you like.

Roman and Kendall look at the room. How do they play it? Tell them to fuck off, like they want to, or . . .

ROMAN

Yeah we're not Dad. We are collegiate motherfuckers. The game goes: confirm the deal is on. Reaffirm structure and the ATN spin-off.

KENDALL

Then: go for the bump the board has requested, which is obviously more challenging given the price drop we suffered post-Dad.

ROMAN

But we fuck-out the idea the post-Dad price fall has anything to do with the underlying value.

Karl and Gerri share a look: Not bad.

Shiv is coming over – Kendall maybe can see her and she arrives past Frank, in the middle of Kendall's pitch—

KENDALL

We want to knock this out of the park. We talk the deck. Parks, sports betting, Living Plus driving growth. There's a path here for us to squeeze an extra three, four dollars a share. Rome and me. Shiv on point here to advise and liaise?

Shiv senses being vaguely patronized.

SHIV

Hey, did I miss the invite? What's the conflab – Boomers and Zoomers?

KENDALL

We're finding out who had the worst Woodstock.

ROMAN

Unscheduled, Shiv. Mom and Dad just stopped by to make sure we have food in the fridge.

SHIV

Uh-huh, cos I wanted to stop by anyway. About the nasty Dad stuff? You seen the stories? It feels like it might be sourced from inside?

Roman's phone pings.

Kendall and Hugo careful to not look at one another. Kendall plays straight and dumb, but is Shiv attuned enough to sense something in the air?

KENDALL

Hugo? What is that?

But Roman has something more pressing—

ROMAN

Um, sorry. But Matsson, asking— He's saying not to freak out?

KENDALL

Freak out? Why?

SHIV

Is he wobbling?

Frank is now entering.

FRANK

Have you just been told? Do you have this?
(*off their looks*)
They're asking for everyone. Requesting us all, in Norway. Plus division heads, three EVPs. I've forwarded.

Gerri has a list of names.

GERRI

He actually sent a list of names?

SHIV

A list? Of— To go?

ROMAN

Okay. So that's sinister as fuck.

KENDALL

What is it do we think?

FRANK

'Cultural compatibility check'.

SHIV

Is it real? It feels provocative. Why did he call Frank? What is this?

GERRI

It's early, but it is smart. Avoid a – a Daimler–Chrysler. An AOL. Bad values-fit.

ROMAN

But why does he want to check cultural compatibility if we haven't done the deal?

GERRI

I guess because we are probably doing the deal?

A significant development.

FRANK

Positive.

KARL

Unless he's looking for a way out?

SHIV

Or invite everyone because he doesn't want just to deal with the B-roll brothers here?

Nods to Kendall and Roman. Will they punch back? No, because they have the power, they can smile. Which in itself bumps Shiv—

Can I see the list? [Am I on the list?]

FRANK

You should all have the list. You're on the list, Shiv.

Shiv looks at her phone. But Kendall is not looking—

KENDALL

What does it look like if we say no, we don't play that weak?

Frank, Karl and Gerri try not to share looks of despair.

GERRI

Um. I guess, in the interests of doing a deal, which we all want— [maybe we play ball?]

Kendall looks at Roman, but they know each other so well all it needs is a flicker.

> KENDALL
>
> Yeah, no. Great. Good. We're playing his game. Let's go get the deal.

Looks and smiles around the room. Shiv watches both parties – the top brass; Kendall and Roman. Trying to figure out where she might sit in all this.

EXT. AIRFIELD – EVENING

Tom, Hugo, Karolina, Ray, Mark, three other divisional heads on the tarmac. The Waystar jet is being readied nearby. (Plus a second one for assistants.)

There are assistants around seeing to arrangements, waiting to get on their plane. Greg comes over from that group to join Tom and gang.

> GREG
>
> Wow. Whirlwind, huh? Why Norway not Sweden?

> TOM
>
> Annual retreat. Anyway, Norway, Sweden, what's the difference? All descended from the same rapists.

> GREG
>
> Right. Well, excited to get a feel for Scandinavia!
> (*then, insinuating*)
> Including the 'hotties'? The 'Arctic foxes'. Bit of 'Norwegian wood'? Ah?

> TOM
> (*quietly*)
> Greg. Have some respect.

> GREG
>
> Because . . .?

Gloomy mood.

> TOM
>
> Because what do you think it is? 'A cultural check-in'. 'Corporate diligence'.

GREG

To help get the deal done?

Karolina has overheard, checking her phone.

KAROLINA

Right! It's not a trip to the Guggenheim, kiddo. It's musical electric chairs.

TOM

To see who they like for after the acquisition. If anyone gets to stick around.

RAY

'Synergies'. 'Efficiencies'. You hear those words? Soon you'll smell burning flesh.

HUGO

Find out who they like. Everyone else – welcome to the lime pit.

GREG

But you? You're not worried, Tom?

TOM
(*aside*)

Me? Well. With ATN spun off I don't have to worry about Matsson. I have to worry about four seconds after our election coverage is over and I get whacked by the cast of *Bugsy Malone* over here—

Tom nods over at – Shiv, Kendall and Roman all now arriving.

With Kendall, Roman and Shiv as they cross, followed by Jess and their assistants.

Roman catches sight of the big Waystar jet up ahead. Kendall sees Shiv is looking too. He feels a wobble—

KENDALL

They refreshed it.

ROMAN

Great. You hang a disco ball in the cabin, my dad still died on it.

SHIV

I thought you were pre-grieved? Dodged the sad bullet. On to the eighth stage of grief – Martinis.

                    ROMAN
No it's not even the emotional – just in terms of simple –.
hygiene.

                    KENDALL
I think, with the extra names, we have to be on the big boy.
Unless we wanna fly scheduled?

*Shiv looks at Roman. A certain nihilism in the absence of her dad and
the meaning he freighted the world with.*

                    SHIV
C'mon, Rome, he's gone, so – Colonel Mustard in the library,
none of it fucking matters.

                    ROMAN
Sure but – the actual *bathroom*.

                    KENDALL
There's like four, Rome.

                    ROMAN
Nevertheless. I might – make my own arrangements.
                    (*clarifying*)
I'll be pissing in bottles.

                    KENDALL
Jess! He's— We might wanna—? Wide necks. Carafes I guess.

Jess nods. Great gig.

                    JESS
Carafes to piss in, check.

INT. WAYSTAR JET – BACK CABIN – DAY

*Pre-take-off. Karl and Frank carefully pull on their knee-high flight
compression stockings. Tom passes.*

                    KARL
Got a problem, Tom?

Tom looks away. Karl and Frank continue to pull them on.

INT. WAYSTAR JET – FRONT CABIN – NIGHT

Mid-flight. Kendall and Roman with laptops, documents. Roman is half-focussed, looking through to the bathroom.

Kendall aggressively engaged with his laptop and Shiv comes to sit by him.

> SHIV
>
> So you two aren't concerned about the Dad stuff? Cos there's been more.

She has it on her phone. Kendall shrugs: What do you want? Not us. Yeah, not us.

> ROMAN
>
> It's not us spinning, Shiv. It's – just – general cultural bile.

> KENDALL
>
> It's wastewater.
> (*re his laptop*)
> I'm sorry I have to focus. Studio overages. *Kalispitron: Hibernation.* A hundred and seventy-five mil sunk cost.

> SHIV
>
> Uh-huh?

> ROMAN
>
> Yeah. Testing at twenty-six. Estimating three weeks of reshoots, which is thirty mil plus forty more on CGI.

> KENDALL
>
> It's a fucking sleepy robot in a cave. How is that a quarter of a bil?

> SHIV
>
> I guess I'm just struck by the number of pieces which knife Dad and imply his kids, particularly his younger sons, have been covering for him for quite some time?

> KENDALL
>
> Hugo! If someone's briefing anything against Dad we'll fucking crucify them, okay? Rat-fucker Sam. Okay? Rome, let's do the Matsson dossier together for angles. Yeah?

> SHIV
>
> Just interesting. How you two look golden?

> ROMAN
> (*'teasing'*)

And, Shiv . . . I'm confused – are you offended that there's messy write-ups about Dad, or that you're not mentioned enough in these fuck-pies?

> SHIV
> (*'teasing' back*)

I'm fine. I like watching you guys Mini-Dad it. Like when the Muppets put on a trench coat and act like they're a real person.

Roman believes this, or chooses to—

I don't care, if you want to burn Dad's legacy – but I actually think it would be better, for all of us, to be together. Like not even with an agenda, just to . . . get through this?

More sincere than usual?

> ROMAN

Shiv, we're trying to prep to get inside his head and squeeze every nickel out of this while keeping the numbers straight across five fucking divisions.

> KENDALL

We're death wrestling with ogres.

She looks at them.

> SHIV

Reading documents, is what you're doing, Ken.

Beat. Then an offer—

> KENDALL

You know one thing? If you want, just to mention, we can cut Tom's throat anytime you like?

> SHIV

Uh-huh. How's he doing?

> ROMAN

He's doing good. He's doing fine. But just in case that would be a nice thing?

Shiv feels patronized. Gets up.

SHIV

Oh thanks so much, guys. That's so lovely.
(*heads out*)
I'm actually up to my fucking eyes in investor conference shit,
so.

INT. ROY PRIVATE JET – BACK CABIN – NIGHT

Tom sits, working on laptop. He has his feet up. White new sneakers on. Shiv enters, all riled up.

SHIV

Nice kicks, Tom.
(*smile*)
So white.
(*more smiles*)
Whiter than an ATN Christmas party.

TOM

You okay, Siobhan?

SHIV

Why you even here do you think?

Tom can see Shiv is in the mood to torture him.

TOM

I don't know, Matsson asked, I guess. We gelled at Sun Valley.
He has a really unpleasant sense of humor.

SHIV

Uh-huh. And how you feeling. About this knife fight? Excited, to
get into it? Stab someone in the back?

This isn't as much fun as she was hoping.

TOM

Well with the spin, I guess I'm out of it. Safe until election night.
Then it's up to you guys, I guess?

She looks at him.

SHIV

You know they'd fire you right now if I said?
(*then*)
They'd like to. Ken and Rome.

                                    TOM
Oh yeah? Okay. Well. That's tough.

Tom smiles. Shiv smiles.

I won't fight you.

                                    SHIV
Jesus Christ. Grow some balls, Tom. It's gross.
                              (*looks at him*)
You're good at your job. You're a great guy. Everyone likes you.
Didn't you know?

She gets up. Nowhere feels right at the moment.

*She heads through to – where Hugo, Karolina, Ray, Mark and Gerri
are discussing the coming events.*

They are aware of her but carry on.

                                    HUGO
I would say, there's a lot to admire. In terms of – in terms of they
have the whole holistic approach, the catered meals, the gyms,
the campus, the incentives?

                                  KAROLINA
Hey could we get another tumbler of Kool-Aid for Hugo—?

                                    HUGO
What? I happen to think we're being acquired by a high-caliber
organization.

Karolina is reading through some printed materials.

                                  KAROLINA
Hugo – did you see their deputy comms is a ski jumper? Ex-
Winter Olympian?

                                    HUGO
Uh-huh. I saw.

                                    RAY
A ski jumper? You can hardly stand up. You're fucked.

                                  KAROLINA
Fulbrights coming out their ass. NASDAQ master race. Just very
impressive serious young people.

                                    RAY
You read what happened when they acquired the video-game
publisher?

                                   MARK
Less than ten-percent retention.

                                    RAY
They went through the place like fire ants.

                                   MARK
                         (*not a good thing*)
Incredibly meritocratic.

                                    RAY
They're insular, weird, brutal motherfuckers. And we're dead.

A very somber mood on the jet. Shiv might head out.

*Gerri takes it in. Makes a calculation – if she's going to survive this,
she'll need familiar faces around her.*

                                   GERRI
Hey. C'mon, guys. Listen. Sure they're young and they're
fit – but they're European. They're soft. Hammocked in their
social-security safety nets and sick-on-vacation mania and free
healthcare. They haven't – they haven't built up immunity to lies
and – fuckery. They may think they're Vikings but we've been
raised by wolves. We've been schooled by a barbarian, exposed
to a pathogen that went by the name 'Logan Roy' and they have
no idea what's coming to them. Okay? Okay!

Beat. It has a restorative effect on group morale.

                                   HUGO
We're snakes on a plane!

That raises a smile at least.

DAY TWO

EXT. AIRFIELD – NORWAY – EARLY MORNING

*An airfield by the water. Scruffy apron – utility vehicles and ground-
support equipment. The two Waystar planes have landed. Maybe*

we see some of the execs arrive from their plane. Or assistants from theirs.

EXT. NORWAY – DAY

A fleet of vans drives through Norway. Granite rock and curved bridges, but also low-density urban sprawl and tourist truck stops with coachloads of older tourists.

INT. VAN – DAY

Kendall crams on his laptop. Roman too. Shiv looking at her phone. Election news.

> KENDALL
> You clock that he's a movie guy? We might need a line. In case he queries the fucking cash-incinerator that the studio is right now?

Roman nods, lets out a little fart.

> Dude?

> ROMAN
> Vans makes me car sick.
> (*then*)
> I'm a little nervous – and you know what happens to my guts.

Shiv has had an email. Early voting indications.

> SHIV
> Hey, Queefer Sutherland. You should be nervous. Early voting sounds lovely and bad for your boy Jeryd.

He shrugs that off.

> ROMAN
> You nervous, Ken?

He is. But will he say? Looks at Roman but in front of Shiv is a little different.

> KENDALL
> Nah. He's just a guy.

> SHIV

Oooh. Iceman.

> KENDALL

I dunno. Maybe, little bit.

This display of vulnerability allows Shiv in—

> SHIV

You're good, Ken. Fucking, every dollar you squeeze makes us stronger when we do Pierce-ATN. Right?

Kendall appreciates it. Nods right.

> ROMAN

I had a dream I sold it and then we looked and the contract was in Turkish lira.
> (*another fart*)
> Apologies. But I'll bust a valve if I don't release the pressure.

EXT. JUVET CAMPUS – TRANSFER AREA – DAY

The Waystar A-team disembark from vans. Their assistants, off behind, handle luggage being transferred to golf carts.

Intel is being shared. Karolina joins Gerri and Ray.

> GERRI

So, it looks like my opposite number – just got back from his second sabbatical in two years? I get the whiff of an HR issue?

> KAROLINA

Their senior comms has been *very* open about her mental health issues. Really brave.

> RAY

Big family man. Five children. Count 'em – five. Can't be easy.

Ray has a photo of a man with his children.

See that's the great thing about me as a value-add – I don't give a fuck about my kids. Empire State Youth Orchestra flautist. Never seen a school concert.

He does a finger lick and sizzle.

Karl and Frank watch it play out from a little way off. Maybe as they climb into a golf cart—

KARL

Well, Frank old pal. Looks like we got ourselves front-row seats at the Hungry Games.

FRANK

Hun-*ger*.

KARL

Huh?

Hugo joins them, scrolling.

RAY

Hugo – looking forward to meeting your Winter Olympian?

HUGO

Andreas Bloc? Sure.

(*then*)

He blew a seven-point lead at the Sochi winter games. He's a possible choker Ray. Possible choker!

There are many staff there waiting to help with the transfer. Some uniformed. But some not. Amongst them – bearded, maybe casually dressed – Oskar doesn't stand out.

RAY

Cuckoo! Thanks, dude, with the other pieces for Ray Hoffheimer?

He tips Oskar, who almost bows in thanks. Hands off the bag.

Roman, Kendall and Shiv arrive out of their van.

SHIV

Hey, hey! Which way to Chairman Matsson's re-education camp?

EXT. JUVET CAMPUS – DRIVEWAY – DAY

Many golf carts carry the C-suite, then assistants and luggage towards the campus, conference center and the rooms.

In the distance we hear shouting in the woods (from Matsson and team's morning 'Shouting Exercise').

> KENDALL
> Where are they? What is that?

Maybe Roman clocks the distant shouting.

> ROMAN
> Dunno, man. Saw a Black guy. Whaling ban?

EXT. JUVET CAMPUS – DAY

Staff carry and drive luggage to the many rooms hidden in the woods, leading the C-suite team to their chalets.

EXT. JUVET CAMPUS – PATH BY MATSSON'S CABIN – DAY

Matsson looks down at the Waystar arrivals.

INT. KENDALL'S CHALET – SMALL ROOM – DAY

Kendall enters and looks at the small room. Luggage already there. On the bed, a GoJo-branded overnight bag and flask.

Looks over to Roman in another chalet, already calling and looking back at him.

Intercut with:

INT. ROMAN'S CHALET – DAY

> KENDALL
> (on phone)
> Like the merch?

> ROMAN
> I'm going to jerk off over it staring at you, you like that?

> KENDALL
> Is yours small. It looks small?

> ROMAN
> It's a bird blind. When a bear shits in the woods he probably uses one of these.

INT. KENDALL'S CHALET – SMALL ROOM – DAY

Jess knocks and opens the door – with a GoJo facilitator.

> JESS
>
> Um, divisional heads et cetera are offered brunch. Matsson has invited the negotiating team 'up top' to get into it? They'll escort us, 'if you want'? How do you want to play it?
>> *(looks at the room)*
>
> Um. 'Cozy'.
>> *(then, she knows)*
>
> I'll make inquiries.

INT. TOM'S CABIN – DAY

Greg and Tom in his cabin room.

> GREG
>
> So, you have a 'decompression brunch', then Gerri, Karl presentations then, all invited to join them for their afternoon sessions then, 'Beyond Holacracy – the Internet of Fungus'.

> TOM
>
> How's the assistant accommodation?

> GREG
>
> Threadbare. Meager. Just this side of insulting.

> TOM
>
> Gotta love that GoJo cost-control!
>> *(then)*
>
> Okay. Greg, listen, today is the start of Operation 'Wambs Beyond Waystar'. So. We might start leaking that I'm 'increasingly uncomfortable' with the tone of ATN's election coverage. Okay? 'The Last Sentinel of Decency', people might be calling me, around the place? Can you let that – waft?

EXT./INT. CABLE CAR – DAY

GoJo facilitator guides Jess, who guides Kendall and Roman, Gerri, Frank, Karl and Shiv into the cable car.

> ROMAN
> (*as they get on*)
> And by the way, what was all the shouting?

> GOJO FACILITATOR
> The shouting? The shouting was The Shouting.

Kendall gives eyes to Jess: Find out what you can. Jess winks.

> ROMAN
> Okay. The shouting was the shouting? Great. Thanks.

Little bit spooky. Doors close. We stay with Jess and the GoJo facilitator—

> JESS
> How's it going? Crazy busy. So . . . how are your guys, good guys?

> GOJO FACILITATOR
> Oh super-good. We have a saying – 'You're either GoJoGo or you're NoNoNo.' They're amazing.

> JESS
> (*Jesus*)
> Cool. That's fun. That's funny.

> GOJO FACILITATOR
> How about your guys?

> JESS
> (*the guys?*)
> Oh yeah. Amazing. Very great people and feeling really good.

Smiles. Neither of them are going to go any further.

INT. CABLE CAR – DAY

Clanking. Roman's stomach is bubbling.

Silence as we look at faces. The Old Guard try to look supportive.

Roman, Kendall check iPads, notes.

> FRANK
> Want to walk the deck once more and talk the angles, the foreseeable unforseens?

Kendall gives him a thumbs up: I'm good.

> ROMAN
> We're good. Good with the plan.

> SHIV
> 'Everyone has a plan until they get punched in the mouth.'

> GERRI
> We've just been around the block a few times so—

> ROMAN
> (*low*)

Sure you have, Ger—

> GERRI
> Just in terms of the dynamics of how these things flow—

> KARL
> You got this. Play it as it lays.

As Karl talks, Kendall writes something on the back of a notebook in Sharpie—

> But I might just add, I have seen guys, going in 'playing hardball' and then not been able to row back. Your dad often led with a joke. Just to establish that however tough it got you know that—

Then Kendall flips it – it just says in big figures: '144'.

> KENDALL
> That's the whole thing. Right? Bring in an offer lower than one-four-four net result: unhappiness. Over one-four-four, net result: happiness.

> ROMAN
> Increasing exponentially with each additional dollar until such time as Karl creams his jeans, while dropping in his golden parachute.

> KENDALL
> Aiming for one-four-seven, hoping for one-four-eight. What with everything, would settle for one-four-five, one-four-six. Right? That's the whole of the game?

Frank nods. Roman's phone goes. He takes it.

> ROMAN
> (*into phone*)
> Hey, Con—? Not now, Con—

Intercut with:

INT. FRANK E. CAMPBELL FUNERAL HOME — SIDE ROOM — DAY

Early morning. Connor on the phone. Willa there by his side.

> CONNOR
> So listen, guys. I'm at Frank E. Campbell and look. Are you okay to talk? Because um. Marcia's been in and given creative direction and I think she's insisted on blusher and she's talking about putting him in a kilt. I'm worried he's going to look like a fucking Bay City Roller.

> ROMAN
> (*relaying to them, freaked*)
> Marcia's been in with Dad, she's talking about a kilt?

Looks at Shiv.

> KENDALL
> Can't he just figure it out? Is it just drama? I bet it's just drama.

Roman puts on speakerphone and hands off.

> CONNOR
> I heard that, Ken – you know, I got a pretty full plate here! I just had to cancel on a room full of working-class whites in Cleveland. I'm genuinely concerned he will look odd and I'll be blamed.

> SHIV
> Con, we appreciate you holding this down. What do you need from us?

> CONNOR
> Carte blanche, if I go into the – the – embalming room and start throwing my weight around. I need to make some asks but I don't want to get blamed.

KENDALL

Anything you need. Con. You're empowered. No recriminations.
Sure, if you need, send photos.

End of call. They ride on. Unsettled. Roman thinks.

ROMAN

Send photos? He's not taking him to the beach, Ken.

SHIV

Maybe we shouldn't have left him with Con. He'd be angry we
left him.

Kendall shrugs. Yeah. Maybe. But. Not anymore. Huh?

ROMAN
(*then*)

Will you guys handle? I don't really want to see anything.

Clank clank. Nerves.

INT. JUVET CAMPUS – GUDBRANDSJUVET – DAY

*The Waystar team (but not assistants) are in the conference center.
Food is laid out on a table.*

*It is a delicious Scandinavian feast. Glistening cinnamon pastries,
piled high, rye bread, eggs, piles of fresh smoked salmon. Fruit juices,
muesli, all looking inviting and fresh.*

*Everyone has loaded up. Perhaps one or two have phones out, still
researching their opposites. Hugo notices something.*

HUGO

Uh-oh – what's this?

*The GoJo top team (ten in total) arriving. Ruddy, healthy, fresh from
outside, in outside gear. They seem younger, hardier, bigger, stronger
than the Waystar gang.*

TOM

Uh-oh. Ambush. You've taken the bait! Fattened for the kill!

People look at their plates piled high.

KAROLINA

Good luck, everyone!

Ray sneaks a fat cinnamon bun onto Hugo's plate, moves his away. They are too far from tables for Hugo to jettison. Motherfucker.

The GoJo gang arrives. Led by Ebba, who's been having a tough day at work.

> EBBA

Hey, guys. Hi. Welcome.

People say 'hello' in general but search out their opposites. Karolina approaches.

> KAROLINA

Ebba? Comms and public affairs.

> EBBA

Hey – Karolina.

> KAROLINA

Exactly. Look at you. You look so well. So *refreshed*!

Tom meets Oskar.

> TOM

Tom. Oskar Gudjohnsen, right?

> OSKAR

Tom. Yes. Tom. Of – Siobhan?

> TOM
> (*'well, kind of'*)

Uh-huh.
> (*then*)

And of ATN. So.
> (*leaning in*)

Not part of the whole, situation here? And if you want a little 'guide to our forest'? The Mighty Oaks of Waystar, and the ahem, 'deadwood', give me a nod? Yeah?

Rasmus passes Hugo, and his large plate.

> RASMUS

Easy, buddy, leave some for us!

> HUGO

You want some of this? I'm happy to share!

(*after him*)
Very happy to accommodate. Super-flexible. Team player.

Andreas arrives with them. Handshakes.

Ah, Andreas? My man. Hey. They tell me you nearly got bronze in Sochi?

ANDREAS
Ah another lifetime.

HUGO
That's almost huge, man. Those darn tenths of seconds huh!

ANDREAS
Hugo Baker. Is it right before this you specialized in spinning oil spills?

HUGO
(*the old line*)
'Clean-up operations are great opportunities for small- and medium-sized businesses'!

ANDREAS
God's work, my friend. God's work.

INT. RIDGE-TOP RESTAURANT – ENTRY HALLWAY – DAY

Up at the top. Kendall and Roman, Shiv, Gerri, Frank, Karl arrive. Matsson is alone to greet them, just one assistant.

MATSSON
Oh. Hey, wow, okay. Look at you all! Rolling deep. Rock Steady Crew.

Bro-hugs.

I can't believe you actually came. What the fuck are you doing here?

KENDALL
Hey. Keen to get into it.

Matsson comes to hug Shiv. But uneasy with women.

MATSSON
What do we do? Am I gonna get a lawsuit if I hug you?

As she lightly, briefly embraces—

> SHIV
>
> Haha, yeah, sorry. Glad it's awkward machismo here too, was afraid you might wear a papoose and respect me.

Matsson smiles, not so confident.

> MATSSON
>
> So you brought the whole gang. Outmaneuvered me. I'm solo. You scared to come talk without the village elders?

He laughs, a big joke. But Kendall and Roman turn to the group. Give them eyes: What do you think? Very quick check-in—

> FRANK
> (*whispered*)
> If you want us don't be intimidated.

> SHIV
> (*quiet*)
> Fuck him. It's dude-bluff.

Roman and Kendall lock eyes. They know the power move—

> KENDALL
> Yeah we don't want to outman you, bro. Let's talk.

Kendall and Roman head in. Leaving the gang anxious outside.

INT. JUVET CAMPUS – GUDBRANDSJUVET – DAY

Tom comes over to Ray and Hugo – whispers to them. Nods over to Ebba who is watching.

> TOM
> You're staying too close to the lox, guys.
> (*then*)
> I think they're watching who's eating the high-fat foods and failing to circulate?

As they talk, Oskar goes to talk to Ebba, who makes a note on her phone, looking at the Waystar folks.

> RAY
>
> Oh motherfucker.

Hugo looks at him.

> I thought he was a grunt. I gave him my bag and under-tipped him!

INT. RIDGE-TOP RESTAURANT — DAY

Matsson, Kendall and Roman head in. Just the three of them. Food laid out. They look at each other, not about to eat.

> KENDALL
> (*whispered*)
> No sudden moves. Don't fart.

> ROMAN
> (*whispered*)
> Oh please. Let's get it done.

> MATSSON
> So. Thanks for coming out. I appreciate. Not ideal.

> ROMAN
> Hey. Not like our dad died yesterday. It was actually a couple of days ago so—

> MATSSON
> At least you didn't find him yourself, BMW still running. Because that can be traumatic.

Roman and Kendall have read about this in the dossier.

> ROMAN
> Right. Yeah. Sure. Um . . .

> MATSSON
> No sorries for Lukas?

> KENDALL
> No, sure, sorry, man.

> MATSSON
> Uh-huh. It's not a competition.

Maybe Matsson shows them to a table of food. There is champagne on ice. But Kendall and Roman demur.

> ROMAN
>
> I see your 'soccer men', the Manchester Red Devils, did a win. Congrats.

> MATSSON
>
> Hey thanks, man. Good dossier. Wanna know what I have on you?

Smiles. What does he have on Roman? Conversation stalls.

> ROMAN
>
> So what's the uh— In terms of schedule—?

> KENDALL
>
> Should we sit down somewhere and talk—?

> MATSSON
> (*mocking them*)
> Ooh – uuh – nervous laugh – hey relax, it's just me. Seriously.

> KENDALL
>
> So. What the fuck is this place? Ten K wedding mill for lawyers' daughters? Family shots by the window?

Kind of joke – friendly. But not.

> MATSSON
>
> Yeah it's bullshit. But it is pretty cool. So. I feel like I want to say shit. Can I get into it? Or do you want me to wait?

Roman looks to Kendall. He might be aware of a slight tremble in Kendall's hand.

> ROMAN
>
> Well. We've come to say, we like your offer, but we don't as yet think it reflects a full valuation of the potential of what you're purchasing.

> MATSSON
>
> Your stock dropped twenty percent Friday?

> KENDALL
>
> And regained ten Monday. Logan was never going to be part of the company going forward. In a valuation sense, his absence is not relevant.

ROMAN

Our key growth drivers are unaffected by our father's passing, the dip is the dip, it's nothing— [fundamental.]

MATSSON

But I feel like I'm going to the checkout during a sale and getting asked to pay more?

KENDALL

If you were willing to pay one-four-four yesterday, shareholders won't like— [you looking opportunistic.]

MATSSON

Look. Let me stop you there. Because I would like to propose a serious offer. I would like to buy your entire operation . . . for the price of – one single dollar.

They look at him. Long beat. Then, he smiles.

No, I'm kidding!

KENDALL

Oh yeah, really good. Funny shit.

Roman looks at him, like: Easy – we're trying to woo this guy.

MATSSON

But I do want ATN.

Kendall and Matsson are in danger of rubbing each other up the wrong way. Roman trying to keep it rolling a bit more.

ROMAN

Well, ATN isn't on the table. Dad carved it out.

MATSSON

But I'm not sure it makes sense and I want it back in.

ROMAN

Why?

MATSSON

Why?

(*then*)

Um, I feel like I don't have to say. Do I? Do I have to say?

(*riding over him*)
It's the original deal. We have the shape, and it can be fast and this way I can give you the sugar you came looking for.

KENDALL

The price is what?

ROMAN

Er, I don't think we're at 'price'—

MATSSON

Like one eight-seven per share. Fifty-fifty cash-stock. For the whole thing.

Kendall and Roman a bit frozen, thinking what they make of it, what Shiv will make of it, Frank, Karl, Gerri, Dad. Who will leave, who will stay? Pierce. Making arithmetical calculations of what that values the whole company at, what the premium is with ATN added back in, a great deal to compute – business, corporate, financial, political, human.

Aren't you supposed to say what you think?

KENDALL

Yeah, man, sure, sure.

Roman looks at Kendall, Kendall at Roman.

MATSSON

Maybe you haven't done this before. How it works is, like:
I say something, then you say something. Cos if you don't say anything, things can maybe get a bit – congealed in terms of—

KENDALL

Yeah fuck off, dude.

Is it a bump? Roman looks at Kendall.

ROMAN

We just, we weren't expecting that. And I'm not sure it works?

MATSSON

It works.

ROMAN

We're not sure it does work.

> MATSSON

It works.

The brothers look at one another.

> (*nods to door*)
> You want to check in with the boiled eggs?

> KENDALL

This is a material change, we'll need to talk to the board, bankers will need to update their analysis.

> MATSSON

Oh sure. But do you like it?

They stay poker-faced. Roman doesn't want to lose ATN, Dad. Kendall would discuss but doesn't want to get pushed around.

> Just between us? You like it a little bit? Right? There's something there? Yeah? You don't have to give me an answer, but, give me an indication? We're in the zone, yeah? Little bit of bubbles?

Matsson is near to or motions to the champagne. Kendall looks at Roman, maybe they could discuss a little?

> ROMAN

We need to take a beat.

INT. RIDGE-TOP RESTAURANT – ENTRY HALLWAY – DAY

Kendall and Roman walk out to join the gang, who wait. Whisper as they come out—

> ROMAN

We say? Yeah?

> KENDALL

Yeah. We say.

They arrive at the Old Guard.

> ROMAN

Offer is one eight-seven. But he wants ATN.

Frank and Karl are very pleased but downplay it. Matsson maybe has some kind of sight line. If so they are all aware and hide their reactions from view.

> FRANK
>
> But he wants the deal?

> KENDALL
>
> He's an asshole. He tried to dominate.

> KARL
>
> Sure, but – excellent news, gents! Excellent!

> GERRI
>
> You effectively achieved a bump.

> FRANK
>
> So, we take it to the board?

> ROMAN
>
> Yeah yeah we did amazing, butter our cocks and serve them with zucchini.

> KENDALL
>
> But we need to run through it first and make sure it's real. We need to talk to the bankers. We need to huddle.

> ROMAN
>
> Where's Shiv?

INT. JUVET CAMPUS – GUDBRANDSJUVET – DAY

A different room has been divided into break-out spaces for informal discussions. Small circles of chairs. Ebba is having an uncomfortable discussion with Oskar.

Whiteboards for the different groups: 'Re-writing Back-ends in Brainfuck'; 'Martin Luther: The Great Disruptor'; 'IM-375: Reflections on a Security Incident'.

Hugo and Ray are checking in at the coffee station.

> RAY
>
> What's going on? When do we give our presentations? They're herding me in with the fuckheads from interactive. What is this?

Ebba, distracted, realizes she needs to move them on to the next activity—

> EBBA

Hey. Thanks, all. Next up, little bit of fun. We'll divide into teams. It's an improvised river crossing and mushroom hunt.

Greg has come to find Tom, showing him a draft of an email—

> GREG
> (*whispers*)
> Uh-oh! Feats of strength for the butter-balls!

> EBBA

Problem solving with an incomplete data set. Pure fun. Just a game.

> TOM

Oh sure. 'Just a game'. Last one across loses their pension.

EXT. JUVET CAMPUS – PATH TO CABINS – DAY

Kendall and Roman.

> KENDALL

It felt like he was trying to fuck with us, right?

> ROMAN

I dunno, not sure that's how he thinks.

> KENDALL

Do you like him?

Roman makes a face: No. But maybe there's some interest or admiration.

> ROMAN

You think he really wants ATN? Or is it a move so we ask to subtract and he goes low?

> KENDALL

Who cares? What do *we* want?

> ROMAN

Well we want to keep it. Right? Do Dad's deal. Keep ATN, add PGN? Me, you and Shiv. Three Fuckateers.

Shiv approaches.

SHIV

Um, so, I just got a bad rumor in my ears.

They look at her.

SHIV

ATN's been leaving an open line to Jeryd's campaign team during morning editorial conference. Dialed in. Did you know that?

ROMAN
(he knew that)

I did not know that.

SHIV

Rome? That comes out, any credibility is blown.

KENDALL

That's not okay. Rome?

ROMAN

I don't know. Cyd? Cyd's in operational charge.
(then)
What? It's a mutual back-scratch. Mencken wins—

SHIV

The numbers I hear, he's not gonna win.

ROMAN

Mencken wins, with us pulling for him. Lot of upside.

Practically an admission.

SHIV

Rome? Jesus. Even Dad had a line.

KENDALL

Shiv, we can— We should get into that. It's not okay. But. We do need to focus. Big picture, we should discuss. What do we think, on ATN folded back in?

Shiv considers and then as a little bit of a 'fuck you' to Roman—

SHIV

Yes. Well. Fuck it, why not. It's a toxic asset.

ROMAN

I mean it is also Dad's pride and joy he died trying to keep?

SHIV

We could just keep one of his old sweaters. Less racist?

KENDALL

(*this might appeal to Shiv?*)

If we don't own it, we can't change it?

SHIV

Yeah but I'm not sure whoever owns it can afford to change it. It's weapons dealing. The margins are too good.

ROMAN

It's a gold mine. Maybe keep the gold mine?

KENDALL

I do think we maybe need to stand up to him? He tried to big-dick it.

Cos he likes ATN or he doesn't like being pushed around? Shiv looks at him.

SHIV

And if he doesn't move? If he walks?

ROMAN

You don't fly Hugo to Norway if you don't want to make a deal.

KENDALL

We can't go in thirsty. He needs to know that if there's no deal, we survive. Thrive.

SHIV

Uh-huh? But can we? Do we?

ROMAN

Well, me and Ken have done a pretty good job.

SHIV

In the last twenty-four hours?

ROMAN

Price has stabilized. Markets seem to like us.

SHIV

Well, the market likes that you're selling?

Karolina has spotted them and is approaching.

> ROMAN
>
> Dad wanted to keep ATN.

> SHIV
>
> Sure, and he wanted to poison Brezhnev and hang Mandela. He wasn't always right. But overall – I think what he wanted really was the deal. So—

> KENDALL
>
> We can't navigate by Dad maps. He's not here.

> SHIV
>
> Well yes I am aware he is not here because I have a hole in my heart and a forty-eight-hour migraine and I don't know whether to shit or cry thank you.

> KENDALL
>
> I'm sorry. Shiv. I'm just—

> SHIV
>
> I honestly, I don't even fucking care. I don't. Let's get it done. Let's just get it fucking done.

Karolina's arrival brings things to a close.

> KAROLINA
>
> Anything, Shiv? Cos we're fighting the good fight.

EXT. JUVET CAMPUS – CREEKSIDE – DAY*

Some of the Waystar team including Hugo and Ray are foraging for mushrooms. Some including a divisional head and Mark are trying and failing to construct a line to cross the river. A couple of assessors are around watching.

Hugo and Ray and Mark watch as Andreas the Olympian easily fords the river or crosses above it on a length of rope.

> RAY
>
> Look at that fucking Adonis.

---

* We had to cut a number of the 'Kill List' trial scenes for time. There was also a tonal choice to be made between focussing on the grief-stricken kids and their negotiations with Matsson, and the more knock-about mood of the executives fighting for their lives.

> TOM

Grade-A grass-fed porterhouse.

> GREG

Such phenomenal technique.

> RAY

He makes it look so easy. Maybe it is. Maybe you could do that, Greg? You're young? Skinny? Be great if just one of us could?

> GREG

Me. Nope, I'm actually fat on the inside. I'm like chicken Kyiv.

> HUGO

What does that even prove? Those are not useful skills in a PR crisis! 'Someone died at a theme park, what shall we do?' 'I know, let's pull a fucking Mack Truck down Broadway with the strength of our own arms!'

Karolina hurries over and talks quietly, as Tom, Ray, Mark, Hugo and a couple of others huddle.

> KAROLINA

Okay. Not great news. A good offer. But he wants ATN folded back in. They're going to the bankers.

A jolt through Tom, who is lounging somewhat.

> TOM

ATN—? *Matsson* wants ATN?

Everyone reassesses their positions.

> HUGO

There's no way these are real mushrooms out here. They've plugged or glued out safe ones. They wouldn't risk it. The lawsuits.

> RAY

Son of a beesting. He cleared it.

They see Andreas has made progress – to the other side of the river – and has tied a rope line for his teammates to cross over.

> HUGO

I thought he was a skier? Now he's some fucking, rope guy? That's cheating. The guy's a fucking ringer!

>   KAROLINA
> What do you think the metric is?

>   RAY
> I'm going to suck ass on the river crossing. I need to kill it on
> fungi. Can anyone help me out with a mushroom?

Tom begins to forage, heads off to some trees. Greg looks to him.

>   GREG
> Buying ATN too? What does it mean, Tom? It means – it
> means—

>   TOM
> I think we just got thrown into the bear pit?

>   GREG
> Okay. Bad.

>   TOM
> No. The bear pit is good. Before I was in front of the firing
> squad.

>   GREG
> Okay. Bear pit better than firing squad?

But Greg is starting to compute . . .

>   TOM
> We're under the microscope, Greg. It's good. It plays. Cos I'm
> dead under the sibs. But with Matsson there's a way through!

>   GREG
>   (*not great, right?*)
> But for me? I guess, actually for me . . .?

>   TOM
> Oh, for you it's bad. I think incredibly bad.

>   GREG
> No. Because? No, because – they're not looking at assistants,
> right, so?

>   TOM
> Unless you're the single highest-paid assistant in the history of
> human civilization?

> GREG

Maybe they'll see that as an accomplishment?

> TOM

No, when some bloodless fuck runs their finger down a kill list you are gonna stick out like a sore thumb.

Greg looks around. Aware of Ebba keeping notes on a phone in the distance.

You're like one of those video-game characters – that when you get shot you explode into a shower of gold coins. The Fabergé Greg.

Greg looks scared.

> GREG
> (*worrying*)

I need a basket.
> (*shouts back*)

I wasn't issued a mushroom basket?

> MARK

We're supposed to be building a bridge! A crossing!

> GREG

I can't build a bridge, okay?! I don't know how to build a bridge!

> HUGO

We might have to use you as a gangplank.

Nearby, Ray inspects mushrooms. He looks desperate.

> RAY

Are these gills or pores? Can someone help me? I have three kids to get through college. Please.

Oskar approaches.

> OSKAR

Need some help, guys? Want a piggyback across? I can ferry you?

Hugo looks to his colleagues—

> HUGO
> *(consulting sotto voce)*
> What do you think? I mean I'd like to climb on his back?

> RAY
> Is it like good strategy. Cooperation?

> HUGO
> I can take the shame if I stay dry. I mean, if we ride them like horses, who's the real winner?

> RAY
> Hold up, buddy? How many of us can you fit?

EXT. JUVET CAMPUS – BBQ AREA – DAY

The teams are gathering. Lots of picnic tables.

There is some axe-throwing off in one area.

Matsson has a high-status table. Just him and Oskar and Ebba. He's got his phone out, discussing something with Ebba. Not happy.

People hover, not knowing where to sit. Tom regards the action with Greg.

> TOM
> We have to play this delicately. Laid before us is a chessboard. Every move is crucial. What you got?

> GREG
> Matsson, pretty cold. When he's fucking randos? He does noise-canceling headphones. Podcasts. Just lies back, cans on, and watches them slide the beanpole.

> TOM
> Okay. And in terms of the cage fighting?

> GREG
> Yeah. Um, well. Some say Oskar, some Ebba.
> *(motions to the two of them with Matsson)*
> In terms of who's keeping the kill list.

> TOM
> So there is a kill list?

> GREG

Oh I have it on good authority there's a kill list, yeah. It's evolving, like eight, nine names.

> TOM

But there's— How many of us are there? It can't be right, I mean there's only ten, eleven of us?
> > (*then*)

But you say target Oskar?

> GREG

Ebba might be out of favor. The shouting was a peer-review session. Her commitment is in question.

> TOM

Okay. Fuck it. I need profile. I'm going in!
> > (*as he goes, back to Greg*)

Keep an eye out. If I need a pawn sacrifice I'll give you eyes!

He walks over towards Matsson's table . . .

Meanwhile – Kendall and Roman are arriving to join Shiv.

> ROMAN

Bankers will give that number an amber, so we have room for maneuver.

As Shiv considers, Greg goes for it with the bros.

> GREG

So, guys, what's the counter?

Roman and Kendall look at him.

Just saying, in case you want to sling some ideas around?

Kendall makes a call.

Just within the safety of—
> > (*tries it out*)

the Quad.

> ROMAN

'The Quad'?

> GREG

The Quad, me and you two, the trio plus Shiv, the Quad Squad. Roy Patrol. The old team.

(*Italian accent?*)
'Da family'.

Tom sits with Matsson. The gravity shifts. Particles like Ray are pulled over, scared but attracted to the power, chance to save their skins . . . some GoJoers too.

MATSSON

Hey, guy.

TOM

May I perch?
(*remember me?*)
We – at Sun Valley, Lukas – we mocked Sundar's cargo shorts, the creases?

MATSSON
(*checks him out*)
Sure, man. We were just discussing.
(*then*)
Is France going to make it?

He looks to Tom. Tom looks over at Greg – pawn needed! Others congregate.

TOM

I'm sorry. As in?

MATSSON

Is France going to make it? Birth rate, youth unemployment. Sclerotic state. Angry fucking Arabs. Will they make it or will they pull a Greece?

Tom thinks, goes for something.

TOM

Well, look, what you need to know from a US news perspective is: we don't give a fuck. USA is late imperial. We don't know cos we don't wanna know. We got our own Paris thank you very much, and when it burns we'll build another.

GREG

Wow, Tom. You know, there was a great article about this recently in *The Economist* . . .

> TOM

Oh excuse me. *The Economist?* Well 's'il vous plaît'. Tell us more.

> GREG

Well. No, just, in terms of education and quality of life and – Old Lady France. Fuckin' don't bet against the fucking old— The – the baguette is mightier than the bagel!

> TOM

Maybe. Sure. I mean the US is full of these fucking millennial crybabies—
> (*motions to Greg*)
chomping on their avocado support animals, asking Uncle Sam for a bailout every time they catch cold. Right *Greg?* You're never at your fucking desk!?

A laugh, as if it's a joke.

> GREG

I know, dude, cos I'm always on the studio floor covering you and making editorial decisions above my pay grade!

They both laugh but not funny in the eyes. Kendall heads over to watch.

Matsson turns to Greg.

> MATSSON

Name the five most mineral-rich countries in Africa.

Greg pauses, mumbles – Ray jumps in.

> RAY

Congo, Zimbabwe, Zaire, fucking, Uganda, DRC.
> (*aside, quietly to Hugo*)
I'm dying. I gotta take a swing.

> MATSSON

Impressive. Zero points.
> (*then*)
It's just a silly question. I like to ask to identify morons. I think DRC and Zaire are the same place, no?

> KENDALL

Maybe that's enough pulling the legs from spiders?

> SHIV

You spend much time in the Congo, Lukas?

> MATSSON

What do Alexander the Great, Cary Grant and Yasser Arafat have in common?

Shiv has had enough, shakes her head – heads off to get a drink or talk to someone.

> KENDALL

Nah. No thanks, man.

> GREG

Um, Cary Grant wasn't his name, and maybe, Yasser – is it – is it they didn't like in a way exist, I mean they did but—?

> MATSSON

Who are you? I don't remember you from the list?

> GREG

Me—? Well, therein hangs a tale – Greg Hirsch. Ory. Gregory Hirsch.

Tom sticks the knife in—

> TOM

He's a cousin. Logan's nephew.

> MATSSON

You're serious?!

> KENDALL

He's good.

> MATSSON

Oh, man! There's more of them? Wait – are you all related?
> (*then*)
This is fucking hilarious.
> (*to Oskar; in Swedish*)
You believe this shit, man?

> OSKAR
> (*in Swedish*)
Six-foot-nine of pure nepotism. Inbred Hapsburg giant.

Tom maybe chuckles along. Greg, watching Matsson and Oskar laughing about him, looks at Kendall and Roman and Shiv, maybe something triggered in Kendall about seeing bullying from the 'big man'.

KENDALL

Enough. Yeah?

Matsson looks at Kendall.

It's fine, I've just seen enough of that shit. But do what you like.

Matsson feels challenged.

MATSSON

Uh-huh. I'm sorry. But look, do you have a counter or what?

They're not about to say.

KENDALL

You wanna do this here?

Matsson gives it a shrug of power play. Roman comes over, gives eyes – Ray and Hugo, Tom and Greg back off. Oskar eventually does, too.

Well. I don't want to pre-empt the board, but my view: it's not necessarily compelling.

ROMAN

We're running the numbers but, we'd like to explore options for us keeping ATN.

MATSSON

Uh-huh. Okay. Bad.

ROMAN

We want to hear you on price on the Dad deal. No ATN.

MATSSON

You don't want ATN.

ROMAN

Uh-huh no sure, but we kind of do.

MATSSON

Sure but you don't. I've been talking to Oskar and we see a way back.

KENDALL

Wow. Okay. You're gonna save our phenomenally lucrative and influential news operation? Thanks, bro.

MATSSON

It's okay, but the graph is horrible.

KENDALL

Look, we're just concerned. About your vision. And with half our value coming in stock, we're gonna lose a ton of value if you screw it up. It's complicated.

MATSSON

Nah. I've seen it. Lot of yelling. Small men, big veins.

ROMAN

Fat wallets.

MATSSON

Look, I don't know what your bank tells you. Probably exactly what you want to hear, that's what we pay them for, right? But long-term, I don't think angry old news works. I'll fold it in. Fat pipe. Straight dope. Bloomberg gray. Simple, cheap, huge. IKEA-ed to fuck. Plus sports, betting, movies. Everything else we figure out later, or break down for parts. Cruises, parks—

KENDALL

Dude – I think maybe you don't understand what you're buying. And maybe that's why there's a disconnect here, on value—

Shiv has spotted things are going off the rails. She heads back to the action to keep an eye on things.

MATSSON

Sure lecture me, Vaulter guy.

KENDALL

No risk, no fails. You look at experiences, look at the ceiling on parks, IP-turboed residential from a trusted brand . . .

MATSSON

Trusted brand? Man! No. No, it's. A parts shop. Good parts, bad brand.

Shiv's back. Matsson doesn't like having to explain himself. Or perhaps he doesn't have all the arguments in his head, without Oskar.

KENDALL

Gotta say, I just think fundamentally you're wrong.

MATSSON

Yeah I don't care what you think, you're a tribute band.

Kendall is going to blow but Roman looks at him. Might've been said in a fit of pique but Matsson is too proud to walk it back.

I'm kidding. I'm joking. Don't dig atoms, man. I just don't love atoms.

ROMAN

We don't mind, dude, that's cool. Fucking Abba – man.

SHIV

We okay?

Kendall might raise a hand – doesn't need her protection.

MATSSON

That was unfriendly. Look, I want to make you fucking rich.

KENDALL

Already rich.

MATSSON

But on the offer I just think, I am what I am what I am?

ROMAN

Okay, Popeye, let us check in and take this back to the board. Because – we would hate this to break down.

But it's icy as Shiv watches Roman try to ease things, and Kendall broods.

MATSSON

Yeah, let's make it work, man. Let's make it work!

Roman leads a bro-hug. Kendall avoids. Everything cool and negative feeling.

In the distance – Oskar is drunk and leading a chant.

OSKAR

Sauna! Sauna! Sauna!

INT. JUVET CAMPUS — SAUNA — DUSK

In the sauna area.

Oskar, three other GoJo guys.

Gerri, Hugo, Ray, Mark, one more Waystar guy.

Europeans are maybe naked, not so we can see their genitals, they might be hidden by legs and towels.

But the American men have their towels tucked around their waists. Gerri under her arms.

The Waystar guys are finding it hard. Ray is trying to ingratiate himself.

> RAY
> I'd have to be cuckoo to go home without picking up a timepiece, right? Totally *cuckoo*.

No one responds. Hugo looks around.

> HUGO
> *(low)*
> I feel we've been demerited, for not exposing. Puritanical refuseniks. I might drop?

> MARK
> *(low)*
> I can't do it, guys. I can't do it. I'm melting.

> GERRI
> *(low)*
> I swear I will boil from the inside before I show weakness here. Christ, Mark, have you been to LA lately?

Mark looks like: Sorry. He stands to leave.

> OSKAR
> You done? No worries.
> *(then)*
> First one out loses their division.

Mark smiles.

> I'm kidding? Head games, yeah? Good for the mind.

INT. JUVET CAMPUS — OUTSIDE SAUNA — DUSK

Outside – Karl and Frank lounging sipping water in dressing gowns.

> FRANK

Poor bastards.

EXT. JUVET CAMPUS — DUSK

Later. Maybe music. Maybe things getting looser. Matsson is with Ebba. They are walking and talking, intensely. At a certain point Matsson spots Shiv and they head over. Shiv is having a drink, looking at the party.

> MATSSON

Hey. Siobhan. Ebba. Ebba's like an estrogen air-freshener we keep around to try to you know, keep us smelling clean?

Shiv looks at her: Okay? Ebba looks back: Part of the job. Ebba smiles. Heard it all before.

> EBBA

It's okay. I keep a note. When I walk, it either goes in my book or they pay me off.

> MATSSON

You'll never walk. You fucking love it.

> EBBA

Oh yeah. Uh-huh. Love it.

They share a look, then Ebba backs off. Matsson looks at Shiv.

> MATSSON

So. How bad was that?

> SHIV

What, the majestic stags? Sparring with their memory-foam hard-ons? Breathtaking spectacle.

> MATSSON

I like to fuck around but I like to fuck around like, psilocybin at breakfast, with money just say the fucking number.

> SHIV

Sure. So straightforward. I'm sure.

> MATSSON

What if I was to say, my business – growth is getting expensive. What with my debt–EBITDA ratio, I wonder if the deal works anymore without ATN?

> SHIV

Then I would say: that makes sense, why not tell them?

> MATSSON

I always wanted it. Now, I think I need it. So I thought it might be nice to ask the big bosses in person?

'The big bosses'? Ouch.

> SHIV

Oh really? So what I'm the messenger girl?

> MATSSON

Nah. No. Maybe with your brothers. I feel like Elvis has died and I'm talking to his pool boys? Mostly.

Shiv nods. A vague offer? She can go hard or soft?

> SHIV

Yeah. Well. They misheard somebody say something a long time ago and got strung out on a dream.

> MATSSON

Do they know they're bullshit?

> SHIV

Owsh!
> (*then*)
They can be guys without being *the* guy.

But Matsson likes the appealing straightforwardness.

> MATSSON

Look. All this Dad shit. Don't come to my house and play with my dick then leave, you know? Is it there, the deal?

He gets up, an offer to follow.

> SHIV

Is it potentially there. Potentially.

MATSSON
Uh-huh? Wanna come hang? Do drugs at the cabin. I'll say
numbers and look at your face?

EXT. ABOVE THE PARTY – NIGHT

*From above. Kendall and Roman look down on the BBQ area or
lights of a rave.*

Maybe Kendall throws a hand axe at a target before he talks.

KENDALL
So, what you think? How does it feel?

ROMAN
Um, yeah. I don't know. Not great. But also, I guess, that's the
thing, right? We're selling. It's like, have we won or lost? It's
kind of hard to tell.

Beat.

KENDALL
Because I think I'd like to tank the deal.

ROMAN
And keep ATN?

KENDALL
I think – tank the whole deal. Kill it. Blow it up.

ROMAN
That's – quite a high-risk piece of fucking sword-swallowing?

KENDALL
I like running the ship and I think we're good at it. And I don't
want to stop. Do you?

ROMAN
Everyone wants the deal. Dad did it.

KENDALL
He's a bad fit and he doesn't get the business and he's going
to fuck it. I've seen him up close and he's a card trick and he's
going to destroy everything Dad built.

ROMAN
Blow it up though? Could be fatal.

> KENDALL

We sell? What happens. We buy Pierce. Crank it, one-hundred-hour weeks. Grow it to fuck and everything goes right and what – ten years, fifteen, twenty, we build it to Waystar size? Are we really gonna spend all our time building back what we already have?

> ROMAN

Wanna chew it with Shivvy?

> KENDALL
> (*no*)

Uh-huh. Yeah. Yeah. Yeah?
> (*then*)

I'm just worried – can Pinky dance?

> ROMAN

I mean no, obviously not. But, um—

> KENDALL
> (*moving on!*)

You like it though, go from fucking weekend warriors, to bossing full time?

And Shiv somehow got forgotten . . .

> ROMAN

It is Dad's deal. I feel – fucking – do the deal. Finish his breakfast. I mean what would he do?

> KENDALL

What would he do? Exactly whatever the fuck he wanted, right? It's already wobbling. Pushy pushy?

> ROMAN

We need to make him walk. Right? But so he feels like it's his call. Cos if the Old Guard smell that we're getting smart, they'll shit their beans – go crying to the board. We're toast.

> KENDALL

Oh sure. It's a tightrope walk on a straight razor. Five-hundred-foot reputational drop.

Kendall's smiling.

> ROMAN

Why does that make you smile? That shouldn't make you smile. Who likes tightrope walking a straight razor?!

Roman's phone goes.

> KENDALL

It's fucking 'feel the force' time. Choose your adventure. Full-bore, fuck the living shit out of the thing.

> ROMAN
> (*into phone*)

Con, what's up?

Intercut with:

INT. FRANK E. CAMPBELL FUNERAL HOME – SIDE ROOM – DAY

Connor is there, with Willa.

> CONNOR
> (*into phone*)

Everything's under control. I've got Dad locked down. Two things – would you like a lock of Dad's hair?

Immediate revulsion. Roman hands Kendall the phone.

> ROMAN

Con's asking if we want a lock of Dad's hair?

> KENDALL

Er, Con. I don't know. Maybe. Can we decide later?

> ROMAN

Did they take it already? Cos if they haven't tell them not to. I don't want them – plucking him like a turkey.

Kendall puts Connor on speaker. Willa is motioning – the hair!

> CONNOR

Also she'd back-combed his damn hair, which I've asked them to adjust. That and the blusher – he looked like fucking Charlie's Angels.

>   ROMAN
> Wait – why are we doing face and hair? It's closed-casket,
> correct?

Kendall feels like he just wants to keep his head in the deal.

> Connor, the casket will be closed, correct?

Roman does not want to see Logan.

>   CONNOR
>   (*losing patience*)
> Roman – this is what I'm being told. They prepare the body the
> same way, open or closed. We have to make a call on hair and
> any other preparations. We have to.

Roman finds it physically uncomfortable to think about.

>   ROMAN
> Okay, well – like, Dad hair. Normal coloring. No blusher, no
> eyeliner. Happy?

>   CONNOR
>   (*businesslike*)
> Absolutely. Eyes open, eyes closed?

>   ROMAN
> Oh my god. Do you even . . . Will he even . . . No. What's he
> gonna do, enjoy the fucking view?

*How long do you . . . keep your eyes? Roman rubs his shut in pained
empathy.*

>   KENDALL
> Eyes closed, mouth closed, hair – normal. We do not want him
> looking like he just came off a log flume, okay?

Roman hangs up. He's been thinking.

>   ROMAN
> Okay. Let's do it. Let's tank it. Let's fucking do it.

Handshake, or hug, or just a moment of togetherness.

>   KENDALL
> Okay. What do we have? What's in the cupboard?

EXT. JUVET CAMPUS – MATSSON'S CABIN – NIGHT

Shiv and Matsson walk towards Matsson's cabin. Shiv gets a text.

SHIV

Ugh. Trying to make decisions about how my fucking dad is buried.

MATSSON

In the ground, yeah?

SHIV

Yes, Lukas, in the ground. Jesus Christ. Unless you want to mount him on your wall, since you fucking killed him?

She can't help laughing. Oh god it's horrible. Maybe they're at the cabin?

MATSSON

So like – I guess honestly, I want to make this work. And I could do with advice.
(*looks disarmingly open*)
I can find it hard to see the angles on people.

SHIV

Uh-huh.

MATSSON

I get into things and then – I dunno. I don't have good boundaries. I'm doing it now.

SHIV

Look. I think a bump gets you over the line.

Matsson nods – considering it.

MATSSON

So you're saying – if I keep offering more and more money, eventually I'll get it? Thanks, top mind. Is this fun?

Matsson smiles. He has a wrap of coke. He offers—

SHIV

I guess. Why the fuck not?

MATSSON

What did you think of Ebba?

                    SHIV
Um, I dunno.

Texts rolling in to Matsson.

                    MATSSON
People around me are freaking. Ebba's not good. She's very—
She won't let me in. What's your Karolina like?

                    SHIV
Yeah she's good. She's solid.

He does a little bump of coke.

                    MATSSON
Yeah. I'm in 'a bit of a pickle'. People judge me.

                    SHIV
Yeah?

                    MATSSON
Yeah. Lot of judging. *Jantelagen. Jantelagen.* No one is better
than anyone else. Except. Haha, sorry. I am. I'm smarter and I'm
richer and I get more pussy, and I'm landing a chopper on you,
so. People get picky. Snitty.

                    SHIV
Yeah. It's not nice having a helicopter land on you.

He has something to reveal, but first, before he says – a truth test—

                    MATSSON
What's up with your husband-situation thing?

Will she be open?

                    SHIV
Um. We're fucked. It's a disaster. I broke his heart, he broke
mine. Lost our footing. I dunno.

Shiv chooses to do a bump. There seems to be a space—

                    MATSSON
Right. So look I'm not going to say everything – but I was seeing
a woman. And after we split up, because of some things we said
when it was very nice, very intense with us you know?

SHIV

Uh-huh.

MATSSON

Yeah as a nasty sort of friendly joke about what I shouldn't do, I sent her some of my blood.

SHIV

Okay.

MATSSON

A vial, frozen. Like, 'Here, like we said would be dumb.'

SHIV

Right. Yeah, not great?

MATSSON

Then, she was, I thought, kind of amused, now she says she wasn't, but I sent her a half-liter frozen blood brick, as a joke.

SHIV

Half a liter? Okay, well, first of all, 'good one', obviously.

MATSSON

She was a little weirded. But I kept doing it. And it became not a joke, then a joke again, now not a joke.

SHIV

Right.

MATSSON

But it's cool. I think because it isn't like it's illegal?

SHIV

No, but this is— Who is this?

Maybe a cigarette tastes pretty good now.

MATSSON

This is— It's actually Ebba. So it's complex. I feel like she's hoarding it and I'd actually like it back.

SHIV

Naturally. Sounds like she's got more of your blood than you do?

MATSSON

So I can just deny it. Call bullshit, lawyer it out?

>   SHIV
> Deniability is hard, with her having so much of your blood.
> Your own head of comms? Man!

He looks a bit lost.

> Yeah look, I don't know who you've got advising you – but
> I would say, however bad they're telling you this is, you need to
> 10X it.

Matsson just sits, impassive.

> People don't know you. If this acquisition goes through, US
> media is going to be all over you. And if you're the creepy
> stalker who writes code in the dark dripping into an IV bag, and
> harassing his direct reports, that has an economic impact.

>   MATSSON
> It is bad.

>   SHIV
> So three-point PR plan, off the top of my head. Point one. Stop
> sending people your blood.

>   MATSSON
> 'Stop doing it.' Seriously, someone should've told me that clearly.

Shiv thinks on it.

>   SHIV
> Catch and kill maybe? Or just a very open meeting. Do *not* fire
> her. Gerri would be good on this. I can give you some informal
> advice if you like.

>   MATSSON
> I would like that. You're cool. You aren't judgy and you know
> what's a joke. Right? Like your dad.

Matsson smiles. Shiv likes the proximity to power – possibility.

Ding. Matsson gets a message.

> Okay. Smart. Maybe your brothers are getting on the beat?

>   SHIV
> Yeah?

> MATSSON

Yeah. They're gonna screen your movie for us?

EXT. JUVET CAMPUS – NIGHT

Kendall with Jess and Greg.

> KENDALL

Greg, I need some help.

> GREG

Well, sure.

> KENDALL

I have a contact, they're calling you on this line.

> GREG

Uh-huh. Any additional context or—?

> KENDALL

You're just telling a journalist the truth, which is that nobody's getting along. Hugo Baker was kind of made to eat poison mushrooms and shit his pants and the two cultures don't mesh and the deal vibes are bad.

> GREG

Okay. Sour vibes to give us juice in the room? Alright. Quad Squad! Quad assemble!

> KENDALL

And Jess – I need you to liaise with their AV guy. A screening – *Kalispitron: Hibernation* rough-cut. Full three hours.

INT. JUVET CAMPUS – SAUNA – NIGHT

Just Gerri and Oskar left now.

Karl and Frank observe. Oskar is really sweating now. Is he going to leave?

> KARL

By god I think she's got him. I think she's fucking sweated out the Viking.

Inside. He finally gets up. Before he exits – highest compliment, to Gerri—

> OSKAR

You make good sauna.

> GERRI

Thank you. You make good sauna.

And Oskar comes on out. Frank and Karl applaud Gerri discreetly.

DAY THREE

EXT. JUVET CAMPUS – MORNING

Next morning.

INT. JUVET CAMPUS – CONFERENCE CENTER – DAY

Inside, a screening for Kalispitron.

We're aware of Oskar, plus Matsson and a couple of other GoJo team watching. Shuffling in their seats. Not going well. We see a couple of bits of the film and temporary effects over their shoulders but mostly their bored and uncomprehending faces. Shiv stands with Roman at the back. Bit agog at how boring it is.

> SHIV

Jesus. I'd heard it was bad but this is – baggy as fuck. Grueling. Is this smart?

> ROMAN

He wanted to see it, so. I guess.

Shiv gets a text message, shows it to Roman – they head out.

EXT. JUVET CAMPUS – CONFERENCE CENTER – DAY

Greg with Kendall.

Shiv and Roman come out to join Kendall and Greg.

Tom is on his phone, with the Gerri, Frank, Karl gang nearby.

> SHIV

Hey. Seen the nasty little gossip piece about out here? No one's getting on? Bad vibes. Where's this come from?

> KENDALL

Shiv?

Looks like: Below my pay grade.

> GREG

Them I guess, trying to put the squeeze on you?

> SHIV

Uh-huh.

Maybe tracks, but she might vaguely sense more going on.

> ROMAN

We heard you were getting close with Lukas last night?

> SHIV

Jealous?
> (*then*)

Just working the case. Looking for our angles.

> KENDALL

Right. Get anything we can use?

She thinks. Looks at them.

Ebba slips out. Give a thumbs up.

> EBBA
> (*escaping*)

Going back!
> (*so boring*)

Intriguing!

Jess heads over. Jess has evidently managed to establish some sort of working relationship and we might clock that Ebba is preparing to give over some useful intel . . .

> SHIV

Honestly, nah, I think he wants ATN for real. So he might go high.

Frank and Karl and Gerri come over.

> GERRI

What's the plan?

> ROMAN

Up on the ridge. Crunch time.

> KENDALL

Pitch is – we retain ATN, and we'll bite at one-four-six. Or – he takes ATN, but we need a crazy premium. Good?

> SHIV

Uh-huh. Good.

> GERRI/FRANK/KARL

Good.

Kendall and Roman head off. The group splits. Tom and Greg awkward.

> TOM

Good morning, Gregory.

> GREG

Good morning, Thomas.

Nods, Greg heads off. Different sides of the deal. Shiv and Tom left.

> TOM

What are you hearing? I hear Jiménez thinks he's going to tap-dance across Lake Michigan.

Shiv feeling once again a little cut out—

> SHIV

You know, you should be careful, Tom.

He looks like: Why?

People are coming down from molly.
> (*then*)

Their pupils are dilated. Your sneakers are like looking at the sun. They're dangerous.

She starts dragging mud from the bottom of her walking boots over his trainers.

> TOM

What are you doing?

> SHIV

I'm helping. This is why no one takes you seriously, Tom. Your shoes are too white.

Shiv's bullying him, but there's a sexual energy to it. Impulsively, Tom flicks her ear. She recoils, 'horrified'.

> TOM

Your earlobes are thick and chewy.

> SHIV

Hey! What the fuck?

She scuffs.

> TOM

Like barnacle meat.

He flicks.

> SHIV

You look like a kindergartner on the first day of school.

She scuffs.

> TOM

Nice chat with Lukas?

He flicks.

> SHIV

Sure I mean he's boring but he's very conventionally attractive. He's broad. I thought you were broad but compared to him you're wiry. You're a fucking spelunker.

INT. CABLE CAR – DAY

Clank clank, up they climb. Maybe a helicopter heading up.

Roman's phone goes. A message from Connor – a photo attached, that we never see.

> ROMAN

Ugh.

> KENDALL

What?

ROMAN

From Con. It's Dad. But it's not Dad. Oh, man. Oh, man.

KENDALL

I'm sorry.

ROMAN

Do you wanna see?

KENDALL

I— No I don't, is it okay?

ROMAN

It's I dunno, man. I dunno. Fuck.

Roman is a bit caged in there now, waiting to get out . . .

EXT. MOUNTAIN RIDGE – DAY

As Kendall and Roman head in, Matsson meets them heading out.

Leads them back out again, onto the ridge, where his helicopter landed.

MATSSON

People are fucking tiny, right?

He leads them on.

Thanks for the movie.

KENDALL

No worries. Early cut. Lot of work but we're excited.

MATSSON

Yeah?

KENDALL

Yeah, needs to be, strategically. Few issues but exciting.

ROMAN

It's all going to be fine is the headline.

MATSSON

But?

ROMAN

Kalispitron: Hibernation. The first two hours are basically a sleeping robot. We can fix it. We're taking control of the cut. But the lowdown – it's spiraling, and tomorrow, soon there will be a press thing about it being – you know. 'In crisis' or whatever, it's fine. Hollywood, always in fucking crisis, right? Their favorite vegan cantina closes – crisis.

MATSSON

Sure. But this is a big one?

KENDALL

Look, the studio is out of control. It's a cultural issue. But it's cool. The fix is easy. We only flag so you know we're not hiding.

MATSSON

Okay?

They walk. Silence.

So, look, are you for real? That movie. Are you Scooby-Dooing me? Is that where you went? Hanna-Barbera fucking business school? Telling me your theme parks are haunted? You tanking the deal?

KENDALL

No, man. Being open. It's just on our models and the banks' models there needs to be more value for the board to get conviction on this.

MATSSON

Oh? The bankers? Yeah yeah yeah.

KENDALL

Well. Sure. But they're skeptical. Also, the pace. We're worried about the pace. We will need to slow this down just a little.

ROMAN

We have the election, then there'll be the transition. And we have some relationships, so in terms of the regulatory [issues we'd face]—

MATSSON

You know I think I preferred doing this with your dad. He was a prick, but he knew what he wanted.

ROMAN

Okay. Pedant's corner – Dad was not a prick.

> MATSSON

No sure. But he was.

> KENDALL

There are just a lot of problems is the honest truth.

> MATSSON

I need to make this happen fast.

> KENDALL

Like I say, that could be an issue. I think we will have to take it easy. We're committed. But this is a marathon, not a sprint.

> MATSSON

I actually think he'd be embarrassed, if he could see this. His two big boys. Playing Scooby-Doos.
> (then)
Am I going to have to go round you, talk to the board, talk to the old ones?

Matsson crosses to urinate. Roman thinks, then finally activates and walks towards Matsson—

> KENDALL

Rome—?

Roman approaches Matsson, urinating against a rock.

> ROMAN

I was just thinking – remember? When you asked me when my dad was going to die?

> MATSSON

It was a joke, Roman.

After a beat, Roman comes up next to him. He gets very close, so that he's talking into Matsson's ear.

> ROMAN

Uh-huh. But you really couldn't fucking reschedule? Ah? You couldn't push by a fucking week? My sister's fucked. My brother's a mess. I'm fucking dead and you drag us out here, you inhuman fucking – dogman?

> MATSSON

Easy, brother.

ROMAN

You fucking killed him. You ground things out for six months, you drained his life, and then you made us come over here because you couldn't wait a few more fucking days?

MATSSON

Hey, bro—?

ROMAN

We're not selling. Okay? We'll grind you down, sand in the gears, every email takes six months and we'll all waste hundreds of millions of dollars and in the end you'll get bored.

MATSSON

Yeah?

ROMAN

Yeah. I fucking hate you.

Matsson looks to him, amused.

And if you tell the board I said any of this I'll say it was a negotiating tactic. And maybe it is. But it isn't. So fuck you.

MATSSON

You just fucked yourself.
(*to Kendall*)
You hear what he just said?

ROMAN

Yeah fuck you. I'm kidding. It's tactics, bitch. It's fucking tactics!

Roman walks off.

INT. CABLE-CAR STATION – DAY

Roman and Kendall.

KENDALL

That wasn't the plan, Rome.

ROMAN

Yeah, well, the plan sucked.

KENDALL

It was dumb. We're exposed.

> ROMAN

Dad would have told him to fuck off, so I told him to fuck off.

Kendall can't really argue with that.*

EXT. JUVET CAMPUS – RECEPTION – DAY

The Waystar team stands by their vans. A GoJo delegation is there to see them off. Ray does some last-minute ass-kissing, shaking hands with a member of the GoJo team.

> RAY

Such hospitality. I tell you, I am just *cuckoo* for working with this team.

> FRANK

What's he saying. What's with the cuckoos?

> KARL

I believe either that beautiful moron thinks cuckoo clocks come from Norway, or that we're in Switzerland?

INT. ROY PRIVATE JET – FRONT CABIN – DAY

With Hugo, Karolina, Ray, Mark, in hushed conversation. Looking at Kendall and Roman.

> RAY

I thought Ken looked – solemn, maybe danger. Maybe no deal?

> HUGO

Ken's unreadable. It's Roman you want to eyeball. He's agitated. I think they got closed?

INT. WAYSTAR JET – BACK CABIN – DAY

Kendall and Roman have laptops and papers spread out in front of them. Kendall engaged. Something on Roman's mind. Finally—

> ROMAN

Jess – I need to make a pee-pee. Could you bottle me?

---

* Once we saw the cut we were able to change the tone of this scene with alternative dialogue used via ADR.

Jess smiles and stands. She goes through to the galley. Pours away a carafe of water. Hands it to a stewardess.

Gerri, Karl and Frank enter, trailed by Shiv.

> FRANK
> (*re phone*)

Matsson.

> KENDALL

Oh yeah—?

> FRANK

Okay. Well thank you. Do you want to— No?

End of call. Phone down.

Revised offer.

A jolt through Kendall and Roman.

> FRANK
> (*this is big*)

One ninety-two—

> KARL

Another five-buck bump. Okay!

Shiv takes this in. The deal she suggested.

> GERRI

He really wanted ATN.

> KARL

It's a home-run, boys. Hail the conquering heroes!

> GERRI

That's – that's— Your dad would be— [proud.] Yeah, that's good work.

Kendall and Roman try not to react.

> KENDALL

Excellent. Let's run the numbers and take it to the board.

> KARL
> (*to a stewardess*)

Could we maybe get some champagne?

INT. ROY PRIVATE JET – FRONT CABIN – DAY

Tom sits, desolate. Shiv enters.

> SHIV
>
> Looks like there's a deal, Matsson takes ATN. Whole caboodle.

> TOM
>
> Okay?

He maintains a poker face.

> SHIV
>
> It's okay to be happy, Tom. The Great Escape!

> TOM
>
> Well, we'll see I guess.

Beat.

> SHIV
>
> Anyway, we think it's time for some moves at ATN. I'm not happy.

What's coming?

> TOM
>
> Uh-huh? Okay, you're really gonna do this?

> SHIV
>
> Cyd's getting too close with Mencken, little bit power-crazed post-Dad. She's gotta go.

He looks at her.

> TOM
>
> Oh, you think?

> SHIV
>
> Uh-huh. You wanna let her know?

> TOM
>
> Sure. Sure.

> SHIV
> (*then*)
> Don't get an erection, Tom, it's weird.
> (*then*)
> Wanna get dinner when we get back?

TOM

Um . . . I don't know.

Shiv gets a phone call. She steps away.

SHIV

Excuse me. Important.

Answers.

MATSSON
(on phone)

Are you with your brothers?

Intercut with:

INT. MATSSON'S CABIN — DAY

MATSSON
(into phone)

Could you take a photo and send me a picture of their faces?

Shiv looks over at Kendall and Roman. She enjoys the feeling of being inside.

We're aware of the rest of the C-suite, the news rippling. Hugo, Ray, Mark, Karolina with Frank and Gerri.

Gerri gets a ping. Interesting. She shows Karolina. Discreetly.

HUGO

Superb. Superb outcome.

But Hugo can see something on the phone.

Is that it? Is that the kill list.

Gerri and Karolina.

GERRI

Jess managed to get a little something. Early draft. GoJo finance list of potential severance costs. Highly provisional. Caveated and subject to change. Would just be an interpretation but—

HUGO

Gerri. C'mon. Don't leave us hanging—

                              GERRI
Okay. If you insist. In seemingly no particular order . . . It would
seem, potentially surplus to requirements are—

Various emotions on all the faces on death row.

Ray.

                              RAY
Godfuckingdammit!

                              GERRI
Mark.

                              MARK
Shit.

                              GERRI
Hugo.

                              HUGO
That slalom motherfucker!

                              GERRI
Frank.

It's what Frank wanted but he doesn't love hearing it this way.

                              FRANK
Naturally. I mean it's speculation.

                              GERRI
Karl.

                              KARL
Let the good times roll!

                              HUGO
What about Karolina?

                              GERRI
Retained.

Karolina says nothing. Just nods. Even more infuriating.

                              FRANK
And you?

Gerri makes a modest face – retained.

> KARL

Tom? Tom must be on the list?

Gerri shakes her head. Nope.

> HUGO

Great weekend. Highly fucking productive.
> *(to Gerri)*

So much for being raised by wolves.

Karl hands around champagne. Ray first.

> KARL

Hey, Ray? You fucking bozo. Cuckoo clocks are from Switzerland.

A beat as it registers with Ray.

Episode Six
LIVING+

Written by Georgia Pritchett & Will Arbery
Directed by Lorene Scafaria

Original air date 30 April 2023

Cast

LOGAN ROY	Brian Cox
KENDALL ROY	Jeremy Strong
GREG HIRSCH	Nicholas Braun
SHIV ROY	Sarah Snook
ROMAN ROY	Kieran Culkin
TOM WAMBSGANS	Matthew Macfadyen
FRANK VERNON	Peter Friedman
KARL MULLER	David Rasche
GERRI KELLMAN	J. Smith-Cameron
KAROLINA NOVOTNEY	Dagmara Dominczyk
HUGO BAKER	Fisher Stevens
LUKAS MATSSON	Alexander Skarsgård
JESS JORDAN	Juliana Canfield
TABITHA	Caitlin FitzGerald
JOY PALMER	Annabeth Gish
JADE	Alli Brown
DENNY	Abraham Makany
LANA	Holly Cinnamon
JAMAL	Micah Peoples
RAJ	Afsheen Misaghi
PETER	John Quilty
LOLA	Maggie Siciliano
ROMY	Eureka Nakano Grimes
SARAH	Katie Lee Hill
DIRECTOR	Lorene Scafaria
CATHLEEN CARMICHAEL	Kelly Nash
STAGE MANAGER	Natalie Woolams-Torres

DAY ONE

INT. WAYSTAR LA – PREP ROOM – DAY

In close, on a screen. Logan is talking to camera.

He's in a mid head-and-shoulders shot. Maybe in a hastily prepared studio. Up against green screen.

> LOGAN
> (*on screen*)
> —what this new product offers is community. Safe, secure community, enriched with integrated interactions with the cherished family of Waystar's movie and TV characters.
> (*then*)
> I'm convinced that the Living Plus real-estate brand can bring the cruise ship experience to dry land, and provide a significant boost to the earnings of our parks division. I couldn't be more excited—

> DIRECTOR
> (*offscreen*)
> Can I stop you there?

She's a professional; someone whispers a note to her. A beat that goes on just a little too long, a murmur off-camera.

> Um, the thought is can we maybe do just one more?

Logan just stares at the director.

> The thought was just maybe a touch more upbeat?

> LOGAN
> That was 'the thought'?

> DIRECTOR
> (*nervous laugh*)
> Just – be good to get it as good as it can be.

> LOGAN
>
> Oh you think we should get it as good as it can be?

Murmur from off.

> DIRECTOR
>
> Like could you maybe sound more excited when you say the word 'excited'?

Logan stares back. There's no way he's going to do that. Gives her a cool look.

Logan is on a screen. Kendall is watching the clip.

In a prep room at the Waystar LA offices with an audio-visual set-up so that Kendall can watch clips and the prepared pieces of Waystar promotional material.

There are paperwork and box files that have been brought in.

On screen – a make-up person steps into frame briefly to adjust.

> LOGAN
>
> Can you *please* stop buzzing around me. You're fucking useless, the lot of you, you're as bad as my idiot fucking moithering kids.

Lana from investor relations, Hugo, Jess, Jade, the event coordinator, and Jamal, the editor, all watch along. Wince at the comment. Maybe share glances but don't catch Kendall's eye.

> KENDALL
>
> It's okay. That's fine. That's a Valentine's card.
> (*then*)
> I dunno. I dunno. I don't really know where we use it? I think it's just me and Rome, right?
> (*to the editor*)
> But Jamal. Can you shoot me a link for that take?

Maybe we end the sequence on a still of Logan on screen, frozen, staring into the camera with displeasure.

INT. SHIV'S JET – DAY

Shiv is watching the clip of Logan. She stays impassive.

Her phone goes.

                    SHIV

Hey.

                    MATSSON
                   (*on phone*)

Hey. So?

                    SHIV

So what?

                    MATSSON

You coming over?

She looks out of the window.

Over across the way we can maybe see Matsson peering out of his jet's window.

                    SHIV

Why?

Intercut with:

INT. MATSSON'S JET – DAY

                    MATSSON

Maybe my jet has recently been swept for bugs and maybe I'm Paranoid Peter who finds it hard to trust?
                   (*then*)
You came two thousand miles, you can't come twenty more meters?

INT. SHIV'S JET – DAY

                    SHIV

I am simply stopping to refuel at a convenient facility en route to our product launch and there's not even any reason for me to get off. So.

End of call. Maybe she waves out the window.

EXT. PRIVATE JET TERMINAL – DAY

We're somewhere in the west – California, Colorado, Utah.

Two private jets are near each other.

Eventually, Matsson comes down his stairs and walks over.

INT. SHIV'S JET – DAY

Matsson comes down the plane to her and sits.

> MATSSON
>
> Tired interior.

> SHIV
>
> Ouch, that hurts. Don't criticize my jet interior!
> *(looks at him)*
> So?

> MATSSON
>
> Nothing. I just thought it would be good to check in and you know – this product launch, investor thing.

She looks like: Yes, what?

> And why you are doing this bullshit?

> SHIV
>
> Well I'm sure we're keeping you fully informed through the proper channels.

Shiv puts on some expensive hand cream.

> MATSSON
>
> Old Father Frank. It's dry. Why? With your dad, the election?

> SHIV
>
> It is on the calendar. If we cancelled a product launch, it'd look like we were just minding the store till you come in.

> MATSSON
>
> You are. Right? I don't need it. I told Frank, I don't need it. Land cruises.

> SHIV
>
> Living Plus.

MATSSON

Land cruises. 'Hey, you know how fucking heartbreaking and shitty it is being locked up on a cruise? How about that but you also get to stay in one place?'

SHIV

According to our market research, people respond.
(*off his look, shrugs*)
People are weird.

MATSSON

It's bullshit. I'm not gonna pursue, so, why announce?

SHIV

Well that's presumptuous.

He takes the hand cream, she takes it back. He looks at her.

MATSSON

You were nice in Norway.

SHIV

I was trying to keep us on track.

He considers – here's the offer—

MATSSON

Okay. Here's my situation. The deal is going through. Velocity. Lots of it, lots of you, I really like. IP, catalogue, facilities, footprint, news possibilities. But. Lots of it I really hate. Lot of rooms I never want to go into. So, someone who knows all that from the inside, but who gets me, could be very valuable.

SHIV

Exciting. Sort of executive museum guide?

MATSSON

Ha! Nah nah nah. Something cool.

SHIV

Such as?

MATSSON

Something amazing.

SHIV

Something 'amazing'? Ooooh! You hooked me, reel me in!

> MATSSON

Hey, I like to work, I like— I'll like spend a whole summer reading GoJoGo consumer grumble tickets – fixing shit. And I like strategy – climb in my time machine right now to neutralize downstream threats with an acquisition or whatever. But I don't need the captain's hat. So. Gap. Possible gap.

There could be a captain's hat going? Shiv isn't uninterested.

> SHIV

Uh-huh?

Maybe Matsson goes a little goofy and mocking of her coolness—

> MATSSON

'Uh-huh uh-huh uh-huh'?? C'mon, can we talk?

> SHIV

Maybe I hate you?

> MATSSON

You can't hate me, you don't know me well enough.

> SHIV

Maybe I'm intuitive. Maybe I just know.
> (*then*)
> Maybe I love my brothers very much.

He looks at her.

> MATSSON

Did they mention about when they went totally fucking mental on me up above Åndalsnes? Totally unprofessional. Totally dumb?

Sounds possible. She maybe felt something had happened but not that. But she's not about to admit anything—

> SHIV

Sure.

> MATSSON

No?

> SHIV

Look. You spoke. I listened. But I should go. I think my flight's about to leave.

(*calling out*)

Start the engines!

He's dismissed. Maybe starts to get up. But there is the next stage of an understanding maybe developing. They play it cool with their words while giving each other enough eyes to tell another story—

MATSSON

Okay. But keep me looped, yeah? My girl on the inside.

SHIV

Fuck you, my boy on the outside. I'm going to tell my brothers everything you said.

MATSSON

Cool. Nothing to hide. Nothing I wouldn't tell them myself.

Also untrue. And he heads off. As Shiv watches and thinks.

INT. ROMAN'S LA HOUSE – BEDROOM – DAY*

Roman heads out. Tabitha is asleep. Roman is all cocky. Bit of a breakthrough last night.

EXT./INT. WAYSTAR LA – DAY

Roman heading in, in his car.

We get a sense of the Waystar offices in LA. Maybe they are on the same lot as the studio or nearby.

In past security.

INT. WAYSTAR LA – DAY

Shiv ahead with her assistant (Sarah).

Tom is with Greg. Gerri and Frank nearby walking the same way, or otherwise in earshot, so their conversation is public—

---

* This episode was a tough one to cut down and in the end we had to lose the entirety of the Tabitha–Roman story and most of the Greg–Tom subplot. These were the strands we chose chiefly because they lifted out so cleanly, but also because the edit generates its own powerful centrifugal force – throwing off material which is further from the show's core questions and concerns.

TOM

After this, I need to be solidly online with New York, okay?
Then, once election rehearsal is done I've got the— I can look at
my speech before, what the investor reception?

*Greg looks for Tom's eye but can't catch it so gives a very overly
straight response—*

GREG

Yes, Tom. I've been helping them. And, it's a really good
space. Great for you to circulate. Good opportunities for
exchanging ideas, comparing of metrics and interfacing with key
stakeholders vis-à-vis business matters.

Spots the odd diction.

TOM

You mean talking to people? Greg, are you okay?

*Greg winks. Karl or Shiv goes into the meeting room. Gerri heads
over to talk to an LA colleague. Meaning Tom and Greg can talk
privately. Greg angles them so they are alone.*

GREG
(*whispered*)

I've hacked it!

TOM

Hacked what?

GREG

The investor reception! I've spoken to the studio and word has
gone out to PRs and agencies and the celebs, the models, the
various assorted hotties, are lined up! It's gonna be like one part
investor to three parts hottie! And when the suits fade away, the
Disgusting Brothers will play!

TOM

Greg. No. Cyd's dead. I've got to give the ATN piece of the
investor day. Matsson will be watching. Like a Scandi Sauron.
I am fighting for my fucking corporate life. No time for
engaging in – degradation.

GREG

Tom? I did this for you, man. You specifically said we should 'take a trip to titty town'.

TOM

To – Greg. No. Polling. Rehearsals, projections. I haven't slept more than three hours a night for four weeks. I should be in six different places.

Greg looks all sad.

What?? Why are you looking so . . .

GREG

I have just done quite a lot of preparation for the launch of Disgusting Bros, LLC. Lickin' Lots of You-Know-What.

TOM

Well *sorry*, Greg. I'd love to be licking lots of you-know-what, but we are days out from a very fissile very historic election.

GREG

I am aware, Tom. My dad texts me three times a day about ATN. He refers to me as 'my son Goebbels' on the family's WhatsApp.

Roman is now there, swaggering past. Maybe he does something rude and expressive of his new potency. A sap touch or hip thrust.

ROMAN

Yo, cucks!

Gerri is outside talking to an LA colleague.

Ger-Bear! Say how do you fare, oh world's biggest square?

GERRI

Fine. You?

ROMAN

Oh good. Tired. Tired.

GERRI

Uh-huh. Jet lag?

ROMAN
(*no*)

Oh sure. *Sure.* Say, listen, G-Spot. Can I get two?

She looks around, she'd rather not. But, sure. They manage to find a space. It's private but Roman is all open and 'honest'.

Yeah, just been meaning to say for a while? An apology.

> GERRI

For what?

> ROMAN

What? For everything. Like in your bathroom. My psychosexual whatever stuff. Hang-ups, act-outs.

> GERRI

I don't have the faintest idea what you're talking about.

> ROMAN

Sure. But – that was all kinda, embarrassing. Childish.
> (*a kind of explanation*)
Tabs is in town. And maybe it's the grief, or whatever, but I'm just – feeling very, potent.

> GERRI

Let the bugle sound.

> ROMAN

I'm exhausted to be honest, Ger. From all the heteronormative vanilla 'how's ya father'. Will you nudge me if I drop off?

> GERRI

No.

> ROMAN

Look. I just have some perspective and it's a horrible time but maybe I'm getting through some stuff, so?

> GERRI

Well bully for you.

Kendall is arriving with a little entourage. They lock eyes. They have a plan.

> KENDALL

Hey. Okay? You good? Ready?

> ROMAN

Ready.

(*for Gerri*)
Standing to attention. Ready to go at it. Hard.

They head in.

INT. WAYSTAR LA – MEETING ROOM – DAY

Inside.

Frank, Gerri, Karl, Tom, Shiv, Kendall, Roman, Karolina.

Kendall and Roman are settling.

> FRANK
>
> Welcome! Welcome, thanks for finding the time. So as
> I understand it. Our CEOs wanted to give us a 'sensitive' in-
> person update, on negotiations, correct?

> KENDALL
>
> Correct. So. Look, overall, very exciting. Questions regarding his
> full understanding of the whole business.

> FRANK
>
> But, still, theoretically, and contingently, exciting?

> ROMAN
>
> Your favorite kind of exciting. Look, we're pleased with the
> offer we extracted. Price is great.

> TOM
>
> Knocked it out the park, you guys.

Karl bangs on his desk a little. Others murmur agreement.

> KENDALL
>
> But. As we are preparing our board recommendation, in good
> conscience we need to give some – confidential – context to this
> senior group and seek your advice.

Shiv switches to alert – doesn't feel right.

> ROMAN
>
> Long story short. Matsson exhibited some – what you'd call
> erratic behavior. That got us concerned.

> SHIV
>
> What is this?

KENDALL

On our final round out there, before we elicited the offer. You should know, Matsson – went a, like little I guess 'crazy', on top of the mountain.

SHIV

What *exactly* happened?

ROMAN

We were pushing him, gently, on what we wanted, how much, and – how would you describe it, Ken?

KENDALL

I'd call it shitting the bed. Meltdown. Human Chernobyl.

ROMAN

Right. He pulled a fuckabout. Carnival of bile and bullshit.

KAROLINA

But, specifically?

ROMAN

He started shouting about how, we didn't know what a good deal was, how he didn't even especially want the deal—

Tom likes the deal.

TOM

He didn't want the deal?

ROMAN

It was his SLT who liked the deal, we 'better take what was on the table'.

TOM

That smells like a negotiating position. Cos he made the offer?

Kendall and Roman look at each other and shrug.

ROMAN

It wasn't coherent. He was like, saying he was stringing us along and he'd pull the deal and come back when we were weakened or leave us to bleed out.

The Old Guard look at one another. Shiv stares at Kendall and Roman.

FRANK

So you think— What do you think?

ROMAN

Honestly, I don't know. He was maybe getting cold feet and wanted us to walk was how it felt?

KENDALL

We're concerned. Loose cannon. We got the sense of chaotic strategy. Misunderstanding of our business. Where we're at and what can drive value.

SHIV

And so what are you suggesting?

Frank is computing, wise old bird.

KENDALL

I guess the question is, can we recommend a deal with – someone of this – character. Given, everything else and so on? Tweets, drug rumors.

(*then*)

Fifty percent in stock – we're exposed.

People consider. This is Gerri's view, but maybe she is more ready to speak because of her Roman exchange?

GERRI

Shall I go? Okay it's a worry. It is a concern and we should monitor closely.

KENDALL

Uh-huh.

GERRI

I don't think it hurts. He's a genius. No one minds a genius acting weird. Warren Buffett could strangle cats and still get a table at Carbone.

TOM

Honestly, kinda probably adds to the mystique?

Frank and Karl exchange looks. Karl wants the deal big time.

KARL

I'd say: what do we know? He's a – generational oddball. But generational talent. Warrior stance. Credible audacity. And we know he made the offer. We know his bank and legal team are progressing in professional fashion.

> GERRI

His reputation is priced in.

Kendall and Roman exchange looks. Should they push?

> ROMAN

Okay, well. Good.

Frank looks a little more concerned.

> KENDALL

Okay, I think we feel covered. Just letting you know and we – we move ahead with what we know, yes?

> FRANK

Thanks for keeping us informed, I'll consider how we handle with the board. Let's make this the start of a conversation, yes?

> ROMAN

Absolutely.

> FRANK

Great. Well, *bonne chance*, for the launch, onwards, and upwards, and other – motivational maxims!

Frank shares looks with Roman and Kendall. More concerned. The meeting breaks. People check in with one another in huddles as they exit.

Shiv is staying looking at papers, apparently.

Shiv is pretty sure she's figured out their game. And it's all a little amusing, and makes her feel better about her own potential duplicity. She has them over a barrel. Kendall can sense she has sniffed them out.

> KENDALL

Sorry we didn't mention. We were hoping to keep things dry.

> SHIV

Uh-huh? Yeah?

> ROMAN

Vanity stopped us, maybe – we were proud of the deal from raising it earlier so—

SHIV

Oh *sure.*

She looks at them. For a while.

KENDALL

What?

She just stares.

SHIV

Do you think I'm dumb?

KENDALL

Hey. Shiv.

SHIV

I know you.

ROMAN

What?

SHIV

I fucking know you!

They look at her. She stares back at them, a little amused.

ROMAN

What?

SHIV

'What?'

ROMAN

What?

Kendall can't quite meet her eye.

SHIV

You're not very good at this, boys. Are you? I know you!
I fucking know you! 'Dad, Shiv spilt chocolate milk in the Range
Rover.'

(*then*)

You're trying to fuck the deal.

Beat. Do the boys share an eye flick?

ROMAN

No.

> SHIV

Oh yeah? But you never mentioned this, this quite fucking interesting incident? Even as a bit of gossip?

Shiv looks to Kendall.

Go on, lie to me, lie to my face.

Then—

> KENDALL

We're not sure about the deal.

Roman: Thanks, pal, left me hanging there.

> ROMAN
> (*aside*)

Thanks, man.

> KENDALL

We were going to say. It was the plan to tell you. We were protecting you.

> SHIV

Oh, thanks, guys, don't get mud on my confirmation dress! Thanks so fucking much!

> ROMAN

It did go nuts on the mountain, Shiv. He was talking shit about Dad.

> KENDALL

We're making plans on the fly. Dad. I dunno, we want to make sure we're not zombie-marching to the funky drummer.

It's a half-truth, mixed in with the honesty.

Listen, will you help? We need you. He's not right for us.

> SHIV

Oh okay? Here's the invite, lost in the mail for a while, but here it is?

> ROMAN

We left you out cos we thought it was for the best for [you to be able to claim]—

SHIV

The idea was, we were getting out, clean, doing Pierce, buying Pierce, together. What happened?

KENDALL

Maybe we can keep it? All of us? And Pierce?

She looks at them both.

ROMAN

This was groundwork. We need you. Gonna be cold for us up there, pitching.

SHIV

Shivvy cheering from the stands?

KENDALL

Let's all get up on stage, Shiv. Me and him, on the product launch. Then all three of us. Unity?

They look at her.

SHIV

You cocksuckers.

Might we wonder what calculations she is making, what side she's playing here?

I have a lot of options.

Roman feels bad, he did want to bring her in . . . so, from the heart—

ROMAN

Hey, Shiv? I am sorry. We are.

She looks at them.

SHIV

Well. You better be. I could fuck you up.

KENDALL

We got overheated. We wouldn't dick you over. Okay?

ROMAN

One of these?

He offers the hug.

Eventually, shuffling, they go in.

How real is it? How real is anything. A few things live at once in all their different skulls . . . Some number of calculations. For Shiv, Roman and Kendall.

> ROMAN

Okay. We should break this up, cos I'm in heat like a German Shepherd and I'll poke one of your eyes out with my hard-on.

Sarah comes to get Shiv.

> SHIV

I have an important meet. But let's touch base about the choreography if we're all going up, okay?
> (*with a smile*)
You know, so it's clear that I'm the most important?

INT. WAYSTAR LA – CORRIDOR – DAY

Shiv's assistant then leads her along the corridor to a room—

> SARAH

Here you go.

> SHIV

Are we all set up?

> SARAH

Think so.
> (*then*)
Investor relations in twenty?

> SHIV
> (*'I know'*)

Yeah. Thank you.

INT. WAYSTAR LA – MEETING ROOM – DAY

Kendall and Roman, considering the alteration.

> KENDALL
> (*re Shiv*)

I think, it had to happen.
> (*a bit of a lie*)
It was just the timing, right?

ROMAN

Yeah. Exactly, we said, we kind of said. It's good. Absolutely. I'm happy.

They head out.

INT. WAYSTAR LA – SHIV'S MEETING ROOM – DAY

Shiv is set up with a box of tissues and her iPhone before her, on a ten-minute countdown.

She has been crying. But now she's in a state of tired emptiness. We stay with her for a beat before Greg comes in—

GREG

I thought we could . . .

(sees Shiv)

Oh, sorry!

Tom clocks and motions for Greg to go.

TOM

Hey, Shiv, are you—?

SHIV

I'm fine.

TOM

Right?

She is hiding. He waits, comes in.

SHIV

We booked this room.

TOM

Okay, well. Let me, leave you to, I thought this was empty for—

Her alarm maybe goes off. She turns it off. The timer is a signal something odd is going on – Shiv fumbles for it.

Yeah – you really okay?

SHIV

I am very busy and I – I am too busy and what with my dad—

> (*'fuck you if you think it's weird'*)
> I sometimes get Sarah to book me somewhere, to have a
> moment – to cry. Fuck you.

TOM

You're scheduling your grief?

SHIV

Yeah well. I'm organized.

(*on the edge*)

Fuck off.

She gets up and presents her back to him. It makes him feel tender.
She's had a tough time.

TOM

Hey. Shiv. Shiv?

He approaches and gives her a hug. Maybe a little sob. She could do
with some human warmth.

They collapse into each other a bit, maybe she turns to him, they're
both in need of a bit of solace.

And then in their human warmth, the quiet room, death, life all
about, their old connection sparks.

They find each other's mouth for a kiss.

It turns quite passionate and hard surprisingly fast.

Maybe their hands seek each other out quite intimately.

And then it's over.

SHIV

Okay?

TOM

Okay.

SHIV

So what the heck was that?

TOM

Well I think you know what the heck that was.

> (*then*)
> And you know what? There's plenty more where that came from.
> (*then*)
> Are you coming to the investor reception?

INT. WAYSTAR LA — PREP ROOM — DAY

Kendall and Roman with Jess on hand.

Materials for the pitch all around. Both reading and mouthing.

> KENDALL
> Does it feel cheesy to alternate? Should we just do block one, block two?

Roman looks like: You're overthinking, it's fine.

> ROMAN
> And what you think on Matsson. If the Operation 'Fruit Loop' doesn't fly?

> KENDALL
> Um. Muster a share block? Board, convince he's a value destroyer? Regulatory shit? Spook him? Hope the price runs away? I dunno.

> ROMAN
> Matsson doesn't have juice past one-nine-two, Tellis says?

> KENDALL
> No one else to shake out? White Knight? Stewy?

> ROMAN
> I'll call one-eight-hundred White Knights, 'Wanna overpay for something we don't want to give you?'

Jess looks at her watch, coughs.

Roman looks.

> Something about this all does depress me.

> KENDALL
> Uh-huh and do you think it's the speech written specifically for our late father or the fact we're planning to warehouse the

elderly and keep them drunk on content while we suck them dollar-dry? Can we flick, J?

Jess moves through the deck presenting images. Something particularly old-school and saccharine comes up, like Doderick shaking the hand of an old man with his grandson.

It is embarrassing. His eye was off the ball.

> ROMAN
> 'Enhanced medical monitoring'.
> *(then)*
> Ugh. I can smell the boiled cabbage. I'm not saying I want to dance – but the pitch, it needs freshening, tightening. Like your vagina.

Jess slightly stiffens.

> KENDALL
> He means mine. 'Personalized longevity programs'. Is that something?

Roman looks like: Dunno?

Can we see drafts, J? The material they drew on and the team available for context and color. Get me the double-click on 'longevity'. I can see everything. Infinite brainbox. Okay?

> ROMAN
> Maybe I'll ask fucking Joy Palmer if the fucking *Kalispitron* director can come on board and make it all more confusing and loud?

> KENDALL
> That now? Sprinkle some sugar. Full of confidence in her. Right? We need movement. That's priority one. Got to up our velocity, man. We can flywheel this. Paint our names in the sky with fire, bro.

> ROMAN
> Oh sure. Green lights all the way down Sunset. Even she must be able to get a mega-hit from a couple of extra content bil.
> *(then)*
> She's gotten risk averse from working the turkey farm.

KENDALL

Break the log jam, get the franchise pump pumping, yeah? 'Full of confidence'.

Roman's making his way out. Kendall is staring at the screen, whirring.

ROMAN

Oh yeah, I'm love-bombing that stuck-up bitch.

KENDALL

Shoot it to the moon, Rome. New cowboys in town!

ROMAN
(*heading out*)
Who wants to fuck! I'm ready to fuck!!! Hooray for Fuckywood!

EXT. WAYSTAR STUDIO – LOT – DAY

Roman arriving for his meeting with an assistant.

INT. WAYSTAR STUDIO – COMMISSARY – DAY

Roman and Joy Palmer, Waystar Studios executive, meet. A couple of assistants off in the distance. Watching. Maybe the tables around have been cleared to give them some privacy.

JOY

Roman Roy! Hey. We'd all like to offer our sincere condolences.

They do two European kisses.

ROMAN

Hey offer refused. I've got all the condolences I need. Yummy. Full.

JOY

Well, haha. You, but . . . You know?

An overfamiliar smile of sympathy. Maybe the hands come for his.

ROMAN

I do.

JOY

Everyone at the studio was inconsolable. I can't imagine . . .

He's not about to get into it with her.

ROMAN

Well thanks I'm actually okay. I'm largely consolable. So, shall we?

But she likes to make a connection.

JOY

It'll hit you. But remember, you will be okay. It's just time. That's all it is.

ROMAN

Uh-huh. Many thanks. Many.

JOY

You will be fine. And where are you staying, you have the place up—?

Something grates about this faux-maternal energy.

ROMAN

Why do you care? You gonna come round and eat my yum yums?

Could be bad, but they smile.

No, I have Geraint's place, in the Palisades?

JOY

Of course. That house is, that's a fantastic house.

ROMAN

Thank you. Thank you re my house.

Smiles.

JOY

And it's all very exciting, about the deal, what's he like?

ROMAN

Lukas? Great. Flaky. Really druggy. Odd. Not focussed. And – yeah, who knows. Honestly, few issues. Sure I can fix but. So! Can't stand still. I have thoughts.

JOY

Of course!

(*'funny' Groucho even?*)

'Everyone does.'

(*then*)

But, no, please, hit me. I remember you were always so keen with Frank. Bursting with ideas.

ROMAN

Yeah. Well, now we're gonna make some!

JOY

Exactly. Leave it to us. Your dad was very good at letting us donkeys do the donkey work.

ROMAN

Uh-huh, message received. So just to get it out the way, *Kalispitron*. I just want to understand who's getting fired for that shit show?

JOY

Ha! Well, it's been— I can loop you in but, it's been complicated. Shall we sidebar that? Particular situation that one, lot of big personalities.

ROMAN

Okay. Well, can't see that happening again!?

JOY

I take it very seriously. I haven't been sleeping.

ROMAN

You should watch the movie. It needs to lose an hour and find an end.

JOY

Right. Interesting.

(*moving on*)

But look, it's going to be great.

ROMAN

Uh-huh?

                    (*'come on'*)

I guess my thing is should we maybe have been alive to the
limited dramatic possibilities provided by a hibernation. Even a
really big one?

JOY

I hear you.

ROMAN

Look, Joy, I'm turning on the money hose. We want to back you.
I just need to hear you're confident you can get the hit machine
pumping?

JOY

Absolutely.

                    (*then*)

I guess there was one thing we were concerned about. The
rightward lean from ATN and the bleed across. I promised
people, I hope it's not inappropriate but I said I would at least
raise, people are really concerned about democratic institutions?

ROMAN

Uh-huh. Well got it.

Then, she looks—

Oh you want more?

JOY

We've been getting a lot of questions about ATN's favorable
coverage of Mencken, hate groups, the O'Malleys – is there
anything you could do, to signal a distance?

ROMAN

From what? It's an election.

JOY

But from a candidate who's on record supporting—

ROMAN

Mmm mmm mmm. Mencken's IP just like anything. Yeah?
                    (*then*)
I don't like him. You don't like him, but, what we gonna do?

JOY

Sure. It's just in terms of talent. The company – you know, we have values in the creative community here.

ROMAN

I know – love the values. Incredibly evolved, ruthlessly segregated city you've built on your geological fault here.

JOY

We're trying.

ROMAN

I feel like you're not listening to me, Joy. I want to dump a ton of money on you, but we want to get the hit pump pumping. Balance between streaming and theatrical. Franchise creation, international marketing.

JOY

You can trust me. Got it. Exciting.

There's something vacant and dismissive in her positivity.

ROMAN

Okay.

He thinks – leave it or get real?

Look. Joy, I get it. You're thinking what the fuck does this guy know about anything? He's not his dad he can't do it, Roman's track record is bullshit.

JOY

No. I'm sure you are where you are for very good reason.

Is she assuming he's not bright enough to catch that?

ROMAN

But I could also fire you so – oh no you're thinking he's freaking out and saying crazy shit, is he spinning out? Well I'm not, or am I? Poor little boy just wants to call his daddy—
(*mimes phone*)
'Uh Dad I'm with that exec you hated, what do I do? Oh you're dead?'

JOY

I think—

> ROMAN

He says you're fired.

She stares at him.

> Our tentpole is bullshit and out of control and you're not gonna
> fix it. I'm calling it. I'm sorry. We're done.
> > *(the right lines)*
> The company wishes to terminate your employment. HR will be
> in touch to start the process of termination.
> > *(then)*
> Come up to the house sometime!

He's off.

INT. WAYSTAR LA – AUDITORIUM – NIGHT

Kendall on stage with Jade, and an assistant, looking at pages.

> KENDALL

The opening remarks are all potato soup. I don't want all this.
> *(points)*
But it probably needs to get said.
> *(then)*
And Jade. Can we get Lana and Hugo on analyst double-check,
who's confirmed? Let's get Raj primed to throw some softballs.

> JADE

Uh-huh?

> KENDALL
> *(re script)*
Shiv can say this. And this. Let her know.

> JADE
> *(doesn't want to tell Shiv)*
Uh-huh. Sure. I can tell her.

Jade makes a note. Kendall reads on.

> In terms of lighting cues – just so we can brief Kush and the AV
> team—

Kendall stands back and surveys the stage for a moment.

> KENDALL

Could we build me a Living Plus house?

> JADE

Uh-huh, as in—?

> KENDALL

Small, plywood with basic brickwork. Nothing crazy. I could walk through it – ATN on here and my face aging on the wall here.

(*re the screen*)

Maybe clouds appear above the house – don't write this down yet – I saw it in Berlin, check it with— Check it, I have the show in my notes. They can do it. If we can't do the house, let's definitely do the clouds. Then we have my dad appear, out of nowhere, boom – hologram. Or we do it with lights – fucking Pepper's ghost. What do you think?

> JADE

I can talk to the team. Denny?

One of the technical team, Denny, is there – freaked out.

> DENNY

(*no fucking way*)

It's certainly an exciting vision.

> KENDALL

Don't say no, Denny, don't say no!

> DENNY

This is for tomorrow?

> KENDALL

Hollywood, though. Right?

> JADE

We'd like a house, practical build, by tomorrow.

> KENDALL

If we do the house, which I'm not sold on, the house needs to be portable because it needs to not be here until after the intro VT, then suddenly – here!

> DENNY

Portable house.

Kendall can feel the resistance.

> KENDALL
> Okay here's the rule. No one can say no. Okay?

Roman appears, waves hello.

INT. WAYSTAR LA — CORRIDOR — NIGHT

Roman and Kendall and team walking back to the prep room.

> KENDALL
> Good pep talk?

> ROMAN
> Yeah. Yeah. Um, good. I think. Good.

He says nothing else, still not quite sure what happened was real. Looking at a stream of messages from Joy.

> KENDALL
> Okay. And look, I've been looking through the launch deck. I have a big— I have a thought.

Way ahead up a corridor, Greg is on the phone to Tom.

> GREG
> It sounds great, how's the Great Dilution? Are there hotties?

Intercut with:

INT. INVESTOR PARTY — NIGHT

Tom is walking up to the investor party.

> TOM
> Not nailed to the exterior, Greg, no. Now I want you watching the main channel and business; those guys have been pimping the Jiménez child tax credit like we're his whores. I want a stream of emails prepped for me to fire. Little comments and suggestions, okay? One every seven minutes. Clever little observations.

> GREG

Could I not come for just a little while? I can draft caustic emails and be disgusting?

Kendall's walking past Greg in the Waystar corridor.

> KENDALL

Yo. Lanko. Follow me. We're recruiting. Dumb flesh for the room. Henchman shit.

> TOM

What's happening, Greg?

> GREG

Um? Ken's asking me to . . .

> TOM

No, Greg! Back in my room. Get the fuck back in there I can't unplug.

> GREG

Ken – Tom's saying . . .

> TOM

Greg, don't leave my election data center okay? Tell him it's the fucking election of the century and you're the linkman through the night?

> ROMAN

In here.

> TOM

Greg?

> KENDALL

Greg?

> GREG

Ken, can you talk to Tom?

> ROMAN

Tell him you're getting plucked. It's the rapture. The Last Temptation of Greg.

> GREG

I'm being plucked, Tom. It's the rapture.

TOM

That's fucking bullshit, Greg, tell him you're a direct report and that you cannot leave your station. The integrity of the reporting of this election may depend upon it.

Greg hands the phone to Kendall.

KENDALL

Tom? Can we grab Greg to brainstorm?

INT. INVESTOR PARTY – NIGHT

TOM

Go ahead, buddy. Squeeze him dry. My pleasure!

Fuck. End of call. With Tom as he sees Shiv arriving.

She walks over to him.

SHIV

Hey. So, am I cramping your style? You wanna 'get amongst it'?

TOM

'It'?

SHIV

The vaginas of the cheerful women who aren't tall enough to be models?

TOM

Nah, I'm good.

They walk through. Shiv looks at the guests.

SHIV

So, who do you like? What would be your first . . . port of call? Shall I guess?

TOM

Could do.

SHIV

Or. I'll choose. You think you could seduce someone here? Is that what you've been doing? Going up and saying things and being all . . . 'hey'.

He's not about to.

TOM

Listen. Shiv. I guess if I could say one thing, from my heart. It would be just – I am sorry.

SHIV

You're sorry?

TOM

I'm sorry I – fucked you up.

SHIV

Oh, you should be so lucky!
(*looks away, then at him*)
You didn't even scratch the surface. I was fucked long before I met you.

TOM

What, with TK?

SHIV

TK, the Washington situation. You were the one after The One and that's always hard.

TOM

I think I got my chisel in on you.

SHIV

Hardly a scratch. Whereas I'm the whole story for you right? I'm the one who twisted your heart up?

TOM

Yeah I guess.
(*someone from college*)
Mary?

SHIV

Mary! Tom. I did a number on you. 'Mary'?! C'mon. You hadn't had a taste of the dark meat till you met me.

TOM

I'd had my times.

They are quiet – but a comfortable quiet. They know each other well, and it spreads its own warmth.

After a beat—

She looks at him with fun eyes.

SHIV

Wanna play Bitey?

TOM

Bitey?

SHIV

Bitey. We never played Bitey? You bite me, I bite you, see who can take it?

TOM

Okay, sure.

They take a moment, then, figuring it out as it goes, maybe Shiv leading as she offers her forearm to him and she takes his and pushes up his shirt to find a spot about halfway up the forearm.

SHIV

Okay? If you stop, the other stops. And you lose. Ready?

TOM

I guess. Bitey?

SHIV

Exactly. One two three: Bitey.

Someone walks past.

Tom raises eyebrows to say 'hi', even as he bites and is bitten.

They bite slowly, slowly increasing the pressure.

Looking into each other's eyes, slowly increasing the pressure. Maybe goading one another with little noises they can utter as they bite.

TOM

Aghh.

SHIV

Uh-huh?

They go on for maybe three, four, five seconds of increasing pressure.

TOM

Aggghgh.

> SHIV
> *(through her bite, without releasing)*
Is that all you've got?

Tom's eyes glint, he bites down and she stops, shocked with the pain.

> SHIV
Aghh. Motherfucker!

She rubs her arm. She laughs. Delighted.

> TOM
Bitey. You okay?

Bite marks. But quite intimate.

INT. WAYSTAR LA – PREP ROOM – NIGHT

Kendall there with Roman and Greg.

> KENDALL
So. My pitch is. It's sizable and it's for our ears only. Maybe not even our ears. We should maybe have our fingers in our ears as I say this.

> ROMAN
> *(re Greg)*
You okay with this, gigantic listening device?

> KENDALL
We can trust Greg. Dead under Matsson. Right, Greggy?

> GREG
Correct. Dead and buried under my nemesis Lukas Matsson.

> KENDALL
So. I've got a thought. If the Matsson weirdo thing isn't going to play.

> ROMAN
Don't think we can pull that statue down right now. His dick's too golden.

> KENDALL
So. I've been through the material and I have a pitch. We make this about us. Show analysts what *we* can do for shareholder

value. Unbelievable growth. Drive the price, we make the deal impossible. I spoke to Tellis.

> GREG
>
> Oh, so all you need is unbelievable growth?

> ROMAN
>
> Hey, Doctor Sarcasmo, did we ask you to squeak? Stand easy, pitch wall.

> KENDALL
>
> If we can drive above one-nine-two, no one thinks Matsson has the juice. He has to walk.

> ROMAN
>
> Chase him out of town on price?
> > (*big reach*)
>
> Okay?

Kendall has some stuff pulled out.

> KENDALL
>
> I think we can get a tech valuation for a real-estate proposition on this.

> ROMAN
>
> Living Plus?

> GREG
>
> It is hard to make houses seem like tech? We've had houses for a while?

> KENDALL
>
> We need to make analysts look at the company differently. This is the killer app. We have relationships with pharma and longevity tech, I think, I think, we fold health, the ARR numbers get explosive. Maximize your physical potential, live . . . well not forever—

> ROMAN
>
> Why not forever?

> KENDALL
>
> Well sure, if not forever, live more, forever.

> ROMAN
>
> Live more forever. Pitch bot? Is it dope?

They look at Greg.

>   GREG
>
> It's kind of dope.

>   KENDALL
>
> Like a robot please, pitch bot.

>   GREG
>   *(after hesitation, like a robot voice)*
> 'It – is – kind – of dope.'

>   KENDALL
>
> We can push this to the moon. Big bump, lets us tell a growth
> story, growth value, in a value company. I mean, sweet potato
> pie?

Roman has the Living+ numbers laid out.

>   ROMAN
>
> The numbers aren't there yet. What can we go to, fracking the
> silver dollar?

>   KENDALL
>
> On projections. Where can we go? I guess the sweet spot would
> be . . . right after they get fucking delicious but just before they
> get fucking stupid?
>   *(then)*
> Greg, get Jess. I need a word person to word this shit up for me?

>   ROMAN
>
> And one of Karl's droids. And Shiv, we fold in Shiv, right?

>   KENDALL
>
> Right. Greg, we have a lot to keep on track. Okay? You have to
> be a big dog and bark for us. Okay?

Roman is flicking through the papers.

>   ROMAN
>
> I like it. I mean I'm not crazy myself, about dying.

>   KENDALL
>
> I know, right? Bullshit.

                              ROMAN

I can't help thinking it was kind of – not— It was very— I didn't
see it coming. For Dad.

                              KENDALL

Very un-Dad.

                              ROMAN

And I think people will be very intrigued if there's another way
through the whole situation?

                              KENDALL

You mean life?

                              ROMAN

Life, death, yeah. Yeah.
                              (flicks)
Get loaded onto a chip. Fired up someone's ass. Float around as
a gas. Live in a tortoise. There has to be ways through. Death
just feels very 'one size fits all'?

Kendall's phone is going.

                              KENDALL

Uh-huh, uh-huh. Right. Greg – audio-visuals. The clouds, yeah?
Chase it!

Gerri enters.

                              GERRI

Roman. I need to talk to you.

                              ROMAN

Sure, Gerri-Berry. Five.

Roman knows what she wants. But tries to play it unworried.

INT. WAYSTAR LA – CORRIDOR SPACE – NIGHT

Roman comes out.

                              ROMAN

Hey. So what is it. I'm busy.

                              GERRI

What happened?

He looks like: What?

With Joy. She's not picking up, and she's got outside counsel
and— What the fuck happened?

ROMAN

Yeah. I fired her. Why?

GERRI

You absolutely cannot fire a studio executive without speaking
to legal and HR and having someone else present in case of—

ROMAN

Er, except, I can, cos I did?

GERRI

What *precisely* did you say because we're open to litigation and
ridicule and we need to discuss how to frame an apology or
row-back or—

ROMAN
(maybe an offer)
I did not fire her I just said she was fired to her.

But Gerri doesn't see it and doubles down—

GERRI

What the fuck does that mean?

ROMAN

She's not gonna be on the street. We'll kick her up to
international or she walks with a fat producer deal, you can
start the sweep-up, G.

GERRI

Do you know how this looks?

ROMAN

Yeah. Gangster. I might poach Kagan. Twenty years younger and
thirty times hungrier.

GERRI

Joy has a lot of relationships and a lot of friends. You're a
weak monarch in a dangerous interregnum. I think you need to
reconsider.

> ROMAN
> It's what Dad would have done.

> GERRI
> Maybe. But you're not your dad.

Can't help but sound like an insult.

> ROMAN
> Well, I'm what's left.

> GERRI
> *(explaining the comment)*
> You're in a more complicated position.

> ROMAN
> Gerri. Here's our thing. You hauling me out of things. Telling me to reconsider good calls. Using the 'F-word' freely. It feels disrespectful.

> GERRI
> *('c'mon')*

Uh-huh?

> ROMAN
> I need you to believe I am as good as my dad. Can you?

> GERRI
> Say it? Or believe it?

> ROMAN
> Look at it this way, I have to believe you believe it. So?

She considers. But decides – this isn't fair. Or healthy.

> GERRI
> This is silly.

She's trying to return the dynamic to something old. But something breaks for him. She will never take him really seriously.

> ROMAN
> You don't treat me with sufficient respect. And that's a problem.

Gerri doesn't say it. It becomes clear she won't.

> GERRI
> That's enough now.

ROMAN

Maybe I'll fire *you too.*

GERRI

Oh sure. I'm not on the kill list.

ROMAN

So?

GERRI

So, Matsson would be very angry.

ROMAN

Fuck Matsson.

She sees he's gone over an edge.

GERRI

Be serious. You're minding shop.

She sees he thinks not. He maybe has other dreams.

Roman, no. You can't win against the money. The money's going to wash you away. Your dad knew. Tech is coming. We're over. Make your accommodation.

ROMAN

This is a simple business decision. You're not good at your job. Maybe my dad did know? Maybe I am firing you for a list of failures that I choose not to outline. But including a failure to close off our liabilities vis-à-vis claims against Waystar Cruises in a timely manner. Maybe that will play nice?

She's almost trying to help him.

GERRI

I *am* good at my job.

ROMAN

Let's get started on that paperwork, Ger, shall we? You gonna do it yourself or shall we get someone a bit fucking sharper on it?

He leaves her behind. She is shocked, also disappointed, bad pupil—

GERRI

Not smart. Not good. Bad move.

INT. WAYSTAR LA – PREP ROOM – NIGHT

Roman comes in, freaked by his risks.

Kendall is there with Peter, Romy, Greg.

> KENDALL
>
> I think we can push push. I think. This is juicy as fuck, Rome!

> ROMAN
> (*maybe queasy*)
>
> Oh yeah. Yeah. Yeah.

Kendall's looking at numbers.

> KENDALL
>
> You okay to show face at the reception? Because I've got the big eye on. Ball's looking fat, bro. I can see everything.

> ROMAN
>
> Uh-huh. Uh-huh. Cool. Yeah.
> (*then*)
> But yeah, you should know I think we should let go of Joy.

> KENDALL
>
> Okay. Yeah? Yeah. Maybe. Yeah?

> ROMAN
>
> Yeah, she oversaw *Kalispitron*, she's running a fucking cult over there, we should get Jeff to run it?

> KENDALL
>
> Well, yeah. I mean, right now, it's kind of all about the moves, so that's baller for me. Let's put an end to Joy. Death to Joy.

> ROMAN
>
> And also Gerri told me not to. So I fired Gerri.

> KENDALL
>
> Fuck off.
> (*looks at Roman*)
> Seriously? Shiv's *godmother*?

> ROMAN
>
> Yeah, but maybe we pull back on that. I dunno. You might have to smooth over, whatever.

He's kind of hoping Kendall will pull him back.

Kendall thinks.

> KENDALL
> Fuck it, bro. Why not! Drop her in the end zone. Who you
> gonna fire next, let's fire them all! Fire Frank! Fire Karl! Fucking
> eat Greg and fire me, man!

> ROMAN
> It feels big. It does feel maybe a bit big.

> KENDALL
> Put on the Dad goggles. It's nothing. 'Dynamic Waystar Duo
> Shake Up Their Senior Leadership Team.' Grumble quote
> grumble quote. Caveat. 'Some are saying these two Young Turks
> might just have what it takes to turn things around!'

But Roman is unnerved as he heads out.

INT. INVESTOR PARTY – BEDROOM – NIGHT

*Shiv and Tom have had sex and pulled clothes or other stuff on.
Maybe they're looking at the party or in a hot tub?*

> TOM
> Nice?

> SHIV
> Nice.

> TOM
> Very nice.
> (*then*)
> What are you thinking about the election party, your dad's
> party? Do you think maybe I should host?

She lets that ride.

Her phone rings. Looks – Matsson.

> Your broad symmetrical friend.

> SHIV
> Let me ask you one thing. You're all in for Matsson, right?

> TOM
> Well, I guess. Your brothers hate me and you hate me, so you'll
> fire me, right? So, yeah.

(then)
Maybe we should host together?

She maybe considers – but high-status, maybe makes a face but moves on with her thought, texting Matsson back.

SHIV

My thing is. I don't totally know what to do.

She looks at him.

TOM

Regarding Matsson?

SHIV

Well we have a connection.

TOM

Oh you have a connection?

SHIV

What? Just – not like that. You think because you want to suck him off I want to fuck him? You think we're all gonna fuck each other and end up living in a big Matsson house singing Matsson songs?

TOM

Still keeping all your options open, honey? Ah? You have to be careful with that.

She shrugs, a truth too deep to be responded to.

SHIV

Ooooh. Truth bombs from the phony man.

Even with all the teasing and the games, it is fun to be back—

TOM

I think I want you, Shiv. I think. I would like this back.

SHIV

Well maybe you shouldn't have betrayed me? Ah? Phony?

Long beat. Tom thinks. Why not say, they're in a new space—

TOM

If I try to say it. If I was to say the truth, it's that, when I met you, all my life, I've been thinking a little bit about money, and

448

how to get money, to – to keep – money. And you didn't tell me, Shiv. You kept me out. I always agreed to – the compartments. But it seemed I was gonna get caught between you and your dad. And I really really really love my career and my money and – the suits, and my watches [and my]—

She snorts. Tsch!

Well. Sure. I like nice things, and if that's shallow, well, throw all *your* stuff out 'for love', throw all *your* necklaces and jewels out for a date at a three-star Italian. Come and live with *me* in a trailer park, yeah? Are you coming?

SHIV
'I'd follow you anywhere for love, Tom Wambsgans.'

He looks at her. Is it real at all? Lots of layers. Kind of not. But maybe the defense is hiding somewhere where it is. They keep on looking until she ducks behind a smile.

And then they both start smiling/laughing at the idea. It's quite funny, that she would say something like that and either mean it – or not.

INT. WAYSTAR LA – PREP ROOM – NIGHT

Kendall and Jade are there with Peter. Maybe another numbers droid, Romy.

KENDALL
What if we doubled that?

Peter makes a little worried noise.

I want to be super-credible.

PETER
Well, I think you know the specific business better than me. But, on units . . . if we go optimistic?

KENDALL
Go explosive, Pete.

Romy hands him more papers, he reads.

ROMY
Peter?

PETER

I guess, the – first wave is Florida, Colorado, Arizona five hundred?

KENDALL

Could that be a thousand?

Peter glances to Romy.

PETER

I suppose? In terms of, yes.

KENDALL

And then the five- and ten-year projections? We've got to be credible, Pete. So – on top of everything else—
(*peers*)
Base-level ARR a thousand dollars per customer.

Peter looks at him.

Three dollars per day to live longer?

PETER

Uh-huh. Okay.

KENDALL

New products and services, machine-learning on the marketing, plus repackaging health data to third parties, easily grow that three percent per month. What does that do to CAGR?

PETER

Um, I – I. Let me see, well it—

KENDALL
(*to a child*)

Does it make it bigger, Pete?

PETER

It makes it much bigger.

KENDALL

CAGR of basically fifty percent per year? Five years, we 10X revenue?

PETER
(*gulp*)

Can I talk to Karl?

KENDALL

No. What's the biggest headline number that's credible?

PETER

I guess, the thing is. Numbers aren't just numbers. They're – numbers.

KENDALL

You're talking gibberish, Pete.

He ruffles Peter's hair. Fucking around. Looks at Peter's numbers.

If it feels scary it's because the potential is scary, Pete.

PETER

Sure. No, good.

KENDALL

I need you to be comfortable because the analysts are going to get into us on this? Are you confident? Are these numbers rock-rock-solid, Pete?

Peter is queasy.

PETER

I – um, I think we can make the argument?

KENDALL

Great. If you're happy I'm happy.

INT. INVESTOR PARTY – NIGHT

Roman says a 'hello' to investors as he passes, on his way to Tabitha. Still a little rocked.

ROMAN

Tabs. Hey.

TABITHA

Roman Roy! My once and future boyfriend. Okay?

ROMAN

I'm actually, I'm good.

TABITHA

Yeah?

ROMAN

Sure. Little wonked. Work shit and – yeah. Stuff?

TABITHA

Dad stuff?

ROMAN

Nah. No. No I'm staying ahead of the sadness. Nope. Dad can't run fast enough to catch me. He's dead. 'Haha.'

TABITHA

Rome. Seriously, we haven't really, had a chance to— You haven't actually said, how you are?

ROMAN

Whoa. Easy there.

TABITHA

I mean how are you really?

ROMAN

Easy, Doctor Freud. I'm fine. Humping like an absolute monster.

She won't let it go.

TABITHA

I guess, I just want to say. It must have been really horrible?

She looks in his eyes and he can't really get away.

ROMAN

I mean it would be dumb to say my dad died and my dick started working . . . but . . .

TABITHA

Nothing? Death of a – parent, but nothing?

He is getting bumped.

ROMAN

Look, let's stop talking, you look offensively dope. If you're so sorry for me, can we not go do the naughty thing grown-ups do again?

TABITHA

But what about all the men, and the pension funds?

INT. WAYSTAR LA – EDIT SUITE – NIGHT

Logan on screen in the edit.

> LOGAN
> (*on screen*)
> I'm convinced that the Living Plus real-estate brand can bring the cruise ship experience to dry land, and provide a significant boost to the earnings of our parks division. I couldn't be more excited.

Greg is with the editor, Jamal.

> GREG
> So what we want. We want him to say – 'a doubling of earnings' instead of a – a 'significant boost'.

> JAMAL
> Uh-huh. Um? Well, I – I – I'm not sure I can do that?

> GREG
> But I bet you can?

> JAMAL
> I might need to talk to a sound editor but, um, without those words, without him saying—

> GREG
> You can build it – out of other bits.

> JAMAL
> Well I dunno if I can?

> GREG
> Yeah you can. I need you to.

> JAMAL
> Well I mean it's just that technically, I don't think I . . .

> GREG
> Look. That's enough okay? That's enough. Just fucking make it happen make it happen or I get in trouble and I don't want to get in trouble I want to get in the good books. So – you help me get in the good books or I punch you in the flippin' nose, yeah? Understand, Mr Snippy Snip?

INT. INVESTOR PARTY — ANOTHER BEDROOM — NIGHT

Post-intimacy. Roman's a bit scratchy.

> ROMAN

So. Ah? I ought to get back. But. Yeah?

> TABITHA

Yeah. I guess? I mean – can we try and get the motor running again, I'll be quick?

> ROMAN
> (*cockney?*)

More, Oliver? *More?!*

> (*sings a little*)

Never before has a girl wanted more!

> TABITHA

Seriously though, Rome? I didn't . . . Right?

> ROMAN

My. Somebody is a greedy goose. Aren't you still full from earlier?

> TABITHA

Seriously though, Rome? Like, it's nice that we've been . . . able to do a bit of like 1950s 'you on me then in me' but . . .

> ROMAN

Uh, think you're describing sex there, Tab. Doing it.

> TABITHA

Some of it. No real foreplay. Middle, briefly. Third act, not so much.

> ROMAN

Middle is the important bit. You can't say I didn't do that. The peni entered the vagini. Sex was completed. Sticker please, Mommy!

> TABITHA

I think one of us, at least one of us needs to come, otherwise it's just – rubbing.

> ROMAN

The bit where we lose control and start flopping around like a couple of salmons in a tub? We can do that in private.

TABITHA

Are you— Does something bother you about putting it in? Are you worried it won't come back out?

ROMAN

Why are you being a bitch?

TABITHA

Please don't use that word.

ROMAN

You do whatever disgusting thing you need to do. Go and fucking frig yourself with your sticky fucking toothbrush in the bathroom, Tabs.

Roman is ready to get some.

TABITHA

Roman, I'm sorry I was in Japan when it happened.

ROMAN

What a weird thing to say. Don't apologize for being in Japan. That's weird.

(getting up)

Look. I've got to get back to saving the fucking company. Apologies if that's not giving you enough vagina sneezes.

Roman is bumped. Tabitha feels bad for him (as she watches him leave)? But still goes to the bathroom.

INT. WAYSTAR LA – PREP ROOM – NIGHT

Kendall is pacing, looking at words. Mumbling to himself. Jess and an assistant in the room waiting.

KENDALL

And blah and bing and bing and dong and dang. Blah blah—

Greg walks in.

We got it?

GREG

Um, so the editor quit and he's talking to his union?

Kendall eats it.

                              KENDALL
Uh-huh. Okay.

                               GREG
I went bad cop and couldn't pull it back, then I went very very
heavily good cop, but. No dice.

Kendall looks at him.

Greg winces – is Kendall about to destroy him?

He looks at Greg. Breathes deeply, can't afford to lose it right now.

                              KENDALL
It's LA, throw money at it. I'm in deep here. Okay? Figure it out.

                               JESS
I'll help, let's go.

                              KENDALL
And find us a sound editor and a picture editor and get them
papered to fuck, okay? And get this out – get the text to Romey,
and Shiv, yeah, I need Shivvy's buy-in.

*Kendall walks out and maybe through the empty corridors and
towards the stage.*

Mouthing things and rehearsing.

DAY TWO

EXT. WAYSTAR LA – DAY

*Dawn. Shiv's car coming in. Ding. Email. She starts reading the
proposed script. Oh dear.*

INT. WAYSTAR LA – SHIV'S OFFICE – DAY

Shiv in an office, with Tom. She dials on FaceTime.

                               SHIV
Privacy?

                               TOM
Can I watch?

Shiv looks at Tom.

SHIV

Hey, Lukas. Hey, Swedey.

MATSSON
(*on FaceTime*)

Hey.

SHIV

Um. So I thought maybe I should mention. We're going to push
Living Plus.

MATSSON

Can you stop that? I don't like real estate and— It's not scalable.
I don't want the hassle of unwinding. Can you stop him?

SHIV

No. Like how?

MATSSON

Like, I dunno, cut the lights? Bomb threat. I don't know. Use
those soft little white hands of yours to strangle him?

*Tom looks at Shiv – 'Soft white hands?' Shiv looks back, not going to
explain.*

SHIV

Lukas. I'm being very generous here. I'm telling you stuff.
Because I feel it is appropriate given the stage we are at. I am
not about to start – dropping stage weights on people's heads?

End of call – what is she to do? Heads out.

INT. WAYSTAR LA – AUDITORIUM – DAY

*Kendall is wiggy and a little scratchy but high on the endeavor,
looking at what the team have put together.*

People are still working.

KENDALL

So how we going?

JADE

Good. The house, the guys couldn't achieve in the end
everything—

> KENDALL

And this . . . Is this the house?

> JADE

It'll be a basic structure.

He looks at it, disappointed.

> KENDALL

This won't be just this, will it?

> DENNY

Well no, we're throwing something over it. We can do it with light?

> KENDALL

How are the clouds?

> DENNY

Really good. We can also use the screen, it's a really strong projection, really precise and dynamic.

> KENDALL

But you've done the clouds?

> DENNY

Yeah.

> (*shouts to an assistant*)

Yeah? Jon, hit it! Hit on the clouds?

There is something which could be a cloud, but really isn't that, which puffs up some from tanks or machinery.

> KENDALL

This is— This isn't a cloud at all. I saw this in Berlin.

> DENNY

We were in touch with them, but yeah, not easy to replicate—

Kendall looks around. He's deep in himself.

> JADE

Okay?

> KENDALL

Uh-huh. Let me think. Let me think.

(*then*)

What you think, Rome? It fits, right? Bing, bang, bong. Me, you, me – us?

Roman is watching, leafing through words for the presentation.

ROMAN

The numbers? The numbers on units and projected sales, Ken, where did they— Where did you get them from?

KENDALL

I got them from up here, Rome.

He points to his head.

ROMAN

From up there?

KENDALL

They're projections, right?

ROMAN

Uh-huh.

KENDALL

I'm kidding. We have it. Pete has it. It's all good. Hockey stick. We're pushing to the moon! Right, Romey?

As Kendall goes to talk to the tech team, Shiv makes it in and over to Roman.

SHIV

What you think of the words?

ROMAN

Uh-huh. Yeah words are okay.

SHIV

And the numbers?

Roman makes a noise.

I mean I get the idea. But. Whoa. Big numbers. I'm worried. He's got that gleam in his eye.

Nods to him on stage.

ROMAN

I think it'll be okay.

459

SHIV

Yeah? Doing his speech from his ramshackle playhouse? And have you heard about Dad?

ROMAN

It's not him, Shiv. It's a file on a computer. It's zeroes and ones.
(*then*)
He's working on synthetic clouds.

Shiv is silent. Then asks.

SHIV

Did you fire Gerri and Joy?

ROMAN

Joy. Yes. Gerri. Not exactly. It was Dad. It was a warning. Kick her to the foundation.

She looks at him.

Might be difficult to row back while maintaining authority.

Too much for now, also she has another aim in mind.

SHIV

This is not good. Rome. But you can save this. He's out of control. You're out of control. This is going down. Shall we pull the plug on today?

ROMAN

I think it is a decent play.

SHIV

Made-up numbers, shooting to the moon? Fake Dad and imaginary clouds. Dude?

ROMAN

It's high-risk. But I think we have to back it.

SHIV

He could do anything up there. And then you're part of it?

ROMAN

I think he might need me. I think I have to go for it.

SHIV

Remember when he was going to write a book that was better than *Treasure Island*? All the blank pages. He was gonna be a marine biologist so he put the goldfish in the bath? I love him but he cracks under pressure. We should protect him.

EXT. WAYSTAR LA – DAY

People arriving for the Waystar investor day.

INT. WAYSTAR LA – AUDITORIUM – GREEN ROOM – DAY*

Jade shows Roman in.

Kendall is standing alone somewhere, lost in thought. Rehearsing what he's going to say

> KENDALL

Hey, man!

> ROMAN

How's it going?

> KENDALL

Good good. So shall we run it? We good. I'm not doing the clouds. We're gonna play an acoustic set. Ken and Rome unplugged? Okay? I think it's right. I've gone even bigger in Colorado. The numbers get crazy good.

> ROMAN

Oh yeah?

> KENDALL

It's enough to make you lose your faith in capitalism.
> (*joke whisper*)
You can say anything!

He clocks Roman's demeanor.

You got the pages?

> ROMAN

Yeah. And I was just – I was thinking, they're great and everything, I like them, I do. But—

---

* The flight jackets used in this scene as filmed were a collaboration between Jeremy and the costume department. Lorene Scafaria and I were aware they were in the works but I was frankly concerned they would seem over the top – but they were a great addition to the scene.

Kendall sees it all.

KENDALL

What? What the fuck?

ROMAN

I wonder if we should do this. Maybe we should postpone?

Kendall looks at him. He needs some support right now. The numbers, the video, the pitch, they're all quite big swings.

Roman turns and walks and maybe sits or crouches in the corner.

Hey, dude, no, it's okay. Or – maybe we dump it on Ray? It's his division. But not do the whole—

KENDALL

This is the – this is the idea though, Rome?

ROMAN

I know, but, I wonder if the idea, isn't a bit— I wonder if I can sell it?

KENDALL

Uh-huh? You think it's nuts?

ROMAN

No! Just. Pitching fucking playhouses and living forever and doubling all the numbers up—

KENDALL

It's time. It's big-swing time. We have to.

ROMAN

Sure. No. I know it. I just think maybe I should leave it to you. You have all the words. And the skills.

Kendall looks at him.

I just think it's your vision. I might fuck it.

KENDALL

Oh, man. Man?

Kendall considers. Hardens a bit.

Okay. What does Shiv think?

> ROMAN
> (*a lie*)

Dunno.

> (*then*)

You don't want to raincheck this – see what else turns up?

He clocks it's a lie.

> KENDALL

You dunno?

> ROMAN

No. I think she's out. Sensible Susan. I dunno. Good luck, man. Good luck.

He gives him a hug or a pat on the arm or something.

Jade knocks and enters—

> JADE

Hey? Okay? It's time.

> ROMAN

It's gonna be great. You'll kill it. Seriously.

> JADE

And Karl wanted two?

> ROMAN

Break both your legs. Break everyone's legs.

Roman heads out. As Kendall comes out there is Karl.

INT. WAYSTAR LA – AUDITORIUM – BACKSTAGE
CORRIDOR – DAY

> KARL

Yeah, just to say, I get it.

> (*quietly*)

On Gerri. Think that will actually play really really well.

> KENDALL

Uh-huh. Thanks. Thanks, man. I gotta—

He nods and they walk towards the stage. Jade leading.

> KARL

And good luck. And just to get some visibility if that's okay,
I just heard there had been more tweaks in my arena?

> KENDALL

It's cool.

> KARL

Could I take a quick peek?

> KENDALL

Karl, man?

> KARL

Or if you could just talk me through just so I feel comfortable,
in my own mind that I've got your back?

> KENDALL

It is all good. Thanks, Karl.

*Karl has been pushed over the edge. Maybe he stops Kendall
somewhere along the way.*

> KARL

Look, I took a lot of shit from your dad, because we'd
been through the mill. But I've been a CFO at major public
companies for over two decades and I know a thing or two
about a thing or two, and if you fuck up his deal – or try to
stand up figures I'm not comfortable with—

> KENDALL

Hey. Easy.

> *(re himself, Karl)*

CEO. CFO. Yeah?

> KARL

Gonna fire your chief financial officer less than a week in, your
dad just gone? Have me walk? You'd be fucking toast. You've
got my dick in your hand, Ken, but I've got yours in mine, okay?
So let's be real. You say something I don't like up there, you
make me look foolish. I fucking squeal.

*Kendall looks at him. Then heads on towards the wings. Karl
switches to say farewell.*

Good luck, buddy.

INT. WAYSTAR LA – AUDITORIUM – GREEN ROOM – DAY

Roman enters. Shiv is already in there. Bit of promo playing, with Karl and Gerri and Frank listing upcoming Waystar titles.

> SHIV
> How's he doing?

They expect disaster.

> ROMAN
> Uh-huh. Good. Pretty good.

A lot of different feelings going on for them. Hugo and Karolina are watching with Lana from investor relations and some assistants. Tom and Greg are in a huddle – Tom anxiously prepping.

INT. WAYSTAR LA – AUDITORIUM – WINGS – DAY

With Kendall as he prepares to go on. The stage manager beside him.

Kendall goes into himself, calm, thinking through his pitch, summoning all his energy.

The short intro that's been playing ends.

Kendall can feel his entrance coming, breathes, adrenaline.

'Harder Than You Think' by Public Enemy plays.

He lets it play for a while.

Then he comes on, it feels good.

We're right with him. The lights, the audience he scans, the music in his ears, his heart beating, the energy of the audience and music feeding him.

Behind him, a short Waystar promo video plays.

INT. WAYSTAR LA – AUDITORIUM – STAGE – DAY

Kendall looks around. Space, lights, attention.

The autocue rolls. He looks at the words but . . . He finds himself riffing, maybe half-planned.

> KENDALL

Hey. Thank you! Okay. Big shoes. Big big shoes. Big big shoes.

INT. WAYSTAR LA – AUDITORIUM – GREEN ROOM – DAY

Shiv and Roman are entering as they see this – a few different screens set up in the green room. Separate zones. Roman and Shiv find their way to a private space.

Exchange a look.

> ROMAN

Big shoes? Big hat? Big nervous breakdown?

Is it okay?

> KAROLINA

Was that cleared, did you okay that?

> HUGO

Did I okay him saying 'big shoes'? No.

Tom and Greg—

> TOM

Never wing it. First rule of speeching.

Then—

> KENDALL

Okay. It says here on my words that I'm glad to be – here. And you know, I almost am. Thanks, prompter!

> TOM

Don't talk to the teleprompter. Second rule of speeching.

INT. WAYSTAR LA – AUDITORIUM – STAGE – DAY

Nervous silence.

> KENDALL

Um, last time I was up at something like this, I was disrupting our annual meeting.
> (*beat*)
> Now I'm CEO. Co-CEO. Huh? Ah? Funny.

Chuckles.

But in truth, um, both ahem 'appearances' share the same root motivation. I'm passionate about this company – what it does and what it can be.

INT. WAYSTAR LA – AUDITORIUM – GREEN ROOM – DAY

Hugo, Karolina watching proceedings on a big screen.

> HUGO
>
> That's good. Is this yours?

> KAROLINA
> *(no, but she looks modest like 'yes')*
>
> Hmm.

INT. WAYSTAR LA – AUDITORIUM – STAGE – DAY

On stage—

> KENDALL
>
> And look, it's sad to be here under such heartbreaking circumstances, but it's also a great honor. And I want to say thank you. To the whole Waystar family. Who have offered us so much love and support over the last few days. So grateful.

He applauds the audience and they applaud back.

> *(looks behind)*
>
> Isn't that right, Dad?

Logan appears on the big screen behind Kendall.

Some applause. Some murmuring.

INT. WAYSTAR LA – AUDITORIUM – GREEN ROOM – DAY

Roman has maybe grabbed Shiv's arm in a sibling's show of appalled, amused shock.

> ROMAN
>
> No. No way!

> SHIV
>
> Oh my fucking god.

TOM

Ohhhhh sshhit.

INT. WAYSTAR LA – AUDITORIUM – STAGE – DAY

On stage—

KENDALL

Dad. We had our differences. But good to see you!

Logan nods hello (to the director of his shoot).

INT. WAYSTAR LA – AUDITORIUM – GREEN ROOM – DAY

Karolina leafs through her version of the remarks.

KAROLINA

He's doing a bit? He's doing a bit with his dead father.

HUGO
(*uncomprehending*)

It would appear so.

KAROLINA
(*leafing*)

This is new. This is all new.

TOM

How do I top this? Hold a seance with Walter Cronkite?

INT. WAYSTAR LA – AUDITORIUM – STAGE – DAY

On stage—

KENDALL

How are you doing, Dad?

LOGAN
(*on screen*)

Let's just get on with it shall we?

KENDALL

For sure! Sure thing.

INT. WAYSTAR LA – AUDITORIUM – GREEN ROOM – DAY

It feels like Shiv's doubts were justified.

> SHIV
>
> Oh my god I want to die. He's dying and I want to die and Dad's dead. Everything's dead!

> ROMAN
>
> *(too embarrassed to speak)*
>
> Aaaaargghhhhh.

> SHIV
>
> I actually don't know if I can watch this.

> ROMAN
>
> She said while watching the fuck out of it. And getting turned on. I can hear how wet you are. It's gross.

> SHIV
>
> Keep it light, Ken. Special speaker from beyond the fucking grave!

> GREG
>
> *(to Tom)*
>
> Okay don't worry about a speech. Just go on and mop up all the blood.

On screen – Kendall, glad that 'bit' is over, takes a drink from a bottle of water. Maybe walks, owning the stage a little more.

INT. WAYSTAR LA – AUDITORIUM – DAY

Frank and Karl watching in a row. Doesn't feel great. They whisper. While trying to look supportive for onlookers.

> FRANK
>
> Strangest double act ever.

> KARL
>
> I'll say.

> GERRI
>
> Fucking amateur hour. Wake me up when it's over.

INT. WAYSTAR LA — AUDITORIUM — STAGE — DAY

On stage—

> KENDALL
>
> So. Listen, today I want to share with you, an extraordinary product my father was working on to the very end.

INT. WAYSTAR LA — AUDITORIUM — GREEN ROOM — DAY

> SHIV
>
> An idea he couldn't exactly remember the name of.
>
> ROMAN
>
> And literally did not give a fuck about.

INT. WAYSTAR LA — AUDITORIUM — STAGE — DAY

> KENDALL
>
> An exciting new vision we call: Living Plus.

Name and image up on the screen.

INT. WAYSTAR LA — AUDITORIUM — GREEN ROOM — DAY

> ROMAN
>
> Also, by Dad, 'Bleeding the Brain-Dead Dry'. 'Florida for Fuckheads'.
>
> SHIV
>
> Now renamed, 'Kendall Goes Woo-Woo'.

As Kendall continues—

> ROMAN
>
> Fuck, if I cringe any harder I might become a fossil.

INT. WAYSTAR LA — AUDITORIUM — STAGE — DAY

Kendall goes for the sell—

> KENDALL
>
> Look. The world's tough, getting tougher. What our incredible new product offers is a sanctuary. A place where it doesn't feel

you or your mom or dad are surviving life. Somewhere you're really living, living *plus*.

Maybe a new image up on the screen.

Our brand-turboed Living Plus real-estate communities are going to guarantee three absolute essentials. One, total peace of mind. Discreet community protection and enhanced home monitoring. You'll have your keys. But you won't need them. Crime-free, hassle-free and respectful.

INT. WAYSTAR LA – AUDITORIUM – DAY

FRANK

Better. Less terrible.

KARL

Nice hooey. Good hooey.

GERRI

Buzzword bourguignon.

INT. WAYSTAR LA – AUDITORIUM – STAGE – DAY

KENDALL

Two, *fun*. Remember fun? That's what we're all about. By a lot of metrics the leading entertainment brand in the world. So. Hyper-local news, movie-themed events, advance screenings, ATN debate and discussions, multimedia events from cooking to premium-access sports. Integrated everyday character IP life enhancement. Maybe a director will come by with a rough cut? Stars certainly will. Shows, movies, rides, experiences to enjoy at home or with the family who will not want to stop visiting. (We can even tell them you're out if you need a break.) We think security plus entertainment is an unbeatable offer, right? Well. One more thing, how about I said it was all going to last forever?

New image up on screen.

INT. WAYSTAR LA – AUDITORIUM – GREEN ROOM – DAY

SHIV

Okay. Leaving planet earth. Glad you're not strapped in?

With Hugo and Karolina.

KAROLINA

Yeah. And it was just getting good.

INT. WAYSTAR LA – AUDITORIUM – STAGE – DAY

KENDALL

Well. I can't. Not quite yet. But, our central extraordinary offer is: health and happiness. Because here's what makes this amazing new product almost irresistible – our incredible links with tech and pharmaceutical companies. Which mean privileged access to life enhancement and extension therapies that right now are the preserve of tech billionaires. But we're going to deliver them at home, at scale, targeted and supported.

INT. WAYSTAR LA – AUDITORIUM – GREEN ROOM – DAY

ROMAN

I mean I would like that? Can we do that?

TOM

Great. How do I follow this? He's telling them they're going to live forever and I'm telling them they might get more local news??

SHIV

Is this flying, Karolina, is it— What we getting?

She is scrolling Twitter, makes a face: Not bad.

Shiv's phone goes. She moves to a private spot.

With Hugo and Karolina—

HUGO

Do you buy him?

KAROLINA

He's buyable.

HUGO

I mean, honestly, he's fuckable. And it helps.

KAROLINA

He's— I dunno. You think he's fuckable?

HUGO

Yeah he's fuckable. Right?

KAROLINA

I mean say what you like, Logan was always, fuckable.

HUGO

Oh hugely. Hugely. It was the eyes.

Shiv has moved to be on her own somewhere and called Matsson.

MATSSON
(*on phone*)

I don't like it. I don't like it.

SHIV

No, you don't want to run prison camps for grandmas.

MATSSON

What's the game?

SHIV

It's gonna die. I think he'll fly off. But. Someone might need to put a stick in the spokes?

INT. WAYSTAR LA — AUDITORIUM — STAGE — DAY

KENDALL

My dad, who'd been around a little bit. Who was conservative on these matters, in terms of earnings growth, has this to say.

Logan on tape, same clip as before—

LOGAN
(*on screen*)

I'm convinced that the Living Plus real-estate brand can bring the cruise ship experience to dry land, and double the earnings of our parks division. I couldn't be more excited.

On 'double' a very attentive listener might notice a quaver of wrong intonation, lips maybe out of sync.

INT. WAYSTAR LA — AUDITORIUM — DAY

Frank looks at Karl. Doesn't quite recall that, nor is it impossible, but feels off, some little looks between them: Hm?

INT. WAYSTAR LA — AUDITORIUM — GREEN ROOM — DAY

> SHIV
>
> Not fucking cool.

Roman doesn't like it either. Seeing Dad manipulated like that. It feels wrong.

INT. WAYSTAR LA — AUDITORIUM — STAGE — DAY

Up on stage—

> KENDALL
>
> Can we really do it? Are people who subscribe to Living Plus support really going to live ten, twenty, thirty, forty years more? Healthy into the hundreds? Well, lot of people think it's coming.
> (*then*)
> But you know, right now, this year if you live in a harmonious community with friends and timely medical interventions, right away you can be looking at up to twelve to eighteen months more of high-quality life expectancy. Maybe that doesn't sound so much? Is it worth it? Living Plus is going to be a premium product. Well, if you ask me would I take an extra year? Right now? With my dad? Say the unsaid? That would be priceless. Miss you, Dad. Love you, Dad.

He sends a kiss towards Dad. Both a real moment and a highly manipulated and manipulative one.

And then . . .

A brief Living+ promotional sting or trail plays. Gated communities. Security. IP. Doderick, Kalispitron. Other characters. Happy grandparents, visiting grandchildren and children. Golf carts. Sunrises and beautiful vistas. It looks good.

INT. WAYSTAR LA – AUDITORIUM – GREEN ROOM – DAY

Hugo and Karolina, with Lana. Calling over to Shiv and Roman.

                         KAROLINA

   Not bad?

                          ROMAN

   How's the buzz?

                           LANA

   People like it.

                         KAROLINA

   General buzz is great. Overall buzz is really good.

                          HUGO

   Oh fuck. Fuck.

He shows his phone to Karolina. We don't need to see yet.

   'Doderick Macht Frei'?

She looks.

                         KAROLINA
                      (*as she computes*)

   Shit.

INT. WAYSTAR LA – AUDITORIUM – STAGE – DAY

Back on stage, Kendall is relaxed.

                         KENDALL

   So I guess we've time to A some Qs, okay. Hey. Mics ready out
   there?

*Maybe around him we get a sense of some people checking phones.
Something spreading.*

Lots of hands from press. Do the questioners move to a central mic?

INT. WAYSTAR LA – AUDITORIUM – GREEN ROOM – DAY

*Shiv and Roman are now crowded around with Karolina and Hugo
looking at a tweet from Matsson. Doderick under a mock-up of camp
wire and a superimposed image of the gate of Auschwitz.*

ROMAN
(*to Shiv*)
Is that, that's a very nasty . . . joke, right?

Her face is deliberately neutral.

SHIV
Hm? Okay. Yes. Holocaust joke.

KAROLINA
Holocaust joke from our acquirer. Could need to strategize?

They look at one another.

What's the strategy?

They turn back to watch—

Can we pull the Q and A? Can we let him know? He's base-jumping into a buzzsaw.

GREG
(*to Tom*)
In a way it's good – cos your presentation – not great – and now – no one will be watching you?

TOM
You said it was a good presentation?

INT. WAYSTAR LA – AUDITORIUM – STAGE – DAY

The promotional sting has finished.

KENDALL
Detailed financials I'll leave to Karl Muller, our legendary CFO . . .

In the audience, Karl looks like: Thanks.

Lots of hands up from press.

But any questions with a broader overview? Um. Okay. Raj?

RAJ

Hi. Congratulations on a great presentation. I was just wondering how you feel about Lukas Matsson's response? His tweet just now?

INT. WAYSTAR LA – AUDITORIUM – GREEN ROOM – DAY

Karolina mutters the 'right' answer.

> KAROLINA
> 'No I did not see that, let's stay in the room and address thoroughly at a later point.'

Shiv goes off somewhere to make a call to/text Matsson.

INT. WAYSTAR LA – AUDITORIUM – STAGE – DAY

Now we're up on stage with Kendall, lights hot, trying to catch up.

> KENDALL
> Sorry I'm not . . . I'm catching up.

> RAJ
> Lukas Matsson's Twitter feed has posted an image of what looks like a comment on the presentation . . .

> KENDALL
> Oh uh-huh. Okay, well, I've been busy up here . . .

Split-second decision to make. Kendall doesn't want to ask more but is aware that now everyone is seeing it on their phones and he is the one person in the dark.

> RAJ
> He's tweeted the words 'Doderick Macht Frei' which is from—

> KENDALL
> Yeah I know what it's from.

Everyone's focus is on a small man on a big stage as he chooses to get his phone out and check Twitter.

Maybe Kendall gets his phone out of his pocket, and we see texts from Karolina saying 'WRAP IT UP!'

Aware his every reaction is being studied, Kendall looks at the tweet. He stifles a nervous smile.

> KENDALL
> Uh-huh.

> RAJ
> What's your reaction?

> KENDALL

Well I'm not gonna fave it . . .

Too glib? Yes. Recalibrates.

Well, firstly, what I would say is – Lukas has his own way of looking at things. Everyone knows we're looking at a deal with Lukas. And I have so much time and respect for what he's built. Now personally I wouldn't have said that. And apologies for any offense caused. You know, he's very – European. And, if and when we complete the deal and he gets into the incredible opportunity this product presents, I think he'll be tweeting something different. But for now, me and my brother and sister have to guide this company – because – well, you know – he's quite, he's quite, I'm not gonna say erratic, but, he's spicy!

INT. WAYSTAR LA – AUDITORIUM – BACKSTAGE SPACE – DAY

Shiv is on the phone to Matsson.

> SHIV

You're getting ratio-d to fuck and that's distracting but not in a good way. You're getting the whole thing more attention than it deserves.

INT. WAYSTAR LA – AUDITORIUM – STAGE – DAY

> KENDALL

Yes, Lola?

> LOLA

He's now tweeted a link to the press conference you gave denouncing your dad as 'a malignant presence'. Why do you think he's done that?

> KENDALL

I know Lukas. He's smart. But we don't always come across as we intend on social media. And one of the things about Living Plus is we see it going beyond. It's kind of like social media but better – it's physical social media.

INT. WAYSTAR LA – AUDITORIUM – GREEN ROOM – DAY

Roman, Karolina and Hugo watch on. Shiv is coming back in.

KAROLINA

That's a fun pivot.

ROMAN

So, it's fucking life then?

Shiv texts Matsson – 'Srsly, cool it on the tweets.'

INT. WAYSTAR LA – AUDITORIUM – STAGE – DAY

KENDALL

It's where you can talk, make real friends in a real-world environment. I think people are really hungry for that connection.

INT. WAYSTAR LA – AUDITORIUM – WINGS – DAY

Tom has arrived in the wings – he's next on. Greg's with him.

TOM

I can't follow that. He just promised them eternal life!

GREG

You'll be great. I'm here, cheering you on! Go go go!

INT. WAYSTAR LA – AUDITORIUM – STAGE – DAY

Kendall looks to the wings – no one's telling him anything.

KENDALL

Oh, they're telling me that's my time. It's been so fun sharing this. Thanks, guys. And thanks, Dad! Now please welcome, ATN President, Tom Wambsgans!

He walks off to warm applause. He passes Tom, knowing he's just sucked all the oxygen out of the room.

KENDALL

Warmed 'em up for you.

TOM

Thanks, Ken!

As Tom walks out on stage he sees Greg embrace Kendall and follow him backstage. No cheering on then.

INT. WAYSTAR LA — AUDITORIUM — GREEN ROOM — DAY

Later. Everyone has retreated to the green room. Kendall comes in. Claps from the room. Frank and Karl and Gerri watch—

> FRANK
> Really good. I mean, just very good.

> KARL
> Uh-huh. I guess the question is, why is he throwing Hail Marys when the game's supposed to be done?

Karl looks at Frank who shrugs. Maybe Frank doesn't mind the price running away as much as Karl does. Gerri shrugs, drinks.

On the screens, Tom is working hard to sell his speech. The following might play in the background of the green room—

> TOM
> (*on screen*)
> You're an ATN Citizen! You're an ATN Citizen! You're an ATN Citizen! I'm an ATN Citizen! Everyone at Waystar is an ATN Citizen! And we here for you! And you here for us! And we love it!
> (*then*)
> Okay. Okay. So.
> (*as news anchor*)
> News just in: Tom Wambsgans, Head of ATN, is beginning his speech! The headlines at the top of this hour: ATN election coverage acclaimed as best ever. ATN Citizens a runaway success. ATN continues to pledge: We Here For You. And, on a lighter note, PGN still sucks! Hahaha! Just kidding, guys.

As Shiv approaches Kendall—

> SHIV
> Well done, Ken. Knew you'd do it.

> ROMAN
> Great work. Proud of you.

> KENDALL
> (*to Lana*)

Uh-huh. Thanks, guys. How are we?

> LANA

Memestock frothing.

> KENDALL

Yada yada. On the reals?

> LANA

Good with buy side. Good vibes with sell. Yeah. Bloomberg has positive snaps coming. Actually seeing some movement.

> HUGO

The king is dead. Long live the king . . . s!

Karl with Frank, and Gerri. They're talking, have probably clocked Kendall's intention, to push the price. But lots of possible interpretations. And right now, Kendall has done good—

> KARL

We're really excited.

Kendall comes and touches Karl on the back.

> KENDALL

Thanks for the pep talk, buddy.

> KARL

Glad it did the business, buddy boy.

Big smiles, Karl with mixed feelings. Kendall at the center of a huddle.

> SHIV

Heil, Kendall!

> ROMAN

Okay? Motherfucker deleted it. He deleted the fucking tweet.

> HUGO

Yeah? Show me.

> ROMAN

I can't show you, dipshit, cos it's fucking deleted.

> KENDALL

Haha, okay. Climb down! Price rocket! Now we're talking.

This feels like a win. Feeling Kendall's growing status, Karl in public at least calculates it works for him to praise—

KARL

Pixie dust on this one. He's special! I know special and he's special!

Kendall gives him a friendly squeeze.

Shiv and Roman look over.

ROMAN

Well thanks, sis. Thanks. Saved me. Thank god you saved me. That could have been me.

Maybe we see Gerri slipping away.

GERRI
(*tight*)

Congratulations.

Kendall can't ignore Gerri, thinks he can fix things.

KENDALL

Hey, Gerri, listen, thanks, um – do you wanna talk? Should we—

GERRI
(*whispered in*)

You're trying to tank the deal? On price?

KENDALL

Just pleased for our shareholders. Pleased for the pension funds, Ger.

GERRI

Good fucking luck.

But Gerri retreats and Greg is there before Kendall can respond.

GREG

Great work, boss man! I was here, cheering you on!

INT. SHIV'S CAR – DAY

Later. Shiv and Tom heading to the airport.

> SHIV

I think, one thing, if we're thinking of hosting, I can't get into all our shit, okay? I think – if it's okay by you, we do strictly party and strategy shit?

> TOM

Strictly. Entirely. Uh-huh. I mean, I can't help it if I find strategy sexy though?

INT. ROMAN'S CAR – DAY

Roman is being driven.

Ding on his phone. He looks. A deepfaked, or badly faked, piece of Logan.

The cadences of the voice make it clear it is assembled from a variety of sources and speeches.

> LOGAN
> (*on phone screen*)

I want to make what I think is a fairly historic announcement. I'm convinced that *Roman Roy*, has a micro-dick and *always* gets it wrong.

EXT. MALIBU – DAY

Kendall is feeling good.

He traces something in the sand with his toe.

It's a number '1'. The waves wash it away.

He heads out into the ocean for a swim.

Episode Seven
TAILGATE PARTY

Written by Will Tracy
Directed by
Robert Pulcini & Shari Springer Berman

Original air date 7 May 2023

Cast

KENDALL ROY	Jeremy Strong
GREG HIRSCH	Nicholas Braun
SHIV ROY	Sarah Snook
ROMAN ROY	Kieran Culkin
CONNOR ROY	Alan Ruck
TOM WAMBSGANS	Matthew Macfadyen
FRANK VERNON	Peter Friedman
GERRI KELLMAN	J. Smith-Cameron
WILLA FERREYRA	Justine Lupe
RAVA	Natalie Gold
NATE SOFRELLI	Ashley Zukerman
MAXIM PIERCE	Mark Linn-Baker
LUKAS MATSSON	Alexander Skarsgård
EBBA	Eili Harboe
OSKAR GUDJOHNSEN	Jóhannes Haukur Jóhannesson
DARWIN PERRY	Adam Godley
SCOTT SAILER	James Van Treuren
CARLY FLIGHT	Ava Eisenson
COOP	Ryan Spahn
JORDAN PARK	Danny Cevallos
CONGRESSMAN JERYD MENCKEN	Justin Kirk
LEN	Shahjehan Khan
LARRY RADFORD	Michael Scott
MARY RADFORD	Brigid Brady
DANIEL JIMÉNEZ	Elliot Villar

INT. SHIV AND TOM'S APARTMENT – KITCHEN TO UPPER
LIVING ROOM/HALLWAY – DAY

Party preparations. A housekeeper is managing caterers and party event staff bringing in boxes of glasses and drinks and food.

Tom has a tray of scrambled eggs. He heads out.

INT. SHIV AND TOM'S APARTMENT – SHIV'S OFFICE/
MIRROR DOOR TO HALL – DAY

Shiv is in her office. But in either bedclothes and dressing gown or stuff for a work-out or hanging around. Tom comes in, all dressed with the tray of scrambled eggs and a gift and a coffee and some paper print-outs.

TOM

Oh Rasmussen? *Rasmussen.*

SHIV

Hey – Tom?

TOM

It's election eve and what has Father Sexmas brought you? Why, hot fresh polling!

SHIV
(already seen)

Yeah Jiménez up four? How will you play?

TOM

Er, I guess, amplify to gin up our maniacs? Or deny, shit on and bury?

Ding. Text.

SHIV

Matsson.

Tom raises eyebrows – him again.

489

TOM

What does he want?

SHIV

Don't worry, only to marry me and have a dozen Aryan children
with me and then we all sing in a choir together—?
(*then, reading*)
Thinks the Living Plus stock bump is fading, wants to know
what else my bros have cooking?

TOM

Is he coming?

SHIV

To the party? No.

TOM
(*shame*)

Ow.

SHIV

He doesn't want to 'swim around my dad's bullshit pre-election
brain-dead AOL-era legacy-media putrid stuffed-mushroom
fuckfest'.

TOM

Oooh. And I thought it was going to be fun?

Shiv looks at her phone.

SHIV

Oh, man. How did I get to be his inside bitch?

TOM

Kind of holding all the cards though?

SHIV

Maybe. It was just nice, when it was nice with my brothers
and— I dunno? That was nice.

TOM

Uh-huh. I get it. I get it, Shiv.

SHIV

Shoot me, but – I like getting on with my family.

TOM

Weirdo.

(then)
Don't you think it could feel like a fresh . . .?
('start' seems too obvious to say)
He's the real deal. Get in there. Together. Or, you first and me
following dutifully. As ever.

Ha. We can acknowledge our shit! Bonding. Hope.

SHIV
I know and I like that. But I'd like to live in the light?

*Tom looks at the scrambled eggs. Shiv is deep in thought. He nods to
the eggs.*

Did you make?

TOM
I carried them *most* of the way from the kitchen.

She's opening the gift-wrapped gift, but distracted.

And this is just a little party prezzie for being such a hot piece of
ass and a foxy little minx.
(watching her open)
And to say I'm glad we're giving this party – together. And
maybe we say, you know, we took a break but now—

SHIV
Yeah, right, that's good and—
(now she can see the gift)
Oh. Okay?

A scary rough-tail scorpion in amber or resin.

TOM
Heh heh. Ah?

SHIV
It's a— What is it, it's a – a scorpion?

TOM
Yeah. Right?

*What does it mean? He intended it to be funny and nice. But is
suddenly alive to the possibility it might not be.*

SHIV
Right? A scorpion. Because—?

> TOM

It's just. It's funny and—

> SHIV

Because?

> TOM

It's a joke – like—

> SHIV

Who's the scorpion?

> TOM

I guess, you? Or – it's just, it's jokey.

> SHIV

Okay? Right.

> TOM

It's just silly, honey. I love you, but, you know— You kill me, I kill you?

> SHIV

Right. Okay. Yeah. I like it, heh.

Does she try to laugh, even though it doesn't feel great?

Get to work! Go contribute to the great toxification!

> TOM

Gotta do my part!

He heads out. On his face – did he get it right?

Shiv looks at the scorpion. Hm.

> SHIV
> (*shouts after*)

Is it because you think I'm a Scorpio? Because I'm an Aquarius!

EXT. COFFEE SHOP – DAY

Rava is meeting Kendall before work. Kendall arrives for a catch-up. He approaches as she looks at her phone, maybe standing waiting for a coffee.

A security guy is there keeping an eye on Kendall at a discreet distance.

KENDALL

Hey. So what is this, because I'm – I'm up against it.

RAVA

Okay? Well sorry. Are you okay? How are you all doing?

KENDALL

I'm fine. We're all fine. This is fine, but if it's legal stuff I really need to keep my head out of that, I'd rather our lawyers—

RAVA

I'll keep it brief. Sophie doesn't want to go to school. She's freaked out, by the election.

KENDALL

Is she okay? What is it?

RAVA

Well, so, on the weekend, someone kind of, she felt, pushed by her a little on the street. She's fine, but – there was a comment she felt was picked up from the— It was— The person had on a Ravenhead shirt, or a quote on the shirt, and yeah. She felt it was racially tinged and she's been upset.

KENDALL

What did they say? What shirt? What?

RAVA

Well I dunno, he was an O'Malley guy she thought. And now at school some kids have this anti-ATN thing, which is supportive but – it's complex for her. So I was thinking maybe you want to speak to her?

KENDALL

Where was she? This incident? Why didn't I know?

RAVA

I think near the park. On Sixth near MoMA and it – it might have been a tourist, she was— It was a muddle.

KENDALL

And why was she out on the street?

RAVA

Excuse me?

KENDALL

I'm just saying like, someone pushed our daughter or whatever, where were you?

RAVA

Where was *I*?

KENDALL

I'm not blaming you, I'm just getting all the information before I make a decision on our course of action. Where were you?

A beat of angry disbelief. Rava's finally had enough.

RAVA

I was raising our daughter while you were running a racist news organization.

KENDALL

Oh yeah yeah, great. Fuck you, come on.

RAVA

No, how dare you interrogate *me*—

KENDALL

Obviously I feel bad, obviously I will do anything to protect her. I am just—

Rava's had enough.

RAVA

Sure. See you later. We'll cope. But maybe call her? Yeah?

And she starts to go.

KENDALL

Well obviously. Jesus.
(*maybe he goes with her for a beat*)
You don't understand the things I'm doing. The things I'm working on. Six continents. I'm breaking my back and it's all for them. To make the world safe.
(*gives up*)
So yeah, go on, walk off!

He tries to call Sophie right away, we see her photo as he calls. But her phone is busy or turned off.

So he collects himself.

INT. ROMAN'S CAR – DAY

Roman makes his call – eventually arrives and gets out to head into the bistro.

> ROMAN
> Yes dig on that, dig to heck on that. Dig dig dig!
> *(listens)*
> Yes we love the deal, but we gotta make sure we know *everything*. On Matsson and on GoJo. There's the due diligence this is – 'undue diligence'. Extra diligence. Okay?
> *(then)*
> And on – Gerri Kellman?
> *(sees it might be useful to explain)*
> There are a number of reasons we might need leverage. She's a very vindictive and terrible person. And I don't want to hear all this either, trust me, but to protect the company. *Anything* could be useful. Movements. 'Martyn'. How many times a week does he go to the gym? Does he show up sweaty or does he shower? Apparently insignificant details could be useful to me, us.
> *(then, as Tomas explains he doesn't feel comfortable)*
> You're a fucking deputy rat-fucker, Tomas, don't object to being a rat-fucker. Okay? It's unbecoming.

INT. BISTRO – JEAN-GEORGES – DAY

The sibs are all arriving. Connor joins Shiv and Roman, standing, some hugs and cheek air kisses.

> SHIV
> Hey, how you doing?

> CONNOR
> Oh, good. Yeah. Just came from seeing Dad.

> ROMAN
> Wow. Again?

> SHIV
> And what, any – change?

> CONNOR
> Looking good. Woke up on the right side of the coffin today, boy!

They look at him.

What? I like to go. You should go.

> ROMAN
>
> And do what? Sit there, like I'm feeding the ducks?

> CONNOR
>
> Cos the weird thing, honestly, is – how much he's not there. It's very strange, to look at someone and they're just— It might as well be this table. I find that consoling.

A beat where they consider this, broken by Kendall's arrival. He's distracted. Looking on his phone.

> SHIV
>
> Here he is. Kendall Plus. The man who led us to eternal life. Waystar Jesus.

Kendall hugs/shakes hands.

> KENDALL
>
> Hey hey. Morning.

> SHIV
> (*brightly*)
>
> You all seen the polling?

> ROMAN
>
> Oh that's why you're perky? Very exciting. I'm sure your Red Guards are all – you know, ready to come round up the thought criminals and turn the police stations into cuddle puddles.

Kendall doesn't find it so funny this morning.

> CONNOR
>
> The exciting part isn't the top line.

They look at him.

In Alaska. I'm exploding, four, five, six percent. Big secession movement. If they ever broke away I could conceivably become the Governor-King of Alaska.

> KENDALL
>
> Right? Guys? Can we? I have a lot of shit on?

Ooooh, big man. Eyes at each other.

> CONNOR

Very well, I hereby convene this funeral management committee? I sent the materials and I assume you've familiarized yourselves?

They have been emailed documents with lists of names and their father's wishes. Some phone looking.

Because, I'm concerned – we're saying 'yes' to all Marcia's wishes, then all your ideas, Dad's requirements. Danger the funeral could turn into a three-day grief-a-thon.

Shiv looks at the agenda.

> SHIV

Just – on Marcia I think I am content to exclude consideration of her wishes entirely?

> KENDALL

Seconded.

> ROMAN

Carried!

> CONNOR

Nevertheless. We really want a tight ninety. And the central question is – who's gonna speak, of us?

He looks – they consider.

> ROMAN

I have no clue. If I want to – I will but I might not. Okay?

> KENDALL

Uh-huh sure. I do think – one of us needs to do the sort of – the facts and figures. The official biog and we should—

> ROMAN

Get our story straight? 'Lovely guy, six-foot-five, wouldn't say boo to a goose, very fond of ham.'

> CONNOR

Ken's right, one of us does The Life and then the rest of us can do the color – the – the—

> SHIV

The beatings, betrayals and psychological tortures?

497

Roman looks at her.

> I'm kidding. I'm gonna do cozy shit. His famous lobster rolls.
> (*thrown away*)
> His ranked lists of the laziest ethnicities.

CONNOR

So who wants to headline main stage?

SHIV

What, before every powerful political, cultural and business interest in the world?

Looks. Roman isn't playing. Kendall and Shiv can feel the power of being the one who sets the record. But neither – out of humanity, deference and a little bit of politics – wants to declare first.

KENDALL

I'm easy. I could speak about Dad?

ROMAN

Uh-huh, your usual 'malign influence' material?

Kendall looks stung. Maybe Roman gives him a touch or a wink or some feeling he might have gone over the edge.

CONNOR

Cos I could do it?

Faces. Bit of a stand-off.

SHIV

I think if any one of us *wants* to do the big number – we should say? Because no one probably minds, right?

Faces wrinkle. They look around. No one wants to be a jerk, or come on too strong. Connor's phone buzzes.

CONNOR

Will you have a think? I'm jumping on the digital battle bus. But tailgate party. Let's nail it down, yeah?

SHIV

Um, yeah on the party? Tom is very – concerned about being fresh for the election and—

CONNOR

Shiv, you can't cancel. Dad threw this before every one – broke bread before doing battle. We have to honor it. God knows he wouldn't have cancelled if we'd died? Right?

SHIV

I know you're looking forward, Con. I just— I'd like us to be respectful, of Tom.

Connor nods. Heads out. Kendall watches. Tough sell here—

KENDALL

Right. Um, one thing from us, Shiv, on the party. We were actually wondering about us, politically, inviting Nate?

Tough sell for Shiv.

SHIV

Nate Sofrelli?! Um, well, me and Tom are— We were hoping it would be kind of—

(*too complex*)

Why?

ROMAN

Well, because. It worked, in LA. Hats off to the Greatest Showman here—

(*fast and aside to Kendall*)

and apologies for the wibble wobble and all due congratulations but—

SHIV

(*picks up the idea*)

We need a plan B if we can't chase him out of town on price?

ROMAN

Exactly – and we think it's regulatory. We go hard on regulatory. DOJ, FTC, FCC, EU.

SHIV

Okay? Since when did— [you two discuss this?]

ROMAN

Well it was always there but now, poll, *if* the Dems win – puke – it's not gonna be too hard to get them to freak about tech overlords ruling the world and destroying the economy and platforming the triggering of the trauma of the whosits.

                          SHIV

Hmm?

                          ROMAN

No?

They look at her, why so skeptical?

                          KENDALL

I think they might just stop it. But even just the threat, creates
a ton more risk for Matsson and kicks the deal down the line,
right?

                          ROMAN

And Nate? He's – right – he's across competition and he's tight
with the Jiménez folks on that.

                          KENDALL

Can we get him down?

Shiv shrugs: Okay.

So we can sell it, on a real level, without lobbyists and all the—

                          SHIV

Due process?

*She looks at them. They're so deep in. Another evolution in her
absence.*

Sure. It's just quite – complicated.

*Roman makes a 'finger going inside a thumb and forefinger' fucky
motion.*

                          KENDALL

Sure, just it's delicate. And face to face is so valuable. Election,
board meeting? Timing is fucking tight?

                          SHIV

What about Gerri? Gerri might be useful on this, cos she
handled all—?

They share a look.

                          KENDALL

You didn't, Rome?

ROMAN

Yeah there's a thing about that but it will be okay.

Then, as Shiv looks—

But, yeah – I fired Gerri.

SHIV

You what? You *fired* Gerri?

ROMAN

But it wasn't a real fire, it was a warning fire. I didn't fire her,
I said she was fired to her. It was a power play.

*Shiv looks between them, maybe something snaps in her attempts to
play fair with them. They're fucking untrustworthy.*

I was just putting her back in her box, and she's so fucking
stupid she misunderstood.

SHIV

Oh, sure, that's the thing about Gerri – dumb.

ROMAN

It wasn't anything, Shiv, this will be fine. It's a Dad play. Keep
the generals worried. I'll fix. I'll smooth it.

SHIV

My godmother?

ROMAN

I got it.

Kendall has things to do.

KENDALL
(getting up)
So is that okay, will you call Nato-Potato, or—?

She looks: What you think?

I got it sure. But will you do— Who's that asshole hipster
Valerie – top of their shortlist for FTC?

She assents, that's right.

ROMAN

Thanks. Thanks, Shiv.

Roman and Kendall head out together. Shiv watches them talk as they go—

KENDALL
(re Shiv)

Okay. Good, yeah?

ROMAN

Good. What else? You okay on any blowback, from the firings? The bloodlust? Throw Hugo at it?

KENDALL

Let's own it. Fifteen percent RIF across global. Street will love. We're throwing off cash like a fucking carnival float!

Shiv decides. Almost as soon as they are out of earshot. Makes a call.

SHIV

Hey, Lukas. Yeah. Listen. They're going regulatory. You need to be there tonight. It's easy. My dad invited you, right?

He sighs: Really?

There are forty thought leaders, pols and officials who'll decide this. And half of them will be there. I'm telling you, you need to be there. To counter.

She's texting on another phone. To Tom, the other pole of her alternative world – 'Sorry if I broke your dick last night.'

INT. ATN – CONFERENCE ROOM/VIDEO ZOOM CALL – DAY

Tom receives. So tired. Types back – 'Nope, still rock hard.'

But he very much isn't. He's wiped out and headachey.

On one or two monitors he has a Zoom screen full of employees.

They are the auxiliary staff – marketing folk, back-office support, accountants, translators, a few producers, back-room technical staff from three or four national (or maybe international) satellite offices of ATN.

Greg watches as Tom goes live.

TOM

So. Um, there's no real easy way of doing this. I've been doing this a few times this week and sometimes it honestly makes me cry. But I just wanted to offer you my heartfelt appreciation and I'm now going to hand you over to a colleague who has more information.

Greg slides into the hot seat. Tom checks his messages.

GREG

Good morning. I'm here to inform you that Waystar Royco has been looking at a range of different options in order to drastically reduce costs and a very difficult decision to restructure the ATN operation internationally has been taken in order to protect the future of the business. This action was only taken after seriously considering all available options.

Tom does crying motions at Greg, then fucky-sucky motions, trying to make him crack up.

But if you're on this call this is confirmation that you are part of the unlucky group who are having their contract terminated with immediate effect on the grounds of staffing redundancy and today is your final day of employment.

Tom motions: Come out fast. I need you. And exits.

Going forward we intend to operate Waystar Royco international news-gathering operations utilizing third-party contract-based arrangements.
(*then*)
I'm getting some confusion in the chat. But yes, if I have been too wordy, yes. We are letting all of you go. You have all been laid off. You. Yes. If you can hear this, you're laid off.
(*back on script*)
Obviously I can't take questions on this call. But this is a very sad day. And can I thank you for your time today and your service to Waystar Royco. Goodbye.

Click! He bounces a piece of paper into a corner basket.

INT. ATN — STUDIO FLOOR — DAY

Greg comes out to join Tom.

Election night rehearsal on the studio floor. An anchor, Jordan Park, is running through a full scenario at the touchscreen.

> JORDAN PARK
>
> —but keep an eye on what's happening here in Maricopa County. Very tight. Remember, this is a growing electorate – with a population of around four and a half million, it's the state's most populous county, in fact it's the fourth most populous in the whole of the United States. That's a chunk of change compared to the much smaller Mohave County in the north-west, or Cochise County in the south-east, both of which strongly favor Mencken. So Maricopa is a significant player on the big stage tonight and one we'll be keeping a very close eye on throughout proceedings. Arizona has come in for some criticism in past elections – some saying it takes too long to count its ballots, others disliking the way it handles its mail-in ballots. There's some feeling, as we've discussed many times and as I'm sure we'll discuss again throughout the course of tonight – that the mail-in ballot system is a system that's open to abuse. There are fears that people can vote multiple times, or use false identities, or vote in the name of deceased relatives or whatever it may be. There's a lot of suspicion around this process, and the fact that it seems to favor Democrats and give them a significant push at convenient moments in the count. Some go so far as to say that even allowing mail-in ballots at all gives an unfair advantage to Democrat candidates since Democrat voters historically favor mailing in their votes in advance whereas Republicans like to show up in person on the day and feel like they're doing their civic and patriotic duty and actually physically taking part in a great American tradition. And being part of a community. But that can be affected by things like ill-health, bereavements, et cetera. So some say the game is rigged. But putting all that to one side here's what we know right now. In the last few hours Maricopa County dropping some one hundred and twenty thousand ballots. These were mail-in ballots that were submitted over the weekend.

Tom and Greg watch from the wings. Tom's exhausted. He yawns.

> TOM

How'd it go, Slim Reaper?

> GREG

Yeah another thirty skulls.

> TOM

Solid. Culling the herd for the angry gods and removing the Cyd stench from the curtains.

> GREG

And tonight we shall toast our kills!

Tom rubs his eyes, anxious. Darwin is heading over.

> TOM

I need to twiddle the human abacus. Can you set me up for a nap in my office?
> (*he's there*)
> Darwin. The Adjudicator! All good? How fares the election decision desk, the nerd herd? Good? Bad? Undecided?

> DARWIN

All good. Focussing now. Just zoning in, hunkering down. It's Diet Coke and zinc from here to Miami-Dade.

> TOM

Great. But listen I just wanted to grab five to say, we all know PGN is going balls to the wall this year on speed. And I just wanted to check you and I are happy? With the rehearsals, in terms of the speed we're hoping for?

> DARWIN

Well, sure but number one, we need to be accurate.

> TOM

Absolutely. But also be great – my POV, new boss incoming in all likelihood – for us to be really fast.

> DARWIN

Sure. Accurate and fast.

> TOM

Fast and accurate.

> DARWIN

I think we're saying the same thing. Accurate and fast.

> TOM

Right. I guess we are saying them in a slightly different order?

> DARWIN

I just wouldn't want to put speed above accuracy.

> TOM

Oh no. No I mean they're almost equally weighted in my mind. I just can't say them both at once. We want to be fast-ccurate?

> DARWIN

Agreed. I get it.

> (*then as he goes*)

Accu-fast.

Tom looks at him as he goes—

> TOM
> (*under his breath*)

Happy last election, dickswab.

EXT. SHIV AND TOM'S APARTMENT – NIGHT

Aerial view of the apartment glowing in the dark, immaculate for the party.

EXT. SHIV AND TOM'S APARTMENT – NIGHT

A smattering of guests beginning to arrive from luxury cars.

There is light security outside.

INT. SHIV AND TOM'S APARTMENT – KITCHEN TO UPPER LIVING ROOM – NIGHT

The party is just beginning. Caterers and servers swarm.

We join Tom as he has a word with the bartender.

> TOM

The German one with this label? The dog that looks like mine? Let's push this okay? Tell them it's a 'light fruity red'. Don't say 'biodynamic' or 'German', just say 'light fruity red', okay? And yes, a little fizz is normal. Sophisticated.

He yawns as Shiv enters and gives Tom a loving pat on the cheek.

SHIV

Wakey wakey. You okay?

TOM

Yeah. Fine. It's a lot, election eve. Turns out! Tired. Pre-tired. Tired of thinking how tired I'm going to be.
(*smiles*)
Someone isn't letting someone get a lot of sleep!

This is really fucking true actually.

SHIV

Haha. Yeah so listen couple extra for the guest list. Matsson is in fact coming.

TOM

Ooooh. Because?

SHIV

Well, because Dumb and Dumber are going to try to stop the deal with regulatory shit, so he's coming to head that off.

TOM

Okay. Well, good. Yeah? I get a chance to dance? Secure my spot? For after the deluge?

SHIV
(*wasn't thinking of him*)

Exactly.
(*deep breath*)
And so, to push that agenda, they wanted to invite, and I didn't feel, tactically I could say 'no', to invite Nate. He's key on tech and trade. So. If that's okay?

TOM

Hm.

SHIV

Yeah. So sorry if— Yeah? I am sorry. Really.

Tom considers. Lot of feelings flash by. But he decides—

TOM

Sure. Nate. Be great to see. 'Nate'.

> SHIV

I can— If you want? I can just say, no, 'you went ballistic'? I feel gross about this. I feel like an asshole.

> TOM

Hey, no. Fuck it. What do I care? Ah?

Maybe this is true. Who won, after all? Maybe she gives him a tender kiss on the cheek. She sees her brothers arriving—

> SHIV

Hey hey hey!

INT. SHIV AND TOM'S APARTMENT – UPPER LIVING ROOM/ HALLWAY – NIGHT

Guests arrive, kisses and handshakes. Canapés and wines.

Polls on phones. Election chatter.

INT. SHIV AND TOM'S APARTMENT – UPPER LIVING ROOM – NIGHT

Kendall and Roman arrive with Shiv to survey the party. Maybe we can see Carly Flight and Larry, Coop, Scott Sailer, Mary.

> KENDALL

Okay! Let's spread some regulatory anxieties, yeah?

> ROMAN

Uh-huh. I used to drop molly and shark for skirt. Now I'm looking to hook up with gray hairs from the Heritage Foundation to talk competition policy.

> SHIV

Okay! Let's get those surveillance capitalism heebie-jeebies cooking.
> *(nodding to a group)*
Don't let me get stuck with the *Journal* op-ed ogres.

> KENDALL

Hey Dad's ideological range was wide. Sure he supped with crypto-fascists and right-wing nutjobs, but he also broke bread with venture capital Dems and centrist ghouls!

Roman's phone buzzes. He hangs back and answers—

ROMAN
Hey, what's up? Not your guy's poll numbers, har-de-har.

INT. SHIV AND TOM'S APARTMENT – UPPER LIVING ROOM/
HALLWAY – NIGHT

Maybe forty or fifty guests have gathered. A wet bar against the wall.

Servers rotating with canapés. A lively atmosphere.

We see a gallery of New York power players, lots of libs but some conservatives too—

Entertainment moguls (the equivalent in our world of David Geffen and Scott Rudin).

Media/journalism, think tanks and intellectual people (the equivalent in our world of Thomas Friedman, Anne Applebaum, Bret Stephens and Bill Kristol).

Magazine/digital publishing icons (the equivalent in our world of Graydon Carter and Arianna Huffington).

Fashion/style power players (the equivalent in our world of Diane von Furstenberg and Cynthia Rowley).

'Socially conscious' investor types (the equivalent in our world of Justin Rockefeller).

Centrist political figures (the equivalent in our world of Michael Bloomberg).

Liberal tech power players (the equivalent of Sergey Brin and Sean Parker).

Guests are dressed stylish but casual. It's a fun dressed-down affair for the ultra-wealthy elite of the city.

Against one wall is a large poster-board grid with the title 'GUESS THE SPLIT' written on top in a giant font.

A large colorful tin of kettle corn rests next to the poster board on a stool.

Tom stifles a yawn. Greg nearby.

> GREG

Maybe have a coffee?

> TOM

If I have a coffee then I won't be able to sleep later. *Think*, Greg.

Greg surveys the room.

What's your game plan?

> GREG

I dunno. Couple of loops, show some face and out. Right? Will they be horrible, these folks, cos of ATN?

> TOM

Nah. Our libs are the good libs. The kind that can take a joke. Locker-room libs.
> (*saying 'hello' to guests as they pass*)
But listen. Matsson's coming.
> (*looks around for privacy*)
So, that's my focus. And you, unless you're a true believer in the Dumpster Brothers, you might wanna sweeten that beat? Yeah?

> GREG
> (*pained*)

Yeah. I'd – I'd like to feather that bed. But I'm team Ken-Ro I think.

> TOM

Up to you, Greg. You wanna nail your dick to the family tree? Or jack into the mainframe with me and the Techtronic Emperor?

He waves to a guy.

> GREG

Wasn't he MeToo'd?

> TOM
> (*as he heads off*)

Lightly. Tempest in a teacup. It didn't take.

Shiv's talking to Valerie. Gives Kendall a thumbs up, going well. Roman joins Kendall.

> KENDALL

Okay, Shiv's hitting Valerie. You seen Nate?

ROMAN

Yeah, no, but Mencken's team called.

KENDALL

Okay? Because? The polling?

ROMAN

Their internals are even worse.

KENDALL

Boohoo. And they want – what, ATN to go full 'They're coming to give your guns hormone therapy, all your guns are gonna be ladies'?

ROMAN

Um, three or four states where Connor's one percent is throwing things. It could be pivotal. If he drops, most of his support goes to them. Con's team is refusing contact. They want me to convince him to drop out?

KENDALL

I mean. I dunno. Fuck that guy, right? Victory vans. Those O'Malley fucks. I think fuck him.

ROMAN

I guess. I mean, it's not bad for us to be tight with them? If it did swing his way? Yeah?

Kendall clocks Roman's possible desire to help Mencken. But it still makes sense.

KENDALL

Fine. I see you. I'll work the libtards, you go help the Nazis.

Nate enters the party only to bump into Tom. Roman and Kendall clock.

Over with Nate and Tom—

NATE

Hey, Tom.

TOM

Hello, Nathaniel.

NATE

I appreciate the invitation.

511

                              TOM

Well, I've missed you.

Hands him a glass.

                              NATE

I'm not staying long. Lot going on. I won't drink too much of
your wine.

                              TOM

Don't you worry. Gobble my gravadlax pal, plenty more where
that came from.
                            (*then*)
Light and fruity. Apparently it's a wine that sorts the
connoisseurs from the weekend Malbec morons?

A partygoer, Len, passes Tom and makes a crucifix with his fingers.

                              LEN

Keep away from him, Nate! Back! Back, foul news demon!

                              TOM
                         ('*fuck you*')
Ha! Good one, Len. Good to see you.

INT. SHIV AND TOM'S APARTMENT – BATHROOM – NIGHT

Roman finds Connor. Takes him into the bathroom.

                              ROMAN
Hey, sorry to interrupt. Con, can I grab you?

They find privacy.

So, listen: kind of a biggie. A bit last-minute, but, Mencken's
team called. And they want to know if you might be willing to
drop out?

                              CONNOR

Of the election?

                              ROMAN

Yes of the election.

                              CONNOR

You are aware the polls open in eight hours?

> ROMAN

Yeah it might be too late to physically remove your name from ballots. But if you were to make a statement? Divert the Conhead stream towards the Mencken river?

> CONNOR

And after all the blood and treasure I've expended, why on earth would I do that?

> ROMAN

Um, they said, maybe for the good of the Republic?

> CONNOR

Uh-huh.

He makes a face.

> ROMAN

No? I mean, you don't want to be the guy who won it for the Dems? They want to, you know, decriminalize crime and – tax your taxes.

> CONNOR

I have principled issues with Jeryd. He's all over the map on recycling. No thanks.

> ROMAN

Okay then I have also been authorized to make the follow-up offer which is: how familiar are you with 'Mogadishu'?

> CONNOR

Mogadishu, in Somalia?

> ROMAN

Because he's very impressed with your talents and he was thinking maybe you'd fit for an ambassadorial appointment?

> CONNOR

In a failed state?

> ROMAN

Con. Yeah? State dinners. 'Your excellency'.

It is a little appealing.

> CONNOR

Little bit car-bomby? Tell him UN. That's more my vibration yeah?

INT. SHIV AND TOM'S APARTMENT – UPPER LIVING ROOM/
HALLWAY – NIGHT

Across the room, Gerri enters.

> ROMAN

She came. That's good. You smoothed that for me, General Franco?

Frank looks at him.

> FRANK

No. No. She's incredibly angry.

A glass clinks. Kendall stands on a chair to address the room.

> TOM

Welcome, everyone! One and all. Ken?

> KENDALL

Um, party people! In the place to be! Welcome to the Tailgate Par-ty!

A warm response from guests. He surveys the room.

Who we got here? Carly Flight, oh shit. The Podmeister General. Larry and Mary, love it. Len. My guy Nate Sofrelli saw the polls this morning and moonwalked here!

Some laughs. Nate smiles.

So listen, it's our first one of these without the big guy. We're still gonna live it up. As always, kettle corn will be shipped to whoever is closest to tomorrow's electoral counts. Thanks to my sis for hosting. But yeah, we didn't know what to do this year. We watch history, we make history, and then one day, we become it. Can I – can I just ask you all for a moment of silence. If we could, in memory.

They bow their heads in silence.

Shiv might roll her eyes. Roman makes a face. Perhaps a jerk-off motion.

Thank you, y'all!

Suddenly Matsson emerges into the back of the party along with Ebba and Oskar.

Surprised looks from Kendall, Roman and other Waystar figures. It throws Kendall at first. But he recovers.

So, okay! VIP in the house! Mr Matsson, how are you, sir? You don't get my sister's home in the deal, you know. Don't get greedy!

Matsson smiles.

MATSSON

We'll see!

KENDALL

Hahahaha. Nice. Nice. Anyway, my dad loved you all. We love you all. So let's have some fun. Let the games begin. Salud!

As Kendall descends from the chair, the siblings all clock each other and move out . . .

There is a new atmosphere in the room. People rearrange themselves to get a look at Lukas, the tech titan.

Whispers and glances.

Kendall marches over to—

INT. SHIV AND TOM'S APARTMENT — MAIN FLOOR BALCONY — NIGHT

Kendall and Shiv. Whispered.

KENDALL

Okay? What the fuck is he doing here?

SHIV

Seriously. Right?

Roman has been to check with a party planner.

ROMAN

I guess, Dad invited, and he emailed a 'yes' like four minutes
before walking in?

SHIV

Do we just throw him out?

ROMAN

I mean, we can't afford to be seen treating him as an enemy?

KENDALL

We hang tough, yeah? Stick to the plan. Regulatory. These
assholes in here? *Our* assholes.

ROMAN

What's his game? He going for a freak-out, or is he flicking the
same beans as us?

SHIV

How do we play?

KENDALL

Shiv— He— There's too much peanut butter between us. Can
you stick close?

SHIV

Uh-huh?

ROMAN

Right. Guide him away from the high-value targets, the meaty
loot boxes?

KENDALL

Refill his glass, run him in circles. Tell people he's looney tunes
behind his back. Keep him from the bigwigs.

ROMAN

Unless he gets sloppy and gropey in which case lead him directly
to the editor of *The Atlantic* and do not pass 'Go'.

Shiv smiles.

Yeah?

SHIV

Sure. Operation 'Nuke the Luke'.

INT. SHIV AND TOM'S APARTMENT — UPPER LIVING ROOM —
NIGHT

*Over in the thick of it — Matsson is surrounded by a sycophantic
Tom.*

> TOM

Yeah tough day. Election prep.

> MATSSON

Uh-huh. And what are you like, more hands-on or overview guy.

> TOM

Huh. Huh. Um.

*Feels like a trick question, it isn't. Maybe Greg swings by and tries to
get his beak in.*

> Interesting. I guess, well, let me ask you this: which do you value
> more highly?

Matsson smiles. Not gonna say.

> Because I like to think I can do both. Dirty hands, clean noggin.
> Multitasker.

> MATSSON

Are you kissing my ass?

> TOM

No I'm not kissing your ass! No. Lukas. You're too smart. You'd
see that a mile off.

Smiles. Shiv approaches Matsson. Cards close to the vest.

> MATSSON

Hey hey, Tom here's kissing my ass. Great place. Who'll get to
keep it in the divorce?

> GREG

Ha! Hahaha.

*Matsson sees Greg and doesn't love what he sees. Tom looks at a
guest and goes off. Gives Shiv a thumbs up, things going okay with
Matsson. Greg is excluded.*

> MATSSON

So. Let's do this! Who do I hit?

*Shiv is hyper-aware of who can hear her. She's playing a careful line –
look like she's trying to chaperone him, while really chaperoning him.*

> SHIV
>
> Nate, Carly, and Valerie first. I'll keep eyes on my brothers.
> (*looks around*)
> And Lukas, I'm sure you've done this before but – don't, like
> don't—

He sees what she's going to say – 'Don't freak people out.'

> MATSSON
>
> Coder man no smash skull? Why coder man no eat human
> flesh? Me like-like?

She smiles. Ebba comes close with Oskar.

> SHIV
>
> Well, you're about to purchase some of the most prized cultural
> assets and political communication channels in America and you
> need to prepare the ground or your many enemies will portray
> you as some heartless jerk-off coder from Gothenburg.

> MATSSON
>
> I am a heartless jerk-off coder from Gothenburg. Right, Ebba?
> (*then*)
> You remember Ebba right?

> SHIV
>
> Of course. How are you?

> EBBA
>
> I'm, yeah. Fine.

> SHIV
>
> This is for later, Ebba. I wonder if you shouldn't fire your
> lobbyists?

> EBBA
>
> Sure. It's not actually my arena. I'm sorry. That's Andreas and—

> MATSSON
>
> Don't apologize, Ebba, it's just information, yeah?

They stare at one another for a long beat. As Oskar approaches—

(*then, to Shiv*)

'Social anxiety'. She's the only flack in the world who hates talking to people.

                    EBBA

I don't love parties but I'm good.

                    OSKAR

Whereas I love them, I do.

                    MATSSON

Number two who's moonbeamed on edibles and a comms who's scared to comm. Great.

INT. SHIV AND TOM'S APARTMENT – SHIV'S OFFICE –
NIGHT

Roman confers with Connor and a freshly arrived Maxim Pierce.

                    CONNOR

So Mogadishu is a no-go. It's a death sentence.

                    MAXIM

Frankly we're insulted.

                    CONNOR

But. I'd like to roll through the options. As a brother, what's the top option?

Roman looks at his phone.

                    ROMAN

Okay, well . . . let me see.

                    CONNOR

Would love to get to Europe. Could I creep up through the underbelly? Come up through the Balkans? Couple of senior departures, Berlin by Christmas?

                    ROMAN

Well I think they could talk Slovenia or Slovakia?

                    CONNOR

Yeah. I think I'm a 'no' on the Slos.

                    MAXIM

What about South Korea?

> ROMAN
>
> Top-ten GDP? Major geopolitical player? I think it's tough.

> CONNOR
> ('fine')
>
> North Korea?

> MAXIM
>
> Easy, my liege.

> CONNOR
>
> I'd be a voice of reason. Get Kim and I together over some late-night bulgogi we could probably hash shit out. Oh-hell, is that a No-bel?

> ROMAN
>
> Con, they're not gonna put you anywhere with nukes.

> CONNOR
>
> Insulting. I'm not sure I wanna go anywhere they don't have nukes.

> ROMAN
> (looks at phone)
>
> Okay, and how familiar are you with Oman?

> CONNOR
>
> Oman?

> ROMAN
>
> Oman. The cradle of civilization. Probably. 'The Venice of . . . the desert'. Fresh dates, fresh oil and fresh oppression?

Connor thinks it over. Looks at a map.

> CONNOR
>
> Oman. Poor man's Saudi Arabia, or a rich man's Yemen? Hm. I need to check. See what my wo-man thinks of O-man?

INT. SHIV AND TOM'S APARTMENT – KITCHEN/UPPER LIVING ROOM/HALLWAY – NIGHT

Shiv there with Matsson and Nate. She looks over at Kendall, like she couldn't help them talking.

Kendall motions: Keep an eye on. Shiv gives a subtle thumbs up.

Greg would like to try again but he sees Kendall. Can't try with him watching. Maybe makes eyes, or hand signals about Matsson being up himself.

MATSSON

Look. Essentially I'm just a self-made guy who made a cool product that people love. And you might want to consider that maybe I'm a better option than the screwy sons of the Canadian-Scottish man who did all the boat rapes?

Shiv makes a face: C'mon, too much.

NATE

I send you my nine ninety-nine a month. I'm no hater. But Daniel is troubled by out-of-control algos, worried you bleep-bloop guys are gonna data-mine us all to death.

MATSSON

I get that. But in terms of – this. The truth is someone's going to pick up these assets. Who? The – excuse me, Shiv – the Failsons?

Shiv makes a face, makes out this is too much.

They'll do what he did, but stupider, uglier, less – amenable.

SHIV

He's amenable.

NATE

Amenable ATN?

MATSSON

ATN, well, honestly, I'm not going to do anything crazy. I want to make money, maybe diversify a little bit, maybe open it to more voices?

SHIV

He's gonna do a Great Replacement.

MATSSON

Nah, but genetic variation. Thin out some of the shouty guys.

NATE

What about leadership?

MATSSON

I'd make major leadership changes at the top of ATN.

A look from Shiv. They look over at Tom.

> NATE
> (*winks at Shiv*)
> Uh-oh! Trouble in paradise!

She looks away.

> MATSSON
> Nate, I like you, I'd like to keep talking, I don't know who's going to run it, honestly, who do you think, I'd love your opinion?

We join a tired Tom by a drinks table nearby. He sees most of his red wine has gone untouched. He makes a face.

Tom looks across the room and sees Shiv and Matsson and Nate all chatting together. It doesn't feel great.

> GREG
> (*frustrated*)
> I can't get any purchase. He's too busy slobbering up Nate with Shiv.

> TOM
> (*defensive*)
> They're just talking, Greg.

The party is in full swing now, servers making their way through with kitschy Americana appetizers with funny little American-flag toothpicks stuck in them.

Fancy guests fill out their electoral-count guesses on the foam board against the wall.

A guy, Larry, is filling in his guess, which favors Mencken.

> ROMAN
> Mencken man, eh?
> (*then*)
> Anyway I guess it's out of our hands but – once he gets his mitts on ATN? Swede? 'Tonight at eight, Reparations Hour with Hurdy Gurdy Third Sex'.

Roman looks over at Matsson as he moves on to Carly Flight with Shiv.

Shiv looks at Roman: What can I do?

Roman makes a discreet signal, finger whirling at temple: Make them think he's nuts. Shiv nods.

> SHIV
>
> Hey, Carly. You've met Lukas?

> CARLY
>
> Hey! Oh how I've tried! How're those subs coming?

Matsson is bumped but ignores, probably nothing, comes in with full smile and handshake.

> MATSSON
>
> Can we try again? I'll be super-entertaining I swear. Or maybe I'll suck, how funny would that be if I just completely bit it?

Carly smiles. He can do it, when he wants. He gives her full attention, and eye contact—

> But seriously, reach out. Love the pod. I sometimes even listen when it isn't about me!

A smile. She's not un-charmed.

INT. SHIV AND TOM'S APARTMENT — ANNEX HALLWAY — NIGHT

Kendall has spotted that Nate has been to the bathroom or another room and maybe has positioned himself to talk to Coop to catch Nate as he comes out . . .

> KENDALL
>
> Hey, buddy.

A hug. Coop is dismissed.

> NATE
>
> Hey, brother. Listen, I know we haven't had a chance to talk? I'm sorry, man. He was— What can I say, but he was— Jesus, I can't imagine.

> KENDALL
>
> It's tough, but, life keeps a-rolling, right? But *you*, man. Throwing off some king-maker vibes. How's Daniel? Can

I shoot you names? You could make a decent cabinet from my
fucking poker night?

NATE

Oh sure, yeah, the activists will love that.

Smiles, but Kendall launches in.

KENDALL

And look, dude, I'm just going to give you my rap straight.
Okay?

(*looks around*)

Because we could be really good for you guys. I'm talking a
major reset of the dialogue. Which I am personally invested in.
But that only happens if this deal goes away.

Interesting. They both look around. Maybe they angle more private.

NATE

Uh-huh. Okay?

KENDALL

Yeah. Board-wise, shareholder-wise, we can't come out publicly,
but the deal is, is headed to the woodshed. GoJo has had
incredible growth and he's a charismatic figure. But he's going to
get wrung out. He's been a playboy at the tables burning zero-
interest cash. The party's over. But. That's gonna take a while to
shake out. We could do with some help. And you know, there is
really legitimate concern here, DOJ or FTC balking at the sports
overlap? The FCC over foreign ownership—

Nate wrinkles his nose.

NATE

Uh-oh. He's pitching me!

KENDALL

Maybe CFIUS would have a word to say about Matsson's, you
know, 'extreme political positions', and fucking, Holocaust
jokes? You thought my dad was bad? Try him. Norse-blooded
and twitched out on *Call of Duty*.

NATE

Like you give a fuck.

KENDALL

Hey, I give a fuck. I have skin in the game, pal. Kids.

Real or manufactured?

I've got some dues to pay, I've got some debts and I intend to repay.

NATE

Okay?

KENDALL

Yeah.

NATE

And so? What?

KENDALL

You come out for regulation pretty soon and we give you a better ride in the first hundred days. Is that not interesting to you?

NATE

Sure. Until what, hundred-and-first day, when you call us commie puberty-blockers?

KENDALL

Really. I'd want to review ATN. I think, we turn the dial down. That frog can get de-boiled pretty fast. Probably got to keep hitting the crime buzzer. But race, the crazy stuff, we just— Let's have a country yeah?

NATE

Doesn't it revert to type though? If leadership doesn't change?

KENDALL

Minnesota Fats? For sure. Refreshed.
(*then*)
All we need is some breathing room?
(*then*)
Whaddya say?

NATE

I think what you say is interesting.

> KENDALL

Because, like, if this happens for you guys. If it happens.
I would— Honestly, we'd need to get a message to the markets
and the board fast, like day after, to put sand in the gears?

> NATE

Uh-huh?

> KENDALL

But could – could you backchannel that? Any hope of like – of
like—

> NATE

What?

> KENDALL

Like, not a deal. But is there an accommodation? An indication
of an accommodation.

> NATE

Man, I forgot how eager you are to get laid at a party.
> (*then*)
Let me check in.

> KENDALL

Love it. Would love to get laid!

INT. SHIV AND TOM'S APARTMENT – GUEST BEDROOM/
COAT ROOM – NIGHT

Shiv and Matsson rendezvous, she angles him private.

> SHIV

Nice wordings. Eminently plausible.

> MATSSON

Really? Yeah? Because I don't always read people great?

It's true. A slightly more open side of Matsson. Shiv soothes.

> SHIV

No, you're doing great. We've hit the A-Team. Now we maybe
build your profile with some op-ed narcissists, and Beltway
psychos?

MATSSON

Bang bang bang. I like this!

Maybe they start to walk.

I think – I think, you know, I thought these people would be
very complicated but in fact, it's basically just – money and
gossip?

SHIV

Oh yeah. It's only money and gossip.

MATSSON

So, take me down to Paradise City!

Shiv scans the room. Can she see her brothers?

SHIV

Sure. I guess my only question at that point would be: great,
I love heaving you around like a great lump of pine and making
you shine. But. What have you done for me lately?

He looks at her.

MATSSON

What do you want? I like talking to you. You know you can
have whatever you want.

SHIV

This situation is not without risk. So if I was to move to actively
engage in assisting you in the acquisition, I would need to know
it leads to a very very very significant role.

MATSSON

Three verys?

SHIV

Yeah.

MATSSON

Okay. Talk to me.

SHIV

I know my way around the company. I know everything. I'm
collaborative and I have the name and I just— I'm hot shit and
I'm ready to go. So? You don't want to be across all the bullshit,

you want to be coding and strategizing in the clouds. So do we just say it's me running shit day to day?

He looks at her.

MATSSON

Can I think?

SHIV

No.

MATSSON

Well I don't want to lose you – so.

They maybe touch knuckles or some other bond. Shiv has a jolt of excitement. Everything right now feels like it might work out. Tom. Matsson.

Can I— I'm going to take five and I'll be back with the dipshits and limpdicks, yeah?

Shiv's Queen of the Party as she walks to join—

INT. SHIV AND TOM'S APARTMENT – UPPER LIVING ROOM – NIGHT

Tom talking to a media mogul named Scott Sailer, drinking red wine.

SCOTT

So, Tom, you gonna imperil democracy tomorrow?

TOM
(laughs, pointing around)
You against the wall, you against the wall, you're a nice guy, you can live! Bang bang bang!

SHIV

You don't have to worry about Mr Mild here. I assure you he's a one-pepper menu item.

TOM

Thank you, dear.

SCOTT

And plans after the deal goes through? I hear you might be headed elsewhere?

Tom looks to Shiv. While bumped, rides it out fast.

> TOM
>
> Uh-huh. Always got options. Where'd you hear that?

> SCOTT
>
> Maybe I misheard.
> > *(sips, not great)*
> Could this be corked?

> TOM
> > *(preoccupied)*
> I don't think so, screwtop.

A flicker of worry from Tom. Scott moves off.

Kendall sees Matsson 'unguarded', catches Greg, who is looking longingly at this power center he's not supposed to approach.

> KENDALL
>
> Hey, Bony Moronie. Need you to lend a hand.

> GREG
>
> What's up?

> KENDALL
>
> Matsson? Can you 'look after' him?

> GREG
>
> Um, he has occasionally expressed a distaste in the past for my particular flavor of, me?

> KENDALL
>
> Find him a blunt. Something stronger? Point his dick in the direction of some fissile material, yeah?

> GREG
>
> Yes sir! I can try!

Roman on the phone, comes to join.

> ROMAN
>
> Okay, well. That's some top-shelf fucking of the rat.

Roman hangs up.

> Hey. The deep-dive dredged up some filthy doubloons.
> Matsson's been creeping on Ebba, his comms. Harassment

sloppy spaghetti. Maybe sending her wackadoo shit – bits of hair and blood?

KENDALL

Mmm num num num! Nate, want in on this?

Nate is nearby.

ROMAN

Wanna hear something nasty about someone terrible?

NATE

Um, sure. I gotta go.

KENDALL

Uh-huh? We good? On the – situation.

NATE

Well. Um. Yeah. Um. Just – lot to hit tonight.

ROMAN

Yeah? You gonna go turn Wyoming purple with the strength of your big blue dick?

NATE

Um, I think, yeah, Daniel's people aren't crazy about me rubbing shoulders with you and – Coop tends to yap and – it looks a little cozy and – yeah. Apologies.

Maybe Nate can see Coop and a couple of others just aware of the temperature of this conversation? Kendall can't see.

KENDALL

But is there still something here? On the – legitimate concerns you might have?

Nate steps away – hands up.

ROMAN

We can make primetime safe for you. All we need is one sentence signaling to the market that Jiménez is skeptical? We'll write it up for you!

NATE

I'm going to be straight with you. I don't feel comfortable with the tenor of this conversation.

> KENDALL

Hey. Don't play hall monitor with me, okay? I know you.
> (*hint of a threat*)

I know who you are, my friend.

> NATE
> (*quietly*)

I don't know what you think this is, but I'm not Gil. And you sure as fuck ain't your dad.

Kendall is backpedaling now. The hard push hasn't worked.

Nate walks away. Kendall looks at Roman.

INT. SHIV AND TOM'S APARTMENT – GAME ROOM – FOOSBALL AREA – NIGHT

Connor explains a possible future to Willa.

> WILLA

And so where would we live, exactly, in Oman?

> CONNOR

In Muscat, I should think. In a compound.

> WILLA

In a compound? In Muscat. But above ground?

> CONNOR

Of course above ground, Willa!

He shows her a photo of the Muscat skyline on his phone.

'Pearl of Arabia'!

> WILLA

Okay?
> (*then*)

And is this one of the – spooky countries? Is it Sharia law.

He scrolls.

> CONNOR
> (*reading*)

Sharia is *one* of the sources of legislation?

> WILLA

Uh-huh?
> *(looks at some words on the page)*
'The Sultan's word has the force of law'?

> CONNOR

At the airport, we'd walk straight through?

> WILLA

And this would be, for Mencken? All my friends hate Mencken?

> CONNOR

Diplomatic plates? You can park anywhere! You can basically drive on the sidewalk. The police can't touch you!

> WILLA

And my family.

> CONNOR

Right. But – Oman's a solid starter embassy. Perky GDP. No theaters of conflict. No theaters at all probably. You'd have a monopoly! 'You must come to see the puckish satire penned by Her Excellency the ambassador's wife.'
> *(then)*
Soak your walnuts in that.

Willa considers.

EXT. SHIV AND TOM'S APARTMENT – LOWER-LEVEL LIVING ROOM/UPPER LEVEL – NIGHT

Oskar is downstairs at the kids' table.

He takes a huge honk on a vape.

> MATSSON

Easy, bro.

Oskar blows the smoke out towards Greg.

Sorry, dude.

> GREG

Fine. No, no worries, just taking five.

> OSKAR

Fucking hanger-on. Fucking dingleberry.

> GREG

Ha. It's cool.

> MATSSON

Nah, man. I'm on a charm offensive. You okay, kid?

> OSKAR

Fuck off, kid.

> MATSSON
> (*re Oskar*)

We should fire him. Ah? Ebba? Shall we fire him?

She shrugs.

> OSKAR

Sorry, is this boring you?

> EBBA

It's fine. I've just seen him cut your balls a hundred times, it's just a little boring.

> MATSSON

Maybe he likes it, maybe that's his job?
> (*then*)

I'd love to fire Ebba I just can't because she has fostered a situation – created a situation where I find it difficult to do what I want. I'm not saying you've done it on purpose but it's interesting. It's like you got tenure, cos we mingled?

Beat. Greg leans in to Matsson.

> GREG

I mean I know you're kidding but.

Matsson looks at him.

I could help?
> (*goes for it, 'kidding'*)

I'd fire her right now if you want. I've recently had experience.

> MATSSON

Oh this guy can help!
> (*calls out*)

Everyone, come watch, this kid is going to fire my senior comms!

Ebba has had enough, walks off, unhappy.

Kendall clocks and nods to Roman.

INT. SHIV AND TOM'S APARTMENT – UPPER BALCONY –
NIGHT

Kendall and Roman have approached Ebba, who has found a secluded spot.

> KENDALL
>
> Hey. All okay? We just wanted to check in to offer support on a human level?

> EBBA
>
> I really, I'm totally fine.

> KENDALL
>
> Well that's great to hear. Isn't it?

> ROMAN
>
> Totally.

> EBBA
>
> We built his whole rep. He's not a coder. Someone handed him a box of tech and he took it to market. 'Bravo'.

Ebba might look at these two guys with no real accomplishments of their own.

> KENDALL
>
> Well, we just wanted to say we sympathize. All the shit.

> ROMAN
>
> Yeah we don't stand for that.
> (*re Kendall*)
> I'm sure you know his record on this stuff? Ally.

> EBBA
>
> Uh-huh. I'm out in February anyway.

> KENDALL
>
> Well that's a shame.

> ROMAN
>
> Because of the – sending you, and whatnot?

How do they know? Not about to discuss.

> EBBA
>
> I would say that's pretty much the least of his worries.

> ROMAN
>
> Right. Because?

> EBBA
>
> India.

She knows the power she has right now.

> KENDALL
>
> If there's something you want to tell us? Get out in front of?

> EBBA
>
> Saying comms misrepresented the sub numbers. That is not correct.

Sounds very big.

> KENDALL
>
> Uh-huh? No, I agree—?

> ROMAN
>
> I think I know this, but what are – the details here?

> EBBA
>
> Oh yeah. I'm gonna give you all the details. Sure.

But she stays. Kendall and Roman look at each other.

INT. SHIV AND TOM'S APARTMENT — MAIN-LEVEL BAR
AREA — NIGHT

Shiv and Tom chat with Coop, who is showing them the ATN homepage on his phone.

> COOP
>
> 'Dem Positive Polls a Radical Disinformation Plot.' Ballsy.

> TOM
>
> Like to keep things peppery.

> SHIV
> (to Coop)
> Did we mention he's very tired? Poor guy can't be across
> everything.
> (then)
> Maybe you should call Pam on that? Everyone here's needling
> me.

> TOM
> Well, then tell them to stop wetting their pants.

> SHIV
> I get it, Tom. But – there was— Did you hear in Phoenix the
> O'Malleys firebombed a campaign office?

> TOM
> A firecracker. A pair of firecrackers taped.

Roman and Kendall approach.

> ROMAN
> May we? CEO shit?

*Kendall and Roman pull Shiv, they're whispery and giddy, as Tom
heads off.*

> KENDALL
> Oh Shivvy! Get ready to Riverdance!

> SHIV
> What? Did you hear about Phoenix?

> KENDALL
> Matsson's numbers are funky!!

> SHIV
> What. What are you talking about?

> ROMAN
> Ebba spilled. Screwy metrics in India.

> KENDALL
> Matsson's been peddling bundles of South Asian packing
> peanuts!

Shiv tries her very best to look happy.

SHIV

I mean, that's— Wow! And, you're sure? Is it big enough to be significant?

ROMAN

We think so, yeah. Yeah.

KENDALL

See. New money. You gotta hold those fresh bills to the light.

SHIV

That is— Fuck, I can't believe it!

She glances down into the downstairs area and sees Matsson hanging with Greg.

INT./EXT. SHIV AND TOM'S APARTMENT – LOWER-LEVEL LIVING ROOM – NIGHT

Matsson and Greg are perhaps sharing a vape pen with Oskar and some other younger folks.

MATSSON

Forty scalps in three days? Mr Nephew. I thought you were backwash at the bottom of the gene pool.

GREG

You may have underestimated me!

MATSSON

So how do you do it?

GREG
(*shrugs*)
I just do it. Jackknife right in there and slit some throats!

MATSSON

Feels shitty?

GREG

Honestly? Not really. HR says the good thing about me is it *looks* like I care, but I don't.

MATSSON

You do have the look.

> GREG
>
> I know! Yesterday I canned this guy named Taylor who's like fifty, and he started crying, 'Ooooh no, I've just bought a house' and I was like, 'Oh man, oh man' and I was like crying but I was thinking, 'Well, maybe you shouldn't have!'

> MATSSON
>
> Not a good person.

> GREG
>
> I am but, you know, gotta do what ya gotta do, you know? It is what it is.

Shiv approaches.

> MATSSON
>
> Hey, there she is. Welcome to the kids' table! The Hate Pit. Is it time to up periscope?

> SHIV
>
> Lukas, can I talk to you for a moment?

INT. SHIV AND TOM'S APARTMENT – GAME ROOM – NIGHT

Shiv gets Matsson private. Makes sure the boys can't see.

> SHIV
>
> So. What is going on with the numbers?

> MATSSON
>
> What numbers?

> SHIV
>
> 'What numbers'?

She stares at him.

> MATSSON
>
> In India?

> SHIV
>
> Uh-huh.

> MATSSON
>
> Is this Oskar or Ebba?

She doesn't say.

Well. Okay. There's a little issue. We're looking into it. With the subscriber numbers. Being bullshit. Not bullshit, but – yeah, a little bit bullshit.

> SHIV

What does 'a little bit bullshit' mean?

> MATSSON

We maybe discovered a metrics error that has been overstating our subs in India. Like maybe if there were two Indias it would make sense.

> SHIV

You *maybe* discovered—?

> MATSSON

But there's only one India. Emerging market, you know, it's all wet cement.

> > (*then*)

Crazy, right?

It sort of feels good to unburden. He might even laugh a bit crazily.

> SHIV

Stock and cash deal, the board would be within their rights to pull out. When— How are you handling? When are you addressing?

> MATSSON

I don't want some dweebs shorting me. I don't like it when people get into me.

> SHIV

It's gonna get out eventually.

> MATSSON

Or. We buy Waystar and it gets lost in the deal dazzle, or there's a hurricane, or a war.

> SHIV

I want to rewind. SEC? DOJ? Is this even legal? How hot is it in hell?

> MATSSON

We close quickly. And then shit's gonna get crazy good. Next quarter, the numbers will probably even be maybe real?

She isn't amused.

Oh, c'mon. It is kinda funny though? I know it's bad. But you can fix it, right?

Shiv leaves him, a bit dazed from the head-spinning news. What has she tied herself to?

INT. SHIV AND TOM'S APARTMENT – UPPER LIVING ROOM – NIGHT

Roman approaches Gerri again, he's on a high.

> ROMAN
>
> Hey. So. Can we talk? I have some thoughts to run and wouldn't mind advice.

> GERRI
>
> No.

> ROMAN
>
> Hey. Gerri? Ger?

> GERRI
>
> What?

> ROMAN
>
> Listen. About me firing you. That wasn't real.

> GERRI
>
> No?

> ROMAN
>
> No. That was heat-of-the-moment, you know?

> GERRI
>
> No.

> ROMAN
>
> C'mon. Gerri? Yeah. Let's go and chat. I can stand in a cupboard and jerk off and you can explain to me what the SEC is.

She looks at him.

Too soon? What do you want? Sorries, cos I got sorries.
> (*dips a knee, low voice*)
> 'So very sorry, Your Highness.'

GERRI

I'm out. I'm done.

ROMAN

Bullshit.

GERRI

No. Not bullshit. I'm going.

ROMAN

C'mon. Dad fired people all the time, I was just feeling a bit 'fire-y', okay?

GERRI

Look. You should know. I have some requirements, several of which have been officially communicated, some maybe it is wise for me to do in person.

ROMAN

Ooooh. Robo-Gerri! Scary!

GERRI

I want money, eye-watering sums, hundreds and hundreds of millions.

ROMAN

Um, well, no.

GERRI

That's easy. That's an easy 'yes'.

ROMAN

Why are you being a sucky baby?

GERRI

I think you and Shiv and so on have correctly made an assessment that I don't wish my career to end with a mess created by you and your sexual incontinence and your strong attraction towards me.

ROMAN

Blurgh. Don't even.

GERRI

But. It's a fine balance and if I don't get these eye-watering, frankly, unnecessary sums, I'll go public.

ROMAN

Oooh, girl power!

GERRI

So the money's easy. I also want control of the story.

ROMAN

'The story'! No one cares, Gerri.

GERRI

I know how these things go. The story and the story behind the story and the story whispered behind that. I've retained personal reputation management. They will be on the line as Karolina gives background briefings off a set of my bullet points?

ROMAN
(tries to go back to saucy)
'I'd like to see your bullet points.'

But he can't get there or even really look her in the eye.

GERRI

And if I get so much as a *whiff* of anything undermining my narrative anytime in the next five years I will sue, and go public with the many many pictures of your genitals in my possession. Good?

ROMAN

Yeah. Well. It was just a real pleasure working with you, Gerri.

GERRI

If you ever wish speak to me again, I'll need Karl or Frank to be present.

She turns and walks away.

ROMAN

Oh you bet, Gerri. Maybe the National Guard should be present too and McGruff the fucking Crime Dog?

GERRI

I could have got you there, Roman. But – no. Nope.

Roman chuckles but it doesn't feel good.

He swaggers through the party, angry and sad. Smiling guests off with a mean look in his eye.

The party has thinned out and he finds Connor at a table with Willa and Maxim, Matsson and Oskar and Ebba and Greg. He's riled up and ready to fix shit.

> ROMAN
> (*to Matsson*)
>
> Hey, man, excuse me. Excuse us.
> (*to Connor*)
>
> Can we settle this?

> WILLA
>
> Everyone is quite freaked out about this political firebombing in Arizona.

> ROMAN
>
> Oh please. The pop-pops in Phoenix? A wastepaper basket caught fire. I heard a file cabinet's in the ICU. Con. Can we draft?

> CONNOR
>
> Well, there's actually been a slight change of heart.

> ROMAN
>
> Connor, you got your bauble, now let's do a fucking statement yeah and wind up the old fax machine and fart it out to your oddball army, yeah?

> WILLA
>
> We wonder, Roman, if he hasn't invested too much in this campaign to drop out now?

He looks at her.

> ROMAN
>
> You tried. You flopped. Find a new thing.

> CONNOR
>
> This is who I am.

> ROMAN
>
> I know. Please stop.

> WILLA
>
> He's fought hard and we want to find out what might happen. He might write a book about it. Or speaker circuit or—

MATSSON
(something he's heard)
Or King of Alaska?

Roman nods to come private. But Connor shakes his head.

ROMAN
Nothing will happen. You'll be a freckle on the scrotum of eternity.

Kendall spots and comes over to calm things.

WILLA
Anything could happen tomorrow, actually.

KENDALL
Is this where the real party is?

CONNOR
That's the beauty of this little system we have called democracy?

MATSSON
Oh yeah? I've been looking for the real party?

ROMAN
Con, man. Eat the fucking carrot, bro. Yeah?
(he's reached the end)
Everyone in this room thinks you're a joke. So tell Willa to shut up, cover her shoulders and pack a fucking bag for Oman. Yeah?

KENDALL
Rome?

CONNOR
There's one person in this room who doesn't think I'm a joke and that's who I'm gonna listen to. Willa?

Connor gets up, led by Willa. They watch them. Shiv comes over and sees them off but then starts to watch the brothers spar with Matsson.

MATSSON
Nice party. Cool family.

ROMAN
Yeah sure. You gonna tweet this?

MATSSON

Ha? So, who's going on somewhere in this shitty fucking town?

ROMAN

Um. Yeah, probably not.

MATSSON

Depressing, right? From up here. You can really see how second-world it is?

KENDALL

I don't know. Pretty happening town, famously?

MATSSON

Next to Singapore or Seoul? It's Legoland.

KENDALL

You know we still run shit though?

MATSSON

Oh, right. 'Only in New York'. Nothing happens here that doesn't happen everywhere, dude.

KENDALL

Cool, man. You should get that printed on a cup. That would look so cool. Sell them in a head shop in Rotterdam, be a good business for you. Cos I know you could do with new revenue streams.

MATSSON

Hahaha. Yeah well. Good presentation, man, I look forward to getting into the projections? Meaty projections, bro.

KENDALL

Oh yeah? Yeah. Exciting, excited about that. Estimates, you know? But your *numbers*. Exploding. Right? Literally unbelievable.

MATSSON

Thanks, man. And congrats to you, but I hear some of your numbers are gay.

KENDALL
(*laughs*)

My numbers are 'gay'?

> MATSSON
> (*laughs*)
> Yeah, man. You have this really cute little valuation that just came out as gay. That's so cool.

> KENDALL
> That's kinda homophobic, man.

> MATSSON
> Just let the wave hit you. Go with it, float out.

> KENDALL
> Nah, I think I am the wave though actually, dude.

> MATSSON
> Oh yeah. Yeah. Cos you like the deal?

> KENDALL
> Are you kidding? Biggest overpay in history. Love that shit. Love it. Love the deal!

> MATSSON
> Let's have a hug, yeah? Love the deal! Man. Yeah, yeah. Night night, sweetie. Love the deal.

> KENDALL
> Love the deal.

They do a little bro-hug. And part ways.

> MATSSON
> Thanks, thanks, guys.

He passes Shiv. Smiles. Tom comes over.

> SHIV
> You guys okay?

> ROMAN
> Fuck it. Yeah.

> KENDALL
> Uh-huh.

Tom looks troubled.

> SHIV
> Okay?

TOM

Me? Yeah. I might just. I'm gonna – bed. I'm bushwhacked. My eyelids are sandpaper.

SHIV

Well maybe we can just see folks off together?

TOM

Shiv? Do you know what my tomorrow looks like?

SHIV

You're not gonna be doing anything, Tom. You'll be watching for shiny foreheads. Just forty-five more minutes.

He snaps.

TOM

I'm just a little tired because the – the fun gossip I'm hearing from pretty much everywhere I go at this party, in my house, is that I'm going to get shitcanned?

Looks at the brothers.

ROMAN

Lot of faith in you.

KENDALL

Always been a loyal servant.

Tom goes to get a glass of water. Shiv follows.

SHIV

Sorry.

INT. SHIV AND TOM'S APARTMENT – MAIN FLOOR BALCONY – NIGHT

They step onto the balcony. People can't hear but they can see their body language.

TOM

I just really do need to get some sleep. I'm sorry. Okay? Shall we leave it there?

SHIV

Uh-huh. Sorry. I'm just— I'm worried. I've nailed myself to the Matsson cross but he might be bullshit. He's – erratic and I'm not sure he's real.

TOM

(*weary*)

Shiv, he's the future. He's real.

SHIV

Right, you're Tinker Bell for Matsson? There's a time-bomb in his numbers and I might get blown up.

TOM

You'll be fine. You'll always be fine.

SHIV

Well no. I'm fucking my family for this!

TOM

The forty most important people in America were here and you were walking around telling them all I'm going to get fired?

SHIV

It was implied, a little, lightly, just as part of – a tactical kind of – like a joke, just a little—

TOM

Funny joke.

SHIV

It's something he said, a thing that isn't true, but we needed to say it.

TOM

But you stood by his side and – he said that and you were like 'Yeah, sounds good to me'?

SHIV

I'm not doing this now.

(*then*)

I'm in serious trouble. That was a play.

TOM

You'll be okay. You're a tough fucking bitch who will always survive. You'll do what you need. You'll do whatever you need.

SHIV

Well. You're projecting. Because that is actually you.

Italy has entered the discourse.

TOM

Should we have a real conversation?

SHIV

With a scorpion? No.

TOM

That was a friendly thing.

SHIV

Yeah. I know. I'm a scorpion. You're a hyena, a street rat. 'Haha'. What's not funny? You're a snake. Here's a dead snake to wear as a necktie, why aren't you laughing, Tom?

TOM

I wonder if we shouldn't clear the air.

SHIV

Well, sure.

TOM

I think – you can be very selfish and you find it hard to think about me. And and – maybe you shouldn't have even married me, actually—

SHIV

You proposed to me at my lowest fucking ebb, my dad was dying. What was I supposed to say?

TOM

Perhaps 'no'?

SHIV

I didn't want to hurt your feelings.

TOM

Thanks. Thanks on that. You've kept me very safe.
(*then*)
Running off to fuck the phone book.

SHIV

Tsch. Hick. You're a hick.

TOM

And then hiding it because you're scared of how awful you are.

SHIV

You were only with me to get to power. So. You got it, Tom. You got it.

TOM

I am with you because I love you.

SHIV

I don't think so. You were fucking my DNA. You were fucking a ladder because you and your family are striving and parochial.

TOM

That is – not a fair characterization.

SHIV

Your mom loves me more than she loves you. She's cracked. You betrayed me.

TOM

You were gonna see me get sent to fucking prison and you fobbed me off with this undrinkable fucking wine cos you won't have my baby because you never really honestly thought you'd be with me for more than four years I don't think.

SHIV

You offered to go to jail because you're servile. You're servile.

TOM

Yeah well you are incapable of thinking about anyone other than yourself because your sense of who you are is *this* fucking thin.

SHIV

Did you read that in a book, Tom?

TOM

You're too fucking transparent to find in a book.

SHIV

You're pathetic, you're a masochist who can't even take it.

TOM

I think you are incapable of love and you are maybe not a good person to have children.

A shift at this partly successful attempt to actually hurt her.

> SHIV
>
> Well that is not a very nice thing to say is it, Tom?

> TOM
>
> I'm sorry.
>
> (*then*)
>
> I'm sorry but you've hurt me more than you can imagine.

> SHIV
>
> And because of you I missed the last six months with my father—

> TOM
>
> No. No.

> SHIV
>
> You sucked up to him and cut me out.

She looks at him.

> TOM
>
> It's not my fault you didn't get his approval. I've given you endless approval and it never fills you because you're broken.

> SHIV
>
> Sure I don't like you. I don't even care. I don't care about you.

Quiet.

> Feel good now? Yeah? Feel good? Glad we cleared the air?

> TOM
>
> Yeah fucking great. Tip-top.

> SHIV
>
> You don't deserve me and you never did. Everything came out of that. It's so fucking – flat.

Tom stares at her. Whatever they had now feels broken beyond repair.

INT. SHIV AND TOM'S APARTMENT – MAIN BALCONY TO UPPER LIVING ROOM – NIGHT

Shiv walks in – aware the room has been aware of her argument outside. Heads to Roman.

SHIV

Jesus. Why did you let me marry him?

They smile. Maybe a hand on her shoulder or a smile. No time or place to get into it, but some support offered.

ROMAN

You okay?

She might just be able to say 'yes' or nod. And switches it up—

SHIV

Okay! C'mon. Wine! Music! Fun!

ROMAN

There she is! The Red Baron claims another kill!

Roman raises his glass to Tom still outside.

His phone buzzes.

Hey.

AIDE
(*on phone*)

Hold for Congressman Mencken.

A little thrilling jolt for Roman. A wait. And then . . .

MENCKEN
(*on phone*)

Dude. What happened? Thought we'd bagged this buck?

ROMAN
(*smiles*)

Hey, fuck you I tried. You shoulda kissed more babies, you freak. Shoulda used your tongue.

MENCKEN

You're in my bad books now, little boy.

ROMAN

Uh-huh. May I invite you to bite me?

A little chuckle. Then—

MENCKEN

Guess we got our work cut out for us tomorrow?

ROMAN

Guess so.

MENCKEN

Didn't think this would come down to a buzzer beater. Hope you've been practicing your jumper.

ROMAN

Better luck next time!

MENCKEN

Nah. I don't fuck with luck.

They can feel each other smiling through the phone.

Catch you on the flip-flop? Let's stay tight? If we land this, you're coming to Spamalot, yeah?

ROMAN

Sure thing. Later.

The call ends. Roman feels a rare surge of real confidence coursing through him. He's the one the great man calls.

INT. SHIV AND TOM'S APARTMENT — GUEST BEDROOM/ COAT ROOM — NIGHT

Kendall and Frank meet privately.

KENDALL

You find ways to have fun out there?

FRANK

More or less. The red wine smelled like wet dog.

KENDALL

Can we do five. Just Franky and Kenny, not CEO and Chair? I want to let you in?

Frank fears what is coming.

FRANK

Oh hell, what are you gonna say? Are you gonna show me dead babies?

KENDALL

I don't think the GoJo deal is in the best interests of the shareholders and . . .

Frank has heard enough and puts his fingers in his ears—

I'd like to explore ways of killing it.

FRANK

Lalalalalalala. I don't want to hear this, Ken!

KENDALL

Frank? What if we were surrounded by clouds of cotton candy? Yeah? Like, 'Ooh look, Frank, there goes a unicorn on a unicycle wearing a unitard. Do you see him, Frank?'

Kendall points, all playful. Frank is putting twenty things together and stays dead straight.

FRANK

I see him.

KENDALL

Exactly. So, in this magical marshmallow world I think, Chairman – tribal elder – I want to fold you in here, Frank.

FRANK

I don't know if I'm foldable.

KENDALL

What if I told you the deal's gonna fall apart? That I don't have the hard details yet but Matsson's bullshit. His subs in Asia are significantly inflated.

Frank considers.

You don't want to quit yet, me CEO, you Chair, five more ride to glory and out?

He raises his eyebrows.

So what do you think?

FRANK

You have become more plausible. Norway, the price bump, product launch.

(then)

But lot of people feel that – a mid-size media company, you got, pardon my French, a mid-size peanut, it just can't hang with the big swinging ding-a-lings.

KENDALL

I'm just gonna hit you with this: what if we run it all the way back?

FRANK

I am tensing my glutes. What?

KENDALL

We go Reverse Viking. We pillage their village. Waystar acquires GoJo.

Huge swing. More than a little crazy. But quite Loganesque.

FRANK

There would have to be major issues?

KENDALL

There are. What if we can slow this down. And we eat Matsson's lunch. Bigger than Dad ever was?

Frank knows Kendall has to be careful with the emotional component here.

FRANK

Roman and Shiv?

KENDALL

Yeah. I dunno. I dunno. Part of my plans. I love them, but not in love with them, you know? One head, one crown. But I'll need ballast. Will you help?

Frank thinks. Then sighs.

FRANK

I don't know what I think. What's my face doing?

He's smiling.

INT. SHIV AND TOM'S APARTMENT – WINE CELLAR – NIGHT

Shiv still dazed from her fight with Tom.

MATSSON

Fun party.

SHIV

Yeah. Oh yeah. Fun party.

MATSSON

Thank you. I know I'm like a pain in the ass or whatever. You okay?

SHIV

('no', covering)

Tom? Oh we love it. We love to fuck in the car we keep crashing. Burton and Taylor being chauffeured by Grace Kelly.

MATSSON

I can do it. The business. But I don't want to . . . I want scale, content, data, revenue. But I don't want to do the gossip, or what committee's in session, I don't give a fuck.

SHIV

Well. That's the job. That's some of the job.

MATSSON

But I don't want that part.

He lets that land. Shiv feels it.

So do *you* want it?

SHIV

The top thing?

MATSSON

You know Waystar. And politics, media, America. That's you. And I stay on – Chairman and Founder and fizz my brain away while you front-face the fuck out of the cultural and political nodes. It's not a horrible shape, right?

SHIV

It is not.

Shiv considers. But she doesn't have to. It's been her aim.

Matsson nods. It seems they've made an informal pact.

MATSSON

Okay. And what else would you need?

                              SHIV
We keep me in the box for now, I don't want a mess with my
family. But once we're closed—
                    (*thinks, then goes for it*)
I'd like to move forward without Tom. It's too tricky for me.

Matsson thinks about it.

                           MATSSON
Right.

                              SHIV
Good.

INT. SHIV AND TOM'S APARTMENT – LOWER LIVING ROOM/
UPPER LIVING ROOM – NIGHT

*Shiv smiles. In some sense her life is in pieces, and yet . . . maybe she's
found her way to a new life beyond the rubble?*

Matsson gathers his gang.

Kendall finds Greg as he is filing out—

                           KENDALL
Hey. You and Matsson. You two were practically touching pee-
pees?

                             GREG
Just – doing my duty.

                           KENDALL
Stick with him tonight, okay? Show him the town. The more
disgusting the better.

                             GREG
Really? Cos. My start time's pretty early.

                           KENDALL
And, photos, yeah? Godspeed, nasty boy.

Shiv and Roman are there.

                            ROMAN
Hey, swell shindig, sis. A peerless assemblage of assholes.

KENDALL

Yeah thanks for hosting. And I guess thank Tom.

Tom sweeps in.

TOM

Hi! Okay, everyone! Bedtime for Bonzo. Sorry, but please get the fuck out of my house now! Party's over! I need to sleep. Thank you very much, terrific night!

A few people laugh nervously. Others look at Tom. Is he joking?

Seriously, I mean it. Go home and cry, enjoy your own beds, I am done, I am done, I can barely stand, I'm fine but that's enough now. Toodle-pip. Thank you for coming!

He makes a shooing gesture and people begin to gear up to leave.

Don't forget your coats! Safe travels!

Circle of guests start to break up and edge away. People collecting their coats and things.

Shiv smiles and rolls her eyes, hiding the sadness.

SHIV

Fuck Tom.

KENDALL

Yeah, fuck Tom.

They laugh, not knowing how serious she is.

ROMAN

So, hey? Funeral? If no one wants to grab it, happy to take the main energy spot?

Shiv and Kendall instantly consider what this might mean.

KENDALL

Yeah?

ROMAN

Yeah. No problem. I got it. Seemed like no one wanted to say. Happy?

Shiv not unhappy but . . .

I've just had some thoughts – appearing and— Yeah.

                        KENDALL
I know that. I know that thing.

                         SHIV
Knock yourself out, Rome, paint it red.

His siblings look at each other and somewhat hesitantly nod.

                        ROMAN
Great. Happy, happy. Headbangerz.

Roman leaves with a satisfied smile. Feeling quite powerful.

EXT. SHIV AND TOM'S APARTMENT – AERIAL – NIGHT

The lights turn off in various rooms.

INT. SHIV AND TOM'S APARTMENT – MASTER BEDROOM –
NIGHT

*Shiv lies down in bed. She turns out the light and stares into the
darkness.*

INT. SHIV AND TOM'S APARTMENT – GUEST BEDROOM/
COAT ROOM – NIGHT

Tom, finally granted his chance to sleep, lies wide awake.

Episode Eight
AMERICA DECIDES

Written by Jesse Armstrong
Directed by Andrij Parekh

Original air date 14 May 2023

Cast

KENDALL ROY	Jeremy Strong
GREG HIRSCH	Nicholas Braun
SHIV ROY	Sarah Snook
ROMAN ROY	Kieran Culkin
CONNOR ROY	Alan Ruck
TOM WAMBSGANS	Matthew Macfadyen
FRANK VERNON	Peter Friedman
KARL MULLER	David Rasche
WILLA FERREYRA	Justine Lupe
RAVA	Natalie Gold
NATE SOFRELLI	Ashley Zukerman
HUGO BAKER	Fisher Stevens
MARK ROSENSTOCK	Brian Hotaling
RAY	Patch Darragh
MARK RAVENHEAD	Zack Robidas
MAXIM PIERCE	Mark Linn-Baker
JESS JORDAN	Juliana Canfield
SOPHIE ROY	Swayam Bhatia
LUKAS MATSSON	Alexander Skarsgård
CONGRESSMAN JERYD MENCKEN	Justin Kirk
DANIEL JIMÉNEZ	Elliot Villar
DYLAN	Michael Broadhurst
DARWIN PERRY	Adam Godley
PAM	Lori Wilner
TRACY LEVINGS	Ashley Rowe
PETER SAMPINO	David Kerley
DAVE	Jason Babinsky
LAUREN PAWSON	Crystal Finn
DELTA PIKE	Sharla McBride
MILWAUKEE REPORTER	Katie Hannigan
JORDAN PARK	Danny Cevallos
SHAW	Kate Arrington
CATHLEEN CARMICHAEL	Kelly Nash
CRAIG HAMILTON	David Briggs
BEN STOVE	Tom Nichols
ZAHRA RAJAVI	Rana Novini

JOHN PORTIS	Iain Page
LOCAL PGN REPORTER	Makayla Montelongo
ANDY	Andrew Barsh

INT. ATN – TOM'S OFFICE – NIGHT

4:54 P.M.

Tom drinking an energy drink.

Election day package running silently.

We see – voting lines, graphics.

Both candidates voting—

Mencken in Long Island.

Jiménez in Denver.

Some disruption and voter intimidation.

Maybe the exterior of Mencken's New York base of operations, a midtown hotel, rival demonstrations.

Greg knocks.

> GREG
>
> Okay, dude? The five p.m.?

Tom stands. Shakes his head. Does some moves to wake himself for the night – stretches his head forward like a tortoise to stretch out his neck – quite a few times and it looks quite weird. Then, geeing himself up, and windmilling his arms to get the blood flowing, jumping up and down on the spot in a little pogo.

> TOM
>
> Rah. Blahhhh! C'mon! C'mon!! C'mon!!!

> GREG
>
> You okay, man? All good?

INT. ATN — CORRIDOR — NIGHT

They head off down an ATN corridor.

> TOM
>
> Is 'all good'?
>
> *(looks at him)*
>
> First post-Logan election? Cyd spitting poison around town like a king cobra that ate Graydon Carter's iPhone. PGN to the left of me. FVA to the right of us. I need to deliver the best election night numbers ever cos my bosses are offering to rip my heart out as a little peace offering to all-comers. So yeah. Bit tense, Greg. *Little bit*, yeah.

> GREG
>
> *(mumbles)*
>
> Only a casual inquiry, man.

They stride on.

INT. WAYSTAR — LOGAN'S OFFICE — NIGHT

Frank, Karl, Hugo, Mark Rosenstock, Ray.

Refreshments on the tables. Outside catering. Maybe a discreet bar with a barkeep has been set up out in the entrance area.

Kendall arrives.

> KENDALL
>
> Hey hey. How we going?

> FRANK
>
> Oh good. I mean, you know?

Nods to the empty desk, empty chair. They all acknowledge the sadness of Logan's absence. But Kendall lets them off the hook, lightens things—

> KENDALL
>
> Huh. Least you can talk this year?

> FRANK
>
> No more 'chatterbox forfeits' from the Big Dog.

> HUGO

I won't get a paperweight thrown at me for 'chewing potato chips like a trash compactor'.

Kendall looks at them, he's invited this – but resets the tone.

> KENDALL

I think I liked Dad's way. Three screens, twelve hours. Total silence.

Karl is looking at the catering. Kendall makes a phone call.

> KARL

Shall we get a few more crabs? Stone crab. Crab cakes? I don't know why, why does it feel like crab goes with elections?

Kendall connects.

> KENDALL

Hey, Tom. You good? Needs to be gangbusters tonight, man, yeah?

> KARL

Chesapeake Bay – Maryland – DC, is – is that a thing? Crab and democracy?

Intercut with:

INT. ATN – OUTSIDE DECISION-DESK ROOM – NIGHT

4:57 P.M.

> KENDALL

Need those numbers, T. Really wanna see those numbers, Tom. Markets watching. First Super Bowl. How we gonna cope without the king? Huh?

> TOM

I got it! All good, Ken.

On Tom looking weary. There are a group of people gathered outside the decision-desk room. Pam (senior producer), Lauren Pawson (below her), Dave (lead director), Mark Ravenhead, Delta Pike, other anchors and pundits and senior journalists.

How we looking, Pam?

Pam is checking two phones.

> PAM
>
> Um, bit of crackle. We have a news van in a bit of trouble in Oregon? Things getting fighty in Milwaukee.

> TOM
>
> You see the – the viral thing about the woman who voted forty times for Jiménez under her dead mom's name?

> PAM
>
> We tracked her down. Not super – reliable. She's not a well person.

> TOM
>
> Still. It's a great example of what could happen, if we're not careful?

> PAM
> (*looks down*)
>
> Oooh. Long night in dress shoes? Cyd used to go for these sort of – slip-ons with a padded sock?

Tom looks concerned. Darwin, Head of the Election Decision Desk, emerges from the room.

> DARWIN
>
> Okay? Shall we?

INT. ATN – DECISION-DESK ROOM – NIGHT

As they filter in—

> TOM
>
> Darwin, you don't do anything special tonight, someone, mentioned adult diapers.

> DARWIN
>
> I think there's always time for the bathroom. You shouldn't be sitting in your own filth as you tabulate the aggregated wisdom of the Republic. I mean I keep a Stadium Pal on hand but that's really just for peace of mind?

He has a Stadium Pal on his desk.

Inside, the decision-desk team, who have been sequestered with the National Election Pool. Twelve or so with binders, laptops, extra screens and devices.

Everyone huddles into the decision-desk room. Group of ten to fifteen senior executives and talent – Tom, Pam, Lauren, Dave, Ravenhead, couple of other anchors. Journalists making notes.

Darwin gives his speech—

> DARWIN
>
> Hey hey, all. So Ts and Cs. Forgive me those of you who know this!

He starts in. But through it, at the back, Greg and Tom whisper to each other—

> GREG
>
> You get *some* rest though?

Tom looks like: No.

> TOM
>
> Marital strife. Dread. Pity. Horror. Felt like I, starting with my tongue, chewed myself up from the inside, then shat myself out as a quivering wretched mass.
> (*then*)
> How was your night?

> GREG
>
> Pretty monstrous. His crew knows some unseemly venues. I danced with an old man.

Tom looks like: What?

> He didn't want to dance. But they made us dance. He was so confused. I drank things that— Things that aren't normally drinks.

> TOM
>
> And did you – figure out my rations, emergency battle dust?

> GREG
>
> Uh-huh. Yes.

> (*looks around*)
> And I er, got the impression— Do you know about, Matsson, with Shiv, their sort of business-alliance arrangement?

> TOM
> (*'yes'*)
> I don't know what you're talking about.

> GREG
> Wanna strategize. You gonna fry her?

Tom looks at him.

> TOM
> (*quietly*)
> Information, Greg. Like a bottle of fine wine. Hoard it, store it. Wait for a special occasion. Then smash someone's head in with it.

Through the above Darwin gives his briefing—

> DARWIN
> (*sing-song, thirtieth time*)
> As you know this information is given to us on a need-to-know basis on terms of utmost confidentiality by the National Election Pool with whom a number of the team have been sequestered. Any leaks could theoretically impact the outcome of the election! Got it?

Faces.

> Can I hear a 'got it'?

Tom and Greg interrupt their discussion mid-flow to join in—

> ALL
> Got it!

> DARWIN
> Thank you! Also. What we are about to tell you is a snapshot of what those who have voted so far have told pollsters – but cannot reliably be used to predict winners and losers.
> (*then*)
> So, what we hear is – and remember this is not decisive, but what we are seeing is Mencken may be overperforming in Georgia and Arizona. And doing well, not surprisingly, with

white men. Jiménez seems to be overperforming among women and people of color and he's specifically overperforming in Pennsylvania, Michigan, Nevada.

Tom and Greg's discussion is over and they focus to hear—

So overall. Our early read would be: closer than polls have suggested. Close. But Jiménez is likely edging on what we've seen.

RAVENHEAD

Boo. Booooo.

DARWIN

But listen, this is privileged information, leaks could suppress or encourage turnout and result in our ejection from the National Election Pool? Okay?

TOM

You heard the man. Zip it okay?

They all exit. A buzz and hum.

INT. WAYSTAR – LOGAN'S OFFICE – NIGHT

Kendall listens, then, still on the line, announces to Shiv and Roman (on their phones) and everyone else—

KENDALL

Tom says. Exit polls say: looks like Jiménez. No leaks!

Groans, murmurs, smiles, winces. Faces. They don't like Jiménez, but Mencken is a bit much.

SHIV

I got four smileys from Gil. They think they've got it.

ROMAN

Well I got eggplant eggplant flag from Mencken.

SHIV

Well four smileys is more than two eggplants?

ROMAN

Four smileys is symptomatic of the complacency at the heart of his out-of-touch campaign.

                              SHIV

Eggplant eggplant flag reeks of the misogynistic bravado which
has so repelled the median voter.
                             (*then*)
I feel sick.

                              ROMAN

It's fun! My team is playing your team. It's just spicy because,
my team wins, they're gonna shoot your team.

                              SHIV

What you hearing seriously, these your Nazi vans?

                              ROMAN

The fun buses? The victory vans.

                              SHIV

In Florida they picked people up, told them they were taking
them to vote and a kid got left by a highway, it's fucking
kidnapping.

Shiv makes a call, heads outside to the area with desks.

Roman makes a call.

                              ROMAN
                            (*connects*)
Tabs. Yeah they're calling it for Jiménez. Big turnout. Few
things. But yeah, get offshore! Get offshore, baby!

Frank and Kendall talk privately.

                              FRANK

I'm worried about our future as a competitive economy. Debt to
GDP. Rome. Constantinople. Vienna. London. Falling towers.

                            KENDALL

Uh-huh. Sure. Spooky.
                          (*looks around*)
But how do you feel about where we're at? Me?

                             FRANK
                          (*looks at him*)
I have been thinking. These GoJo numbers. Enough to talk to
the board. What do you have?

KENDALL

I'm digging. But so far – a hunch. A strong hunch though, Frank.

FRANK

A hunch? Well I'm not Quasimodo's chiropractor so that's of no interest to me.

KENDALL

(*again checking on others*)

Our price is nudging up. Maybe we're the natural daddies. Everyone was hot for tech, but he's going to get taken to the woodshed. We've taken our medicine and we can bring hygiene to his hordes of overpaid devs cooking up crazy moonshots. Maybe we Daddy it? Yeah?

INT. WAYSTAR – OUTSIDE LOGAN'S OFFICE – NIGHT

Shiv, being careful to be discreet, is on FaceTime with Matsson.

SHIV

Hey, Lukas. Looking like Jiménez. So. Good for democracy.
(*turns away so even her lips are hidden*)
Great for us.

MATSSON

(*on FaceTime*)

Okay.
(*little bit disappointed at the lack of action, fun?*)
Fine.

SHIV

But I think either way, we think about, your funky numbers, tomorrow, day after, get ahead of the numbers, I'll come up with some language—

MATSSON

Yeah. I was thinking about that – me and Oskar with Gregory Peggory – last night. Cos I don't know?

SHIV

You talked to *Greg* about this?

MATSSON

He was a part of a conversation, as a normalist. And yeah, I just wonder maybe we keep my terrible secret, secret?

She gets a call.

> SHIV
>
> I think – I think that's— I have to go but let's talk yeah?

Switches calls or on another phone—

Intercut with:

INT. JIMÉNEZ'S SUITE – NIGHT

Busy multiple-room hotel suite. Nate is in the comms room.

> NATE
>
> Are you in at ATN, Shiv?

> SHIV
>
> Upstairs. We leave that to them, you know Dad's rule?

> NATE
>
> They need to be covering the intimidation, it's pretty dark, Shiv? Who watches the watchmen, you know?

> SHIV
>
> Who watches the watchmen? I fucking do! Are you getting good numbers.

> NATE
>
> Good. Just, watching the weather channel – storm clouds in Nevada. We have people in line. Um, disturbance in Wisconsin. But.
>
> (*then*)
>
> Yeah. Scared but good. Precinct data is— Yeah, Pennsylvania, Arizona, could be tough.

> SHIV
>
> Okay.

> NATE
>
> Yeah.
>
> (*then*)
>
> You okay?

Is this about her fight with Tom at the party? It better not be . . .

> SHIV

Good, yeah.

A strange bubble of emotion. Someone she used to be close to. Used to tell things to.

And it's gone.

> Well good. You're good. I'm here. And this all goes good, let's talk yeah. Let's keep this channel open on Lukas and me and new ATN and all things good yeah?

Shiv looks through to—

INT. WAYSTAR – LOGAN'S OFFICE – NIGHT

Kendall and Roman huddle up around Logan's desk, away from the execs who are watching the TVs down at the other end.

> ROMAN

Jiménez wins, I guess, he waves through the deal, does he? And we— I guess, last-ditch is board or shareholders.

Roman gets a text.

> Okay? Jeryd wants face-to-face?

> KENDALL

Me?

Roman texts.

> ROMAN

Should you try Gil or direct to Jiménez?

> KENDALL

Feels kinda sweaty. Maybe today is not the day?

> ROMAN

I guess – today is the day the rooster puts its head in our hands, right? The hosepipe goes through our hands . . . moment of maximum leverage?
> > (*then*)
> He says it might be a bit tight over there for two of us?

Kendall's phone goes.

> KENDALL

Ha. Fuck him. Go. Go. Sure.

Kendall makes a non-committal nod. Takes the call. As Roman heads out past Shiv, giving her a hello.

Hey, Rav?

Intercut with:

INT. SUV – NIGHT

Rava, with Sophie next to her.

> RAVA

Hey. Hey, Ken. Listen, we're all okay but we're a bit freaked out.

> KENDALL
> (*suddenly alert*)

Are you okay? Where are you?

> RAVA

We're good but I am scared. There's an SUV, we think there's an SUV— It's following us, Ken. Gordon thinks so too. There are guys trailing us. Can we come to the office, do you have good security at the office?

> KENDALL

What's the license plate?

> RAVA

T-three – is TR-three um, I can't see – Gordon has texted you.

> KENDALL

Is it— Because it is probably mine.

> RAVA

Well no. Gordon is driving us.

> KENDALL

Yeah. I was going to tell you. I didn't want Sophie to freak so I just actioned it. They were meant to be discreet.

> RAVA

What the fuck?

KENDALL

Just an extra layer of bubble wrap. For her and Ivey.

RAVA

You're having me followed? Covert surveillance, to show you care. The fuck?

KENDALL

Is she there, because this is not appropriate to discuss in front of Sophie.

Sophie looks like/motions: Can I talk?

RAVA

Your hired goons got a problem with that? She wants to talk. Sophie wants to talk.

KENDALL

Of course. I was trying to address an issue. Are you okay? Is she okay?

Sophie thinks again – no. Motions: Not now.

SOPHIE

Can I talk to him later? I feel anxious.

RAVA

She doesn't. She's— She'd like to talk later. I'm scared, Ken. She's scared. There's shit burning, there's intimidation.

KENDALL

Rav. Will you relax and tell Sophie I love her and that is why I do everything I do. Okay. Okay, Rav? Nothing is going to happen.

(*then*)

Tell Sophie I love her.

INT. WAYSTAR – LOGAN'S OFFICE – NIGHT

On Kendall. Who thinks for a long beat, shaken. Makes a call.

Just calling to say good luck. Great numbers.

Intercut with:

INT. JIMÉNEZ'S SUITE – NIGHT

Nate is still in the comms room of Jiménez's suite.

> NATE
> Thanks, man.

> KENDALL
> And um, apologies if things got a bit heated.

> NATE
> Lot of shit going down, 'victory vans'. His shitheads kicking off
> in Milwaukee? ATN going to cover?

> KENDALL
> I'll talk, but gotta let them do their thing but yeah.
> (*then*)
> Listen, you got Daniel there?

*Nate knocks on a door. Daniel Jiménez is in a room next door with
his family and his chief-of-staff. Hand over phone—*

> NATE
> Dan, you here for Kendall Roy?

Jiménez makes a face. But takes phone.

> JIMÉNEZ
> Hey, Kendall?

> KENDALL
> Hey, Dan. Hey, man. Just – best of luck.

> JIMÉNEZ
> Thanks, man. Great to speak.

> KENDALL
> Good to chat. Good luck.
> (*then, dives in*)
> But when this is over there needs to be a big conversation about
> tech is all I'd say.

Is he going to say anything?

JIMÉNEZ

Great to speak. I'm gonna put Nate on.

KENDALL

Sure. And may the best man, the best man, who you know, will protect American jobs and rein in tech and is called Daniel win. You know!

JIMÉNEZ

Hahaha. Let's catch up! Have a good one, man.

KENDALL

Sure, man. Today, my eye is just here. Making sure it's *fair as fuck*.

On Kendall looking concerned – can he trust team Jiménez to help? He and Shiv smile as she re-enters.

INT./EXT. ROMAN'S CAR – NIGHT

Roman, with his security, is being driven to see Mencken. We might see protestors against Mencken and his supporters.

INT. HOTEL – CORRIDOR – NIGHT

Roman walks along a hotel hallway towards Mencken's suite. Many people. Some Secret Service agents identified by their pins.

INT. HOTEL – MENCKEN'S SUITE – NIGHT

Dylan, press guy, and another staffer greet Roman.

DYLAN

Hey. Come on.

Roman is guided through the suite. Everything is abuzz. We can maybe glimpse a communications room and the boiler room – for receiving and interpreting data. They maybe head through an outer room to where a door is closed. The inner sanctum.

Dylan knocks and a staffer opens—

Perhaps in there Mencken and his wife and child, his chief-of-staff, three or four other aides.

ROMAN

Hey hey hey. Look at you! Losing it like a massive loser.

MENCKEN

I blame you. Couldn't deliver Connor, ah? ATN scared to run all
the fraud going on?

ROMAN

Hey, fuck you. I keep my hands out. So, what is this. Cos I'm
busy.

MENCKEN

Oh *you're* busy!

ROMAN

Fuck you. Yes. What? I don't run around town like a fucking
food-bike guy you know?

Mencken gets him somewhere private.

MENCKEN

Look. I just wanted to say a couple of things very directly.
(*then*)
We still think we can win. But. I'm very focussed on losing.

ROMAN

Okay?

MENCKEN

Winning is easy. Winning would take care of itself. But if I lose
I need to work on, what assholes would call 'the narrative'.

ROMAN

Okay? Like: 'insurgent campaign, unfairly maligned as extremist
by the coastal masturbation factories'.

Mencken clocks Roman is fast – has seen the angles.

MENCKEN

Exactly. If I lose I want it correctly characterized as a huge
victory. Overperformed. I want to be the president and I want
you to be a partner in that and if it isn't tonight, it will be next
time.

ROMAN

Hey, 'Even if you're not going to be *the* president, you're going
to be *our* president.'

MENCKEN

Exactly. 'Me you, we'll go far . . .'

ROMAN

'Over the road and into the bar.'

They shake or hug. Roman heads out feeling more Dad-ish than for a long while.

INT. ATN – CORRIDOR/TOM'S OFFICE – NIGHT

6:55 P.M.

On screen – Countdown to 7 p.m. polls closing in Georgia, South Carolina, Virginia, Vermont, Indiana, Kentucky.

Tom and Greg walking to Tom's office.

GREG

So, listen, at some point tonight can we do a chat in terms of – the me of things and—

Greg is looking around at the many bodies that are about tonight. Tom is preoccupied with two phones pinging.

In terms of. Like. After this. How to play it because well, Matsson – he – he treated me quite abominably. But it felt like trusting and he was talking a lot and so, I guess how I thread that needle in terms of the Quad of it all, the family Quad and whether that still works or—

TOM

Enough! Greg. Hey. Yeah? I cannot. Where's my coffee?

GREG

Tom? I don't do coffee anymore, man—

TOM

No. Greg. C'mon! I need to be clear? I get drowsy, miscall Colorado? Instability. US loses credibility. China spots opportunity, invades Taiwan. Tactical nukes. Shit goes big-kablooey. We're all back to amoeba. It's a long way back from pond life cos you failed to get me a double-shot, yes?

GREG

Okay. Do you want some of what you asked for?

He pulls out a wrap of coke.

TOM

No, I don't think— What do you think?

GREG

I think, maybe no? Election night?

Tom goes to the door and locks it or stands against it.

TOM

Okay. Hit me. But this doesn't go in a book, okay? This is not a thing. Is that understood?

Takes a tiny snifter of coke off his hand. Offers Greg—

GREG

Uh, no thanks. I'm *just* feeling normal after last night.

TOM

Oh so you'll do it with Matsson but not me? I don't want you looking all judgy. Go on.

GREG

I need a clear head. Also I sometimes fear I could get a taste for it and—

TOM

Shut up, Greg, don't be Mom.

GREG

I don't want to. Please.

TOM

Greg? It is medically good for your brain. Or are you saying the Aztecs are all stupid? Don't be a racist little bitch about this.

Greg goes to toot. A little bit. Maybe misses.

Are you pretending? Are you pretending to take coke?

Greg has some and Tom spots something.

Greg? Excuse me?

He comes in.

What the *fuck* is that?

There is some sushi on Greg's desk.

GREG

They were ordering some for folks and I said why not get you one?

He inspects the pack, without touching.

TOM

Bodega sushi? Are you insane?

GREG

I think Samson was on that?

TOM

No. *No, Greg.* Not Samson, I want you Gregging. You're busted down back to Greg tonight. Okay? For tonight, my digestive system is basically part of the Constitution. Microwaved milk and ginger shots. Bottled American water, spaghetti and olive oil. Okay?

His phone goes – Connor.

Intercut with:

INT. CONNOR'S SUITE – NIGHT

6:58 P.M.

Willa, Maxim, Connor, several consultants.

TOM

Hi? Con.

CONNOR

Tom, I got this crew here. And they're 'shooting da stuff' but none of it is 'makin' da show', dude? Is there any film in these cameras?

He looks at the TV.

TOM

I think we're planning on featuring, Con?

CONNOR

Well no because I'm watching. I expected to be frozen out by all those other mooks, but you guys? Come on! Give me some sugar, man. Maybe everyone voted for me. We don't know?

                                    WILLA
Schrödinger's cat.

                                    CONNOR
Till we open the boxes, I'm just as much president as the other
two, yeah? So c'mon? If I do it, that's the story of all time?

Greg is pointing at his watch.

                                    TOM
Con, I'll see what I can do, okay? I gotta go. Polls closing, yeah?

Phone down. Connor raises his eyebrows.

                                    MAXIM
Okay, well. If it's going to happen anywhere, it's going to
happen in Kentucky.

                                    WILLA
Anything can happen. *Anything.*

                                    CONNOR
Anything can happen!
                                    (then)
So glad I didn't drop. It just makes an election so much more
interesting, when you're in it?

                                    WILLA
'You gotta be in it to win it!'

                                    CONNOR
Anything could happen!

*They all cross fingers as they watch the ATN polls closing graphics
and listen to—*

INT. ATN – STUDIO – NIGHT

7:00 P.M.

The anchors discuss the first results of the night.

                                    TRACY
And it is seven o'clock on the East Coast, which means polls
have just closed in half a dozen states. The most closely watched
state at this hour is Georgia, which Representative Mencken
almost certainly needs to win if he's to secure the presidency.

As of this moment too early to project a winner in this crucial battleground.

> PETER
>
> It's also too early to make a call in Virginia. However. Our decision desk can announce—
> (*dramatic pause*)
> Jeryd Mencken will defeat Daniel Jiménez in the Commonwealth of Kentucky and the state of Indiana.

INT. CONNOR'S SUITE – NIGHT

Connor turns off the TV in disgust. Silence.

> CONNOR
>
> Gah. It was never gonna happen. Why didn't I drop out!

> WILLA
>
> Fuck Kentucky, Con.

> CONNOR
>
> No. No. I shan't become that. No. Alas, Kentucky, Willa. Alas, vanity!

INT. ATN – NIGHT

Time passes. Election coverage from the streets. The newsroom floor.

INT. ATN – TOM'S OFFICE – NIGHT

8:55 P.M.

Greg and Tom watching TV.

Tom twitchy with his pick-me-up? Pam comes in.

> PAM
>
> As we heat up, Tom, how much do you want to give to— Fair bit of intimidation. His folks and ours.
> (*then*)
> So like fire in Wisconsin, in Milwaukee that could be nasty. Could be electrical failure. Might be Menckenists.

Tom wrinkles his nose – nah.

Camera smashed and crew harassed in Portland. That's them.

Tom nods – sounds like a story.

> TOM
>
> I trust you.

All this over the anchor on TV—

> ANCHOR
> (*on screen*)
>
> So with polls about to close in fourteen more states, let's take a look at north-west Pennsylvania, Jordan, how does that look on the map? Daniel Jiménez has clocked up sixty-seven electoral college votes. Jeryd Mencken standing, as of right now on seventy, correct.

> JORDAN PARK
> (*on screen*)
>
> Well, um, if we take a look. If we take a look.

The touchscreen TV doesn't respond as it should. Tom notices in horror.

> TOM
>
> The touchscreen is malfunctioning! The touchscreen is malfunctioning!

Tom runs out.

INT. ATN – CORRIDOR – NIGHT

Tom is followed by Greg and Pam.

> TOM
>
> The touchscreen is malfunctioning!

Tom runs into the control room.

INT. ATN – CONTROL ROOM – NIGHT

9:00 P.M.

On screen – polls are closing in Arizona, Colorado, New Mexico, Wyoming, Louisiana, Minnesota, New York, North Dakota, South Dakota, Michigan, Kansas, Texas, Wisconsin, Nebraska.

Soon after, Jiménez wins New York, Mencken wins South Dakota, North Dakota and Wyoming.

Tom bustles in, cokey.

> TOM
>
> The touchscreen is malfunctioning! What's going on. What the fuck's going on!

> DAVE
>
> We're on it. A graphics generator shat the bed. Where's my touchscreen! On main desk, on main desk.

> TOM
> *(scared he's losing it himself)*
> You're losing it, Dave. Don't lose it tonight, Dave! Don't lose it!

Intercut with:

INT. WAYSTAR – LOGAN'S OFFICE – NIGHT

Kendall is on the phone to Tom.

> KENDALL
>
> What the fuck's going on with the touchscreen, Tom?

> TOM
>
> I'm on it!

Tom hands the phone to Greg.

> KENDALL
>
> Figure it out. Figure it out!

> GREG
>
> Hi, Ken, it's already happening.

> KENDALL
>
> We're about to get another batch, Greg, and if we drop numbers now I'm going to come down there and fucking explode okay?

Pam takes Tom out.

INT. ATN – OUTSIDE CONTROL ROOM – NIGHT

> TOM
>
> Where's that touchscreen, Pam! Is it loaded up?

> PAM
>
> It's loaded up.

> TOM
>
> Get it on air! Get the new one on air! We'll be hemorrhaging, we'll be a laughing stock.

> PAM
>
> We're on it, Tom. Okay? It's in. No one will notice, okay? We've done this before. We have three and they're all lined up.

Tom's phone goes.

INT. WAYSTAR – LOGAN'S OFFICE – NIGHT

Shiv has one phone in hand, one on desk on speaker to Nate.

> SHIV
>
> Tom, the fire in Wisconsin? You got this?

Kendall is nearby, the Old Guard down at the other end.

INT. ATN – CORRIDOR/TOM'S OFFICE – NIGHT

9:05 P.M.

On screen – Michigan and Wisconsin are too early to call.

Tom is returning to his office.

> TOM
>
> Uh-huh, I think I have that. Electrical.

Intercut with:

INT. WAYSTAR – LOGAN'S OFFICE – NIGHT

> KENDALL
>
> Why aren't we covering, Tom?

> TOM

Well, I think it might not be so interesting to our viewers.

> SHIV
> (*into other phone*)

Electrical failure?

> NATE
> (*on speakerphone*)

Not what we hear.

> SHIV

Not what Nate hears.

She puts Tom on speakerphone too next to the Nate phone.

> TOM

Well bully for Nate.

We stay in the Waystar office as the two phones side by side speak to one another—

> NATE
> (*coolly*)

Hey, Tom.

> TOM
> (*coolly*)

Hello, Nate.

> KENDALL

We need to be all over this, Tom.

> TOM

It's important for us to keep our unique perspective. We have conflicting reporting.

> SHIV

Oh do you? What about the actual pictures, of it happening I can get on my fucking phone?

> TOM

We have to make choices on what to cover, Shiv. Just because something's on fire that does not make it news.

> KENDALL

If these nut-nuts are going paramilitary we can say that?

                    TOM
Uh-huh. We just need to respect our viewership.

                    SHIV
By not telling them anything they don't want to hear?

Roman arrives back, off phone—

                    ROMAN
Hey. You got this about Antifa firebombing in Milwaukee?

                    NATE
No. We hear his people, Mencken's.

                    TOM
Look, if it becomes a story, we'll do the story.

                    SHIV
And what, this is a vote-count center?

INT. ATN – TOM'S OFFICE – NIGHT

In Tom's office. Pam comes in. Greg's there.

                    PAM
Tom. They're evacuating, we've got a local chopper up, and a
reporter on the way.

                    TOM
Guys, I've got to manage this. I'll keep you looped yeah. Talk to
Greg yeah?

INT. WAYSTAR – LOGAN'S OFFICE – NIGHT

On screen – Mencken wins Louisiana.

                    GREG
                 (*on speakerphone*)
I can keep you fully abreast, guys, happy to be the link-up guy
here . . .

Kendall ends the call.

                    SHIV
If it's Milwaukee, if it was deliberate, it's Menckenists.

ROMAN

False flag? Could be.

SHIV

Oh shut up.

Her contempt resonates but somehow reflects worse on her, in this corporate environment.

Kendall is reading Twitter and other social media.

KENDALL

Guys?

Shiv, Roman, Kendall watch a news report on ATN from the Milwaukee fire—

REPORTER
(*on screen*)
The fire was initially thought to have been caused by an electrical failure, but now claims and counterclaims are being made by groups who were protesting alleged voting irregularities outside the vote-count facility.

Kendall is looking at his phone.

KENDALL

How the fuck are we behind social media on this. We need to be leading this.

INT. WAYSTAR – LOGAN'S OFFICE – NIGHT

9:18 P.M.

On screen – 'FIRE IN MILWAUKEE COUNTY DISTRICT BUILDING'.

Shiv is on the phone with Nate.

SHIV

Are the ballots intact?

Roman is on with Mencken—

ROMAN

Where are you at?

Intercut with:

INT. HOTEL – MENCKEN'S SUITE – NIGHT

Dylan, Mencken's press guy.

> DYLAN
> Depends how many votes have gone.

> ROMAN
> But ballots have been lost?

> DYLAN
> Oh yeah. We're chartering planes to Milwaukee. A ton of
> number-crunching by our analytics team. Trying to check the
> Milwaukee County voter rolls to see who has voted so far.
> *(then)*
> But listen can you help us on the messaging?

INT. WAYSTAR – LOGAN'S OFFICE – NIGHT

Roman thinks, slips out of the room.

Shiv on with Nate.

> SHIV
> Have you got all the bodies you need?

She spots Roman leaving.

Intercut with:

INT. JIMÉNEZ'S SUITE – NIGHT

> NATE
> We have bodies. We have a SWAT team on it, they're interfacing
> with the Wisconsin campaign.

Shiv spots that Roman has left. Goes after him.

INT. ATN – NIGHT

Roman makes it down corridors.

INT. ATN – OUTSIDE CONTROL ROOM – NIGHT

Tom is outside talking to Greg. Spots Roman approaching.

> TOM
>
> Roman? Rome? No brass on the battlefield please, yeah. That's in Logan's Geneva Convention, right?

> ROMAN
>
> Just a pop-in, what's going on? They've evacuated the count center, right?

> TOM
>
> I do not know, I have lost another touchscreen, Roman, I am down to my last fucking touchscreen!

Shiv is arriving downstairs.

> SHIV
>
> Hey. What's going on?

> ROMAN
>
> Nothing. Tom thinks China has hacked his tech.

> TOM
>
> I do not. And I really think you guys would be more comfortable upstairs? Greg, yeah?

Atmosphere between Shiv and Tom.

> SHIV
>
> Hello, Tom.

> TOM
>
> Hello, Siobhan.

> SHIV
>
> Are the ballots still in there?

Then Kendall is arriving there too now.

> KENDALL
>
> Hey, man, can we catch up, where are we?

> TOM
>
> Greg. Please. Can we get— Can you get these guys upstairs?

Pam comes out.

> PAM

Reporter on the way. Three, four out.

> ROMAN

We'll see that and what's going on, then – back upstairs, okay?

Tom walks off wearily.

> SHIV

Hey, Tom. Tom?

INT. ATN – PRIVATE SPACE – NIGHT

Tom has three phones. Two buzzing. Plus his brain is on fire. Shiv wants to get them back to somewhere more normal so she can eventually tell him something she needs to tell him. Maybe now, maybe soon.

> SHIV

Um. Listen, just fast I wanted to just to apologize, for some of the things that I said, at the party?

Hard front from Tom.

> TOM

Okay.

> SHIV

And give you a chance. Also to— [You might want to retract some of what you said.]

> TOM

Uh-huh?

> SHIV

Well, look, I can't do it to—

He looks all hard.

that.

> TOM

How should I frame my face?
> (*then, looks at her*)
> What, you might want some advantage from me? Scared I'll blab about you and Matsson?

SHIV

No. Jesus fucking Christ.

(then)

Tom, my father has just died. My father just died, okay? And for *a number of reasons* I have been a little, off-kilter. Maybe I can get some margin of consideration on that?

TOM

Sure.

SHIV

What does that mean? 'Sure'.

TOM

It means, you hated him, Siobhan.

SHIV

I did not hate him. I loved him.

TOM

Well, it was complicated. But you certainly hated him sometimes and also, sort of, killed him.

SHIV

Fucking hell, man.

TOM

Sort of. Sort of.

SHIV

Yeah that's the bit I'll remember. Thanks.

(then, 'fuck you')

Yeah, well, also, I am pregnant, by you. And there is never a good time to say but eventually you need to know so, okay? Now you know.

What the fuck?

TOM

Right.

(then)

And is that even – true?

SHIV

You— What?

Her – unbelievable he should ask that.

He – is hardly asking, maybe more of a protective shield of words, but he finds he still asks—

TOM

Is that even true or is this a new position or a tactic – or – what?

That she would lie about this? Unbelievable. She fixes him for a beat, then departs.

On Tom – biggest night of his career. Kind of accidentally on drugs. Now gonna be a father. Brain on fire.

INT. ATN – CORRIDOR – NIGHT

Roman and Kendall are scrolling in the corridor. Greg on a phone.

JESS

Guys? They have an area?

Roman and Kendall shake their heads. Shiv joins, full of feelings.

KENDALL

Okay?

SHIV

Uh-huh. Uh-huh. Yup.
(*then*)
Yeah. I mean. I think obviously everyone knows. But I wanted to acknowledge that things are tough. With my situation and Tom. I want to get into it but I can't get into it now okay?

ROMAN

You want us to kill him, I'd love to kill him?

SHIV

(*shrugs, 'maybe'*)
I think. Maybe he's just a piece of filth and – there's— I need to fill you in on stuff. But – you can't trust him. You know that, right?

KENDALL

No need to say it, Pinky. We got you.

Tom comes down the corridor towards the siblings. Who look at him with hard eyes. Maybe Roman 'boos'. Shiv smiles hard at Tom who can barely look her in the eye. Shakes his head.

INT. ATN – CONTROL ROOM – NIGHT

They follow Tom in to watch – a reporter is doing a two-way interview with an anchor.

> REPORTER
> (*on screen*)
> In terms of the fire, it's still burning and crews are struggling to contain let alone hope to extinguish.

> ANCHOR
> (*on screen*)
> Any reports of injuries?

> REPORTER
> None right now, fortunately. The building was evacuated immediately. All staffers are accounted for.

> ANCHOR
> And in terms of the ballots? The votes?

> REPORTER
> There's a lot of confusion. It looks like all the ballots had been received here at the vote-count facility. But election workers were evacuated unable to back up the tabulators or save the paper ballots. So we have a certain amount of confusion and debate over the way forward here.

> KENDALL
> Who's responsible. That's the story right, who burnt this place down?

> ROMAN
> For me it comes down to coupla old favorites. The Blacks or the Jews.

He looks around. Only Tom, Shiv and a couple of people close by could hear.

> Kidding. I'm *kidding*!

> TOM
> Please? Greg, can you—?

Greg offers them a direction out . . .

INT. ATN – CORRIDOR – NIGHT

Roman gets a call. As they are walked down a corridor—

ROMAN

Connor?

As Shiv, Kendall and Roman walk—

Intercut with:

INT. CONNOR'S SUITE – NIGHT

CONNOR

Rome. Um. Jeryd isn't picking up?

ROMAN

Yeah, somewhat busy, perhaps.

CONNOR

Because I wondered if what we talked about. Might still be on offer? Ambassadorship-wise?

ROMAN

That was kind of a yesterday offer. If he doesn't make this. You're going to be partially fucking responsible. Okay?

CONNOR

Rome. I've spent like a hundred mil here? Can't I get a sniff of even a little guy. Organize a little coup down in old Peru? Put me in a van to Tajikistan? Could I just be our fun guy in Uruguay?

ROMAN

Your rhymes are compelling. But what's in it for him, Con?

CONNOR

Oh I don't know, maybe just one of the finest political operators of his generation sorting shit out?

Roman hovers outside the exec room as Kendall and Shiv go in. He gets another call.

INT. ATN – EXEC ROOM – NIGHT

11:01 P.M.

On screen – polls closed in California, Oregon, Washington, Idaho. Jiménez wins California, Mencken wins Idaho.

Shiv is on the phone.

> SHIV
> (*reporting*)
> So, under state law, the vote is not certified until absentee ballots are counted. No Wisconsin result is valid until the absentee ballots are counted.

> KENDALL
> Uh-huh. And how is Daniel feeling?

> SHIV
> Confident but terrified. Yeah. Is that a— I don't know if there's a name for that feeling?

Roman comes in.

> So, Rome, under Wisconsin law . . .

> ROMAN
> Mencken says we're done. Wisconsin is done. That's their position.

> SHIV
> Well no. Like a hundred thousand absentee Milwaukee ballots are missing. So we have to figure out how to go forward and—

> ROMAN
> Go forward to undermine Mencken's lead?

> KENDALL
> Does he have a lead, is that right?

> SHIV
> Artificial lead. With a hundred thousand Milwaukee ballots missing? Every vote must be counted.

Roman makes a dismissive noise.

> KENDALL
> I think that is maybe right, man?

> ROMAN

They can count all the votes they have. However, unfortunately, some have been lost. So.

> SHIV

'Some have been lost'? Meaning fascist fuckheads burnt them.

> ROMAN

We literally don't know that. It could very very easily have been your fucks, they love fires.

11:05 P.M.

On screen – fire. Pennsylvania and Georgia are too early to call. Storyline of political night has taken shape – as the focus hones in on the battleground states, and the tea-leaf reading begins.

> SHIV

You are making hay from political violence.

> ROMAN

Or, your guys knew they were going to lose, so they did something crazy to call it into question and get a revote.

> SHIV

You don't believe that.

> ROMAN

Maybe I do?

> SHIV

Jiménez is going to take like Pennsylvania, Michigan and Arizona so I don't even know why you're even getting uppity about this shit.

> ROMAN

Well why are you getting so uppity about this shit if you're so confident?

> SHIV

Because – because if Mencken wins it's the end of the world and so I'd like a little fucking cushion.

> ROMAN

Listen, let's get real. Jiménez won't block the GoJo deal, so fuck him. Yeah?

Roman looks at Kendall who won't catch his eye.

SHIV

Who knows, maybe he would. But we cannot let that be the—
That's not the thing here, right, Ken?

KENDALL

Hm. Hm. I don't know.

SHIV

Ken? Don't get cynical.

KENDALL

Not cynical. No. But blocking the deal? I'm a realist.

SHIV

Says the man who cuts his son's throat to eat him on the high
pass.

KENDALL

We can all say nasty shit, Shiv.

Tom comes in.

TOM

Um, so, FVA is saying they have enough vote reported to call
Wisconsin. FVA, VeraNews are gonna call it for Mencken.

ROMAN

Okay? Wow. Well? Can't get outflanked. And we want to be
fast? We're gonna need to call it right?

SHIV

No!

KENDALL

Tom. Where's— What does like an independent— Can you get
us – Decision-Desk Darwin?

INT. WAYSTAR – LOGAN'S OFFICE – NIGHT

11:30 P.M.

*On camera – Jiménez giving a statement – respect the process, follow
the administrative process, no result until they have all the results. A
partial result isn't a result.*

Karl and Frank and Hugo watch.

INT. ATN – EXEC ROOM – NIGHT

Darwin is led in. He has papers. Tom kind of avoids Shiv's eye and she his.

> TOM
>
> Dar. Thank you so much. So we have some questions and some thoughts and—

> KENDALL
>
> Do you have a result as it stands in Wisconsin?

> DARWIN
>
> Well, we've tallied the vote totals so far—

> ROMAN
>
> And?

> DARWIN
>
> The margin for Mencken, is significant. It couldn't be made up by outstanding existing uncounted votes, only the ones destroyed.

> ROMAN
>
> Well we're not waiting for the burnt votes. So you can call it.

> SHIV
>
> I think they'll have to hold it again. A revote?

> DARWIN
>
> Well I would say a revote is incredibly rare and complex – because while we theoretically know everyone who requested an absentee ballot, we don't entirely know how many turned them in. And there's nothing in Wisconsin law that really covers what to do so—

> ROMAN
>
> Exactly. You can't do it. Boom. Mencken. Thank you!

> DARWIN
>
> But we of course, we think, the team knows, we know, how the missing votes would have broken down.

ROMAN

They're gone! We can't know what was on those ballots.

SHIV

Well we do know. That in past elections Milwaukee votes would go—

ROMAN

You know, what they *might* have been, but we don't *know*.

DARWIN

Sure.

(*then*)

I just basically do know.

ROMAN

Well you don't know.

DARWIN

I do know.

ROMAN

How do you know?

SHIV

We do know.

ROMAN

You don't know. Why do you know?! Cos you're so 'plugged in' you know how all the little peasants vote and what's in everyone's heart? Well no.

SHIV

Rome?

ROMAN

Ballots get lost every election. There's no way to get burnt ballots back.

SHIV

Bullshit. Bullshit bullshit.

TOM

Shiv?

SHIV

What?

Electric between them. Eyes. Her ready for him to mention. Will he?
No, he stays on track—

                          TOM
You are sounding a little unhinged.

                        KENDALL
You fucking watch it, Tom.

                         DARWIN
We do know.

                         ROMAN
It's not for us in here to say how they will have voted? I mean
why don't we just run your model and not bother with all the –
people, huh? Is that what you're saying?

                          SHIV
We're saying historically . . .

                         ROMAN
Historically people used to burn witches, should we start doing
that?

Everyone getting text messages and calls. Roman looks at his phone.
He's exchanging messages with Mark Ravenhead.

                          SHIV
Look. We know, we just know the fire will have destroyed a lot
of Jiménez ballots. Right?

                         ROMAN
So, the fire was biased? 'Fire favors GOP' claims mad witch?

                          SHIV
We just know.

                         ROMAN
They can't rerun the election, right? If the Right got wrongly
blamed for this, what would that do? If the Left did? Could get
nasty?

He gets up.

                          SHIV
Where are you going?

ROMAN

I am going to the bathroom, to shit? Do you want me to livestream it?

He goes.

SHIV

Ken?

KENDALL

I just think it is hard.

SHIV

If the lost votes were counted, Jiménez would take the state.

Tom, off his phone.

TOM

There is this piece of it that the Dems knew they weren't going to get the votes they needed so they torched it.

Greg has an email.

GREG

Um. There's a press release, a tech firm thinks they can figure out votes even from ashy residue?

Pam knocks in.

PAM

Um, guys, I think, I think Mark's commenting directly, ATN voice. Roman's given him talking points?

They turn to the TV, Ravenhead's statement. As Shiv rushes out.

INT. ATN – STUDIO – NIGHT

11:38 P.M.

On screen – Jiménez has won Washington ('Key Race Alert').

RAVENHEAD
(*on screen*)

Look I just want to address something directly here. We don't know who conducted tonight's firebombing, and nor does anyone else, yet. You can see people speculating across other outlets. And *we're* the bad guys? Because we want to count the actual votes, not rely on the estimates of a bunch of professional politicos who time after time come up – isn't *this* funny – with polls which undercount support for traditional values. So yeah, maybe some of their crazies heard they were underperforming and decided to stop the count, destroy the evidence? And so, yeah: 'Just stay quiet, we'll guess what we think was on those ballots. *We'll* decide'? Yeah? They know best, and you'll eat what's for dinner. Because they don't really care for folks who ask too many questions. Innumerate residuum! We'll figure it out. And issue you with your new government to march into your homes and take whatever we want in the way of your mechanisms of self-defense and tell your son she's your daughter or the other way round.

Shiv reaches Roman who is watching from by nearby.

And now apparently Daniel Jiménez is accusing the fire of being biased. That sounds right? It only burnt Democrat votes. Yeah? You know, one of those picky fires? I'm sorry, *what*?

> SHIV
>
> Fucking bullshit! Bullshit! Roman. Fuck you. This is not okay. We need to even this up, we need an opposing viewpoint on this—

Kendall comes to find Roman as Shiv gets a call, heads off.

> ROMAN
>
> 'Powerful commentary'. Heh?

> KENDALL
>
> I don't feel good necessarily about this, Rome. I need to think.

Shiv takes the call.

> SHIV
>
> Hey, Lukas.

Intercut with:

INT. MATSSON'S HOTEL SUITE – NIGHT

> MATSSON
>
> What the fuck is going on?

> SHIV
>
> Yeah. Pretty scary.

MATSSON

Is this okay? Do I need to hustle? Do I need to get ready to be cozy with this Mr Scary?

SHIV

I can handle, I can handle, Lukas.

MATSSON

Yeah because Greg tells me it's getting kinda hairy in there? Don't let them break my toy will you, Shiv, ah?

SHIV

I'll be in touch.

INT. ATN – OUTSIDE CONTROL ROOM – NIGHT

11:45 P.M.

On screen – Mencken wins North Carolina. Arizona and Michigan are too early to call.

Shiv approaches.

SHIV

Hey. Greg. Time for a word, bud?

INT. ATN – CONFERENCE ROOM – NIGHT

Shiv gets them in there and closes the door.

SHIV

Hey, um so. I just wanted to— It's so busy but I just wanted to check in.

GREG

Right. On election day?

SHIV

Did you have a good time last night, with Lukas?

GREG

Shiv. I just went for a drink with him. That's not my fault.

She looks at him. Leaves it an uncomfortable beat.

SHIV

Do you find me attractive, Gregory?

GREG

I don't— I wouldn't think about things such as that.

SHIV

I thought you were a 'Disgusting Brother'? That a little too disgusting for you?

GREG

I don't think this is appropriate.

SHIV

Because, I am just letting you know, if you try to fuck me, I'll kill you.

GREG

Sure. Uh-huh. Got it.

(then)

I guess, my only question would be. If anything did come to pass. In terms of you. And he? You know, silence is golden. But how golden? Like – is there an offer?

She looks at him.

SHIV

Yeah I have an offer. How about I offer for you to keep all your internal organs on your insides, rather than I pull them out your asshole?

He decides – okay, well, nothing more to be gained.

Go on. You're lumber. Keep your nose out. Okay?

INT. ATN – EXEC ROOM – NIGHT

12:10 A.M.

Roman comes in.

ROMAN

So?

Kendall's deep in thought.

Look, Mencken will block the deal. But he'll kill it, if he wins he's willing to refer it to FTC, whatever, new law, foreign ownership tightened, whatever, he'll screw it up, in exchange for our support tonight.

> KENDALL

Okay. What, in, in, so many words?

> ROMAN

In those words.

> (*then*)

So? Shall I get Tom, shall I get the human abacus, shall I do it? Yeah?

On Kendall – agony of indecision.

INT. ATN – TOM'S OFFICE – NIGHT

12:15 A.M.

On screen – Jiménez wins Pennsylvania ('Key Race Alert').

Roman slips into Tom's office. Tom, Greg and Darwin waiting.

> ROMAN

Hey thanks for this, guys, so. We have the votes. Can't rerun fairly, can't let Lefty terrorism affect the thing. Let's call it.

> TOM

But – on what precedent, by what authority?

> ROMAN

By the power of me, the CEO of Waystar telling you what to put onto the telly-box mouth people.

Tom looks at Darwin.

> DARWIN

Um, I don't think we can, guys?

Maybe Greg starts eating from the sushi, squeezing wasabi out and eating to relieve tension.

> ROMAN

I think we can, Dar.

> DARWIN

If we call it – if we call it – and, you know, the others, went his way—

ROMAN

Look, we have outstanding states. Michigan, in Ohio, Georgia, Arizona. It's not that big a deal.

DARWIN

I'm worried that it's a decision that I couldn't necessarily—

ROMAN

Uh-huh and thank you. Everyone respects you, Darwin. But it's really not a numbers thing.

DARWIN

But I don't think I can call it. I mean, the Wisconsin Elections Commission and Milwaukee Election Commission will go to court and the camps will litigate – it'll be a jurisdiction fight that I *think* Mencken might shade but I can't, we just can't—

ROMAN

Uh-huh. Great. But I'm just gonna say, we're good. It's on me. The votes that exist have been tallied and they give Mencken the state.

TOM

But you don't make the call. I make the call.

ROMAN

We'll be making the call together, Tom.

DARWIN

You can't make the call without me making the call!

ROMAN

Look, I don't want to make you do anything. But what if we were to say, this is the situation in Wisconsin, how would it feel if we said it wasn't a – a call-call, but a call – that was—

TOM

Pending? We could call it pending?

ROMAN

You could explain, we could get the camera, in on you and you can explain?

Darwin would love a way out. He has a little vanity, has potentially always felt he could be on-screen talent.

> DARWIN

I *could* explain. And could there be a graphic to make it clear – the call isn't a like – a call-call?

> TOM

'Pending call'.

Beat. Darwin opens a laptop. With his fists clenched to not make contact he nudges away a box of sushi open on the desk, he doesn't notice but smeared along the rim is some wasabi.

> DARWIN

Oh, man. Okay?

He rubs his eyes with his knuckles.

A strange sensation grows. He groans.

> ROMAN

What is it? Are you—?

> DARWIN

My eyes. My – eyes?

> ROMAN

What?

> DARWIN

I've got something in my eyes!

> TOM

Greg? Wasabi.

> DARWIN

Is it wasabi? Is there wasabi in my eyes! I've got wasabi in my eyes!

Darwin has his head down, blinking and moaning. Rubbing eyes. Shiv comes in, hearing shouts.

> DARWIN

Argh. It's gone more in! It's gone more in! It's on my hands.

> SHIV

What the fuck are you doing to him?

> ROMAN

We're good.

                              TOM
      Darwin, are you okay? Greg?

                            DARWIN
      Fuck me fuck me fuck me, it stings! It stings!

                              TOM
      Greg, get him water.

*Greg pops a can of La Croix lemon water. Darwin has his eyes
clenched shut. But hears the pop.*

                            DARWIN
      Sweet mother! Oh mother of god fuck me gently this smarts.
      Water.

                             GREG
      Here. Here you go. Here.

Darwin puts his head back, but cups his hands.

                            DARWIN
      Pour it— Water—

But Greg has already poured La Croix in Darwin's eyes.

      Argh! It's washing it in! It's washing it in!

                              TOM
      Not lemon! Greg?!

                            DARWIN
      Is it lemon? Is there lemon?

                             GREG
      It's clear! It's La Croix!

                            DARWIN
      Is it lemon? Argh.

                              TOM
      It's lemony, Greg.

                            DARWIN
      Jesus H. Christ!

                             GREG
      It's La Croix, it's natural – like medical? Here, here's water.

> DARWIN

Lemon? Argh!

Darwin washes, takes a beat. Blinks.

> ROMAN

Are you okay to call it, Darwin?

> SHIV

He can't call, Roman!

> TOM

We're making the call, Shiv. He called it. Greg. Don't put any more lemon water or wasabi in his eyes, okay?

Tom and Roman head out.

INT. ATN – CORRIDOR – NIGHT

Tom walks on. He is digesting the news about his child. It's likely true. Does he even start to smile a little before . . .? he doesn't allow that and there—

Is Connor being escorted down the corridor by a security guard?

Tom passes.

> TOM

You shouldn't be in here, Con?

> CONNOR

A very good evening to you too. Rome?

Tom walks on.

> CONNOR

Rome? One thought. How about I concede in his direction? Could that be of interest?

Roman stops in his tracks.

INT. ATN – CONTROL ROOM – NIGHT

12:23 A.M.

On screen – Ohio was just called for Mencken.

> TOM

Pam, we're calling Wisconsin for Mencken, get the graphics up.
Let them know, Dave, five out from calling Wisconsin.

INT. ATN – EXEC ROOM – NIGHT

12:28 A.M.

On screen – Wisconsin is called for Mencken ('Key Race Alert').

> ANCHOR
> (*on screen*)

And ATN is therefore ready to make a call. That Jeryd Mencken
has won Wisconsin. That Mencken takes the ten electoral
college votes of Wisconsin and edges closer to that magic two-
seventy—

Kendall and Roman watching with Connor.

Roman gets a text. From Mencken. He turns to Connor.

> ROMAN

Okay, man. Okay. There's something there.

INT. ATN – MAKE-UP ROOM – NIGHT

Connor is being made ready. With Willa – she reads his speech.

Watching the anchor too.

> WILLA

You really wanna?

> CONNOR

Slovenia, Willa?

> WILLA

Uh-huh? I am torn. He's very right-wing.
> (*she looks*)
But – Vienna for lunch. Venice for dinner?

INT. ATN – STUDIO – NIGHT

Connor is recording his concession speech.

CONNOR

Thank you. It's becoming clear tonight that as far as we can tell – Mr Jeryd Mencken will be the next President of the United States and I for one wish him well. For although I set out a clear and compelling path, America in her divine wisdom has chosen to take another. Well. Good luck. You have turned your back on low tax, a small state and high growth and near-guaranteed national happiness for another path. Perhaps a better one? I doubt it. But, you never know. But tonight is not a night for recriminations. Tonight is a night to thank my campaign staff. Tonight is not a night for excuses. Even though the first of my debates passed without the moderator offering me the chance to speak. And I'd like to say to my first running mate, who I will not dignify with a name-check, but had *that woman* not dropped out and then, had I not had to replace her with another figure who turned out not to be able to bear the weight of public scrutiny. Had I not been betrayed by those two, jackrabbits. Who knows? Who knows, my friend. But honestly, America. You flunked this one big time. I guess you're gonna have to find some other poor mook's paps to suckle on as the corrupt bipartisan system zombie-marches on. And so I call out to my friends tonight, to my people, the loyal Conheads. And I say Conheads, I salute you, it doesn't stop here. No, I say America, be afraid, for the Conheads are still coming!

During the speech, we cut around to—

INT. ATN – EXEC ROOM – NIGHT

Roman watching.

INT. WAYSTAR – LOGAN'S OFFICE – NIGHT

The Old Guard watching.

INT. ATN – SHIV'S OFFICE – NIGHT

And Shiv watching.

INT. ATN — STUDIO — NIGHT

Connor steps off. Pumped up.

> CONNOR

Good?

> *(looks at her)*

No?

> WILLA

Yeah. No. I mean, didn't feel super concession-y.

> CONNOR

Well it was a concession speech. So?

> WILLA

You ended it with 'be afraid'. You told everyone to be afraid of you?

> CONNOR

Yeah it just came to me. I thought it went well. It had good cadence.

INT. ATN — EXEC ROOM — NIGHT

12:50 A.M.

> TRACY
>
> *(on screen)*

Just — want you standing by, Ben, because we are able to make an important call tonight. And that is the ATN decision desk is now projecting that Daniel Jiménez has won the state of Michigan over Jeryd Mencken.

> PETER
>
> *(on screen)*

And that's fifteen electoral votes. So our tally goes to two-sixty-two for Mencken and two-sixty-two for Daniel Jiménez. And polls will be closing soon in Alaska, with three electoral votes. The only state yet to be called other than Arizona and its eleven electoral votes.

Tom comes in with Darwin.

> TOM

Um, guys. Just a heads-up. We hear— We're hearing the campaigns are getting it from the data nerds. Dar?

Roman gets a text.

> DARWIN

Arizona is going to go red.

> ROMAN

And that, that would be it, right?

> DARWIN

Well, no. Not— I mean. We are kind of boxed in. With Wisconsin. But I don't feel comfortable, calling it because—

> ROMAN

But I mean, if PGN is going to call it?

> DARWIN

It's just obviously, we're boxed in – because if we call it, because of Wisconsin, we called Wisconsin pending, so—

> ROMAN

We called Wisconsin, that's over, forget that. We can't un-call it, can we? That would make us all look quite unprofessional.

> DARWIN

So, Arizona, that means calling the election?

This lands heavily on Kendall.

> KENDALL

Tom, will you guys give us a minute?

Tom and Darwin head out.

> ROMAN

That's it.

> KENDALL

I don't know, Rome. I think. I might like— Can we think on? Maybe we – maybe we can revisit – Wisconsin and— Because, yeah, we— That was—

> ROMAN

Are you gonna pull a big-brother?

KENDALL

No. Like what?

ROMAN

Like when, if you wanted roast chicken, and I wanted steak, we always had chicken?

KENDALL

Because you'd freak out. You'd tantrum, so they thought—

ROMAN

I would tantrum cos we never had a fucking steak!

KENDALL

Well I think they got scared if you tantrumed, then you'd think you'd won so they couldn't let you have a steak.

ROMAN

Well it was bullshit. I never won. I never won. Always chicken.

KENDALL

So because we had so much chicken when we were kids, I have to elect a fascist?

ROMAN

Yeah. Basically.

(then)

Look. If we don't call for him early, if we don't get on the train, and he still wins – which is perfectly possible – but without us, tonight, or going legal, think about that? With FVA and VeraNews backing him, we're left the most dickless eunuchs in cuck town?

KENDALL

It's fucking real, bro.

ROMAN

Nah.

KENDALL

We call it, we call it, if we push it – maybe it happens?

ROMAN

We give it to Mencken. Mencken blocks the deal. He's not fucking wishy-washy. He's a guy.

KENDALL

But. But I don't know. My kids. The whole, the whole – thing?

ROMAN
(*mockingly wet-eyed*)

'Oh America!'

KENDALL

It's just a – nice idea, you know? All the different people together?

ROMAN

What would Dad do?

KENDALL

I don't know.

ROMAN

C'mon! The guy in the pocket? The guy who's gonna answer our calls? The fucking guy who's gonna print us dollars? It's all upside.

KENDALL

Apart from the matter of him smashing the country to pieces?

ROMAN

Don't be a Prissy Peter? Maybe we could do with a dose of that? Just a nice little dose of the frighteners? Wind shit back twenty?

KENDALL

Somebody pushed Sophie—

Roman waits, respectfully.

ROMAN

And she's okay?

KENDALL

Yeah. People will say shit, Rome. A lot of tiresome shit, forever.

ROMAN

Mmm? Sure but think about the fucking – action, the fucking, choo-choo of it. We'll be in the fucking West Wing. Nothing matters, Ken, nothing matters. Dad's dead and the country's a big pussy waiting to get fucked. I'm serious. Let's get fucking. Do shit! We're not chin-stroke motherfuckers. Action! We can

pay for any damages. Let's jam our heads in the bosom of history and just—
> (*shakes his head between imaginary breasts*)
blurghghghg!

It's a bit funny. But Kendall is caught.

KENDALL

Uh-huh?

ROMAN

Or. Or what? Sit on our hands like a pair of damsels in distress watching our chance slip away?

Kendall heads out – but full of thoughts and feelings.

INT. ATN – SHIV'S OFFICE – NIGHT

On screen – PGN – calling Arizona.

KENDALL

Hey, Shiv. Can we talk.

She's wary. What is this?

SHIV

We're fucked. We're fucked, Ken. Because we called – it's fucked.

KENDALL

Yeah. I don't know what we should do. I feel like my head is— I – can't get the scale of things, one with another, what's real and—

SHIV

I think we— Can we recant? He's a bad bad man.

KENDALL

His team are being very direct. They'll block Matsson's deal.

Shiv is uncomfortable. She doesn't really want to directly lie.

SHIV

He *says* he will.

This hits.

KENDALL

We call it for him, that gives him legitimacy to declare, we're in bed with him, I think yeah?

SHIV

Maybe. Yeah. Yeah?

KENDALL

You think he's the full – horrible? Because there is a persuasive view he's just a management consultant who does fash-drag?

SHIV

It feels dark.

KENDALL

Uh-huh. But it will get ground out in the courts, whatever we say?

She feels very compromised, with him right there, so open.

SHIV

Right. But – yeah?

KENDALL

Uh-huh.
(*looks at her*)
Speak, speak more, Shiv. Speak. You can say?

SHIV

I dunno. I hate him but. It's complicated.

KENDALL

Because?
(*looks at her*)
Are you feeling, have you felt cut out?

SHIV

I guess?

KENDALL

Uh-huh. I, look – shall we be totally honest in here?

SHIV

Uh-huh?

KENDALL

I have – I have sometimes felt like I could do it. Like I can do it, me. And that's not to say I haven't loved the feeling of all of us together and that I don't feel that something has happened with us, but – it can be messy, we're very different?

> SHIV

Uh-huh. Sure.

> KENDALL

Yeah? So, so, um, yeah. I guess. I'm just going to say it – I have wondered if I could – push through, honestly. But I don't want that to be a, an – end to a family thing, I would like to talk openly about that feeling maybe? What I think I can do?

> SHIV

Uh-huh?

> KENDALL

So – I just want to be honest about the context.

> SHIV

I appreciate that.

> KENDALL

And so yeah – honestly it's all complicated. Mencken is Roman's guy, so that's complicated?

> SHIV

Right.

> KENDALL

I feel threatened maybe by their relationship. So I want, a bit of me wants to not support that? Maybe that's in there pulling away from Jeryd?

> SHIV

Yeah and also – you're a – good guy.

It is nice to hear that. Of course, Shiv has a few reasons for saying it . . .

> KENDALL

Thank you. I dunno.

> SHIV

You are. Essentially.

> KENDALL

But we all want to stop Matsson, right?

> SHIV

Uh-huh.

He can feel the hesitation. Even she herself doesn't quite know how much she might be willing to admit.

> KENDALL

Go on?

Shiv feels compromised. But okay, let's go for it. She feels this is for the greater good—

> SHIV

I – er, I, guess I would say, that whatever the advantage for us, as as, corporate players short-term in such a move, he's – he's the nightmare. Plausible in – a – a – a decadent era. You know, the whole what we have is— People think it's a thick wall they can just throw endless rocks at to register their general disapproval. And the edifice, people hate will just – just stand. But you know, things break, it's not a wall, it's perishable – vegetation. People have no idea, *no idea* how bad things could get.

> KENDALL

I dunno. He sometimes seems like a bit of a Halloween-costume guy?

> SHIV

He says the bad shit. He believes the bad shit. He's a— Yeah. What can I say?

> KENDALL

We wouldn't actually be making him president—

> SHIV

We might not be able to crown him, but we can stop him. He gets momentum tonight, that makes it possible. He needs our call.

> KENDALL

But I want to – I want to—

But it dies on his lips.

She looks at him.

I'm not sure I'm a great dad.

> SHIV

You're okay. You've tried. It's all we can do.

> KENDALL

Maybe the poison drips through?

> SHIV

Nah, man. Nah. And I think even Dad wouldn't back him tonight.

> KENDALL

Do you give a fuck what Dad would've done?
> (*then, also*)
He basically picked him.

> SHIV

Sure but – an early call? It's bad business. We throw the papers and the whole thing in for him? And then the courts go the other way in a week, a month, and we're essentially done as a news organization?

> KENDALL

It's just hard to think we'd give it all away to Matsson.
> (*then*)
Could we try, could you try, once, direct to Nate to get *something*? To stop the deal?

She looks at him, nods. She takes out her phone.

I know it's a mess. Thank you, Shiv. One of these?

He offers a hug. She feels bad. But they hug.

> SHIV

Hey? Hey, Nate?

INT. ATN NEWS – CORRIDOR – NIGHT

Shiv walks out into the corridor.

Kendall watches her speaking into the phone through glass.

> SHIV

Hi yes, just calling with an inquiry. A check-out.

We hear a message from the other end: 'This number is not in service, please dial again to connect your call.'

Shiv smiles to Kendall.

INT. ATN – EXEC ROOM – NIGHT

On screen – numbers discussion. Alaska has been called for Mencken. Score is Mencken 265, Jiménez 262.

Roman there with Tom. Kendall walks in.

> KENDALL
> So, um, Shiv's seeing what we can get from the Dems.

> ROMAN
> Oh please?! What? C'mon.

> TOM
> I need to know what we're doing, guys? If we stick with Wisconsin and call it?

> KENDALL
> One moment, Tom. One.

Tom heads out. As Shiv enters—

> So?

> SHIV
> Yeah. I think there's something there.

> ROMAN
> Nooo. Man?

> KENDALL
> Like?

> SHIV
> I— They might be— They are willing to think.

> ROMAN
> Oooh. They *might* be willing to *think*?? It's deep-fried bullshit.

> SHIV
> They're just not – so. Direct? I think we can probably get them to stop it.

> ROMAN
> Sorry. No. Game over. C'mon, we have to call it. It's cast-iron from Mencken.

SHIV

Roman. Even Dad – even Dad – in this situation would
respect—

ROMAN

Dad did what the fuck he wanted. One fax and he took a
government out. 'Screw Lyle.' That was enough. Canada. Here.
He did what he wanted.

SHIV

He liked stability, he pushed and— But he never wanted shit to
unravel. He helped end, he ended wars.

ROMAN

Only ones he'd started. He didn't give a fuck!

KENDALL

What did they say, Shiv. What did Nate actually say?

SHIV

Um, he would talk and – and they could see the arguments. It
was encouraging.

Kendall gets up. Gets out his phone.

What are you—?

KENDALL

I'm gonna call, I'm just gonna be very direct. We need just a
little bit more and—

SHIV

Don't call him.

KENDALL

Why?

He looks at her. Weird. Kendall makes the call.

SHIV

They're – busy.

Walks out. He connects to Nate.

Roman talks, Shiv watches Kendall – preoccupied.

> ROMAN

Can't have uncertainty. The markets. The chaos of trying to rerun an election could send the country into meltdown.

She's on autopilot, fearful of where Kendall's call will lead.

> SHIV

Bad faith. Bad-faith argument.

> ROMAN

Can't have uncertainty. China is coming.

> SHIV

Oh now China is coming?

> ROMAN

It's not the final – final, anyway. There's court shit and— It'll fuzz along. It's just—

Now outside, Kendall, call over, asks Greg.

> KENDALL

Greg. What the fuck is going on with my sister and Matsson? Huh?

Greg looks in – time for that wine? Shiv sees them connect. Fuck.

INT. ATN – EXEC ROOM – NIGHT

Kendall comes in.

> ROMAN

What they give you. What they promise you – unlimited social security spending with this one weird trick?

> KENDALL

Shiv?

> SHIV

What?

> KENDALL

'I think you're a good guy.'

She sees that her lie about Nate is up.

> SHIV

I found it hard to get Nate so I summarized some impressions.

Kendall looks at her, nods, mock-earnest.

> KENDALL
> Oh right, right, smart, really good, Shiv. But you lied?
> (*then to Roman*)
> She didn't get anything from Nate – she didn't speak to Nate.
> And she's in with Matsson, right?

> ROMAN
> What?

> SHIV
> No. We all— We agreed I would get close to him, to help—

> KENDALL
> Shiv's fucking us. Right, Shivvy?

> SHIV
> No. No. I – I – I— (just got close to him and then you two—)

> KENDALL
> 'I – I—I – I'—
> (*then*)
> I fucking asked you some real questions, Shiv. I wondered why
> you looked like a goose trying to shit a house brick, you piece
> of – dirt.

> ROMAN
> Have you got a side deal?

> SHIV
> No. I have some options – and, did exactly what we said. I was
> getting cut out, so—

> ROMAN
> Well. Mencken. It's Mencken, right?

> KENDALL
> Mencken.

> SHIV
> No.

Roman goes to the door, calls or sends for an assistant.

> ROMAN
> Tommy Two-Tits!

SHIV

Look. I – I have fostered a relationship. I have but, you – said yourself, you said yourself, you've thought—

KENDALL
(*nods along mockingly*)
Uh-huh, uh-huh, uh-huh? Sure, sis. Sure.

SHIV

Please, listen, aside – from all this, aside, it's not the right thing—

KENDALL

Aside from the fact that you lied to us and doing what you want, *precisely*, plays into your own interests, yeah aside from that?

SHIV

Ken? Please. C'mon. Who are we?

ROMAN

Will no one think of the children!

SHIV

I am not going to let this happen. There comes a time—

ROMAN
(*highfalutin*)
'A time, in the affairs of man, to get fucky-fucky with Matsson'?

SHIV

Seriously, this is real. My concern for the state of – the Republic and – pluralism and the future – is—

ROMAN

You're boring, Shiv.

SHIV

Fuck you. Ken?

KENDALL

He's right.

Maybe he does a yawn.

ROMAN

And, you don't have a pass for in here.

> SHIV

I don't have a pass for in here?

> ROMAN

No you don't have a pass for down here, just as a matter of fact.

> SHIV

I might go public. I might go to the papers, to people with what you're doing.

> ROMAN

If you keep on talking hysterical shit we might have to ask you to move. People are trying to do serious work.

> SHIV

Fuck you. This is about the future of the Republic.

> ROMAN

Nah, it's because you've broken up with your boyfriend.

> SHIV

You prick.

Tom comes in.

> ROMAN

Tom. Call it. We can call it.

> TOM

We're calling it?

> ROMAN

We called Wisconsin. Now we call Arizona, so we call the election.

> SHIV

No, Tom. No. This is a terrible mistake.

A look between them – does she appeal to all the things that the future is freighted with now? He's not available. Even a little cruelty in his announcement—

> TOM

Hey, not my call. Not my call. Your call, guys. If you say so.

> SHIV

Fucking – Pontius Pilate!

> ROMAN

No one knows what you mean! No one cares. No one cares!!

Tom makes a phone call to Greg.

> TOM

Go tell them I'm coming. I'm calling it – we're calling it for Mencken. Tell them I'm coming.

INT. ATN – CORRIDOR – NIGHT

1:20 A.M.

Greg ends his phone call.

Crosses Jess.

He looks weird. He stops for a beat.

> JESS

You okay?

> GREG

Yeah. Yeah. I have to go – tell them, I think, we're calling it for Mencken. Yeah. So. I should—

> JESS

Right.

> GREG

I'll be in trouble if I don't go.

> JESS

Okay, dude. I mean—?

> GREG

Yeah. I mean, I don't really have a choice.

> JESS

Sure. Yeah.

> GREG

I'm just pressing the button – not even pressing the button? Asking them to prepare to press the button.

> JESS

Right all it does is – launch the nuclear attack?

> GREG
>
> It's not gonna change anything, if I don't?

> JESS
>
> Couple of minutes?

> GREG
>
> Right. But realistically?

He's off.

> Whoa! Crazy one. What a crazy one!

INT. ATN – CONTROL ROOM – NIGHT

1:25 A.M.

Tom comes in to call the election. Darwin stands, heavy-hearted. Greg has given advance notice.

> TOM
>
> So, Pam. He said, yeah? I'm calling it for Mencken.

Beat. Weight in the room.

> PAM
>
> Okay. Well then, Dave?

> DAVE
>
> Okay. Lydia – get me 'Mencken Wins'! Get the ticker going on ATN Citizens, let people know two mins, ATN is going to call it. Drum roll. In the booth, ninety seconds till we are projecting.

> PAM
>
> Dar, let's put the checkmark in – we good? Dar, Dave, Steve. Tom, we're confirmed?

INT. ATN – EXEC ROOM – NIGHT

Kendall and Shiv and Roman watch.

> ANCHOR
> (*on screen*)
>
> ATN is ready to make a projection in the state of Arizona. Arizona has just been called by ATN, which means ATN is

projecting that Jeryd Mencken is elected next President of the United States!

INT. ATN – EXEC ROOM – NIGHT

1:40 A.M.

On screen – Mencken in a hotel ballroom. His supporters cheer and watch—

> MENCKEN
> (*on screen*)
>
> It's now clear that I have won sufficient electoral votes to be declared the next President of the United States and I find the responsibility awesome. I know there are some who feel that there is something left to contest. But votes have been cast, the votes have been tallied. On another day, in another time they might have fallen in another fashion. But tonight we only know what we know what we know – the election has been called for me by an authority of known integrity.

During the speech, we cut around to—

INT. ATN – CONTROL ROOM – NIGHT

Darwin, head in hands, rocking.

Tom and Greg watch—

> TOM
>
> Maybe we find a history guy? A brain. A real brainiac. To say why this sort of thing has happened before and it's all fine? Greg, get them to dial us up a history asshole?

INT. WAYSTAR – LOGAN'S OFFICE – NIGHT

The Old Guard, agog.

INT. ATN – EXEC ROOM – NIGHT

> MENCKEN
> (*on screen*)

Those partisan operations run and funded by my rivals might try to drag this out but, I think all fair-minded Americans will accept the plain result. And let me say, to my critics. I'm not a demagogue. I am a defender of democracy. The democracy I believe in is about togetherness, not division. I believe not in turning on one another in arrogance and judgment but binding ever faster together, in truth and unity. One America. But democracy, it has this tendency we have to beware, to become mere transaction. I give you this. You give me that. I come begging for your vote. My welfare checkbook out. Crowning the welfare kings and queens till everyone has become a little tyrant, crowned by the state. No, the model I follow isn't from the scorched marketplace where cunning men haggle for the best price. That's not me. The democracy I believe in is drawn from the folkmoot – from the forest green where a leader emerged from the people. A leader was – willed almost into being, brought forth by the great sweetness of the virtue of the combined wisdom of the good people of this Republic. Don't we long sometimes for something clean once in this polluted land? That's what I hope to bring, not something grubby with compromise but something clean and true and refreshing, something proud and pure!

Kendall and Shiv and Roman watch. Maybe through some of the above—

> KENDALL

He's a guy we can do business with.

> ROMAN

He's gonna play ball. You should hear him talk semiconductors.

> KENDALL

We're holding the leash. We have him by the leash.

> SHIV

You've done something bad here.

> ROMAN

We've just made a night of good TV, that's what we've done. Nothing happens.

> SHIV

Things do happen.

Roman gets a call – Mencken. Displays the name.

> ROMAN

Oooh. President calling. Cool.
> (*answers*)
Yo. Hocus-POTUS. You sitting in the POTUS position? Whuddup.

> MENCKEN
> (*on phone*)

Hey, man. No time but just thanks. Yeah? 'You and me, we'll go far—'

> ROMAN

'Over the road and into the bar.'

End of call. Roman all glowing.

INT. ATN – CONTROL ROOM – NIGHT

1:55 A.M.

Tom with Pam and Dave.

> PAM

The legal process is going to be lengthy.

> TOM

When do you think it'll all be over?

> PAM

I don't think we're gonna be able to take our eye off the ball for at least the next seventy-two hours. Could be going on for the next three weeks?

> TOM

Uh-huh. Right. Right. I am incredibly tired.

> PAM
>
> I mean the fact is, he is going to be amazing for numbers. That's just a fact.

Greg comes in. Watches the coverage. Maybe we can see a few marches and disturbances.

> GREG
>
> Your phone is red hot, Tom. A lot of very important people want to—
> (*then*)
> A lot of very important people want to scream at you.

There's a picture of Tom on screen at PGN. And Shiv and a photo maybe of all of them with Mencken.

> TOM
>
> That just feels very – pointed?
> (*then*)
> Can you check on the numbers?

> GREG
>
> From where? From Wisconsin?

> TOM
>
> From Nielsen. Fast overnights, Greg. Numbers. Soon as.

> GREG
>
> On it.
> (*then, a text*)
> Um, Darwin's wondering if there'll be time for him to do his caveats soon?

Tom looks like: I don't think so.

We stay on Tom's face – what a night. Unbelievable.

INT. CONNOR'S SUITE – NIGHT

2:30 A.M.

Willa and Connor have arrived back.

> CONNOR
>
> Oh, man. Mencken wins. We're going to Slovenia. Ding. Jiménez pulls it back—

(*thumbs to himself*)

Hero to the Left. Dong! Speaking tour! Either way, four percent in Alaska! Ker-ching. Every lever we pull is a jackpot, honey!

INT. KENDALL'S CAR – NIGHT

3:15 A.M.

Kendall being driven home. He's tired. Puts Rava on speaker and holds the phone flat. He doesn't mind Fikret hearing.

> KENDALL
>
> Hey. Can I come see them?

> RAVA
>
> (*on speakerphone*)
>
> They're asleep, Ken.

> KENDALL
>
> I can wait.

> RAVA
>
> I should be asleep but I can't. What's going to happen?

> KENDALL
>
> Nothing, Rav. His bark's worse than his bite, there'll be a lot of— Dane Harrington will likely be chief-of-staff. They won't scare the market. The market has its eye on this, okay?
>
> (*then*)
>
> He's gonna stop the takeover and that would be good.

> RAVA
>
> Uh-huh?

> KENDALL
>
> I can hear that tone. I had to make a tough call.
>
> (*then*)
>
> Big picture, I'm gonna remake the company.

> RAVA
>
> Uh-huh. Great. Great, good to know.

> KENDALL
>
> Sophie will be fine. He has values. It was one guy. We're literally gonna help pick the cabinet, Rav.

                              RAVA
Uh-huh. Thanks, Ken.

                           KENDALL
See you at the funeral, Rav. See you at the funeral. Okay?

Kendall hangs up.

Some people just can't cut a deal, Fikret.

EXT. STREET – NIGHT

3:40 A.M.

Shiv walks the street.

                           MATSSON
                         (*on phone*)
Jesus fucking Christ! What's going on?

                             SHIV
Those funky numbers. I'm sending words, let's get them out next
twenty-four. Lot of fucking news.

Intercut with:

INT. MATSSON'S HOTEL SUITE – NIGHT

                           MATSSON
You guys are crazy!

                             SHIV
It's more than fucking crazy, Lukas.

                           MATSSON
Yeah but it's craaaaaazy!

                             SHIV
We are going to do a number on them. We are going to fuck
them so hard. We're gonna fix this. Yeah?

                           MATSSON
                      (*'cool it, Shiv'*)
Oh, that why I'm buying your company?

SHIV

No. But – this is out of control.

MATSSON

Should we reach out to Mencken? That's the logical thing, right? Shall I do it, or you?

On Shiv. Doesn't want to do that.

SHIV

Nah. That's not the play. No, let's take his legs out before he can goose-step his way up Fifth.

Episode Nine

CHURCH AND STATE

Written by Jesse Armstrong
Directed by Mark Mylod

Original air date 21 May 2023

Cast

KENDALL ROY	Jeremy Strong
MARCIA ROY	Hiam Abbass
GREG HIRSCH	Nicholas Braun
SHIV ROY	Sarah Snook
ROMAN ROY	Kieran Culkin
CONNOR ROY	Alan Ruck
TOM WAMBSGANS	Matthew Macfadyen
FRANK VERNON	Peter Friedman
KARL MULLER	David Rasche
GERRI KELLMAN	J. Smith-Cameron
WILLA FERREYRA	Justine Lupe
KAROLINA NOVOTNEY	Dagmara Dominczyk
HUGO BAKER	Fisher Stevens
JESS JORDAN	Juliana Canfield
MARK ROSENSTOCK	Brian Hotaling
RAY	Patch Darragh
RAVA	Natalie Gold
SOPHIE ROY	Swayam Bhatia
IVERSON ROY	Quentin Morales
COLIN STILES	Scott Nicholson
STEWY HOSSEINI	Arian Moayed
SANDY FURNESS	Larry Pine
EWAN ROY	James Cromwell
CAROLINE COLLINGWOOD	Harriet Walter
KERRY CASTELLABATE	Zoë Winters
SANDI	Hope Davis
LUKAS MATSSON	Alexander Skarsgård
PETER MUNION	Pip Torrens
CONGRESSMAN JERYD MENCKEN	Justin Kirk
EBBA	Eili Harboe
OSKAR GUDJOHNSEN	Jóhannes Haukur Jóhannesson
DYLAN	Michael Broadhurst
MARIANNE HIRSCH	Mary Birdsong
SALLY-ANNE	Nicole Ansari-Cox
CARDINAL	Fr. Dennis J. Yesalonia
FUNERAL DIRECTOR	William Villanova, Sr.

DELTA PIKE	Sharla McBride
ZAHRA HEYDARI	Rana Novini
OFFICER MILLER	Rachel Paula Green
PROTESTOR	Mark Fichera

INT. ATN – TOM'S OFFICE – DAY

Close on Tom.

He's tired. So, very tired. Drinks coffee. Maybe does some hops on the spot to try to wake up. Some roars. Colleagues passing by ignore.

The day after election day (or the day after that).

We're in his full ATN office (not his war room down near the newsroom floor). He's watching ATN.

> DELTA PIKE
> (*on screen*)
> President-elect Jeryd Mencken is denouncing attempts to derail the democratic process. In a speech from the new Mencken transition headquarters in New York City this morning, he announced . . .

We cut around—

INT. SHIV'S APARTMENT – DAY

Shiv watches, laying out her funeral wear. She has some shoes ready.

> DELTA PIKE
> (*on screen*)
> Daniel Jiménez's team is seeking a court injunction to prevent the certification of election results until all absentee ballots are tallied. President-elect Mencken is dismissing ongoing attempts to challenge the election result, stressing that a revote would likely cause Wisconsin to miss the Electoral College's mid-December meeting date. The Republican-led Wisconsin Legislature, meanwhile, is vowing to step in and name a slate of Mencken electors to ensure the state is not disenfranchised in the selection of the next president.

She changes the channel to PGN.

INT. CONNOR'S HOTEL SUITE – DAY

Connor prepares.

> MENCKEN
> (*on screen*)
> There are no do-overs available for an election. No mulligans.
> Ya get the result, and real men take their lumps. They don't cry
> about it. Let them do the sour grapes, cos I'm measuring the
> drapes!

INT. ROMAN'S APARTMENT – DAY

*Roman is in his mourning wear. Watches same piece of Mencken. Bit
folksy but impressive.*

*He leaves the TV, looks at a number of note cards – he has a funeral
eulogy that he has run through a few times. He's hitting it once
again—*

> ROMAN
> My father – Logan Roy – was a great man, in the true sense
> of the word. Born, the middle child of three, he was sent away
> during the Second World War to—

*As he walks the apartment declaiming, he knows it all now, he feels,
so he summarizes and freestyles as he goes, nodding through the
points—*

> Bing bang *BONG.* Sad sad sad.

He checks himself in the mirror, then like it is part of the speech.

> I look good. I look good.

*Looks at each card, the three or four bullet-pointed prompts for the
speech, carries on talking as if this is part of the speech as he nods
through the words on the cards, but winking into mirrors, counting
off the points on his fingers.*

> I am the man. I am the man. As you can see, here I am. Talking
> loud, about my dad.
> (*with the cadence of a speech, all grave*)
> And don't I, perhaps, remind you all of him, just a little?

(back to the bullet points)
Chicago Daily, '81. Launches *The Correspondent*.
(all serious or mock-serious, English accent?)
'A passion for human communication'.
(then, back to himself)
I am King Dong. The King of Dong. Please bow down. I picked
the president. Can you see his pecker sitting here in my pocket
now?
(then, new card)
Pearl Cable. Sandy Furness.
(points, he will do this for real in the church)
Hey, Sandy. Guess you won, hahaha.
(sad face)
End of first marriage.
(then, new card, all real and earnest)
Communication. *Connection*. Nothing is more important!
(then, second-to-last card)
See Shivvy cry, see Kenny lie. See Roman the Showman light up
the sky!
(then, last card)
Last years. New adventures. Was he, maybe – tiny nice voice –
losing it a bit at the end? Kerry? Selling up? Who knows? *But*.
Great man.
(back on script for final lines)
His demise was carried, written in fire. Pulsed electric, in a
flash, over seven continents, into newspapers he started, across
networks he founded, through fiber he had laid, satellites we
launched. A great man indeed.
(then)
You want to applaud. Not really appropriate in here, but fuck it,
g'wan, let rip!

He bows.

Phone goes.

Intercut with:

INT. KENDALL'S CAR – DAY

Kendall riding to rendezvous.

> KENDALL
>
> Hey, man. You okay?

> ROMAN
>
> Yeah I'm okay. I'm good. I'm actually, honestly, I'm excited.
> (*then*)
> Sicko right? But. Mencken wins. Kills the deal. I mean, it's just *interesting times, bro*!

Kendall looks out – at the windows being boarded up. Bad vibes.

> KENDALL
>
> Sure. Listen, just one thing. Do you think, we've got the hotline, you have, I guess, and I just think, for business, for everything, can we, get Jeryd to turn the heat down? Turn the volume down a little?

Protestors gathering. Maybe something odd or disquieting. A gas can? Someone helping someone put a mask around their face. Or some guys bent over a bucket with a bottle in it. Just a little furtive and odd.

> ROMAN
>
> You don't like these fucking ratings, dude? 'Conflict is Bonflict.'

> KENDALL
>
> Sure, just. Hard to get fucking paid when the banks are all on fire? So today—

> ROMAN
>
> (*neither 'yes' nor 'no'*)
> Uh-huh. My thing, for today, is, and good to check in, but, the board all there? Time to poison the well on Matsson, right? Whichever way the courts go. Kill it before Jeryd even has to do anything political. Get into all those fucking saggy old board earlobes. Waystar stock's up. Political connections secure. Get them all jangled up and frightened off – so we never even need to take it to a board vote.

KENDALL

Uh-huh. Yeah?

(*static*)

I mean. It is the funeral?

ROMAN

He'd fucking love it! We might get him out of the box if he knows there's a little bit of fucking *shenanigans* afoot?!

Kendall tries to laugh, it's sort of true, but he's not on that frequency today, things feel heavy.

He gets a call – Rava.

KENDALL

Okay, I hear you. Just. You know. Just a little – Queasy Gonzales?

ROMAN

See you at Shivvy's yeah? To roll deep?

Roman is on his way out. End of call.

KENDALL

Hey?

RAVA

(*on phone*)

Um, Ken. I just wanted to say, I am concerned – everyone's saying there are going to be major disturbances.

KENDALL

Rav. It's rumors. I'm with Fikret. I'm going with the sibs but he'll pick you guys up and then—

RAVA

Yeah, I'm not sure. I think we might head upstate today and I'm really sorry. But that's my decision.

KENDALL

What?

RAVA

We're going to go to Travis and Robert's and then—

Kendall sees it all and doesn't need to talk anymore.

> KENDALL
>
> Are you on the road? Have you left?

> RAVA
>
> No. But we are—

He ends the call mid-sentence.

> KENDALL
>
> Fikret. I want to be at Rava's in three – I'll figure out fines and violations – get us there now, okay? Sidewalks, one-ways, get me there.

Kendall breathes as maybe Fikret pulls out and around towards oncoming traffic and swerves back.

INT. SHIV'S APARTMENT – DAY

As Shiv watches TV, she tries to put on some shoes that have become too tight for her swelling feet. She has to return to the closet to find some other wider, flatter shoes. She puts them on. Here we go. She looks at ATN playing and calls Matsson.

Intercut with:

INT. MATSSON'S HOTEL SUITE – DAY

Members of his team are buzzing around. As Matsson watches—

> MATSSON
>
> Fucking shit show. *Shit show!* Are you watching?

> ZAHRA HEYDARI
> (*on screen*)
>
> And to repeat the news that broke just a little earlier this morning: outgoing Senator Felicity Montarelle will shepherd cabinet appointments through the Senate confirmation process. While Kenton Petkus, the Washington attorney who made his name defending US Marines from debunked war crimes charges, is taking on the key role of chief-of-staff.

SHIV

Uh-huh. So, I think you need to get your bad numbers out.
Because this is just an amazing day to bury bad news. It's a
freebie. And who knows how long this will last?

MATSSON

Uh-huh? I still think, if you have a little dicky, maybe don't go to
the nudist beach?

SHIV

A tsunami just washed everything away. No one's checking the
dicks. Seriously. I know this. Do it.

MATSSON

So, forceful!

(then)

How do we get around Mencken, though? It's real, blocking the
deal, over regulatory?

SHIV

I don't see it. I think the courts stop him. He's just – he's out of
tune with like some deep – sentiments of this country and—?

MATSSON

(interrupting)

You've only been a democracy for fifty years.

SHIV

Well no, no, not—

MATSSON

What, unless you don't count Black people? I know that's
traditional in your land, but it's a bad habit.

SHIV

Yeah, but—

MATSSON

I'm just saying, you're nearly as mature a democracy as
Botswana. These things are possible. So I need to reach out.
How did that go?

SHIV

Cleanest is just stopping him? Activate, donate, motivate. Can
you talk to – your – to your buddies. Get the algos pushing the
straight dope?

He makes a 'maybe' noise.

> Look. I gotta go. I'll see you there. He'll be there. Okay. Lot of angles. You gonna tell Ebba to bury those numbers. It's just so golden.

He thinks – yes.

MATSSON

Ebba!!

EXT. RAVA'S APARTMENT – DAY

Out on the street.

Kendall's car drives fast.

We see Rava's staff loading up into a Suburban. Staff putting some stuff in the back.

INT. KENDALL'S CAR – DAY

Kendall motions for Fikret to slow safely and then—

KENDALL

Block her. Block her in there, Fikret. Block the car.

EXT. RAVA'S APARTMENT – DAY

Kendall's car comes in at an angle, blocking Rava's car. She is outside the car. He gets out.

RAVA

What are you doing, Ken?

She shuts the back door with Sophie and Iverson in there behind the tinted glass.

KENDALL

What the fuck is going on?

RAVA
(calmly)

We are just getting out of town.

KENDALL

That's hysterical bullshit. You're not bringing the kids to their grandfather's funeral, are you insane?

RAVA

I don't consider it safe. I don't want to—

KENDALL

Leave them with me.

RAVA

I don't consider it safe.

KENDALL

Do you realize how nuts you sound?

RAVA

No.

KENDALL

Well you do. You sound nuts.

RAVA

It doesn't feel safe in the city.

KENDALL

I don't believe you.

RAVA

It does not feel safe today and I don't feel they will necessarily be safe with you.

KENDALL

Fucking horseshit. What fucking unbelievable horseshit.

RAVA

Well, I'm sorry but you don't know, you don't know what's going to happen.

KENDALL

You're too online. You've lost context. Everything is fine.

RAVA

You said things were going to be okay, you said Daniel would win. You said—

KENDALL

You can't go.

He tries to open the door but it's locked. His kids inside.

> Open up. Open the door. Soph, open the door! We're going to
> the funeral.

RAVA

I don't consider it safe.

KENDALL

Bullshit. Pretext. You're trying to hurt me. It's my father's
funeral.

RAVA

We're going. I am sorry. There will be a memorial and—

KENDALL

He didn't want a memorial. I'm going to go to court to get an
emergency court order to stop you leaving the city.

She goes to get into the front, does he come close or block her?

RAVA

Are you gonna touch me? Is that next?

Does a passer-by clock?

KENDALL

Can we please discuss this?

RAVA

I'm sorry.

KENDALL

I'm gonna lie in front of your fucking car.

But he's not.

She gets in. They reverse. And pull out around Kendall's car.

INT. ATN – TOM'S OFFICE – DAY

Greg and Tom.

*He has a newspaper spread out (NYT?). Graphic representation of
the ATN newsroom and decision desk, the executive viewing room. A
minute-by-minute analysis from insiders of how the call was made at
ATN. Pictures of key players.*

TOM

Who gave them the timeline?

GREG

Lot of people know. Lot of people don't want to go to The Hague for war crimes?

TOM

Oooooh! Get him.
                    (*then, looking*)
Nothing on me? Big graphic of Darwin? This— It diminishes my role. I'm tarred with the Mencken brush so I may as well get the goodies, right? No point joining the party if you don't get your little dacha?

Greg looks at his watch, breathes out hard.

What?

GREG

I just, the funeral. I feel for closure, I would love to—

TOM

Well I need to too. I'm a wheelman.

Greg: What?

I'm a casket wheelman. I'm on front right. Fucking front-right wheelman. Highly visible. Front right.
                    (*jumping in*)
'Closure'. You little – fucking. So you can dip your beak in the honeypot, make some arrangements?

GREG

I think for you too—

TOM

We'll go late. Court rulings. Possible riots. Something changes every five fucking minutes. The Republic is wobbling like a fucking panna cotta. And I'm harvesting eyeballs like a fucking eyeball hoover.

GREG

Fine. It's just. Shiv hates me and Roman— And – now it's looking – like, what Mencken wins, blocks the deal? There's just a lot of angles?

Tom looks at Greg.

> TOM
>
> Fine. Fuck off.
>
> (*then*)
>
> But save me a space. Yeah? Good space. Second row. And let Mencken's people know I made the call. Tell Mencken I swung it, yeah?

And Greg heads out, taking out a black tie.

> It's gridlock. You'll be better off walking!

EXT. SHIV'S APARTMENT BUILDING – DAY

Kendall pulls up.

Gets out. Discombobulated. Some security around. Roman waits outside.

> ROMAN
>
> Hey.

Chauffeur opens the door. Roman and Kendall hug or touch.

INT. FUNERAL LIMO – DAY

Inside – frosty atmosphere.

> SHIV
>
> Hey.

Kendall doesn't know where he stands with Shiv.

> KENDALL
>
> Sorry I'm late.

> ROMAN
>
> It's fine. Just been sitting here with Lady Liberty crying for all the taxes she won't be able to pay.

> SHIV
>
> Are you really gonna do that shit today?

> ROMAN
>
> I can say what I like. What you did was terrible. You betrayed us.

She looks at Kendall.

> KENDALL
>
> I have strong feelings. I don't want to go there.

> SHIV
>
> Oh you have strong feelings? Look what you've done to the world, you've set it on fire! *You* have strong feelings??

> ROMAN
>
> You're sore. Because Mencken is smart and will never let a foreigner run our wonderful company.

> SHIV
>
> Uh-huh. And is he coming, Mencken?

But does something land with Shiv?

> ROMAN
>
> Is Matsson?

She shrugs. But clearly 'yes'.

> Doesn't know when he's beat.
> (*then*)
> You should be pleased. Mencken wins and blocks the deal, we stay in charge.

> SHIV
>
> You do.

> ROMAN
>
> Well, the idea is a family – family – situation. So. Big picture. All is good.

Kendall has been quiet.

> KENDALL
>
> Yup. It's just a great fucking day.

> SHIV
>
> You okay?

> KENDALL
>
> Yeah. Good. I don't know.
> (*then*)
> Um, Rava's taking the kids out of the city. She's 'concerned'. So.

ROMAN

Well that's dumb. And shitty.

SHIV

I'm sorry, Ken.

Looks. Shiv could say, 'Told you so.' But, no.

KENDALL

It's fine. I dunno. Fuck.

She looks at Roman. Tension.

Roman longs for a reset.

ROMAN

You get Mom's invitation for 'a Caribbean air-clear'?

SHIV

Oh now Mom suddenly wants to play mom? Fuck off.

KENDALL

Yeah I'm a hard 'no'.

Kendall and Shiv in agreement, but turned away.

Then, is it a tactic or just because she has to—

SHIV

So, also. I've been wanting to tell you. And I'm likely telling
Mom today, so, I may as well say, I'm actually pregnant.

Beat. Wow.

ROMAN

Is it mine?

SHIV

Uh-huh, haha.

KENDALL

Really? Fuck.

(*then*)

Shiv. Wow. And, um—?

He doesn't need to say—

SHIV

It's Tom's. Like four months. So.

Hm. So she's had a big secret for a while?

KENDALL

Okay, well. Congratulations.

ROMAN

You're having a Wambsgland? I thought you'd just been eating your feelings.

SHIV

Great, yeah, good stuff.

ROMAN

You know, I'm not going to stop— [doing jokes.] I see you breastfeeding I *am* going to jerk off.

SHIV

Jesus fucking Christ, man.

ROMAN

What? I'm pleased!
(*re Shiv*)
One less sibling to compete with.

SHIV

No. My kid will kill you. I'll train my kid to kill.

ROMAN

Pregnant chess pieces can't play chess, Shiv. Too heavy. They just fall over and roll off the board.

SHIV

Uh-huh. Sure.

ROMAN

Yet again your arch-nemesis, your vagina, has foiled you.

KENDALL

Guys, can we—? Today. Shall we. For the funeral? Just cool it?

ROMAN

What? Funeral truce?

Shiv and Roman look. Nod.

KENDALL

Yeah? Today is just about today?

                              SHIV
     Sure.

Call comes in – Connor.

                            ROMAN
     Congratulations.

                           KENDALL
     Con?

Intercut with:

INT. CONNOR'S HOTEL SUITE – DAY

                            CONNOR
     Hey. We have a problem. I just got a call, funeral details are
     on social media. The security team thinks it could be a target,
     threats.

                            ROMAN
     What sort of threats?

                           KENDALL
     Is there hard intel?

                            CONNOR
     They have the time and location. As a part of the new
     administration I could be a target.

                             SHIV
     Well, it is not a new administration.

Kendall looks at her: Funeral truce?

                            CONNOR
     They advise against a funeral procession. NYPD can't guarantee
     protection for the cortège today.

                             SHIV
     God, you really have ruined Dad's funeral.

                            ROMAN
     Well we're not the ones who have made the day all about
     ourselves and all the cum we've hoarded are we?

                    CONNOR

Can we please try to have a bit of – decorum? Maybe we lead
by example?

                     SHIV

Spoken with the gravitas of a man who gave a blowjob to
become ambassador to Slovenia.
                    (*then*)
Sorry.

                    CONNOR

Look. I'm gonna, I suggest, you go, we go directly to the church
and the casket – they may have to loop round, so. Up and
around to avoid some closed cross streets. Yeah?

They look at one another. Probably best.

                   KENDALL

Sure thing. Okay. See you there.

                    CONNOR

Okay. Happy Funeral.

                    ROMAN

Happy Funeral.

                     SHIV

Happy Funeral.

EXT. NEW YORK – STREET – DAY

They drive through the city.

Windows boarded up.

*Groups of protestors happy in gangs, placards not aloft yet, greet,
walk.*

INT. FUNERAL LIMO – DAY

Jess calls Kendall.

JESS
(*on phone*)
Hey. Listen, they're saying there's a gathering, a march is
gathering from the park and FDR is gridlocked and— I can
meet you on— I've dropped a pin, I can guide you?

He's going to relay.

EXT. NEW YORK — STREET — DAY

Greg cycles on a Citi Bike up a cycle path.

EXT. NEW YORK — STREET — DAY

Limo pulls up. Jess is waving.

They all get out. Kendall puts on dark glasses.

ROMAN
Glasses. Smart. You can cry in secret, hide all emotion, and thus
emerge, victorious, as the winner of the funeral.

JESS
Hey, guys. I think from uptown it's easier— But yeah there's a
lot of confusion.

Shiv and Roman march off.

Kendall is looking at his phone. Some solace in arrangements.

KENDALL
Listen. I think I want – like early next week – I want to speak
with some family lawyers. Custody.

JESS
Okay?

KENDALL
(*peering at iCal*)
Tuesday? Let's do— What's this— What's this meet with you?

His antennae prickle.

JESS
Don't worry about that.

KENDALL

Let's bump that – what is that?

JESS

I'll reschedule something.

He looks at her.

I'd just like to do twenty and – I'd like to put that in for later in the week. But don't—

KENDALL

Sure. Like what?

JESS

Shall we do it when we do it?

KENDALL

Well don't be weird.

She's going to have to say something.

JESS

. . . I want to talk about my situation.

KENDALL

What about your situation?

JESS

Ken. It's a big day, I don't want to do this today.

KENDALL

Well now I'm thinking all kinds of things. C'mon, what?

He's not going to let her up. So. Her prepared speech, all couched to keep him sweet and get out elegantly—

JESS

Well, you've always been really supportive of me and my aims and ambitions and I really appreciate that so I'm sure you'll understand that it might be a good time for me to move on to another position.

KENDALL

Okay? Wow. Okay. Fine. Of course.

JESS

Great. We can chat more when . . .

KENDALL

Can I ask why?

JESS

Just, yeah – feels like time.

KENDALL

Is this about Mencken?

Yes. But she doesn't want to get into it. Though, nor actually, does she feel she owes him a lie. This is his mess.

JESS

I've been thinking about it for a while – so.

KENDALL

Well fine. I just have to say. Like where has this come from? Because we'll need to figure out the transition. What role exactly are you moving to?

JESS

I'll do what I can but I think I'll be going on a relatively tight horizon. So, yeah, sorry.

KENDALL

Well there's no need to be sorry.
                    (*then*)
This is ridiculous. This is fucking ridiculous, Jess. If you feel sorry about it you should reconsider.

Nothing, smile from her.

Fine. It's fine. I wish you good luck. I do. I like you. I just think you're in for a very rude awakening.

JESS

Uh-huh maybe.

KENDALL

Do you have any idea how much I've done for you?

JESS

I just think it's time.

KENDALL

Is it Mencken? Because – I'm working shit all over.

> (*then*)
> I like you, Jess. I actually like you.

KENDALL

JESS

Thank you.

KENDALL

Do you like me?

JESS

It's just been a hard time.

KENDALL

This is fucking dumb. I'm sorry but, I've given you extraordinary access.

She looks at him, refuses to give more.

> You have no idea how things will turn out and it's very juvenile. Just dumb, Jess. Really dumb.

JESS

Well I'm sorry you feel that way.

Silent awkward resentful walk, then—

KENDALL

Lovely day to tell me. Fucking nice touch. Really thoughtful.

EXT./INT. CHURCH – DAY

Maybe there is a system of barriers to let only some cars come near the entrance to the church.

Mourners are filtering in.

Discreet security checking people. Whether gate metal detectors or handheld.

EXT./INT. CHURCH – DAY

Kendall makes it in.

Hugo is there. Has good news!

> HUGO

Um, Ken? Not for now. But I have something to keep you updated on.

> KENDALL

Uh-huh. What?

> HUGO

Not for now, but – GoJo. Matsson has slipped out that they've got deeply bullshit subscriber numbers all across South Asia! But it's not for now.

> KENDALL

Well you are in fact telling me now?

> HUGO

Well, it's not to engage with, just to know.

It all feels too much. The fucking and counter-fucking. Kendall looks around the church, the many people he knows. All feels a bit threadbare and awful. And yet—

> KENDALL

Go on. Where did they slip that out? Shoot me links. We will need to amplify that, okay?

Hugo nods. Good stuff.

> HUGO

Horrible day.

Kendall looks over to—

Shiv with Connor and Willa. Shiv's looking at an email on her phone.

> SHIV

But we agreed Roman would do the eulogy, Con?

> CONNOR

But we said we could consider? If we wanted to—

> SHIV

Sure.
> (*re the email*)
I'm just worried – this is, it's so long. And also actually hard to follow?

WILLA

It's formally inventive. That's one of the things we like.

SHIV

The middle is very vindictive? Overall it just reads as something of a – of a bitter screed?

CONNOR

Pierre Trudeau is getting the treatment! Reinhold Niebuhr is *finally* getting the treatment! The Ulsterman is getting the treatment!

SHIV

I worry your eulogy could leave us open to legal action?

CONNOR

Okay. Fine. I'll take a look!
(*then*)
And – congratulations.

SHIV

Oh, thanks. Yeah, I was going to say. I was about to say.

WILLA

Congratulations.

SHIV

Thanks. Yeah. Can't really understand it. But yeah. My spite baby. I'm thinking of getting in-utero plastic surgery. So it comes out only looking like me.

Roman is approaching with a funeral director.

ROMAN

So, there was a warning someone was gonna try to zip-tie themselves to the casket? Lovely folks you got out there.

SHIV

Is he okay?

ROMAN

It's fine. Nearly here. I'm gonna do a little bit of – handshaking, okay?

SHIV

Why not. Network heaven. Whole board, half the Senate, quarter of the House?

ROMAN

I hope you're not going to get all bitter. With a sour little white-woman life, moaning about gerrymandering and researching which garbanzos are most organic.

She looks at him. It lands a bit as he heads off and—

Kendall comes over.

KENDALL

So. Heard that besides Dad we're also burying your boyfriend's fraudulent numbers today? Nice.
                    (*then*)
Funeral truce?

SHIV
                    (*not quite a denial*)
Not everything is connected.

KENDALL

Uh-huh. Well.

Possibly true. But also, maybe weary, he lets it go.

                    (*re Roman*)
The eulogy is good, right, he did good?

SHIV

He's on top of the world. Target-rich environment. Buttering up the butterballs.

KENDALL
                    (*including Shiv*)
Lot of fucking money-changers in the temple.

Now as they watch – Roman moves on and is giving Frank a pat on the back.

Roman with Frank, looking over at Kendall—

ROMAN

Yeah, Frank pal. Hey. We've had our battles huh, but – this – puts it in perspective don't it?

FRANK

Sure. Life is short. We should all love one another.

(knows there is a part two)

Go on?

ROMAN

Nothing. Just an observation. I think Ken's lost his stomach for the fight. He's getting kinda teary about 'the Republic'. Too much late-night Ken Burns. Which is lovely. But Mencken is gonna block the deal. And if Ken's lost his stomach for the fight – which I really hope he hasn't – well, if there's gonna just be one cherry on the cake. I'll be, you know, rounding up a posse?

Then, with a phalanx of Secret Service and aides, including press aide Dylan, in comes – Mencken. Shaking hands and giving two words, two minutes to folks.

SHIV

You're tied to two dirty little fuckers.

They look over at Roman shaking hands and sharing friendly words with Sandi and Sandy.

Nearby also is Colin, with his wife.

You know he's having therapy?

KENDALL

Colin?

That opens a lot of possibilities, not great. Kendall's head spins.

SHIV

Apparently. Who knows what dirt he did for Dad, ah? We should put the shrink on the payroll.

And now Matsson is arriving too – with Ebba and Oskar.

Want to touch base with Lukas?

KENDALL

I don't want to be on maneuvers at my father's funeral, Shiv.

He watches Roman work the room.

Greg arrives, sweaty, looking around all anxious for allies, approaches Roman.

> ROMAN

Gregory.

> GREG

Hey, man. Hey. Sad day. Wow.
> *(looks at Mencken)*
There he is, ah? Would you introduce?

> ROMAN

Mencken?!

> GREG

I mean, I was one of the – amongst the – crowning committee
so?

That is true. But no. Roman motions to Ewan.

> ROMAN

Maybe. Later. You're on Ewan watch. Okay? He wanted to
speak but – sadly—
> *(jerk-off motion)*
no time. So. Yeah? He starts unfurling a banner or singing union
songs, license to kill.

Roman motions to cut his throat.

Karolina, Gerri, Sandi. Karl returns with news—

> FRANK

Nearly here.

> KARL

They ask you about carrying the box?

> FRANK

With my back? Are you kidding. You?

> KARL

I've been carrying him for twenty years.

Naughty smiles.

> FRANK

This is it, ah. He's gone. He's really gone.

> GERRI

How much of you is glad?

> KARL

We had our fights but. He – he had some fucking heft to him. I miss him.

> GERRI

Stockholm syndrome. Crossed with a little bit of China syndrome. I don't think a single person in this whole room actually looked forward to seeing him.

> KAROLINA

Moving tributes. I might put that in the press release.

Roman comes over.

> ROMAN

Hello, fellow saddos. How are you holding up?

> KAROLINA

We were just saying that . . . he was one of a kind. No one that met him will ever forget him.

Gerri turns her back. Roman is all alive with possibility. Splits Karl off.

> ROMAN

Yeah, Karl, I just wanted to talk to you. On options if and when the deal gets blocked. How I see things. Because, I really think – don't know how this can be put to the board for a final decision with all the uncertainty? Mencken would block foreign ownership. So, I wonder, if in terms of planning, we don't wait for the courts and just – chart our own course?

> KARL

Sure I mean personally I am thinking about golden parachutes, wide rivers?

> ROMAN

C'mon? How many salmon can you catch, Karl? It's the same fucking fish the Parks Service ships around the country for old-timers to hook?

Karl looks at him.

Wouldn't you like to boss a young fucking numbskull around the halls of power?

Maybe, maybe there could be some fun left?

Kendall watches. Can't stand all the politicking right now. Full of grief and tiredness. Bereft of children. The church so high-ceilinged and august. He smiles off people who approach. Caroline arrives.

SHIV

Okay. Here we go. Mommy dearest. Are we freezing her out?

KENDALL

I dunno. One down? Be nice to the other in case she drops dead of a broken heart.

(*sad, sibling-connecting, joke*)

Or, not having a heart?

SHIV

Sure. It's her big day. Don't want to rain on her parade?

As Caroline arrives with them Kendall gives her a kiss.

Hi. Hello.

CAROLINE

Hello.

Caroline looks Shiv up and down. She knows right away. Maybe it's the shoes.

Oh. *Well.* Hello, darling. Okay?!

Shiv lets her know with her eyes, and face, she's right.

SHIV

Yup.

CAROLINE

Yes?

SHIV

Yes.

CAROLINE

Blimey!

SHIV

I know.

CAROLINE

Well I never.

SHIV

Yup.

CAROLINE

Right.

(*then*)

Well then. Well well!

SHIV

Thank you.

CAROLINE

Exactly.

(*she is pleased*)

Well we can get into all that later. And you didn't think to— [tell me?]

SHIV

Well I have to be careful giving you information. You might use it against me?

Caroline decides to ignore and see Peter instead.

CAROLINE

Peter?

(*then*)

Peter's incredibly excited. I think he's brought an autograph book.

Roman arrives to greet/kiss his mom.

Peter approaches.

PETER

Hello. Hi, all. So sad.

(*ironized, but perhaps insufficiently*)

'Daddy's here!'

ROMAN

Hello, Peter.

PETER

Sorry for your loss. Sorry for your loss.

SHIV

Thank you.

                              KENDALL
    Thanks.

Peter's barely able to conceal his interest in all the opportunities and connections offered by the people present.

                               PETER
    I'm going to – I'm just going to, excuse me one second.

He heads off.

                             CAROLINE
    He's going to go and roll around like a Labrador in a lovely big
    pile of senators.

                               SHIV
    How respectful.

                             CAROLINE
    He's actually rather sad. He's written a poem.

                               SHIV
    About Dad?

                             CAROLINE
    And he wanted me to ask if he could read it?

                              ROMAN
    Here? Um, no.

                               SHIV
    No. Absolutely not.

Shiv walks off. She spots Gerri.

    Hey. Thanks for coming.

                               GERRI
    Well, you know. Used to see him around the office so . . .

                               SHIV
    And I want to say. I am sorry – how things have worked out.

Shiv didn't always play nice, but she means this and Gerri can tell.

                               GERRI
    It was probably inevitable.

Shiv shrugs.

         (*with a mix of rejecting pity and true sympathy*)
And I want to say. I'm sorry – how things have worked out.

Gerri nods over to Kendall and Roman.

With Roman and Kendall. Roman is full of moves.

ROMAN

Who have you hit?
         (*evidently no one*)
Because, it's great that Mencken's a racist and won't let a dirty foreigner buy the company, but I still think we need to get the board and brass rallying round the poor orphans here. Right?

KENDALL

Sure, dude. Sure.

Roman spots Marcia—

ROMAN

Marcia's looking chic. Hubba hubba.

Kendall winces.

     What?

         (*then*)
She's a sexy woman. A sexy funeral lady. Dude, I tell you what, if you are weirded out by that, wait till I have sex with Marcia, on Dad's coffin.

Almost funny. Kendall tries to smile. But Roman's potency is a little threatening.

     Ken. C'mon, we both know one of us will, it's tribal. It has to happen.

He looks over at Matsson, Oskar, Ebba as Shiv approaches.

Shiv has had some iron put in her soul.

SHIV

So, the numbers pieces starting to come out. No significant blowback, right?

MATSSON
         (*doesn't like being bossed*)
So far. Uh-huh.

(*but it was a good call*)
No, it's good. It's working. Gold star.

SHIV

It might get worked into this profile on you. The writer made contact for a phoner but I'm thinking—

He looks like: No. He looks over at Mencken.

MATSSON

What we think? He's gonna win it out, is he gonna cock-block me?

SHIV

Well. Obviously the whole thing is unimaginable.
(*then*)
But. I did have one idea. If he comes through. Mencken?

MATSSON

Oh yeah?

SHIV

I guess, rather than walk away. Would it be smart to see if—?

MATSSON

Uh-huh?

SHIV

Well, you've toyed— What about, what about, you offer him a US CEO for the US properties at least? Give him a win on that, let him have that as a media win?

MATSSON

And if we made that offer. A US CEO? Who would you have in mind?

SHIV

Oh I dunno. *Anyone.*

MATSSON

Right, anyone.

They smile.

SHIV

You know who could be good?

MATSSON

No. No I do not.

SHIV

Um. Shiv Roy?

MATSSON

Oh yeah? She hasn't really got any experience, has she?

SHIV

Well, political acumen, knows the world. Can cut a deal and
delegate. Just very fucking clear-sighted.
(then)
Plus, apparently she's got the chairman that sad Swede basically
pulling her strings anyway?

MATSSON

Does she?

SHIV

Uh-huh. She's Lukas Matsson's total puppet, they say.

MATSSON

Isn't she, isn't it right she might drop a kid?

SHIV

Yeah. But she's one of these hard bitches who's probably gonna
do like thirty-six hours' maternity leave. Emailing through her
vanity Cesarean. Poor kid will never see her.

MATSSON

What a hard-ass.

SHIV

I know. Not widely liked. Highly effective. Not well-liked.

MATSSON

Oh, cos I hear, once you get to know her – you know?

SHIV

Well maybe, maybe there's a heart under there somewhere. Who
knows?

They look over.

MATSSON

I guess the question is, will he buy it? Cos you two, hatey-hatey,
right? Could you make him like you?

677

> (*a challenge*)
> Can you intro?

Stung by the sense her politics reduces her power here, Shiv rises to the challenge.

> SHIV
> I can do anything. My dad's dead.

The funeral director comes to find the family to tell them that the hearse is there.

Roman comes to get Shiv. Maybe doesn't mind breaking up this particular party.

> ROMAN
> Okay? He's here, guys. Headline act.

The funeral director ushers people to their seats and key family and friends out to the back.

INT. CHURCH – DAY

As people move into rows of pews.

Caroline sees Kerry. With a man.

> CAROLINE
> Kerry? Is it Kerry? Come. Come and sit with me.

> KERRY
> Yeah? Are you sure – is that okay?

> CAROLINE
> Of course and who's this?

> KERRY
> This is my brother. And my friend who is a lawyer. I thought there might be an issue, in terms of entry – or something.

> CAROLINE
> Are you alright?

> KERRY
> Yeah. I'm okay.

Marcia is nearby – Caroline is leading them towards the front.

> CAROLINE

Sally-Anne! Come and join us! Sally, do you know Marcia?

> MARCIA

Hello, Sally-Anne.

> SALLY-ANNE

Hello, Marcia. Hello, Caroline.

> CAROLINE

Sally-Anne was my Kerry, so to speak. All water under the bridge!

They settle.

> MARCIA

At least he won't grind his teeth tonight.

Little smiles. They all know that teeth-grind.

Kerry starts crying. Caroline's unexpected warmth overwhelms her. Marcia maybe offers an arm.

Nearby, Greg is calling Tom.

> GREG

Okay, dude. Final call. This is it, you're gonna miss it.

Intercut with:

INT. ATN – DAY

Tom still at ATN.

> TOM

Fires ~~in Baltimore~~. The president, is going to make a statement. Darwin might resign. Online is peaking. I'll be as fast as I can. But let them know it was me!

INT. CHURCH – DAY

> GREG

Can I inquire about front right?

But the call is over.

A funeral director comes to get Shiv and Matsson, near Caroline.

Greg spots and goes to inform.

> Hey, Lukas. Um, Shiv, I think Tom's not going to make it.

MATSSON

> Where's your Tommy?

SHIV

> Lot of news today. In the grindhouse.

Matsson clocks. Tom is prioritizing work. Monster work ethic.

GREG

> But that means. That means there is a wheel free – on the casket. You're down a wheelman.

CAROLINE

> Peter would take a wheel?

GREG

> Tom says – Tom kind of offered me the wheel?

The family gathers at the back.

Pallbearers bring the casket up the steps and position it, feet first, onto the trolley.

The cardinal plus three of his team walk down to bless the casket and cover it with the pall.

They lead the procession followed by funeral director, the casket and the family.

Greg, Frank, Karl, Ewan wheel it.

Connor, Kendall, Roman, Shiv walk behind.

INT. CHURCH – DAY

And as the coffin proceeds down the aisle—

Antonio Vivaldi, Violin Concerto in D Major RV 234 'L'inquietudine' 3. Allegro molto (Philips recording of I Musici Chamber Orchestra).

For a half minute or so we follow as the coffin is brought down the middle of the church's central aisle.

We are high and wide like a coronation or state occasion.

With a long lens we find faces as they feel the coffin pass and steal looks at the four children who follow.

INT. CHURCH – DAY

Family fills front rows, Ewan and Greg's mom and Greg together. The kids. The Old Guard, Cyd and Gerri. Frank, Karl, Ray, Mark, Hugo, Karolina.

Roman motions for Greg to keep an eye on Ewan.

Greg offers to let his grandpa go first. He's eyeing him suspiciously.

> GREG
>
> Here you go, Grandpa.

> EWAN
>
> Thank you. But I'd rather go on the outside.

Greg looks at him: Why?

> GREG
>
> Would you mind— You might be more comfortable on the inside?

> EWAN
>
> My legs, are long.

> GREG
>
> Well mine too.

Stand-off.

> You're not going to make a scene are you, Grandpa? There is concern and— Yeah? Please?

> EWAN
>
> I have no plans to make a scene, Greg. I want to sit in the aisle, alright?

Greg looks at him and judges he can trust him.

In front of them – the siblings whisper—

> CONNOR
>
> It's— I've got it down.

> SHIV

What to?

> CONNOR

Like twenty pages.

> KENDALL

Con, I really think, we said— Shall we leave it to – Rome.
I think?

> ROMAN

Could we bump Frank and you do first reading?

> CONNOR

I would consider that. Can I freestyle?

> ROMAN

'Freestyle', dude, it's not fucking snowboarding?

Shiv goes to tell Frank he's bumped.

INT. CHURCH – DAY

*After the processional hymn. The cardinal performs the Introductory
Rite.*

> CARDINAL

. . . We ask this through our Lord Jesus Christ, your son, who
lives and reigns with you and the Holy Spirit, one God, for ever
and ever.

> CONGREGATION

Amen.

> CARDINAL

Please be seated for the Liturgy of the Word.

Connor takes the pulpit, reads Wisdom 3:1–9.

Eyes Frank who is a little unhappy.

> CONNOR

A reading from the Book of Wisdom.

The souls of the righteous are in the hand of God, and no
torment shall touch them.

They seemed, in the view of the foolish, to be dead; and their passing away was thought an affliction and their going forth from us, utter destruction.

But they are in peace.

For if to others, indeed, they seem punished, yet is their hope full of immortality.

INT. CHURCH — DAY

A little later.

The Communion Rite (the Lord's Prayer, Doxology, Sign of Peace, Agnus Dei, Communion, Communion Hymn, Antiphon, Post-Communion Hymn, Post-Communion Prayer).

> CARDINAL
> And now a word from those who knew and loved Logan best—

Roman is about to go up when . . .

Ewan stands up. Roman turns, Greg is behind.

> ROMAN
> *(quiet)*
> Greg? Stop him.

Greg looks with horror, maybe gently grabs a sleeve.

> GREG
> Like how?

Roman looks at him.

> What do you want me to do? Take out his legs?

Greg approaches Ewan too. Shiv too.

> GREG
> *(whispers)*
> Grandpa. You promised.

> EWAN
> I'm not making a scene. You are.

> SHIV
> I think you might not be on the program here?

                         EWAN
Thank you. I'm going to speak.

He makes it up to the lectern, puts on reading glasses.

Greg, Shiv decide – better to retreat.

                         EWAN
Good morning.
                 (with an eye to the siblings)
What sort of people would stop a brother speaking for the sake
of a share price?

*He draws a handwritten speech from his pocket. He refers to it
sometimes. Though he has taken care over it and knows it mostly
by heart. Occasionally, he loses his spot, or adds an emphasis or a
clarification he sees might be useful in the moment and off-the-cuff.*

It's not for me to judge my brother. History will tell its story.
I can just tell you a couple of things about him. You probably
all know, we came across, the first time, during the war. For our
safety. But the engines on our ship gave out and the rest of the
convoy left us floating. They told us – they told us children – if
we spoke or coughed or moved an inch the U-boats would catch
the vibrations off the hull and torpedo us and we'd die in the
drink, in the hold there. Three nights and two days we stayed
quiet – a four-year-old and a five-and-a-half-year-old speaking
with our eyes.

*We see the siblings. The versions they know, if any, of these stories are
a little different. Maybe Kendall and Connor make faces. Not quite
right, right? But for Roman, the thought of a young, helpless Logan,
a frightened boy, breaks something inside him.*

                      (briskly)
So that's a little sob story.
                      (then)
And once we were over. Our uncle who, was shall we say, 'a
character' he— They, they had a little money, and they sent
Logan away to a 'better' school, and he hated it. He just hated
it. He wasn't well. He was sick and he mewed and he cried and
in the end he got out and came home, under his own steam,
without permission. But once he got back our little sister – she

was a baby but she was there by then – she, he always believed,
he brought home the polio with him which took her. I don't
even know if that was true. But our uncle and aunt certainly did
nothing to disabuse him of the notion, they let that lie with him.

(*then*)

So. Those are two things. I don't know what weight to give
them. I only say them because I know them and I have a mouth
to tell.

(*then*)

I – loved him, I suppose, and I suppose some of you did too, in
whatever way he let us and we could manage. But it should be
said, he has wrought the most terrible things.

(*getting this objection of Logan's out of the way*)

The cheapest comfort we can give ourselves is that the world is
a big ball and its turn isn't much affected by our actions. But if
such a small quibble is all we have against our responsibility, it's
not much to sling on the balance.

(*then, the case for the prosecution*)

I suppose in the way we estimate these things, he was a Great
Man. But – I can't help but say – he fed the bad part of men.
He was hard in his own heart – and in the end it doesn't matter
why. He was a man who has here and there drawn in the edges
of the world; now and then, darkened the sky a little; who
closed down hearts, and fed that bad flame in men, the mean
and hard-reckoning part that keeps their hearth warm while
another goes cold, their grain stashed while another is hungry.
And even dares to tell that hard – funny, yes, funny – but *hard*,
joke about the man in the cold. You can get a little high, a little
mighty, when you're warm. You can imagine all sorts of things.
It's pretty to think all sorts of things. He didn't, I'm afraid, share
an open spirit, didn't love or foster the finer impulses.

(*then*)

I can hear him in my ear now – the, excuse me, the old bastard –
asking what these finer impulses are exactly, what they mean?
But they are in us, they are, and I don't know why he never
found solace in that. He found solace in the other: in the
meagerness of things, in the baseness of metal, in the few hours
in the day. Yes he gave away a few million of his billions, but
he was not a generous man, he was mean. He made but a mean
estimation of the world. And he fed a certain meagerness in

men. He needed to, perhaps, because he had a meagerness about him; and maybe I do about me too, I don't know. I try. I try.
> (*then*)

I don't know when, but some time he decided not to try. He let himself off. Decided nothing applied. He let himself go and it is a terrible shame.
> (*folding his speech and departing*)

God bless you, my brother. God bless you.

In the front pew. Roman looks at Kendall.

Roman is feeling concerned. Kendall clocks—

> KENDALL

Yadda yadda. You okay?

Roman nods. It feels to Kendall like the moment when a son must defend something, or nothing will remain. A moment where something will be erased for good if it is not spoken. A rather sacred duty. Does Roman understand that?

> KENDALL
> (*cont'd*)

You've gotta – say – the other side yeah? That's not everything, right?

Roman probably does. But it's not his style to meet that sort of gaze. He makes a brittle joke, but his heart is heavy—

> ROMAN

I'm good. I might try to make a pass at Marcia as I go.

He winks and gets up. Kendall, Shiv, Connor give him a touch, a pat, or just eyes of support where they can. He must respond for the sake of their father's immortal honor.

Frank is behind, gives him a pat.

> FRANK

Okay, son?

As he squeezes out he winks, whispers, covering a growing sense of trepidation—

> ROMAN

Pre-grieved. I already gave at the office.

He walks up, and the churchy air thickens around him.

He passes the coffin. And maybe he puts a hand on it or thinks about it and something cracks that he's been keeping at bay.

He heads on up. But as in a dream, progress feels slow, hard to make. He can feel his throat thicken – become hardly wide enough to let air pass.

Up the steps. The huge crowd is very vivid. Stretching in expectation, waiting for a public oration of substance. A great responsibility. Normally, always, he would duck, weave, joke, hide, but there is nowhere to hide. It's just them and the world and his father dead in a box right there.

The microphone makes a pre-hum of sucked-in expectation. It all threatens to overwhelm. Maybe the words can help. He looks at the card.

ROMAN

My fath— Logan Ro—
    (but his throat is too thick, tries to force it out)
was a grea ma—
        (he's overwhelmed)
in the true senses, sense—

Maybe if he tries not to do the speech which swims before his eyes and looks far too long?

I, um I loved my— And . . . He's gone, but—

Tears, or the effort of stopping tears overwhelms.

I'm sorr—

And he – breaks – either just on the inside or outside too but he knows he can't carry on.

Maybe he tries again but he can't say the words, feels he has frozen – he must get down, away. But also maybe suddenly that he can try again, maybe what feels like an hour has just been a second and now it will all click back? But he needs very much to not be the focus for one second. As he looks up it seems unreal that when he is feeling the worst, the most, he has ever felt he should be expected to do something, anything. Unfair.

He edges down the steps and stops at the front – can he try again? Will he? Kendall comes to him. Caroline is rooted. Shiv and Connor come out too.

> KENDALL
> Just have a moment. Have some water.

He crumples a little, maybe can't quite accept their touch.

> ROMAN
> I can't.

He's catapulted back to something basic, a question he can't not ask. He knows but he feels he needs to ask—

Is he in there?

His siblings give him a touch, or a look: Of course.

Can we get him out?

A quick huddle – eyes amongst the group – what's kind; what's possible; what's necessary?

> SHIV
> What do we—? Can you—?

> CONNOR
> Um – I don't know—

> KENDALL
> I can. I could.

> SHIV
> Yeah?
> *(permission?)*
> Go on. Yeah. That's not it all. What Ewan said—

> KENDALL
> Uh-huh. I know.

Roman has the cards and fumbles, passes them to Kendall.

> ROMAN
> I'm sorry.

> KENDALL
> It's okay. You're okay. I got you.

As Kendall composes himself. He makes a note on the back of a card.

On the Old Guard—

Looking at Roman, crumpled, maybe crying, or holding back tears, helped and supported by his siblings.

Kendall prepares.

Roman in the cloak of a deep fear – he couldn't perform.

The eyes of judgmental society. People give each other half-smiles. Poor kid. Poor guy.

But also something elemental and more brutal. A son not stepping up. A man who is still a boy.

The village elders harden in judgment, the town has made its estimation.

People give supportive, closed-lip smiles to him as he passes, and then to each other – Frank, Gerri, Karl, Karolina, Hugo, Cyd, Stewy, Sandi, Sandy. Jeryd. Dylan. Matsson. Oskar.

The nods and smiles to him have empathy and pity. But the eyes to one another say: Oh, he can't do it. And perhaps: He's toast. Does Karl whisper/mouth this to Frank?

By the lectern. Kendall prepares himself. He flicks the cards. Do they work, these words they all agreed?

Roman is composing himself. Gerri leans forward as he settles back.*

>   GERRI
> You okay?

>   ROMAN
> Uh-huh. Uh-huh. Man. I don't know what happened. Fuck.

>   GERRI
> It's okay.

That lands.

>   ROMAN
> I got hit by a wave.

---

* I quite wanted to give Roman this moment of comfort but in the cut he seemed too far gone to be reached.

                    GERRI
    It's okay. You're okay.

                    ROMAN
    I fucked it, huh?

Gerri looks at him with some tenderness.

                    GERRI
    No.

                    ROMAN
    No?

Gerri decides to tell the nice lie—

                    GERRI
    No, it's okay. People understand.

                    ROMAN
    These hard – these stone-cold money fucks?

                    GERRI
    Funeral doesn't count. You get a freebie.

Wouldn't it be pretty to think so?

                    ROMAN
    Funeral is a freebie?

                    GERRI
    Funeral is a freebie. People get it. It's okay.

He looks at her. He knows she's lying but – it's nice.

                    ROMAN
    Thanks, Ger.

                    GERRI
    You'll be okay. This is fine.

*She gives him a touch. He winces, retracts, shrivels, too many
emotions. Gratitude, guilt, self-pity, self-loathing, lust, fear. He goes
back in on himself.*

                    ROMAN
    Yeah, fuck off.

And he makes it back to the pew.

Kendall's gone steely. What Ewan said isn't the whole truth and he can't let it stand. It's a lot to try to counter, but he's bolstered by a swell of indignation—

KENDALL

Um, I'm going to try to – just to stand in for my brother and— I have his, our, words, my sister's and my brothers' but – I'm— I – I want to— Some things have been said, and I want to, to respond or, um, excuse me, I will try to find the words.

He has some notes now but they are key words.

I don't know how much I know. But I knew my father. And – I've said it, I've said, it out loud, and maybe I regret it, but I said it and it is true – what my uncle said is kind of true. My father was, a, a brute. He was tough.
>   (*then*)

But.
>   (*then*)

He – *built* and he *acted*. And, there are many people who will always tell you no, and there are a thousand reasons, there always are, not to – to not act. But he was never one of those. He was full of a vitality, a force which could hurt, and it did, but . . . My god! The sheer— The lives and the livings and the things he made.
> (*and one thing he's not saying that perhaps he should*)

And the money. Yes, the money.
>   (*why shouldn't we say it?*)

The money. The lifeblood, the oxygen of this, this wonderful— This – civilization we have built, from the mud. The money, the corpuscles of life, gushing around this nation, this world, pumping life into every capillary, every village, filling men and women all around with, with desire, quickening the ambition, to own and make and trade and profit and build and improve. Great geysers of life, he willed: of buildings that wouldn't stand, of ships, steel hulls, amusements, newspapers, shows and films and life, bloody, complicated life. He made life happen. He called – stuff – into life, and he pushed, and heaved it on. He made me and my three siblings. And yes he had a terrible force to him and a fierce ambition, that could push you to the side,

but it was only that human thing – the will to be and to be seen and to do.
> (*then*)

And now people might want to tend and prune the memory of him – curb that force, that magnificent awful force of him, but my god I hope and think it's in me. Because, if we can't match his – vim – then god knows the future will be sluggish and gray.
> (*then*)

That was what he was for in the end: the light, the air, fun, *entertainment*. He did not, in the end, take the world more seriously than it deserves. He had it maybe in the proper proportion. He found it I think, a – a playground and he took a mighty go-around every amusement, looked at every interesting thing. There wasn't a room – from the grandest state room where his advice was sought, to the lowest house where his news played – where he couldn't walk, and wasn't comfortable. He was *comfortable* with this world and he knew it. He knew it and he liked it. God bless you, Dad.

Kendall heads down.

Connor, Roman give him a pat. He did enough. He said something both consoling and not untrue.

Shiv nods in respect. Makes her way out. Whispers to Kendall and Roman – she's going to speak. One thing that was in their eulogy – but she is going to say it in her own words now—

SHIV

Um, with how it's all gone, we didn't— It's okay, Rome, and thank you, Ken – we didn't get to say everything so I am just going to— Sorry, we're nearly done! Um. My father.
> (*reaches into herself*)

My father. We – we couldn't. We'd play outside his office. I think we wanted him to hear. And he'd come out, he was terrifying.
> (*does she smile and a few people smile?*)

He was so – so terrifying to us, and he'd tell us to be quiet. '*Silence!*' What he was doing was so important. And we couldn't conceive what it was. Presidents and kings and queens and diplomats and prime ministers and world bankers, I felt the whole world was in there with him, and it often was. Nixon, China, Gorbachev, Thatcher, Reagan. Wars and famines and revolutions, yeah. I don't know. He kept us outside. He kept everyone outside. But when he let you in, when the sun shone, it was warm. It was warm in the light.

(*then*)

But – um, it was hard to be his daughter. It was, he – was hard on women. He would say I think, he loved women, and he did I guess and he loved me his – his Pinky, his little girl.

(*close to the edge?*)

But yeah – he was— He – couldn't fit a whole woman in his head. I suppose he couldn't get it, that I was just like him. That I could contain as many, as fierce, desires and skills as him. He couldn't, or he wouldn't, get that. So that's my— That's for me. But he did okay. You did okay, Dad. We're all here. We're all here and we're doing okay, we're doing okay. Goodbye, my dear dear world of a father.

INT. CHURCH – DAY

Recessional hymn.

INT. CHURCH – DAY

The congregation files out.

At the back the family is gathered. As they exit, several people pat Kendall on the back. He has a new energy.

Roman is the object of some sympathy. He's gone in on himself. Can't really bear it all, shrivels from people's touch. Everything feels phony to him.

Mencken makes it past Roman to shake Kendall's hand.

Kendall looks around, he accepts condolences with a political ease. Feels something swelling. That he's found his voice.

Shiv makes the rounds and thanks people for coming.

Hugo talking to Ebba.

> KENDALL
> (*to Jess*)
> Okay, everyone who's coming on knows where the cars are, yes?

A nod from Jess. He's the CEO of the funeral. Accepts handshakes and condolences.

Hugo is in his ear.

> HUGO
> Will fill you in later – but interesting conversation.

Kendall looks: Yes now.

> Ebba. Shiv floating a US CEO to placate Jeryd.

> KENDALL
> Right. Good fucking luck.

> HUGO
> Details to follow.

Kendall looks round. Can he see Shiv? That? Here? But of course.

EXT. NEW YORK – DAY

The funeral cortège weaves through the streets of New York – places are boarded up. Streets quiet.

EXT. CEMETERY – DAY

Funeral cortège makes its way into the cemetery.

EXT. CEMETERY – MAUSOLEUM – DAY

A smaller group is here.

Just the family and close friends. People exit the cars.

Funeral directors on hand. The cardinal and his assistants.

Maybe Kendall and Shiv starting to feel that the pressure of the worst part of the day has passed and that they did their part.

Kendall regarding Shiv. Weighing.

Roman still suffering and subdued.

They approach the mausoleum.

ROMAN

Oh, man.

KENDALL

Look at this thing. Jesus.

CONNOR

He never send you pictures? You never saw?

As they consider—

He got it on a deal. He was really pleased. It was a – it was a dotcom pet-supply guy who built it, I believe, but that guy decided against.

SHIV

Are you serious? It's an off-the-shelf mausoleum.

CONNOR

Yeah, Dad sort of, I think he didn't want to go in the ground and he didn't want to think about it too much – so. I think he just went in for it at auction and – boom.

SHIV

Catfood Ozymandias.

CONNOR

I think it was five mil all in. Great spot.

SHIV

Good deal.

KENDALL

Good deal. I guess, good deal.

The casket is set up by the entrance.

As people gather – Kendall, Connor, Roman and Shiv look inside.

There are, as well as the sarcophagus where Logan will go, wall chambers up the wall. Kendall looks at them. Four on one side.

So weird, they find a space to talk a little lightly—

KENDALL

You interested?

SHIV

Chance to get to know him?

CONNOR

I'll have to talk to Willa. I was crazy for cryogenics, but yeah—
(*then*)
I wouldn't say no to top bunk. You?

KENDALL

Man, I dunno. Yeah. I had trouble finishing a Scotch with him.

ROMAN

He made me breathe funny.

KENDALL

I might check out somewhere a bit more chill for eternity you know?

CONNOR

I think I'm gonna jump in if that's okay by you guys?

Connor backs out.

Willa, you interested in a spot?

WILLA
(*looking at her phone*)
I'm sorry. I just got – I got an email. About maybe them holding a reading, for my play? Wow.

CONNOR

Uh-huh. Cos I know you'll have a life once I'm— And I want you to. I want you to fall in love again.

She's excited.

WILLA

Oh thanks, baby. Ooh. Attendance fee!

CONNOR

Right. Maybe you'll want to be buried with me? Because you know the guy after me could turn out to not be a good guy?

WILLA
(*still thinking about the reading*)
Aww, no. No.
(*but she can't stop*)
Plus 'involvement in casting'. '*Involvement*'?

CONNOR

So just to say. I'll be in here waiting and you can always join me.
So, just you know, going forward. Bear me in mind.

WILLA

Oh, honey. Thank you.

She's all excited.

The group assembles for the internment service . . .

EXT. CEMETERY – MAUSOLEUM – DAY

*The service ends. The casket is taken in, or men start to assemble to
lift the casket into place. Then—*

SHIV

I'm intrigued to see how he gets out of this one?

The boys smile.

KENDALL

Is Hugo crying?

SHIV

Probably got MeToo'd.

Peter nips up to the sarcophagus. Drops a letter in.

ROMAN

What the fuck was that?

CAROLINE

He wanted to pop something in there.

SHIV

Well what is it? A shopping list? Forty-eight things to see in
purgatory?

CAROLINE

I think it was his poem.

SHIV

Well can someone get it out?

KENDALL

Oh, man.

                              SHIV
     I know. Jesus.

                             (then)
     I guess he got away with it?

                             ROMAN
     With what?

The casket is lifted into the sarcophagus.

                             ROMAN
     Man oh man. It's too much, man.

*Roman has a physical reaction and backs away. Kendall tries to
comfort him, but it doesn't feel right to Roman. He's filling up with
dark feelings, suspicions. Shrugs him off.*

                              SHIV
                    (to Frank and Karl)
     Dad, he didn't ever – really. What was the worst. How bad was
     Dad?

They look at one another.

                             FRANK
     He was a salty dog.
                             (then)
     He was.
                             (then)
     But he was a good egg.

                             KARL
     What you saw was what you got.

                              SHIV
     Yeah?

                             FRANK
     Yeah.

The kids head off.

Do Karl and Frank look at one another?

                             KARL
     Right?

It's complicated . . .

FRANK

Right.

They carry on looking at one another. How much is there to tell?

Marcia passes Shiv.

SHIV

You okay?

MARCIA

I loved him very much. I miss him very much. He broke my heart and he broke your hearts too.

Mourners get into their cars.

(*to Caroline*)
Shall we take a car together?

People leaving. Kendall approaches Hugo. His head is bubbling.

KENDALL

H. How you doing?

HUGO

Who, little old me? I'm fine. You know. Big day.

KENDALL

Uh-huh. Come here. So. Listen, I wanna brief media on background.

HUGO

Then I am the droid you are looking for!

KENDALL

Uh-huh. That Matsson's acquisition doesn't have the support of key members of the family.

Hugo looks: Who?

You don't say who. Matsson is trying to steal the company for a song. Board is thinking of voting down the deal. It's feeling like, Living Plus, et cetera, the price soaring post-election ATN pumped, it undervalues Waystar. Premium's too low. And the shocking subs revelations, *shocking*, have sent a shiver of. Anxiety, panic, perhaps through the board.

> HUGO

I got it.

> KENDALL

Well write it down.

> HUGO

I have the gist, the argument.

> KENDALL

Yeah but I don't trust you.

> HUGO

Right? Well, you should because—

> KENDALL

I trust you to snake, I just need to be sure you relay precisely my arguments.

> (looks at him)

Look, Hugo. Life isn't nice. It's contingent. Everyone who says they love you also fucks you. This is a plan to fuck the deal. I need Mencken to come out fast with something public. I want to rule the world, and you can come. But it won't be a collaboration, okay? You'll be my dog. But the scraps from the table will be millions. Happy?

> HUGO

'Ruff ruff'.

Kendall gives him a pat and goes to get in the kids' car.

INT. FUNERAL LIMO – DAY

Roman aching. Looks out the window.

Kendall primed. Ready for action. Discreetly looking at phone.

Shiv primed. Ready for action. Discreetly looking at phone.

Then, catching each others' eye, a little smile. Is it the shared inappropriate phones? Is it the shiver of their coming conflict? Or a nasty math – Roman is down, so they are up?

EXT. ST. REGIS HOTEL – DAY

Barriers. Police.

Mourners head in.

Then—

Maybe something thrown. Or a scuffle off on a street corner. A firework or gunshot.

The shatter of glass from around the corner.

People duck. Cower. But then carry on. Maybe a firecracker?

A group can be heard or seen just making off around the corner.

Mourners head in.

INT. ST. REGIS HOTEL – DAY

Mourners heading in.

> WILLA
> It could just be a really great opportunity is the thing, Con?

> CONNOR
> Sure. We can fly back. Drink some cheap white wine and say 'hi' to all those cool guys who hate me.
>   *(under breath)*
> And want to sleep with you.
>   *(then)*
> We can make a weekend of it!

> WILLA
> I guess it just makes me think. Will it be hard to have a playwriting career, in Progressive New York Theater, from Slovenia? With us working for an authoritarian strongman?

> CONNOR
> We'll be tempering him! And you'd be – a *lady ambassador*!

> WILLA
> Sure, just – the theater is my life. I'm a playwright.

> CONNOR
> Grace Kelly stopped acting when she became a princess. Ambassadortrix is better than playwriter. It's just objectively better.

Willa not sure.

Let me talk with Jeryd. Let's see what flexibility we have. Maybe Mexico City is an easier commute? I'll talk to Jeryd.

Kendall approaches Colin.

> KENDALL
>
> Hey, big man. How you doing?

> COLIN
>
> Yeah. Sad. Sad day.

> KENDALL
>
> Uh-huh. I know. How you doing though, in yourself? You okay?

> COLIN
>
> Sure.

> KENDALL
>
> Good. Good.
> (*then*)
> Cos I hear you were talking to a head-shrinker?

> COLIN
>
> That's supposed to be confidential.

> KENDALL
>
> Well I'm sorry, dude. But it's not!
>
> (*then*)
> No that's cool. Just. People just talk. Big guy like you going to talk about his mama!

> COLIN
>
> My wife suggested it.

> KENDALL
>
> Right. That's nice.

> COLIN
>
> Your dad paid me off nicely but I got time on my hands.

> KENDALL
>
> Uh-huh. I tell you what I think. I think you come work for me.

Colin looks at him.

Big strong guy like you, what you fucking gabbling about, ah?

COLIN

I don't love it.

KENDALL

I know. Come work for me. Come work for me. Yeah? Talk to
me! Yeah!

INT. ST. REGIS HOTEL – DAY

*Shiv with Matsson and Ebba, looking over at Mencken – he has
Dylan plus four other aides marshaling those who want face time.
Plus Secret Service all around. Shiv is not looking forward to what
she needs to do—*

SHIV

Uh-huh. Okay. Wanna come watch me scuba in his bullshit.

Kendall arrives. Hugo nods to where Mencken is.

Kendall makes it over and is admitted to the charmed circle.

MATSSON

Stand down, Red, he's eating your falafel.

Shiv, Roman, Connor, Greg, all aware.

KENDALL

Hey, man. I guess, what, sort of like, congratulations-pending-a
grueling-jurisdictional-knife-fight!

MENCKEN

Ha. Yeah. Confident.

KENDALL

Exciting. I know you're harvesting names. Kenton?

MENCKEN

Exactly. Give them to Kenton. Many thanks.

KENDALL

No worries. And so – yeah I guess, given – what we – have, you
know, how we've been pleased to cooperate in terms of shared
vision, I guess I wanted to touch base.

MENCKEN

Uh-huh?

> KENDALL

Wanted to talk and get my thoughts to you.

> MENCKEN

I thought you were the sound system, now you wanna choose the track?

> KENDALL

Not one-way traffic, dude.
> *(he can say this much)*
Like when might you be dropping something publicly about your regulatory concerns, vis-à-vis Foreign Tech and Great American Corporations?

> MENCKEN

Well I've said I'll try to help.

> KENDALL

Oh, 'try to help'?

Greg comes over. He makes it through.

> GREG

Hi. Greg Hirsch. ATN with Tom.

Kendall looks at him: Fuck off, dude.

> KENDALL

Er, Greg? [Not appropriate.]

Roman watches. Everyone's swarming his guy. His guts are empty. But is he going to just leave it all?

> GREG

Just wanted to say, Tom and I, proud to be in there last night pulling for – for the correct result.

> MENCKEN

Uh-huh, thanks.

> KENDALL

Dude?

Looks at him like: You look ridiculous. Maybe says it.

Roman decides he can't be excluded any longer, gets through.

ROMAN

Hey, Daddy Long Legs. Go and kick your grandpa will you?

GREG

Tom called it, I relayed so. No thanks required. Just doing our jobs.

ROMAN

Big-boy talk. Fuck off. Yeah?

MENCKEN

Hey hey hey.
                    (*he has a bully's eye*)
Hey, it's the Grim Weeper. Tiny Tears. Kidding. You good?

Kendall looks like: Too much. But even that is painful.

GREG
                    (*retreating, slipped in*)
That's funny, Mr President!

ROMAN

Just – in touch with my emotions unlike you psychopaths.

MENCKEN

You know there's a tape, tape of you a-screeching and a-sniveling?

ROMAN
                    (*last fragments of vim*)
Well have fun jerking off to that.

KENDALL

Easy yeah, man, today?

Does Kendall try to put an arm around and get rejected, as—

CONNOR

Um, hey. J-Man. I just wanted to grab five to – talk macro Slovenia, micro, travel budget.

KENDALL

Con? No.

CONNOR

What? I am trying to talk with my colleague. To bat some ideas.

> (*to Mencken*)
> Like, what if I said to you pan-Hapsburg Mitteleuropean American-led EU alternative, what would you say to me?

Everyone is giving Mencken eyes. Shiv comes over and—

SHIV

Mr President, follow me. I'm your extraction team. These people may bore the very life from your body.

Mencken, having been boxed in, is eager to escape.

MENCKEN

Excuse me.

He moves and his bubble of aides and protection does too.

SHIV

Can I invite over Mr Matsson?

KENDALL
(*to Roman*)
You heard what Supermom's got planned?

Roman puts his hands up: Not now.

CONNOR

Literally no plan for Slovenia. *None.*

Shiv and Mencken find a spot.

SHIV

Well my thing would be, you're done talking to your side, chance now to open out. Big-tent this shit?

MENCKEN
(*leans and whispers, kidding but not*)
Some motherfuckers I don't want in the tent.

But Shiv takes it as a joke. As she gives eyes and Matsson comes to join—

SHIV

Quiet the rhetoric though. The country has a headache.

MENCKEN

You know the scary thing about me? The shit I say, I actually believe it.

Matsson arrives. Maybe Mencken gets Dylan, etc., to back off for privacy.

SHIV

Here we go.

MATSSON

Yeah. You're not gonna be comfortable at the twentieth-century table. You wanna feel the real deal.

MENCKEN

Look at us, a blond, a brunette and a redhead walk into a bar – a liberal, a conservative and a – what's your philosophy exactly?

MATSSON

Pussy pasta privacy?

SHIV

Anarchocapitalist parmigiana.

MATSSON

So, congratulations. We're both busy but here's my story. I want Waystar. I want a piece of the news, sports, archive and library, IP and talent and yeah, I really like the deal.

SHIV

So – I guess what we want to think about is what would make you, assuming, you make it, what could reassure you about his ownership?

MATSSON

I want to be very frank that I want you to feel comfortable.

MENCKEN

I guess the thing, was, whatever our frictions. There was an ideological sympathy with Logan.

SHIV

My dad had deep ocean currents swirling his gut. But on specifics? He liked winning. Money. And gossip. That was about it when you got down to it.

MATSSON

I mean, across GoJo, GoJo socials, and in terms of the whole communication environment, we're in that place where we make the thing that everyone has and nobody knows how it works.

There's a small group of people who are thought leaders in that space. It's worth getting our take. Also, fun.
(*nods – re Ken and Roman*)
Couple of little men in your pocket or – a gateway to broad and growing cultural influence?

MENCKEN
(*the bullshit*)
Well, it's really all about the regulatory framework and CFIUS considerations – yeah so it would be out of my hands. National interest and domestic—

MATSSON
Oh sure. Of course. But, just to say, the stuff I'm interested in, I don't need to be too inside day to day. So, like would an American CEO, keep it feeling culturally aligned?

MENCKEN
Uh-huh, what, Kinder, Küche, Kirche here? I thought you hated me.

SHIV
I do. But Dad was flexible. I'm flexible. I get how things go.

MATSSON
And you'd be glad, right. To see him win?

SHIV
My feelings are irrelevant. Our audience loves Jeryd. And I respect our audience.

Kendall looks over. He sends Hugo out to gather intel.

INT. ST. REGIS HOTEL – NIGHT

Greg is walking, spots Ewan. They look at each other.

GREG
Hey, Grandpa. So. You lied to me. Nice.

EWAN
Ooooh! Big man. I said I *wouldn't make a scene.*

GREG
I'm not scared of you, Grandpa. I fired a hundred guys last week.

EWAN

Proud of that are you?

GREG

Little bit. They weren't productive. Maybe they'll be happier where they are productive?

EWAN

Disgusting.

GREG

So Mom and I were talking and we think we won't be coming for Christmas this year.

EWAN

You've become a firing machine. Are you firing me as your grandpa now? Because you can't.

GREG

I can. You lied, you disinherited me, and you don't even like me.

EWAN

I like you well enough.

GREG

Well. Funny way of showing it?

EWAN

Likewise.

GREG

As in?

EWAN

You never come to stay!

GREG

You made it pretty clear you didn't want me.

EWAN

You complained there was no TV. But there was a TV.

GREG

You called me Mike TV. You wrote it on my forehead.

EWAN

I took you fishing. I saw you hurt a frog. You were ungrateful regarding gifts.

GREG

I asked you for Power Wheels, and you gave me a stick. I asked you for a lawyer and you gave me Pugh.

EWAN

I think you misremember. I used to read you to sleep, I taught you how to whittle with a penknife. You liked it.

GREG

I wasn't allowed to flush the toilet unless I did a poo.
(*then*)
What do you want me to do, do you want me to say that Power Wheels aren't awesome? Because they are.

EWAN

I sent you a bird book. But you don't remember that.

GREG

I do. I do.

Fought to a standstill . . . Then—

Thanks for the bird book.

Kendall over to Stewy—

STEWY

What's up. You okay, brother? Come here.

They hug.

KENDALL

I'm okay. I am.
(*making connection*)
I mean the widows are doing Dad orgasm noises. 'The wail of the banshee.' But yeah.

Kendall smiles, so does Stewy.

I need to talk.

STEWY

Oh fuck! You got that gleam in your eye!

KENDALL

I'm talking to my boy Jeryd. He's gonna come out against the deal.

STEWY

Yeah. In bed with him? Do the jackboots not chafe your pretty legs?

KENDALL

So. Uncertainty. And I want to kill the deal fast. Fuck it out.

STEWY

I don't think so. People are bought in.
(*calculations*)
Dewi? Can you get Shiv and Roman?

Kendall motions one of the two.

The big shareholders . . . Connor, Josh, the Ulsterman? Probably not, right? Everyone wants out.

KENDALL

GoJo is a bubble. Matsson is unstable. These India numbers they're sneaking today – very bad. Super-bad. Hyper-bad in Hyderabad.

STEWY

Maybe. I guess. Maybe? It's just a little. Depressing? We stick with the same old? Yeah? Maybe you make us jam tomorrow. *Maybe.* Out the same old fucking depressing jam factory. Or, you know: cash. Plus a piece of the Swedish AI streaming social sex robot.

KENDALL

Uh-huh. I see that. But what about – we stab him in the face? Take them over.

STEWY

Okay. We're leaving for Venus.

KENDALL

We have the borrowing capacity. We have the credible track record. We can manage their assets but they can't manage ours. GoJo shareholders, everyone's losing faith in the maestro. The retail base is starting to flow out. Okay? We maintain the synergies and upside for our shareholders.

STEWY

The prices are pointed in the right direction I guess.

> KENDALL

Exactly. Kill. Put in my people, destroy their C-suite. Forty, fifty, sixty percent RIF in GoJo. I strangle him on the floor and absorb his power. Full reverse fucking Viking.

> STEWY

I mean the bad news is I'm hugely unpersuaded.

But he smiles a bit. He is not uninterested.

> The good news is my hair's not on fire and I haven't shat on the floor or called the cops.
>
> (*then*)
>
> Talk to me.

INT. ST. REGIS HOTEL – NIGHT

Tom arrives. Comes over to Shiv. She's in turmoil, deep-rooted guilt somewhere. It manifests as icy.

> SHIV

You made it.

> TOM

Uh-huh. Yeah. I can only stay for twenty.

Tom has a weird look about him. Haunted from fatigue?

> SHIV

Ballsy. Whole new Tom. You'd never have dared not come to his funeral when he was alive.

The implied criticism allows him to wearily stab back—

> TOM

Yeah the thing about your dad is, he's lost quite a lot of influence over the past few days.

Champagne is going around, Tom takes one but doesn't get one for Shiv.

She coughs, decides she's taking one.

He looks at her. She stares him down and sips. Daring him to say something. After a long beat and a couple of sips.

> It's fine. That's fine.

SHIV

Well I know it's fine.

A silence. He looks at her. Will he say anything? Yes.

TOM
(*then*)
So – go on. Are you ever going to explain, what happened?
How— Why you didn't— [tell me?]

SHIV

I wasn't sure I wanted to keep it, then I wasn't sure it was –
okay.

He looks.

But it is, by all accounts, so.

TOM

Why didn't you tell me?

SHIV

It seemed too sad. Then we had a bit of a honeymoon and
I dunno?

TOM

Taking the potential dad for a test drive?

Caroline makes it over.

CAROLINE

The happy couple! Congratulations, Tom.

TOM

Thank you. Yeah. If it wasn't such a total fucking disaster it
would be a dream come true.

Smiles.

CAROLINE

Are you going to be okay? It is very— It's hard.

A bit of weakness admitted – so they go a little playful.

SHIV

Oh I'm hardly going to see it, the family way.

CAROLINE

Oh yes, it's lovely when you don't see them, that works fine.

                         SHIV
They don't grow up emotionally stunted?

                      CAROLINE
Oh I shouldn't think so, darling, would you?

                         SHIV
Can we talk actually, Mum. About – plans? If there's – an air-
clear – you might help me with?

Caroline looks: Tell me more, shall we discuss?

I'll text you.

Caroline reads the look of her daughter in an instant.

                      CAROLINE
Look at that, Tommy. Some filthy little stratagem! All over my
head. I'm too innocent for this world!

And Caroline heads off. Tom shakes his head. Some mom.

                          TOM
Wow. I'm sorry, Shiv.

                         SHIV
Meh, you disassociate fairly early.

*Things start to overtake Tom. He's so tired and sad. And he also
suddenly feels a little guilty.*

                          TOM
And not to be here. I would have. I just . . . I am so so tired. And
I've been awake so long. I – I felt like I couldn't leave?

*Maybe he thinks he is about to start to cry. He doesn't really
understand it, it's physical, he's not going to cry, but crying might
happen to him. He presses tears or potential tears away with his
wrist.*

I was the first one in with him when, after he died. I said – did
say a goodbye.

                         SHIV
You're exhausted.

*She knows him very well. He's gone a bit childlike. She comforts him
physically.*

Why don't you go back to the apartment? Just for a few hours. I don't care. Sleep. The blinds are working.

He can't imagine this. This is heaven.

> TOM
>
> Now? I – I can't now? We're right in the middle.

> SHIV
>
> You can. You were going to be here, now you're going to be there. This is going to go on for months.

Tom checks the time. He imagines. There is a world where this is possible. He is moved by this.

> TOM
>
> The hotel people know me and I hate it.

> SHIV
>
> Just hide for a while.

The greatest gift in the world. He leaves – to get some sleep.

*Matsson approaching.**

Hey? So. This fucking *Vanity Fair* guy. Still texting at my dad's funeral, you really have to respect the disrespect.

She looks in his eyes. News? Yes—

> MATSSON
>
> It's a 'yes'.

> SHIV
>
> Yes?

> MATSSON
>
> Yes.

> SHIV
>
> From, yeah? Okay. Good. Smart!

> MATSSON
>
> Yeah. They think they're interested. I think I could make a US CEO work.

---

* We had to put Matsson in a car because of some scheduling issues – but it turned out to be a good way to construct the scene.

SHIV

Okay? Let's make a meatball burger!

Big smiles.

Kendall approaches Roman. Hugo has given Kendall a briefing on some rumors.

They look over at Matsson and Shiv.

KENDALL

Romey, you okay, man?

ROMAN

Look at her. In her fucking pomp. Fucking glowing. All dope and one in the chamber.

KENDALL

Uh-huh. I might need your help, bro.

ROMAN

If only we could put my fighty sperm in your working dick or sew your working dick on to me instead of my broken one?

KENDALL

So. It's possible Lukas and Shiv— There might be an accommodation with Mencken.

ROMAN

Nah. No.

KENDALL

Well, yeah. So.

ROMAN

We have an agreement. He'll block because—

KENDALL

Well, we don't have a lot of leverage at this point. So we might need to – to make some moves. And I might need your help.

ROMAN

I don't feel so good.

KENDALL

Uh-huh. That's because you fucked it.

ROMAN

Hey. C'mon.

KENDALL

It's okay, man. It happens. You fucked it. With Jeryd.

ROMAN

Well, no. If he welches on the deal to block – we can – we can –
we can hurt him with ATN, cry foul—

KENDALL

Well yeah. He's got our dick in his hand. We should have his
dick in our hand. Yeah?

ROMAN

But—

KENDALL

Uh-huh. I'm sorry, man, but it's fucked. I should have stopped it
so I blame myself. But it's on us, dude, okay? If we don't wanna
say 'bye-bye' to Waystar, one chance left. We fight Shiv at the
board okay? The Roy Boys versus Shiv the Shiv.

ROMAN

Um.

KENDALL

It's okay. I've got it. I have a plan but I'm gonna need you to –
just – yeah, help me here and we can do this. Okay, dude?

He gives him a hug. Not entirely consensual.

You fucked it. But it's okay.

On Roman. He feels very alone.

Shiv working the room.

Kendall too.

*Looks at Frank and Karl who smile at him, but tinged with
something.*

EXT. NEW YORK – STREET – NIGHT

Roman has left the wake. He walks out, ignores his car.

EXT. NEW YORK – STREET – NIGHT

Farther down he's walking with a manic swagger, eyes wild looking for trouble. To avoid, or something else.

There is a police outpost, a couple of cars, some cops (including Officer Miller) talking to each other.

> ROMAN

What's up? All good?

> OFFICER MILLER

Yeah you're good. Kind of a bull run on Fifth.

> ROMAN

Keep up the good work.

EXT. NEW YORK – STREET – NIGHT

Roman heading along a cross street.

At the end there are maybe some lines of barriers and cops.

Beyond it on the avenue, protestors walk. Some jog.

Roman quickens his walk towards it.

He makes it to the police lines, there is a loose straggle across the street, behind crash barriers.

The rush of people beyond in the dark is chaotic. Protesters, some who have not done this sort of thing before. Some politically organized and then a rush of people who are wearing vaguely similar stuff. Black, hoodies and jeans. Some with face coverings of one kind and another.

The people rush – it feels as he gets closer like a rush of humanity, Roman is right there getting close.

> ROMAN

Fuck you.

No one can hear.

Nor can the cops.

Fuck you fuck you fuck you! Fuck you fuck you fuck you pricks.

He makes it to the barriers and either climbs up so he can stand or leans over and tries to get some attention.

Fuck you all, fuck you all.

The bodies rush close. It's a confusing mess.

OFFICER MILLER

Hey?

Then Roman either hops off from the top rung of the barrier, or hops over it.

ROMAN

Fuck you.

And as the people rush around him he is buffeted back, people collide with him, not much interested, he stumbles back, in amongst the thick of it, getting buffeted by the wave of humanity but trying to stand up and curse as it washes away with him or he goes down on the ground.

Episode Ten
WITH OPEN EYES

Written by Jesse Armstrong
Directed by Mark Mylod

Original air date 28 May 2023

Cast

LOGAN ROY	Brian Cox
KENDALL ROY	Jeremy Strong
GREG HIRSCH	Nicholas Braun
SHIV ROY	Sarah Snook
ROMAN ROY	Kieran Culkin
CONNOR ROY	Alan Ruck
TOM WAMBSGANS	Matthew Macfadyen
FRANK VERNON	Peter Friedman
KARL MULLER	David Rasche
GERRI KELLMAN	J. Smith-Cameron
WILLA FERREYRA	Justine Lupe
KAROLINA NOVOTNEY	Dagmara Dominczyk
HUGO BAKER	Fisher Stevens
COLIN STILES	Scott Nicholson
STEWY HOSSEINI	Arian Moayed
SANDY FURNESS	Larry Pine
EWAN ROY	James Cromwell
CAROLINE COLLINGWOOD	Harriet Walter
SANDI	Hope Davis
KERRY	Zoë Winters
LUKAS MATSSON	Alexander Skarsgård
DEWI SWANN	Robert S. Gregory
PAUL CHAMBERS	David Patrick Kelly
SIMON EDGERTON	Jeff Blumenkrantz
PETER MUNION	Pip Torrens
CYRUS TELLIS	Kevin Changaris
EBBA	Eili Harboe
OSKAR GUDJOHNSEN	Jóhannes Haukur Jóhannesson
SONYA ADEYEMI	Carole Denise Jones
DIANE LIU	Midori Nakamura
BARMAN	Anthony Simone
STEVE COX	Wayne Pyle
JONATHAN	James Furino

DAY ONE

INT. WAYSTAR – BIG MEETING ROOM – DAY

Kendall arrives. Room of key bankers and lawyers. Kendall is keeping everything cooking by force of energy.

Maybe we have some visual representations of the reverse Viking deal – financials and structure.

KENDALL

Hey! Okay, Telly! Let's run this board presentation again shall we?

Tellis is ending his call. Bad news.

TELLIS

Uh-huh. Great. Yeah.

KENDALL

What?

TELLIS

Just Stewy. That was his guy.

Kendall looks.

Yeah, I don't think we got him.

Big blow. Fuck! But – Kendall eats it. He's got to keep this thing alive.

KENDALL

Uh-huh. That's cool.
          (*keeping up the front*)
Really? *Man.*
            (*then*)
Where is he? Get me him direct. It might be smokescreen. I think that will be smokescreen. I can pull in Stew.
          (*to someone*)
Dial him up.

                    TELLIS
Uh-huh. I don't think we have the shareholders and I don't think
we have the board numbers, Ken?

                    KENDALL
I'll get the votes.

                    TELLIS
If we had more time but, tomorrow, Ken? By tomorrow?
                    (*then*)
You wanna just outline the path here – and how . . .

                    KENDALL
I got fucking me. I got Ewan, I got Paul, I got Dewi. *Locked.*
So—

                    TELLIS
                (*they're not locked*)
Uh-huh. Good. And—?

                    KENDALL
And I got— I still think – I can get Stewy. Then I think, maybe
Sonya. I think, maybe, Frank. We have multiple routes.

Tellis doesn't see it. Not good.

                    TELLIS
Uh-huh. Because. Right now you have four and one of those—
Is Roman even gonna show?

                    KENDALL
Don't worry about Roman.

                    TELLIS
Good, because I wouldn't mind getting him some materials—

                    KENDALL
I'll forward. I'll handle.

                    TELLIS
Cool. But like as a point of interest in terms of logistics where is
Roman exactly—?

The last straw, Kendall can't keep this in the air on his own.

                    KENDALL
I don't know.

(*then*)

I don't know. I don't fucking know okay?! I don't know. That make you feel better?

A passive-aggressive stew of anger, and a need to keep things going, the loneliness of being The Man—

But I got him. Okay? I fucking got this, Telly Bear. So help me, don't fucking hinder me, yeah? Let's push things forward? I love you. Okay?!

Tellis smiles: Okay. Who's he in bed with here?

INT. MATSSON'S HOTEL SUITE – DAY

Lots of activity but this is the hub. Lawyers and advisors.

Shiv is in full bloom and feeling full strength, off the phone—

SHIV

Okay! I think they lost Stewy! He's wonked. I think – we have Ken in the trunk. We have him trussed up and ready to fucking bake!

Matsson is a little bit unsettled. Not quite focussed. What is it? The big deal coming up?

MATSSON

Ja ja. Das ist gut.

SHIV

You worried?

MATSSON

Nah. Nah. Nah. Good.

Shiv analyzes and thinks he needs reassuring—

Maybe she has a whiteboard, or other visual representation. Grabs a pen, tallies off on a for/against chart.

SHIV

Cos we got me, obviously. Simon, Frank. Sandy and Sandi locked. I think Stewy's not gonna split. He says all sorts of shit but: money, honey. Diane Liu, Sonya? We're there. With margin. We peel off Ewan, Paul, Dewi? It could, end up being just fucking Ken. And Rome against. If Roman even shows up from whatever jerk dungeon he's getting pity-spanked in?

Matsson gives a small smile. Why not more happy?

Happy? Yeah?

He does a weird smile.

> MATSSON
> (*aggressive*)
> Yes this makes me happy! Success. Okay? Sorry. I just like—
> (*rubs fingers*)
> stuff. I'm not a big maneuvers and fuck-fuck guy.

> SHIV
> Well sure. That's me. I love fuck-fuck. You do stuff. So. My list is: you looked at the revised draft announcement Karl sent? That's all good. I'm checking in with Frank if you wanna do the old-school signing still? Ebba?

Ebba nods.

At Waystar? Them and you – and me, US CEO?

She wonders what else is ailing Matsson.

What's yours? Wanna talk Tom?

Tiny shiver of reaction from Matsson – what? He covers, shrugs.

I know you're thinking about ATN? And it's not a big deal for me.

> MATSSON
> Yeah we've done couple of vibe meets.

> SHIV
> I know, he's shitting it!

> MATSSON
> Right. Well, the delta between a guy and a 10X guy is life and death, and ATN is central, so. What you think? On Tom?

> SHIV
> Lukas, sorry. That has to be you.

He looks at her.

But, okay, he's a, you know— He's a very competent guy but, with no, agenda, I think, if it's simpler to kill him, if he irks you, or – it's complicated, it *is* okay. He's very plausible corporate matter, but also a highly modular interchangeable part. And I would say that to his face.

> MATSSON

Okay?

> SHIV

But. If we, with all the changes, you like continuity? Well, ATN is going gangbusters, and he's well-liked, he's an insinuating worm. If he stayed on, for me, that also would not be a problem, okay?

> MATSSON

Uh-huh?

> SHIV

Tom is – separate from my feelings – Tom will, honestly, suck the biggest dick in the room. That's my assessment.

> MATSSON

'Love is in the air, dah-dah de dah dah.'

> SHIV

Personal feelings aside.

Shiv gets a call – 'Mom'. Hides it.

As Shiv takes the call, Matsson calls Ebba over and asks in Swedish to find out the details of the cartoonist of something he has before him—

The big profile of Matsson in Vanity Fair. *But the illustration is Shiv pulling his strings – him as a puppet.*

Excuse me.

Intercut with:

INT. CAROLINE'S BARBADOS HOUSE – DAY

We will likely only hear Shiv's end of this and not see Caroline till the end of the call.

But it might go like—

> CAROLINE

Hello, darling. How are you doing?

> SHIV
> (*then, turns away, stands*)

Uh-huh? I'm fine. Good thanks.

> CAROLINE

I just wanted to see if there was any chance at all—?

> SHIV

Well it would be lovely. But I just think. Schedules. You know?
Board.

> CAROLINE

Uh-huh. But just to say – there is someone here who I think
you'd like to see? I promised not to tell. But put it this way, he's
your brother and it's not Kendall.

> SHIV

Okay? Well, I'll see if I can crack the code! Um, let me think.
Can I get back to you but, thank you and let's try to make this
work, shall we?

Caroline puts the phone down.

INT. MATSSON'S HOTEL SUITE – DAY

Stay with Shiv. She thinks. Big news.

*Something's up. The cartoon. Matsson flicks his eyes at it. Says
something else to Ebba – to do it fast.*

> SHIV

That okay? The profile bullshit?

> MATSSON

The cartoon? Oh sure. It's funny.

*Maybe he pretends to be her puppet for a beat, and does puppet
limbs—*

'Doop-di-doop'. It's a perfect cover story, so.

> SHIV

Great, because [I could look into]—

MATSSON
(*interrupting*)
People get at me, they like to get at me, they always have, that's
fine. Ebba! Let's get it framed! We're finding the cartoonist.

SHIV
Sure.

MATSSON
Let's send him flowers! Shall we send him flowers, like every
hour on the hour. For a year?

Ebba looks weary. This again.

SHIV
Uh-huh. Listen. So – that was – an associate, indicating they
have a fix on Roman.

MATSSON
Okay. Well, can we get him. In case?

SHIV
(*numbers on the board*)
I think we're all, set here? And you have— You're all diary-ed
out on internals for the rest of today so— [there's nothing for
me to do.]

A flicker from Matsson.

I wonder if I do go nail Roman too?

MATSSON
Sure. I mean I don't mind a fight—

SHIV
Sure, but just if we could get unanimity on the board, or close,
all smiling in public? Just for the start of our – reign – it would
be so nice?

MATSSON
Well, whatever the lady wants!

SHIV
For the corporate narrative? Like if we're on separate sides, me
and the bros, it's *Lady Macbeth Part Two*? Media loves that shit.
It would just be so nice, if it was a really clean start. Abundance
of caution?

731

MATSSON
Sure. Abundance of caution. So safey-safey, aren't you? Mrs
Nicey-Nicey!

A good thing? Surely yes.

SHIV
That's me. Sugar and spice. Fully contactable. Find me wherever,
whenever. Okay?

Shiv heads out.

INT. ATN – TOM'S OFFICE – DAY

Tom is running facts with an overworked Greg.

He has materials on Matsson, including the Vanity Fair *profile and
cartoon illustration.*

On screen – Steve Cox's business show.

STEVE COX
(*on screen*)
And in terms of M&A action. We're hearing that GoJo and
Waystar could seal their long-gestated deal as soon as tomorrow
to create that all-singing, all-dancing tech-news-entertainment
conglomerate some analysts have been so hot for. Word is that
regulatory concerns have receded, so Lukas Matsson may soon
take control of the deceased Logan Roy's empire to add to his
streaming, betting, sports and socials everything app.

TOM
Okay. Okay. Born 1976, Gothenburg. Team. Manchester United,
AKA the Red Devils, 'crazy season, dude'! Father suicide. Can
mention. The. The sort of – the topics – the good topics to steer
onto to build rapport? You didn't just google these did you?

GREG
I mean, is Google not allowed? I – I'm not – Mossad, I'm just Greg?

Tom's phone goes.

Intercut with:

INT. PLANE – DAY

Shiv is on a plane, or getting on, or arriving at the airport. With her close team.

                              TOM

Shiv? What you hearing?

                              SHIV

Roman's at my mom's. I'm on my way to bag him. I'm looking for unanimity.

                              TOM

Okay. At your mom's. But – did you talk to Lukas? Am I for the chop?

Greg leaves. He's picked up useful information.

                              SHIV

I'm trying.

                              TOM

I've just got a bad feeling. He's booked in a third 'hang'. It's excruciating. I'm scared he'll want to play a game online, I'll just run into a wall for hours.

With Shiv – she has a mental to-do list. Tom is on there.

                              SHIV

Tom. Can we have a real conversation?

                              TOM

Uh-huh?

                              SHIV

Look. I don't know about Matsson. I'll do what I can. But with us. I wanted to get a few things straight.

                              TOM

Yeah. Well. I want to be very nice. Czechoslovakia it. Just lovely, velvet, parting of the ways—

                              SHIV

So, for you, there's not anything – left?

                              TOM

Well. How do you mean?

SHIV

I guess I thought it was worth raising— Are there any positives about – the nightmare we've shared?

Tom clears his throat or swallows.

TOM

As in?

SHIV

One way of looking at it – we sort of killed each other. But also we've had a – a controlled burn. And that can be healthy?

TOM

We said some pretty terrible—

SHIV

I know. But I guess if there was anything there.
> (*with a smile, knows this is awful/comical*)

It would just be so, very convenient.

TOM

Oh sure. It would be incredibly convenient. You'd be married to your husband.

SHIV

Think of the scheduling?!

TOM
(*not unkind*)

Oh. You've fallen in love finally? You're in love with our scheduling opportunities?

SHIV

And also, I guess I would— Like, I'd love to be able to – to not—

TOM

Not to have failed? At marriage? You don't like to fail a test do you, Shiv?

SHIV

Look. We have said the worst things.
> (*wants to say something real*)

I have always been scared, I guess in relationships of – the underneaths and all the— What's the worst thing a person thinks? But we know. And that's bad. But. Once you've said and done – the worst. You're sort of – free? We'd be building on bedrock. I guess the question is, are you interested in a real relationship?

INT. WAYSTAR – KENDALL'S OFFICE – DAY

Kendall is on the line, leaving a message.

> KENDALL
>
> Stewy. Bro. Don't hide from me. I can see you from up here. Come with me, Stewy, we can win this.

Hugo comes in as he ends the call.

> HUGO
>
> Roman. From Greg and Rat-fucker Sam.

Slides him paper. An address—

> KENDALL
>
> Okay?!

He dials.

> Hey, Mom. So I hear Romey might be there?

Intercut with:

INT. CAROLINE'S BARBADOS HOUSE – DAY

Caroline on the other end.

> KENDALL
>
> I'm sorry I couldn't make your get-together. But I need to speak to Roman very urgently. No recriminations. But it's life or death. Is he there?

> CAROLINE
> (*doesn't want to lie outright*)
>
> I mean, I can't say.

> KENDALL
>
> Oh you can't say? Well, he needs to come back. Is he planning to come back, for tomorrow?

> CAROLINE

That's for you all. He's fragile.

> KENDALL

Uh-huh. And is Shiv there? Is she coming?

> CAROLINE

I don't want to get into a lot of business. I just wanted to see you all? But if it's going to be thumbscrews I'd rather it wasn't—

> KENDALL

Is Shiv coming to you? Mom?

> CAROLINE

I'd love to see you. But I would like to have a family time and not a whole – debacle.

> KENDALL

I'm coming. I'll be there, Mom.

On Caroline. A certain amount of regret?

INT. WAYSTAR – KENDALL'S OFFICE – DAY

End of call.

> KENDALL

I have him. We have him. I'm flying out. I'll be back, tonight, early tomorrow latest, small team. I put this together on the move okay? We roll in thirty! Momentum, Hugo, momentum!

Kendall is up, anxious, ready to go.

EXT. CAROLINE'S BARBADOS HOUSE – DAY

Shiv arrives.

> SHIV

Hey hey! Hello, Blimey. You okay?

Roman has a fucked-up face. Some painful bruising, fading now, and some stitches above his eye. But less vivid and painful than they were a day or two ago right after funeral night.

ROMAN

I'm fine. I'm good. 'You should see the other guy.' Not a scratch on him – but huge issues with toxic masculinity.

Caroline comes out. In the distance Shiv's assistants and lawyers are getting out of a car.

CAROLINE

Hello! How lovely. And look, how lovely, you've brought all your lawyers with you.

Shiv is looking at Roman.

SHIV

Shit, man, what did you—

ROMAN

Just – got into a discussion with some of your pals about the merits of liberal democracy.

SHIV
(*she has an agenda*)
Well, listen, I think it's good you're here. Good to rest up.

Looking at his eye, but then pulling away—

CAROLINE

It's much better. I couldn't look at him when he arrived.

ROMAN

True. Peter did my eyedrops.

CAROLINE

I just— Eyes. They disgust me.

SHIV

Eyes? Like we all have, human eyes?

CAROLINE

I don't like thinking of these little wet balls rolling around in people's heads. Face eggs. Come on in – come in!

As they go—

The place is the same as ever. Water gets in everywhere. It's a money pit.

EXT. BARBADOS – DAY

Kendall's car driving towards Caroline's house.

INT./EXT. KENDALL'S CAR – DAY

Kendall makes it across the island with his assistant.

> KENDALL
>
> Hey, Stew? Well good, because I didn't buy it. Good man! And I've found Roman. I always had Roman, but this is just – like nailed nailed.
> (*listens – interesting shit*)
> Okay? Lawrence? Lawrence Yee? What shape does that make? Talk dirty to me, Stew.

INT./EXT. CAROLINE'S BARBADOS HOUSE – DAY

Kendall barrels in quite hot.

> KENDALL
>
> Hello! Hello-o! Hide and fucking seek, Romey! The – hunt for *Red* fucking *October* is over!

He heads through the house to the terrace.

> Where are you? What's going on, Romey? What's going on?

Shiv is there. Has been sitting next to Roman.

> Okay. Well look at this fucking family scene! What's going on? Rome, are you okay?

Shiv gets up and stands between them. They talk fast and messy—

> SHIV
>
> Hey. Easy. Easy. He's – fragile.

> ROMAN
>
> Fuck you, fragile. What?

> SHIV
>
> Back off, man.

> KENDALL
>
> Back off? I'm just arriving for a cup of fucking tea.

(*past Shiv to Roman*)
Let's go talk. Let's go, Rome, yeah – let's head home, we need to talk, they're fucked.

ROMAN
Well no, fuck you, don't talk to me like that. You're fucked. We're fucked. So don't bullshit me.

KENDALL
(*to Shiv*)
Did you get your little screwdriver in on him? Have you pried him open? Have you got to him.

SHIV
No, what?

KENDALL
Because that's bullshit, we're in this, Rome— She's doing a number on you, man.

Caroline arrives.

CAROLINE
Hello what's going on? Are we alright?

KENDALL
Hey. Hey, Mom. Yes. I just need to talk to Roman.

Time for a kiss or touch as he keeps up his assault—

All a bit on top of one another—

CAROLINE
I'm looking after Roman, Ken, so—

ROMAN
Well not looking after—

KENDALL
(*to Roman*)
You promised me. You promised me you wouldn't change, dude.

ROMAN
Yeah well 'sorry'. I don't give a fuck. I don't care.

Blows a raspberry. Kendall not unkind but exasperated.

> KENDALL

Rome? The fucking— The world's pivoting on you, dude? The world's turning on a clown here.

> ROMAN

Well fuck you sorry but you're a clown living in a dream world. You don't have it. You don't have it. You don't have it you don't have it, so why are you trying to – fucking, get into me?

> CAROLINE

Roman needs— [a bit of quiet and attention.]

> ROMAN
> (interrupting)

Roman needs everyone to fuck off. I'm fine. I had a very violent fight which I won and I am fine, I'm not the fucking sad sack here – so back off.

He gets up.

> KENDALL

Just tell me how you are voting. You're with the man team, yes? Tell me that and we can go.

> ROMAN

No. Don't talk to me like that okay? I'm taking a boat out. And don't follow. I'm gonna be crying and jerking it. My absolute favorites.

He heads out towards the beach. Shiv pats him but he shrugs her off too.

Just fucking – leave me!

Beat. Three of them left. A breath.

> CAROLINE

Are you staying for dinner? Or in and out with all the shouting? I would just love it if it wasn't a horror show.

> KENDALL
> (thinks)

There is— I have, there's a huge board meeting, Mom.

CAROLINE

Oh, *an important board meeting.* That's never happened to me before, an important meeting has never previously rolled over all my plans.

SHIV

To be fair, Ken and I have different attitudes, but it is a very important one.

KENDALL

Like end of the fucking world.

CAROLINE

Uh-huh and then there's something else and another grand endeavor, and everyone stays rich and busy and sad, forever. Are you staying for dinner?

Shiv – thinking about Roman.

SHIV

I'd love to stay.
(*to Ken*)
You probably have people to call, right? Busy, losing?

Kendall would like to keep moving, but without Roman, there's nothing. Thinks.

KENDALL

That would be nice, Mom. We're good. I got nowhere to be. I'm sorry. I am. It's just – it's nuts. I have people to call. Can I take the Red Chalet for my folks?

SHIV

My folks are actually in the Red Chalet.

CAROLINE

You can go in the Boat Houses. They've been redone. And talk to each other about the internet. I pay a fortune and I know it doesn't work and I can't bear to hear any more about it, alright?

INT. GALLERY – DAY

A private art opening at a fashionable gallery.

Tom and Matsson together with wines, looking at a picture. Oskar and Greg there as hang buddies.

>   MATSSON
>   What do you think, man?

>   TOM
>   What do I think? The colors go well.

Matsson walks off to check something.

Greg is there with Tom.

>   Ughhh. Fuck fuck fuck! 'The colors go well.' Is that a sentence?

>   GREG
>   'The colors go well'?

>   TOM
>   'The colors go well.'

>   GREG
>   'The colors go well, together.'

>   TOM
>   'The colors go well.' 'The colors go well.' You're here for the
>   hang, Greg, to jump in if there are little – you know, awkward
>   beats. Fucking social putty. Yes? You're fucking letting me
>   swing!

>   (*he looks over to Matsson*)
>   He's gonna fire me. I know it.

Matsson and Oskar come back to join.

>   MATSSON
>   I don't know. Visual art? I always feel like I'm faking it.
>   Imagining what someone who was me might think, yeah?

*Matsson looks at him. Is he mocking him? A little. He seems to enjoy
some gentle teasing.*

>   GREG
>   'Art-bot three thousand, malfunction'.

>   MATSSON
>   Asshole.

Greg tries to judge the moment.

>   GREG
>   You asshole!

742

Matsson laughs, enjoys the fuzzing of boundaries. Maybe a high five. Greg feels there is a connection.

Matsson looks at him. A cold eye.

> MATSSON
> (*to Tom*)
> So listen. What you got on, dude? You wanna extend the hang?

Tom thought he might be going well. More??

> TOM
> Extend the hang? Happy to hang?

> MATSSON
> Relax. It's only your career, man! You'll get another gig if we axe you!

Tom laughs.

> You know a good place, for dinner? Like, real nice, but not all—
> (*makes a face*)
> Yeah?

Tom tries to figure out what he means. What would be just right – too fancy or too down-at-heel?

> Hit me up, I'm just gonna pull up some weeds. Okay? Let's roll through!

Matsson heads off with Oskar.

Greg huddles with Tom.

> TOM
> (*with foreboding*)
> Another hang. A further hang. More fucking hanging than a dictator's birthday.

> GREG
> It's good. You're vibing!

> TOM
> Well, you're vibing. When— I need - ears open, eyes open, on the assistant loop, Ebba— Is he planning to kill me. Don't – overly vibe, yeah?

> GREG
>
> You asked me to vibe, I vibed.

Tom looks at him, feeling a flash of irritation.

> TOM
>
> You know if he comes in, if he wins. You are fucked.

> GREG
>
> He likes me.

> TOM
>
> You on two hundred K for fucking latte runs and executions? New management, bro. You're getting busted down. Twenty, thirty, forty K. *If* I even stick around. I get fired? I think you're fucked. Family death march. Yeah?

> GREG
>
> I don't do coffees anymore, because I'm looking at strategy.

> TOM
>
> Yeah – ass – strategy.
> > (*then*)
>
> What is the best restaurant in New York? The actual, not what people say it is, but what actually is it?

Greg has some ideas—

> GREG
>
> Nougatine, Eleven Madison, Musket Room, Luthun, Daniel, Carbone?

> TOM
>
> Uh-huh. But scientifically, Greg. Like *amazing*, but not bullshit or 'fe-fe-fe' or 'nim nim nim' but just—
> > (*makes a click*)
>
> *Yeahhhhh!* You know. Like: Oooh! You know?

EXT. BARBADOS – EVENING

Sun goes down.

EXT. CAROLINE'S BARBADOS HOUSE – TERRACE – NIGHT

Pre-dinner. Shiv is waiting, having a juice. Kendall arrives.

KENDALL

Okay. Early bird catches the Rome?

SHIV

Uh-huh. Well. You know?

KENDALL

Just, coupla things, you might be interested in – I got Stewy back.

SHIV
(*shrug*)
Even if he's telling the truth. And you get Rome. Seven plays six. I'm not sweating.

KENDALL

And, according to my sources, Matsson is meeting with Lawrence Yee? Vaulter Lawrence.

Mini bump for Shiv. Is it a lie? But she eats it. Shrugs.

So?
(*scoping her out*)
You knew that?
(*he can see not*)
Just interesting. Like – I mean, he doesn't like us all very much, Lawrence. But you knew?

She rides it as Roman comes down.

ROMAN

Hey. Look at this, fucking, scorpion party! Who wants a piece of me? Come on, pay a dollar and, take your pop at the human fucking vote. Why don't I cut my arms off – give you one each to take home with? Then you can fuck off?

Shiv has a tactic in mind—

SHIV

Here's one thing I did think. Guys, just to spitball. When it goes through. For you two. The Hundred, remember how hot you were for that and could I [relinquish my part of the IP and]—

ROMAN

That is so thoughtful, you'd like get us a job at the mall so we could learn the value of real money?

Kendall smiles. Roman leaning his way?

> SHIV
>
> Rome. Yeah. I'm trying to be realistic, about nice shapes, for when I'm in there. I want you two to—
> (*a dream*)
> I would love to have you two support me actually?

> KENDALL
> (*cold*)
> Uh-huh?

> SHIV
>
> What? Just cos I'm moving forward, my kid loses access to its uncles?? To all the – horrible sexist and homophobic jokes you know.

Shiv smiles. It all feels unbearable to Kendall.

> KENDALL
>
> Don't fucking try and play us, Shiv. Stop fucking gloating. It's not pretty. You've got your hands on my throat yeah? So don't act so fucking Mammie Prim.

> SHIV
>
> I don't know what to say. You two grabbed the crown. Dad died and you grabbed the crown and pushed me out. So I don't know why I'm the cunt here?

> KENDALL
>
> Cunt is as cunt does.

> SHIV
>
> Amazing. Cicero on the wheels of steel. Fuck off. Okay? I won. Sorry for winning. Sorry sorry. I'm tired of being sorry. I just fucking worked it better, so why don't you take it like a man, ah? And just fucking eat it?

A chilly beat.

> ROMAN
>
> My, what a lovely evening on the terrace!

INT. RESTAURANT – NIGHT

Matsson is there with Tom.

TOM

How's your pollock? These cod cheeks were – a worthy opponent. You know?

MATSSON

Good. Yeah. Sometimes I feel every fish in this city is the same piece of Xeroxed branzino. You know?

TOM

Totally. I think we may have been badly advised. Greg fucked it.

Matsson smiles.

MATSSON

So, dude. I feel like I've gotten to know you a little bit. And I like you.

TOM

Well thank you, and I may return the favor and say I like you.

MATSSON

So how would you feel about soft-pitching me?

Tom looks like: What?

On Tom. Give me the main slide.

TOM

On me? As – in terms of my value, to keep me? Well. Sure. I can sing for my supper hahaha!
(*then*)
No, well. As a manager? Er, I'm simple: squeeze costs, juice revenue. Follow the boss. I digest strategy and I implement. So, cruises for example, firefighting and shit-gobbling.

Matsson eyes him.

MATSSON

Num num num.

TOM

ATN is money. I'm just cutting heads and harvesting eyeballs. It's pretty simple. Bring the customer what he wants. Not my place to give dietary advice. Red meat and boiling tar? Bon appétit!

MATSSON

And on the hang-level who are you?

TOM

Who am I? Huh? That's a good one. I'm a grinder. I grind because I worry. I – I worry all night about everything. All the threats, to me, to my division and my physical body. I have an excess of vigilance and an incredibly high tolerance for pain and discomfort.

MATSSON

I noticed you didn't come to the big guy's funeral?

TOM

Work, man. Work. Wasn't like he was gonna un-die if I made it?

Matsson likes that.

MATSSON

Can I be frank with you, Tom? Can you be discreet?

TOM

Fuck yeah.

MATSSON

Yeah so the thing is. With Shiv, and— We can, for voting, and so on, can we— Can we keep this close to our chests? Till I know my numbers. Yeah?

TOM

Uh-huh?

MATSSON

I think it's all good. It's fine, but. It's just I've got a thing which is, with her. Is it kind of too much?

Immediate readjustment. The world turns upside down but Tom's gyroscope can handle and he sails on, into a new world.

TOM

Okay?

(*then*)

The cartoon?

MATSSON

No. Not the cartoon. No, fuck. That was funny. But. She was pushy on the India tactics. She's— I thought the family and

continuity could be upside. She's very, smart, you know. But –
I have plenty of ideas. I don't know how many more I need?
I think she talks to journalists. And I don't want so much
politics. I was a little in need of the political – sort of – the
connections. But you know what, it's easy and – Ebba? I just
know – I basically know everything!

TOM

Hahahaha. Yes you do! You do, man.

MATSSON

Plus. With Shiv, you know?

TOM
('no')

Uh-huh?

Matsson's final test?

MATSSON

Honestly, she's somewhat— There's a little clickety-clickety?

TOM

Right – what like—

MATSSON

And a little bit – I want to fuck her – little bit. And maybe, not
to be weird, but I think, right situation, she might want to fuck
me.

Will he take it?

TOM

Uh-huh?

MATSSON

Sorry to get weird.

TOM

No. We're men.

MATSSON

But yeah, that, I don't need that. Mess. So, I got to thinking, if
I could have *anyone in the world*, you know? Maybe I get the
fucking guy who put the baby in her, not the baby lady? Haha.

TOM

Hahaha! Right.

(*switches to dead straight*)
Well I could do it, I could definitely easily do it.

MATSSON

I need an American. I don't want to scare the horses. ATN is the
profit center. Mencken likes you, if that happens. And you're
super-talented. But I honestly, I don't need a partner, I need a
frontman. We'll be cutting shit to the fucking bone. To the *bone*,
man. Nasty. Yeah? So I'll need a pain sponge while I get under
the hood. You wouldn't mind?

TOM

Nah. No, man. Nah!

MATSSON

So what do you think?

Tom's head is popping off.

TOM

Head up Waystar Royco, I could do that.

MATSSON

Logan Mark Two, this time he's fucking, sexy bro!
(*then*)
Okay. Drinks? Yeah? Party fucking gang!

They head over to the bar.

Greg gets up to greet Tom.

GREG

How was it? Was the mahi-mahi to his taste?

TOM

Motherfucker.

GREG

Is he— Are you – are you – keeping your job? Am I?

TOM

We *might* be okay, Greg!!

GREG

What is it?

Tom mimes mouth zipped.

> TOM

I mean, you are gonna get fucking castrated on pay, like *decimated*. But I *might* be able to keep you??
> *(then)*

Keep an eye on. Piss man, out!

He leaves for the bathroom.

> OSKAR
> *(in Swedish)*

Yeah, what you think?

> MATSSON
> *(in Swedish)*

Yeah I like. I think it works.

Greg – on his phone, as they talk, next to them. Discreetly gets out instant voice translator. Discreetly sets Swedish to English. On the bar.

> OSKAR
> *(in Swedish)*

How do you play it?

> MATSSON
> *(in Swedish)*

Fucking Shiv?

> OSKAR
> *(in Swedish)*

Yeah when do you tell her it won't be her? Because the lawyer says since it's US CEO, I think we have room for maneuver.

> MATSSON
> *(in Swedish)*

Uh-huh, check, I think all we need to do right now is take her name out of the draft? Let's check.

Matsson breaks, looks at Gregory. Covering his phone.

Hey, Gregory Peggory. Why so serious, dandelion dick?

Greg smiles as he recalibrates.

INT./EXT. CAROLINE'S BARBADOS HOUSE – TERRACE/
DINING AREA – NIGHT

CAROLINE

So. It's going to be hearty fare but modest rations.

SHIV

(*quietly to Roman*)

Surprise surprise.

Shiv is looking to ally with him and maybe he can tell?

CAROLINE

I knew you wouldn't be hungry in the heat. We can fill up on brekkie tomorrow at that horrible place where I heard the man from Pink Floyd did a poo in the swimming pool.

KENDALL

Yeah, we'll need to be getting back, Mom. To stop Shiv selling our birthright.

Look to Roman?

SHIV

Well, actually to follow through on Dad's last plans and wishes.

Pitch to Roman?

CAROLINE

Can we not? I'm just glad you're all here. Whatever the motives. And I just wanted to say I am so sorry about your dear old dad. We had some very bad times and we had some decent times and I feel, you know, a lot of my friends, their children are gone, on – drugs or – booze or sex. And well. Here you are, so well done.

SHIV

(*Ken*)

Drug addict.

(*Roman*)

Sex freak.

(*herself*)

Emotional war crime.

CAROLINE

You're all still in play. You're within bounds.

> KENDALL

Well, thank you, Mum.

> CAROLINE

Yes, well, so that's perfectly vomit-inducing but I've done it.

> ROMAN

Say you love us and win a prize, Ma!

> SHIV

Don't say you love us, Rome will try to hump you.

> CAROLINE

Please don't be disgusting.

Little look between Caroline and Shiv? Directed to Roman a little?

So. That's that. And I do think – for what it's worth, I don't want to get my snout in, but I do wonder if – perhaps this offer from that awful man isn't a really good time to say farewell and open a new chapter?

Kendall looks.

That's always been my view as, you know. And—

> KENDALL

Italy? Are we gonna get an apology?

Shiv has a big swing to make and does it very straight.

> SHIV

Well. If she thinks we should sell – in some ways, in a way there is a continuity.

> CAROLINE

That's my view. And I'm sorry and I'm sorry if you've been determined to make that into something squalid.

He looks between them.

> KENDALL

Is this a set-up? Shivvy? Are you trying to tie Mummy's apron strings around Romey's nuts?

> CAROLINE

Listen. I'm going to get Peter. And Peter's friend Jonathan? Peter!

Peter heads in.

PETER

Hello. Hello, all!

CAROLINE

Because Peter's got an idea for an investment opportunity he
wants to share with us. Him and Jonathan who is a whizz, but
has been having a really shitty time recently.

ROMAN

Jonathan? Jonathan's had a hard time? Tell us more!

KENDALL

Rome, man? You see this? Put the squeeze on, sell up? And,
what, invest with Uncle Credit Card Fraud?

Jonathan appears. Peter's age.

ROMAN

Unbelievable. Did you know about this?

SHIV

Amazing. Hi, Jonathan!

*Kendall's phone goes. He gets up and leaves – motioning for Roman
to keep his eyes on what's going on.*

JONATHAN

Hey, guys.

PETER

Now I know it may not feel appropriate but your mother has
kindly let me get to you before the vultures, and the margins are
so creamy I honestly would feel like a terrible shit if I didn't give
you the opportunity to come to the party.

ROMAN

Oh wow, yeah this sounds fascinating!

CAROLINE
(*to Peter*)
He's taking the mickey, darling. Jonathan—

INT. CAROLINE'S BARBADOS HOUSE – NIGHT

Kendall makes it out of the room.

Intercut with:

INT./EXT. GREG'S LOCATION – NIGHT

Greg in a cloakroom or on the street or in a car.

> GREG
>
> Hey. Ken, so. Okay. I have something huge.

> KENDALL
>
> Uh-huh?

> GREG
>
> I'm at the center of the fucking universe with – like knowledge to bring down solar systems.

> KENDALL
>
> Sure, man. Great.

> GREG
>
> But. Um. Yeah. Oh, man. I need almost some advice but – yeah.

> KENDALL
>
> What is it, Greg?

> GREG
>
> I guess. Um. If I told you something incredible would you give me something amazing?

Easy.

> KENDALL
>
> Yeah sure. What.

> GREG
>
> No but seriously. It is amazing.

> KENDALL
>
> Sure, that's why I'm going to give you something incredible.

> GREG
>
> But like. What kind of incredible?

> KENDALL
>
> That depends on what kind of amazing?

> GREG

Um. It would involve— I'd need. Basically I guess, can you guys win, you and Rome if— And could I Quad it up, like full Quad? Because I have some news and some evidence and—

> KENDALL

Take your shot, buddy. Come on.

INT./EXT. CAROLINE'S BARBADOS HOUSE – TERRACE/ DINING AREA – NIGHT

> PETER

Now our facilities won't offer all the bells and whistles you might dream of from a fantasy care home. But it will afford what I call a 'really solid basic level of care'. It's not necessarily what one would like for oneself, but there are, sadly, a lot of people who haven't thought ahead – and we're going to be there waiting for them. And what the tax-wrapper around this vehicle offers, is a way of turning these residents into a sort of collateralized investment opportunity.

> JONATHAN

Now, obviously we're going to be skating relatively close to the wind in terms of financial regulation, but I'm absolutely confident no one can, in layman's terms, 'get us' on this.

Kendall back in. With huge news.

> KENDALL

Shiv? Um. Apologies. Apologies but I need to speak to Shiv in private?

> SHIV

What?

> KENDALL

Rome? Shiv. Please. It's serious. Mom?

> CAROLINE

I'll serve up. Will you hurry because it's gone a bit gummy already?

Maybe Kendall leads them somewhere private or they reorient on the terrace.

756

KENDALL

Shiv. So. You'll want to call – you'll want to confirm. But – I have had it confirmed that Lukas is interviewing for an alternative US CEO. He's fucking you.

SHIV

Bullshit.

ROMAN

Ken – how?

KENDALL

A source, a number of contacts. I'm sorry, Shiv.

SHIV

Oh yeah you're fucking sorry. Bullshit.

KENDALL

Call. Call. It all checks out. Lawrence, bunch of vibe hangs? Have you noticed a little cooling?

She dials.

I wouldn't call Matsson so we can figure out [how we respond and]—

SHIV

Already calling.

ROMAN

Shiv?

SHIV

Fucking *desperate* shit.

KENDALL

Not answering. That's interesting. Does he normally?

SHIV

No. He rarely picks up. So. This is so fucking pathetic.

KENDALL

Okay. Well – yeah, I guess it would be if it wasn't true. Do Karolina, because they have erased you from the new deal-announcement draft. It's shitty, Shiv, it's shitty.

She goes to make calls.

ROMAN

Oh fuck. Man. Yeah? For real?

KENDALL

Yeah.
(*quiet*)
Greg. One hundred percent.
(*then*)
Ebba. Frank. I called Lawrence, they're all— None of them could lie right. He's fucking her. So.

ROMAN

Fuck. Who instead?

KENDALL

Sounds like he's speaking to a few faces. Lawrence? Klein?

Roman is making some calculations on board votes.

ROMAN

Fuck. So. I mean – okay. Um. Well – okay? I guess. With her. Things are – are back – yeah?

KENDALL

As long as she can recalibrate, it's game on.

Slammed door upstairs.

SHIV
(*muffled shout off*)

Motherfucker.

INT. CAROLINE'S BARBADOS HOUSE – BEDROOM – NIGHT

Shiv looking at an email draft – after 'Chief Executive Officer, US Operations:' it says 'XXX'.

She sits on the edge of the bed. Breathing and thinking, thoughts of revenge and feelings of terrible rage. Looks around the room. Too real. Focusses on little details.

KENDALL
(*off*)

Shiv? Can we talk.

SHIV

Fuck off. It's not right.

KENDALL
(*off*)

Can we come in?

ROMAN
(*off*)

Shiv?

They come in – Shiv looking at her phone.

SHIV

It's not right, necessarily. I think someone's not straight here.

Kendall tries to be gentle.

KENDALL

It doesn't seem right, no?

SHIV

Oh don't come the nice guy. Don't come the fucking nice guy,
Ken!

A call back to her phone.

SHIV

Go on fuck off. Fuck off!

EXT. CAROLINE'S BARBADOS HOUSE – TERRACE – NIGHT

Kendall on a terrace, or outside one of their rooms or bungalows.
Finishing a call.

KENDALL

It's just hard for her.

Roman is reading emails.

ROMAN

Man. Okay. It's real, yeah?

KENDALL

I think – I think we just lay it out for her.

INT. CAROLINE'S BARBADOS HOUSE – BEDROOM – NIGHT

Shiv has been thinking. The world has changed. But she can think.
She is a fast thinker.

EXT. CAROLINE'S BARBADOS HOUSE – TERRACE – NIGHT

Shiv comes through to find them.

> SHIV
>
> Okay. So. What are we going to do?

They look.

> ROMAN
>
> Did you talk to him, to Lukas?

> SHIV
>
> I don't want to talk to him. I don't want to – I don't want to—
> > (*to Kendall*)
>
> Don't look at me.

> KENDALL
>
> Hey I'm sorry.

> SHIV
>
> No you're not shut the fuck up.

> KENDALL
>
> I— What can I say?

> ROMAN
>
> Nothing. We might get— Shall we get someone? Laird or Tellis?

> SHIV
>
> Not fucking Laird. And not Tellis. I detest Tellis. Tellis is the
> fucking worst.
> > (*then, thinks for quite a while*)
>
> Call Tellis. We obviously need a read. Call Tellis. He's not getting
> even a fucking tiny piece of this.

Maybe as Kendall calls they shift to a spot where they can all be
around the speakerphone.

> KENDALL
>
> Shiv. You okay? To do this?

Kendall gets Tellis.

> SHIV
>
> This is ugly. This is fucking bad.

> KENDALL
>
> Well. Uh-huh. But – we're a powerful bloc. This was sloppy. It was careless. We're ready to fucking kill him.

> SHIV
>
> I think you're chasing rainbows. I think he has it sewn up.

Tellis answers. We stay with the kids.

> KENDALL
>
> Telly. Thanks, man. You got my message? So look, this is non-prejudicial, this is friend-level briefing, clean of upside, downside or legal action. Side effects may include bloating, seizures or a fat fucking consultation fee. So yeah. This make sense about US CEO – him changing lanes?

> TELLIS
> *(on speakerphone)*
>
> Yeah. I mean, from his point of view it makes sense really to go for someone with more—

> KENDALL
>
> —Shiv's here.

> SHIV
>
> Fuck you, Tellis.

> TELLIS
>
> Sorry, Shiv, no I mean in terms of – the names which are being discussed, they make— Just I mean –

> SHIV
>
> Uh-huh. Cut to the chase, blondie.

> TELLIS
>
> Okay. Big picture. Here's where you are now, right? Prices are increasingly reflecting reality. The market has lost its tech-growth-dream boner. His outfit is feeling fakey, India subs et cetera?

> SHIV
>
> Shaky, maybe.

TELLIS

So. If it's you three as a voting bloc. And on top you have you say—

KENDALL

I have Ewan, Paul, Dewi. I think. I think.

ROMAN

You think? You said they were cast-iron.

KENDALL

Yeah I was lying.

(*smile*)

But they'll be in. They'll be in if we can win. And then I think Stewy?

Shiv looks at Roman.

TELLIS

I believe actually, I can have conversations, it's not impossible, with certain inducements. You three stick together. Um, Sandy or Sandi or Stewy as you say. Diane? I mean as a voting bloc, you can probably threaten to kill it? So, yeah, you have the whip hand.

SHIV

And what about leadership?

TELLIS

Well, yes. You need to present a coherent plan to the board including your leadership candidate.

SHIV

And like could a combination at the top or a – trio or troika or – a – combination or—

TELLIS

(*after a beat*)

Ummmm. Um. Um?

Gap in the air.

ROMAN

You can fucking say, man . . .

TELLIS

I think it hasn't been great for credibility, the Incredible Fuck-Brother Bandwagon?

ROMAN

Who calls us the Fuck-Brother Bandwagon?

SHIV
(aside)

Everyone.

TELLIS

You need it to look like a united choice with a coherent plan that's, not a cop-out at the fudge factory. One strong name for CEO, either combined with chair or a chair with business chops. Is what I would say. Off the record.

ROMAN

Did he get to you, Tellis?

KENDALL

Thanks, Telly, we stick together, we can stop him. One name. Thank you. We might be in touch on some moves here?

Ends call. Looks at them.

SHIV

There's a few ways through this.

KENDALL

Call Laird. Call anyone. Anyone would say, right? We go into battle with our own version of the future. With a king.

ROMAN

And pray tell . . .

Kendall's pitch—

KENDALL

Matsson's a fucking prick, he practically killed Dad, dragging him over. He's capricious, cold, doesn't understand the business. He's a prick.

SHIV

I would like to kill him.

ROMAN

I too would be strongly interested in fucking him to death.

KENDALL

And, if we are going to be real. We'd need— It would be me.
Right?

Beat. Will Roman say it?

ROMAN

Well, Dad said it would be me.

KENDALL

Rome? Man, you were all about jerking off and crying out.

ROMAN

Well, Dad just did say it should be me.

KENDALL

When?

ROMAN

We were getting close again, before, you know this, mostly
and – I was texting and he was warm and he said when I was
with him, late one night, that it should be me.

SHIV

That's persuasive. What else did he say when no one was
around?

KENDALL

Shiv, don't be all – pissy because, oh, sorry, what's this? Oh it's
Dad calling me.
          (*picks up an imaginary ghost phone*)
Ghost phone. Spooky.

ROMAN

Hey? C'mon.

KENDALL

Sorry what's that, Dad?
          (*reporting*)
He's saying, he's saying, yeah it is Roman. Okay, Dad. What—
          (*'listens'*)
Kill . . . Shiv . . . That doesn't make any sense?

ROMAN

Enough. Dad – Dad wanted he said—

SHIV

Sure I mean. Wait, Dad's calling me now?
                    (*picks up ghost phone*)
Princess Di? You shouldn't be on this line! Is my dad there? Dad,
we're getting a big order from Shake Shack, what you want?

ROMAN

Well, it's true. So, I don't know what to do with that.

SHIV

He offered it to me too, Rome.

KENDALL

He fucking promised it to me. Promised. When I was seven.
Seven years old. Can you imagine?

ROMAN

Pics or it didn't happen.

KENDALL

That was something. He shouldn't have done that.

*Shiv knows or has heard or can just tell this is true, and she knows
how it feels.*

SHIV

No. He shouldn't have said that.

ROMAN

Yeah well that doesn't count.

KENDALL

I am simply saying, he said a lot of things. And he said them to
me first.

ROMAN

And me last.

Kendall has something building.

KENDALL

Rome. It's not.

> (*then*)
> Do you even want it? The funeral, yeah? You're not— You're a
> good guy. But – up there? You didn't do the rounds, you kinda
> shrank into your shell, and that's, that—

ROMAN

So, I shed a tear at my father's funeral and now I'm fucked
forever? Didn't see that in the terms and fucking conditions.

KENDALL

That absolutely does not make you a bad person. Maybe that
makes you a good person, that you weren't snaking at the
funeral. Maybe you're well-adjusted and I'm a business psycho.
> (*then*)
> I dunno, man. It's a fucking horrible job that kills you. I'm just –
> honestly I'm just – trying to guide us through the years to some
> truth here, man.

ROMAN

Cheesy.

KENDALL

I'm serious.

ROMAN

Serious cheeseball, is what you are.

Roman walks off down to the beach. Or pool.

KENDALL

He doesn't want it but he can't say it.

Beat.

SHIV

And me?

KENDALL

I love you, Shiv, I love you. But we simply cannot walk in there
and say we're blocking his offer, and we have this compelling
vision, and say that leading it is you, when yesterday you were
singing his song. We simply can't. And we can't say it's Roman
because he lacks heft and he, he looks pathetic, and he might
flop. So. Obviously I want it to be me, but anyone would say,
anyone, objectively would say – LA, my – profile, experience,

position, desire, public pronouncements. It's me. If we want to hold on to this company for us, for my kids, for yours, it's me.

Shiv looks at him, then shouts down to Roman—

SHIV

Hey, Rome, guess who Kendall thinks it should be? It's going to blow your fucking mind!

EXT. CAROLINE'S BARBADOS HOUSE – STEPS TO BEACH – NIGHT

Maybe some minutes later on the beach. Kendall and Roman and Shiv. They maybe have grabbed some beach clothing from by the pool. Maybe Shiv has changed into something comfortable for the beach or a splash.

KENDALL

We can find a cool structure. Fiefdoms. Kingdoms. We pull off a reverse Viking, guys? Huge. Shiv, seriously, take ATN, take all of news – save the world. Roman, social media you try to blow it up again. It'll be fun?

ROMAN

Are we actually going in?

They look at him.

Cos. You know?

Kendall knows what he is worried about.

KENDALL

No bad sharks in Bim, baby. They're North Atlantic.

ROMAN

Yeah, well they can commute. All the seas, in case you didn't know, are connected, it's a huge water subway for things that want to eat me.

They start preparing for a wade or a dip.

EXT. BEACH – NEAR RAFT – NIGHT

Roman and Shiv standing nearer shore. Bobbing a little, feet on the sand. Kendall is a way along – lying on a little raft.

SHIV

So?

ROMAN

What you think? We could fuck it. Get out? Sell to Matsson, let Lawrence or some business-school dry-cleaner sit in the throne?

SHIV
(that doesn't feel good)

Hm. Yeah. Closing time. I dunno?

ROMAN

Uh-huh.

(then)

It can't be him. But it really can't be you.

SHIV

Uh-huh. Well. I hate him, but I fear you. So. I mean, I think he'll be unbearable. But you'd be a disaster.

ROMAN

He'll be— It will be so terrible. But. I dunno? I can, sort of, unfortunately, see it. Whereas you?

SHIV

Matsson took me seriously.

ROMAN

Or he played you like a big fiddle, like a pregnant cello.

SHIV

He will unravel. If we don't give him it.

ROMAN

Meh. So?

SHIV

But if we do give it to him, he'll be unbearable. But if we don't he'll be unbearable and angry and might kill himself . . .

ROMAN

Which would be – good?

Smiles.

SHIV

Well you say that. But. Then we probably go mad and –
I dunno. Not great.

> ROMAN

Who do you *actually* think Dad wanted to give it to?

> SHIV

I don't know if he kind of gave a fuck about anything except one foot in front of the other?

> ROMAN

I don't think he wanted to give it to any of us.
> (*whispered*)
And he found him kind of annoying.
> (*then*)
But, probably, closest? Most often? I guess? We give it to him?

> SHIV

Unless?

> ROMAN

Unless?

> SHIV

. . . We kill him?

They smile at each other.

> ROMAN

Okay? I like killing him. That is intriguing. What would we do?

> SHIV

Just a bit of horseplay gone wrong. Bonk. Biff. Coconut to the noggin.

> ROMAN

Roll the seal off the rock. You stand on one end, I stand on the other, till it goes limp. What goes around comes around?

> SHIV

If we killed him, we could go to bed?

> ROMAN

But he'd be such a dick if it went wrong.
> (*self-pitying*)
'Dude, did you try to murder me? That's so not a thing you're actually meant to do and is not a good thing to do, man!'

> SHIV

'You shouldn't have murdered me. You guys are the worst!'

They smile, then—

ROMAN

Shall we?

They swim over.

What's it like. Being pregnant?

SHIV

Um?

ROMAN

Is it like being fat? Like just fat at the front?

SHIV

Er, I dunno. I – I guess.
(*then*)
It's weird, I've always been very much a one-person unit. But I've doubled my occupancy. And it's— I'm very private, but now I have another person on board.

ROMAN

And what's it like getting big bazzoomas? Do you feel like it might make you fall over?

SHIV

Not a huge issue. No, pretty far down the list of concerns. But good one.

ROMAN

Okay. Just interested.

SHIV

Maybe if you don't go run GoJo socials. You could become an obstetrician? Seems like you've got a real interest in the area.

EXT. BEACH – BY RAFT – NIGHT

They arrive.

KENDALL

Hey.

SHIV

Hey – we were thinking of murdering you.

                    ROMAN

Well don't tell him!

                    SHIV

But too much prep. Too much murder admin.

                    ROMAN

No stomach for the admin.

                    SHIV

Okay. So.

                    (looks at Roman)

We anoint you.

                    ROMAN

You get the bauble. Congratulations. It's haunted and cursed and nothing will ever go right, but, enjoy your bauble.

Kendall tries to look humble.

                    KENDALL

Thank you.

                    SHIV

You *can* smile.

                    KENDALL

Thank you.

                    SHIV

Look at him, he can't get his face right. You can smile, bitch!

INT. CAROLINE'S BARBADOS HOUSE – KITCHEN – NIGHT

They come back looking for food.

                    ROMAN

If we're going to anoint him. First he must complete a task!

                    SHIV

Walk upstairs naked and say 'I'd like a quiet word, Jonathan. In my ass!'

                    ROMAN

Eat a spoonful of cinnamon!

> KENDALL

Uh-huh, that's what they made Lee Iacocca do when he took over at Ford.

> SHIV

Lick the inside of the toilet bowl. Or, no, Rome: meal fit for a king!

> ROMAN

Yes! We're gonna make you a meal fit for a king!

Roman opens the fridge. Shiv goes to the cupboard area. They start to get things out.

> ROMAN
> (*at fridge*)

Oooh. A real bounty!

> SHIV

I'm actually starving – is there – there something for a sandwich?

> ROMAN

Mm! Mama, with this pair of sprouting potatoes, zero-percent milk, and wartime pickle you are really spoiling us!

Shiv has armfuls of dried goods and powders and condiments, mustard and ketchup from the cupboard.

> SHIV

Meal fit for a king! Meal fit for a king! Meal fit for a king!

She opens the top and starts to pour them into a mixer.

Roman encourages Shiv—

> ROMAN

Chuck it in, mate!

> SHIV

You are going to be such a great CEO. If this doesn't kill you. Which it definitely will.

Kendall is laughing. Mayo, cocoa powder, sugar, old Branston Pickle, milk.

> KENDALL

I am actually starving.

SHIV

A little bit of Tabasco.

(*tipping in*)

Oooh *a lot of* Tabasco!

Kendall enjoying it. They are all giggly and high.

Caroline comes in in her dressing gown.

CAROLINE

You're back then? I have to say that was rather rude. Jonathan came from Monaco and he has to be really careful with his days.

Kendall and Shiv catch eyes.

ROMAN

Mom, I know how you feel about best-by dates but you have pterodactyl eggs in here. You have soup cans with Andy Warhol's fingerprints.

CAROLINE

What's going on, why are you up?

KENDALL

We're celebrating.

SHIV

We are *not* celebrating. We're in mourning. We're trying to kill him.

KENDALL

We're voting as a bloc to keep the firm. We're gonna stay in.

CAROLINE

Blimey.

She looks at Shiv – not what they had thought.

SHIV

I've had some negative news. So, we were having a friendly discussion about who it should be?

This throws off some plans and thoughts.

CAROLINE

Oh. Right. Well. I see. Fine.

Roman has found some cheese.

Oh, please don't eat Peter's cheese, darling.

> ROMAN
> There's not a ton of – food. And Ken's hungry and I'm—

> CAROLINE
> Not his special cheese. There's some Cracker Barrel at the back, have the Cracker Barrel you like that.

> KENDALL
> Yeah, I love that because I'm still eight.

> ROMAN
> We could order in. Do you have a number?

> CAROLINE
> No, darling. It costs a fortune and arrives cold and they get the address wrong and please don't order. We've got plenty in.

Caroline looks in the freezer, or motions.

Peter doesn't like the knobby, so I freeze them. Help yourselves.

Roman looks in the bottom freezer door.

> ROMAN
> Oh, it's a bag of frozen knobbies?

> CAROLINE
> Loaf ends. And listen. Peter will be disappointed but – I am happy things are nicer. But quiet if you can? Jonathan's above and he desperately needs some rest.

They blow her kisses as she exits.

Then, when barely out of earshot—

> KENDALL
> 'Peter doesn't like knobbies, darling.'

> ROMAN
> 'Bovril and knobbies, sweetheart?'

They start Frisbeeing knobbies at one another as Shiv whizzes stuff up in the blender.

> KENDALL
> 'Oh, don't eat Peter's cheese, darling.'

Pulling out an open yogurt.

SHIV

'Don't touch Peter's Müller Corner, sweetheart, I brought it over in a hankie.'

Shiv dribbles her saliva in the meal-fit-for-a-king concoction, gives them a wink.

Roman smiles, now he has Peter's cheese, a fat piece of Isle of Mull cheddar.

KENDALL

'Don't eat Peter's cheese, darling!'

Throwing bread and getting a bit hysterical.

ROMAN

I'm so sorry, Peter.

Roman licks the cheese.

KENDALL

'Oh don't lick Peter's cheese, darling.'

ROMAN

'Oh, I'm sorry, Mummy, I licked it all over. I am so sorry.
            (*licking*)
I can't stop licking Peter's cheese. What shall we do?'

He throws an egg. Kendall and Roman start gently throwing the egg to one another, they don't want to break it – but they surprise one another and do feints and surprise, gentle, throws. Over to Shiv and around till it splats as—

SHIV

Okay. Here we go! Meal fit for a king!

She hands it to Kendall.

ROMAN

Congratulations. You fuckhead.

KENDALL

This is gonna be alright. We're gonna be alright, right?

Beat. Could be a moment but—

> SHIV
>
> Drink it and shut the fuck up!

DAY TWO

EXT. CAROLINE'S BARBADOS HOUSE – DAY

Early morning. The kids depart. With their entourages.

EXT. NEW YORK – AIRPORT – DAY

The kids are arriving back. Assistants have coats and bags to greet.

> KENDALL
> (*on phone*)
> Yeah Ewan is best – just left to it. He votes the status quo. Yeah and I have them here. Stewy, I'll go wherever whenever for Stewy.

> ROMAN
> Paul's good. Paul's rock. Paul doesn't trust tech.

> SHIV
> (*to the other two*)
> Con wants to know if we're making the Great Reallocation?

Kendall looks at her as he speaks. Shrugs.

> ROMAN
> Do we care – do we have time?

> KENDALL
> (*hand over phone*)
> Are – are Frank and – Karl gonna be there – cos could be—?

> SHIV
> He is kinda losing his shit? He's— He wants to clear out?

She shrugs.

Roman, hand over phone –

> ROMAN
> (*tells Kendall*)
> We can do thirty? Yeah?

(*then*)

To the Great Reallocation!

(*connects*)

Dewi! Hey, man. Roman.

KENDALL

Fucking Lukas baby! We're a-coming!

Cars leave for the city.

INT. LOGAN'S APARTMENT – DAY

Connor is with Willa.

He is addressing a group—

Shiv, Roman, Kendall. Tom, Greg. Kendall is preoccupied with phone messages and emails.

CONNOR

Now, as you know. My father left us a hell of a task – 'personal effects distributed as my survivors see fit'. I mean, thanks, enjoy the knife fight!

ROMAN

I got Hearts. Does anyone want to swap a soccer team for a bottle of wine?

CONNOR

Thank you, Roman! Please. I know many of you have ahem – somewhere rather important to be this afternoon. But the system is pretty simple. As you move in a clockwise direction around the apartment, you affix your stickers to objects you covet. Affix as you see fit – one sticker each on a number of different articles or many on one prized item. Subsequent circulating mourners then apply their stickers. After two stickering perambulation circuits—

SHIV

(*aside*)

We call them SPCs.

> CONNOR

Objects will be assigned to the higher sticker bidder. Where sticker claims are tied, we move to the second, tiebreak sticker perambulation circuit.

> SHIV
> (aside)

The TBSPC.

> CONNOR

After which all un-stickered items will be pooled and distributed by reverse alphabetical order other than those stickered by the second-tier, excuse me, bereaved.

He nods. In the room down a few steps wait Kerry, Colin and family, and a couple of other friends and associates. Holding small rolls of stickers.

Connor pats some sheets stapled in the corner – lists with some items also having little thumbnail pictures.

Emotionally resonant items from the Summer Palace, and the Toronto, London, Gstaad, LA and Montecito houses are listed here and are subject to an additional secondary-residence bonus fifty-sticker quota. Do I make myself clear?

> KENDALL
> (looking up from phone)

It's a good system.

Kendall and Roman walk Logan's apartment.

They each hold a roll of stickers in their hands.

Everything is laid out. All the regular furniture and decorative items but also in the dining room the big table is covered in household and personal items.

Pictures are stacked and placed around the walls.

In other spots, heirlooms, pictures, trinkets, high value and low, are arranged.

Objects from Logan's life everywhere.

Kendall, considering the treasures laid out, not entirely straight—

'What profits a man if he gains the whole world and lose his soul?'

ROMAN

I dunno, about a thirty-percent return on investment?

Roman stickers a letter opener.

Kendall stickers the same item.

Roman stickers.

Shiv comes over and stickers.

ROMAN
(*cont'd*)

It's all going to break down over a letter opener.

SHIV

Con?! Where are the medals?

He comes over.

CONNOR

Ah. Yeah there was a first round. An initial round.

ROMAN

And who was present at that?

CONNOR

That was myself, solely.

They maybe giggle a little.

ROMAN

O-kay!? And so – does it all have to go, do you not want to—

Willa is there too.

WILLA

I'd really like to get rid of pretty much everything, you know? I have some pretty cool stuff coming in. Cow-print couch. Yea long.

ROMAN

And, Con – you don't want to keep more of it for—

CONNOR

Well, um, we're planning on. If, when Mencken comes through, we're actually thinking of experimenting with—

WILLA

I have a play reading, in six to eight months and so, Con's going to go to Slovenia and I'll be working on that and we're—

CONNOR

We're really excited for how that long-distance thing will add another dimension and—

WILLA

Yeah, keep the spice alive even as we, you know, get deeper into the marriage.

ROMAN

Uh-huh, the second-week itch.

CONNOR

Rome. We're excited.

SHIV

You saw the Wisconsin court thing?

WILLA

(*mild alarm*)

Sorry? What court thing?

CONNOR

Hiccup. Just a hiccup for Jeryd I think.

SHIV

Uh-huh. Or maybe Mencken won't do it, ah? And maybe you'll get to keep him all to yourself!

Shiv smiles at Willa. Mixed feelings.

Connor nods to the TV in the dining room.

CONNOR

Virtual dinner with Pop?

On it plays a camera-phone recording of a recent lunch.

Logan, Frank, Karl, Gerri, Kerry eat together a couple of months back. Logan gets them to do their party pieces: Karl sings 'Green Grow the Rashes', Frank does his retirement speech for Karl, Gerri *her dirty limerick. Logan lists the losing presidential candidates in reverse order. Kerry does impressions of each of the kids. And they all drink.**

ROMAN

Oh, man.

INT. LOGAN'S APARTMENT — LIVING ROOM — DAY

Greg has a couple of stickers. Greg looks at a picture – about to sticker. Now Kendall appears behind him.

KENDALL

Hey!

GREG

Hey?

KENDALL

Nice try, my friend. This is a masterpiece. You might be more comfortable in there with the knick-knacks?

Greg looks at him. Is he kidding?

Go on.
(*whispers in his ear*)
Treats ahoy. Treats a-fucking-hoy for a fucking Quad Bod.

Winks.

Elsewhere – Shiv is looking around.

SHIV

Hey.

---

* This was one of the last full pieces of the show I wrote. It started out as a bit of additional flavour to play on a TV in the background of the sticker-allocation scene which might or might not make the cut. I tried to find character-appropriate 'party pieces' for the dinner guests. 'Green Grow the Rashes' was a happy accident. My wife happened to send me a link to the heartbreaking Michael Marra performance as I was writing and, knowing that David Rasche has a good singing voice, I asked if he'd be willing to give it a go. It was very affecting on the day, but I still feared we might have to lose it for time. Watching Kieran, Sarah and Jeremy react to the camera-phone footage (shot by Justine Lupe) though, its place in the final edit started to feel more assured. The full scene we filmed – a last moment with Logan – is included as an appendix at the end of this book.

                              TOM
     Hey.

                              SHIV
     You okay? You're not getting canned?

He would prefer not to lie.

                              TOM
     Um. I don't – I don't think so. Good luck.

                              SHIV
     Oh. No. No.
                           (then)
     That's all fucked.

Fear in Tom.

                              TOM
                           (squeak)
     Yeah?

                              SHIV
     Yeah. Matsson either changed lanes or was stringing me along
     the whole time. Yeah. So. We're gonna try to fuck him on the
     vote. But yeah. It's not gonna be me.

                              TOM
     Oh. Wow. Whoa. Wow. Are you sure? Who— How did that— Is
     it even true?

                              SHIV
     Yup. Greg.

                              TOM
     Oh. Oh wow. Wow. Man. Man oh man. What a thing.
                         (processes)
     That's – terrible. And – like, do you know who he would— Who
     it would be?

                              SHIV
     Tech pal? Big hitter. Lawrence maybe?

                              TOM
     Fuck.
                     (could this work)
     Well, maybe you should vote it through? If it's all set and—

SHIV

What?

TOM

Yeah, no. No I was just thinking, if it was— But no. Wow.

Shiv looks at him. He looks away. He goes through about sixteen different permutations.

Um. Shiv? You should probably know.

She looks at him and, maybe a fraction before he says it, maybe suspects.

It's me.

SHIV

It's you?

TOM

Uh-huh.

SHIV

Bullshit.

TOM

You might as well know. I mean, you're gonna— It's gonna come out in—
                    (checks watch)
And you should— I wonder if actually you know – you should—

SHIV

Fuck you, really? Fuck you. What?

TOM

Yeah. Yeah.

And Shiv can see.

SHIV

You fucking— He went for an empty suit. Jesus.
           (mocking his duplicity)
'Maybe you should vote it through'?

TOM

Shiv, c'mon. *I know you.*

> (*then*)
> Like you wouldn't – if it was the other way about?

SHIV

Uh-huh, well, good luck. Motherfucker. Good *fucking* luck. Because we have the numbers!

Tom goes to talk to Greg.

Shiv walks to get the boys who are watching Logan heckle Karl singing on TV, keeping his emotion in check by being rude.

SHIV
(*cont'd*)

It's fucking Tom.

KENDALL

What?

SHIV

It's fucking Tom. Let's go. Let's go. Let's run our numbers, come on, let's fucking go.

ROMAN

Oh, man. Man? Fucked by the dry-cleaner!

They head out. Kendall and Roman giving Tom stares as he brings Greg around to the under-stair area.

TOM

Er, Greg, would you mind, can I talk to you in here one moment?

GREG

Um?

TOM

Just a, corporate, matter. Tactics.

Greg considers, then steps into the small bathroom.

INT. LOGAN'S APARTMENT – BATHROOM – DAY

Then—

TOM

Did you tell?

> GREG

What?

> TOM

Did you fucking tell! You bastard? Ah. I was this close and they've had a chance to fucking pull the fucking opposition together, you fucking prick, you fucking—

Maybe Tom slaps Greg. And Greg slaps Tom right back and very quickly there is a flurry of a kerfuffling and grabbing and slapping and commotion in the toilet. Like a pair of birds flapping around in a confined space. Whirling arms, their jackets flying. Confusion.

Then it is all over. Quiet. They look at one another. And Tom steps out.

INT. LOGAN'S APARTMENT – DAY

Tom pulls out phone, dials.

> TOM

Problem. Big fucking problem.

He gets in the elevator.

> CONNOR

Your stickers, Tom? Tom, you have unused stickers?

INT. MATSSON'S HOTEL SUITE – DAY

Action stations.

> MATSSON

Activate. Fucking activate. Ebba, phones. Phones. Yeah? Where's Frank? Ebba, talk to their – person.

INT. WAYSTAR – UNDERGROUND CAR PARK – DAY

The kids' cars head in. Kendall's car arrives.

Shiv and Roman's too.

> ROMAN

Stewy?

> KENDALL
>
> Yeah wobble. Wobbly fucking bastard.

> SHIV
>
> Let's hit them. Let's round them up. Fucking Tom.

INT. WAYSTAR — HALLWAY — DAY

The kids and assistants exit the elevator on their way to . . .

INT. WAYSTAR — EXECUTIVE FLOOR — DAY

Kids back on the executive floor.

> KENDALL
>
> Where do we do Stew? Mine or yours or—?

They nod to Logan's.

INT. WAYSTAR — OUTSIDE LOGAN'S OFFICE — DAY

Shiv is the first through. Kendall checking in with his new version of Jess. Roman talking to Paul on the phone.

Karolina is there to greet, talks discreetly.

> KAROLINA
>
> Hey. So. How you doing. You gonna be able to block you think?

Shiv looks like: Yes but not gonna get into it with you.

> Great! I think it'll be great, you guys. A chance for – change to the culture, the – backstabbing? I'd love a new era. And I just wonder if, between us, to say now, before everything blows up, if a big part of that could be, getting rid of Hugo? Just wanted to plant the seed?

Shiv looks – not totally appropriate, also, not a bad idea . . . as she and Kendall head into Logan's office.

Roman arrives, ending his call.

> KAROLINA
> (cont'd)
>
> Congrats.

Roman looks at her.

> Shiv said you have it. And can you say who's— Who did you
> pick – as the name, as top dog?

ROMAN
I mean it couldn't be Shiv, because—

KAROLINA
Sure. Matsson. So? What did you—

She doesn't know who it is – him or Kendall?

ROMAN
Well, yeah it can't be me, because: 'Your new CEO: Barfight
O'Horrible'.

*He points to his face. Karolina blinks, gets it, or makes out she gets it,
that it would not be politic to push.*

KAROLINA
Right. No. Sure.

*Roman moves off in. Karolina heads off to find Frank, who we might
see jogging to find Karl.*

INT. WAYSTAR – LOGAN'S OFFICE – DAY

Roman nods over—

ROMAN
Looks like they've heard their testicles might be on fire?

HUGO
Can we help prepare the ground?

ROMAN
It's going to be a fairly explosive mega-fuck, so, yes.

SHIV
GoJo deal is gonna die. Maybe Frank pulls the vote. Or maybe
they push it and get humiliated?

HUGO
Okay! Big day on the salami line!

> KENDALL

Yeah, um let me. I'll get you the materials – the details on the financing.

He wants to look at a computer.

Kendall looks at Logan's seat.

Do I dare?

Roman and Shiv look at one another.

> ROMAN

Sure?

> SHIV

Whatever.

Sits down gingerly.

> STEWY

Hey hey hey. How we looking!

> KENDALL

Dude. We have it. We have it.

Stewy looks around.

> SHIV

You're coming with us huh?

> STEWY

Well, I have certain questions about riding the vegetable train. But. Like. I'm kind of a selfish person. So?

> SHIV

Uh-huh?

> KENDALL

You know one thing I would maybe— As – as our shape comes together, and this is for the team here. Do we invite the Stewpot in?

> STEWY

Working nine to five in the typing pool?

> KENDALL

Get him inside. Non-exec chair. The fucking activist backtivist.

> STEWY

Chair? Guys? I like weird sex, I like bad drugs. I'm a complicated individual.

> KENDALL

Bullshit. You like pancakes and waffles and you kiss guys on molly, you're not the heart of darkness you're a grilled cheese with a sucked dick, we can clean you up.

Stewy looks around the room. Maybe does a little circle high-fiving with all of them.

> STEWY

You know. Shiv, I do think, if we gave Sandi a tug, she's also somewhat foldable?

Shiv shrugs. Maybe. Trying not to react to Kendall in Dad's chair, but her eyes keep on flicking.

> SHIV

Sure. Sure. Shall we?

Shiv and Stewy head out to make contact.

As Stewy passes Roman—

> STEWY

You did a good one, man.

What? Roman watches him join Shiv.

Sees Gerri far across the office. With surprise.

> ROMAN

What's she in for?

> KENDALL

I think, we're paying her off big time so it's not a lock-out? Right?

Catches Gerri looking over at him in there. He feels self-conscious.

> ROMAN

I don't really wanna see her. Should she be around?

He suddenly feels a rush. Of what?

> KENDALL

Sure. Let's fuck her out.

> ROMAN

Yeah.

> *(feeling growing)*

I don't really want to see anyone.

He checks a mirror.

> KENDALL

You okay?

> ROMAN

I might call in. Call in the vote.

> KENDALL

I think, man, it's— People know you're here. Show of force, man. Are you okay?

> ROMAN

Uh-huh. Yeah.

> *(looking)*

It's better, than I thought. It's so much better.

> KENDALL

Uh-huh.

> ROMAN

I just feel. People are going to be saying, why isn't it me?

> KENDALL

It could have been you. Just, marginal-presentation shit. You'll have something shit-hot. Socials.

> ROMAN

Right. It's just the optics.

Maybe Roman rubs at his scar. A little obsessed.

It's dumb. The stitches. They're good stitches.

> KENDALL

It's ninety percent about the visuals.

> ROMAN

Uh-huh. I mean, just if – like. If people think I pussied out though, so maybe I won't—

> KENDALL

Yeah?

> ROMAN

Yeah I just. I look kinda okay? It's dumb but. Why isn't it me?

> KENDALL

Bro. Hey.

Kendall offers a hug. Kendall takes the back of Roman's head and holds it. But we see the grip tighten and Roman allows it. Presses his face and especially his eye socket into Kendall's shoulder.

Kendall grinds it in.

Roman knows what's happening. Half struggles, half lets it happen.

> ROMAN

Hey, man?

We're close in and we can see the stitches tear a little, blood seeps, the wound inflamed. The grind goes on a painful beat as Roman grimaces and Kendall is on the verge of tears of gratitude and connection and Roman in self-loathing, self-pity and gratitude.

You fucking bastard.

> KENDALL

I love you, man.

> ROMAN

I fucking hate you.

> KENDALL

We'll be okay. We're gonna do good.

Roman is recovering his poise. Still a little undone. Maybe now dabbing his eye with a tissue.

> ROMAN

Teamwork makes the dream work.

INT. WAYSTAR – ELEVATOR – DAY

Shiv travels up. She has some feelings, but she hardly lets them become known to herself. Stick with the plan.

INT. WAYSTAR – OUTSIDE BOARDROOM – DAY

The board assembles.

Outside. Not quite two groups. But Kendall hits his folks. Stewy, Paul, Ewan, Roman.

Karl and Frank. Karl will make the deal presentation.

Kendall with Dewi.

Also Sandi, Sandy, Simon, Diane and Sonya.

The doors are opened and the board assembles.

Taking their seats, eyeing one another.

INT. WAYSTAR — BOARDROOM — DAY

Frank opens the meeting.

> FRANK
>
> Let's call this meeting to order. I note that all the directors are present. The agenda and information packs have been circulated and I would like to take them as read. We have a revised offer to consider from the GoJo board and a lot of work has been done to get us to a position where we're ready to sign if the board agrees.
> (sigh)
> As you're also of course aware, we will be hearing from our co-CEOs on a strategic alternative.

Roman dabs his wound. Kendall in a prominent position. Next to Frank. The way he moves, the way he looks, the way he makes eye contact with person after person on the board. A little wink, a smile. A solicitous (mock?) humble offer to pour coffee or water. Shiv clocks.

She looks at Roman. Lost in a world of his own.

Everyone lost in a world where their concerns are paramount. Shiv feels a wave of disassociation.

Kendall from his place eyes the room like a hawk circling, he feels all his senses are at their most attuned, can feel the vibrations in the room. Looks and clocks the board members weighting how to play it today, in the future.

FRANK
(cont'd)

I will call upon each director today to give their view on the appropriate way forward for the company. We will devote appropriate time to assess the GoJo position with input from our advisors and then I will call on Kendall to offer an alternative way forward. Karl?

INT. WAYSTAR – OUTSIDE BOARD ROOM – DAY

Assistants and lawyers watch them.

We see snatches from outside. The arguments for the GoJo offer and then Kendall takes to his feet.

INT. WAYSTAR – BOARDROOM – DAY

Kendall. Makes a decision. Feeling not so much Dad vibes as freedom of movement. That thing that was his dad's, that you can say anything. And then it's said. No one can shove the words back down your throat or strike it from the record. So.

KENDALL

Yeah. Um the GoJo offer. Yeah. Um this deal, the deal is a bad deal, the GoJo offer. We were proud, me and Rome, we know it inside out. But it's a bad deal and if you want it to go through you'll have to fire me and find someone else to take it through.
(then)
I think you have your packs here, with the structural arguments and the financing options, and – look it's a thick pack and we've knocked it out of the park. And GoJo, Matsson is flailing, we know that. So, look, I've spoken to you all. We know each other. I like and respect every one of you, but no one is going to have their mind changed in here. So. I suggest, we move to the vote. Kill this – excuse me – GoJo bullshit. And let's figure out how to eat their lunch?

FRANK

Oh, Ken?

> KENDALL

What, you want me to read it out? For due process? We have the votes. Let's do it? Okay.

> FRANK

I'd really rather . . . Simon.

> KENDALL

Let's do it for my dad, guys, yeah?

How does Shiv like that?

> FRANK

Would anyone object to moving directly to a vote?

Assent.

Um. Very well. Simon? Yes?
> (*looks to the deputy general counsel*)

Very well. Can I ask each of the directors, if you are in favor of accepting the GoJo bid at one-nine-two, to indicate in the affirmative.

Through the above – Kendall is concerned about Stewy – but very much about Roman. He looks to Shiv – is he okay?

> FRANK
> (*cont'd*)

So, yes.

> KENDALL

You know my vote. No.

> SANDI

Yes—

> (*looks to her dad*)

And yes.

> DEWI

No.

> EWAN

Nay.

> STEWY

No.

On Roman. Dabbing his eye. How will he go?

ROMAN

Nope.

Kendall was a little tense.

KENDALL
(under his breath)

That's fucking right!

Maybe he puts his feet on the table and winks at Shiv.

She coughs.

FRANK

Shiv?

Shiv gets up. Beat. She has some water.

KENDALL

Er, Shiv?

Time slows. Is this – what is this? A tiny bump, a glass of water. Or the collapse of something substantial?

She heads out.

Shiv?

Kendall follows.

INT. WAYSTAR – OUTSIDE BOARDROOM – DAY

SHIV

I just need one second.

She walks over and heads towards a small meeting room, semi-obscured from the main one.

KENDALL

Are you okay. Are you scared? It's okay, Shiv, we have it. We have it – we look— We have it – we have it?

SHIV

I'm not scared.

She walks off—

INT. WAYSTAR – SMALL MEETING ROOM – DAY

Shiv heads into the small room. Kendall follows.

SHIV

Can I have a moment please.

Roman follows.

ROMAN

Shiv, are we good? What are you doing?

SHIV

I, um. Don't know. I want to think.

ROMAN

Well – can you do it fast?

KENDALL

Think about what? Whether you want us to keep the company or
hand it over to Tom and that piece of shit who killed our dad?

SHIV

I might have changed my mind.

*Tries to get it right between playing cards and adopting arguments,
seeing if there's room for movement and just letting it all flood out.*

KENDALL

What the fuck?

ROMAN

Shiv, I fucking jumped. I jumped.

The idea forms. And sticks. This feels better.

SHIV

I have changed my mind.

KENDALL

What?

SHIV

I can't stomach it.

ROMAN

Shiv, you can't fucking just—?

KENDALL

Why?

SHIV

I can't stomach it.

KENDALL

I'm good for this company, I'm good for this company. We all vote
we keep control . . . We don't then everything's over for, forever.

SHIV

Uh-huh. I have changed my mind.

KENDALL

Why?

SHIV

I can't stomach you.

He tries to keep control.

KENDALL

Is it trust. On your jobs? That's fucking easy, let's put it in
writing. Let's get a lawyer. Shiv, that's easy!

SHIV

I can't stomach it.

Swallows. Can he persuade her?

KENDALL

I am a cog built to fit one machine, Shiv. If you don't give me
this— It's the thing I know how to do.

SHIV

It's not all about you.

KENDALL

I know.

SHIV

You are not the most important one.

KENDALL

I don't think I am.

SHIV

Yes you do. You do you do you do.

KENDALL

But, Shiv, it's so fucking crazy not to just, let me. It's stupid. We
all get something here. You're voting against yourself.

> ROMAN
>
> Fucking let me swing, Shiv, c'mon, I jumped!

> KENDALL
>
> Shiv. I could do this now.

She looks at him. Maybe he could actually.

> SHIV
>
> I don't think you'd be good at it.

> KENDALL
>
> I don't believe you.

> SHIV
>
> I don't think you'd be good at it. I don't think you'd be good at it.

> KENDALL
>
> For – fuck's sake – I mean for fuck's sake, it doesn't make – logic.
>
> (*then*)
>
> I sometimes feel. If I don't get this I think I might die?

He looks to Roman, who just wants this all to be over.

> ROMAN
>
> Shiv, it's the fucking plan, I jumped.

> SHIV
>
> You can't be CEO. You killed someone.

> KENDALL
>
> Which?

> ROMAN
>
> 'Which?' Oh you killed so many kids you forgot which one?

He looks at them. He can't lose Roman too.

> KENDALL
>
> That's not an issue.

Roman looks at him. Kendall has to make a calculation. He jumps.

> That didn't happen.

> ROMAN
>
> As in?

> KENDALL
>
> That's just a thing I said.

They look at him.

It was a difficult time for us and, and I think I – mussed up something from nothing because I wanted for us all to bond at a difficult moment—

ROMAN

No.

KENDALL

There was a kid, but I had one toke and a beer and, not—

ROMAN

Bullshit.

KENDALL

I overthought it, I think. And I felt bad, and – I false-memoried it.

ROMAN

That was a move? Ken, c'mon?

KENDALL

You don't need to worry about that, nothing happened. That's not an issue.

ROMAN

No, man.

KENDALL

It doesn't matter. What's important is, I can say it didn't happen. I'm clean skin.

ROMAN

Did it happen or not?

KENDALL

It. Did. Not. Happen.

ROMAN

Fucking bullshit.

Frustration building—

KENDALL

Fucking . . . Vote for me. Vote for me!

SHIV

No.

> KENDALL

Yes!

> ROMAN

No.

> SHIV

I love you, but I cannot stomach you.

> KENDALL

This is fucking disgusting. It's disgusting. You're, this is— It's inhuman, it's fucking nuts, it doesn't make any sense.

Shiv shrugs. Infuriating.

I'm the eldest boy. I'm the eldest boy and you know – it mattered to him. He wanted something to go on.

> ROMAN

Well she's the bloodline?

> KENDALL

What?

> ROMAN

She is the bloodline.

> KENDALL

What? I'm the bloodline, we're all the fucking bloodline.

> ROMAN

No. If you're gonna play that card, Dad's view was, yours aren't real.

> KENDALL

What the fuck did you say?

> ROMAN

Not real-real.

> SHIV

Rome?

> ROMAN

I am just saying what Dad said.

> KENDALL

Well don't say it. You fucking – cuck.

Roman is stung and enunciates without a lot of emotion.

ROMAN
They are a pair of randos. One is a buy-in, and one is half Rava
and half some filing-cabinet guy.

SHIV
That's too much.

Kendall comes to Roman to hold his face.

Shiv gets up. To leave.

Kendall tries to stop her leaving.

SHIV
Hey!

KENDALL
No!

SHIV
Hey, get the *fuck off of me.*

ROMAN
Hey, Ken, no!

*A tussle. Shiv pushes Kendall, Kendall goes for Roman. Kendall tries
to stop Shiv again. She picks up something from the room, a lamp,
jug or piece of phone apparatus.*

*When he comes again she throws it and it hits the glass wall. Maybe
cracking it or just bouncing off.*

The board outside sees the tussle. Undignified. They look at one another.

Shiv emerges, disheveled.

Kendall composes to Roman—

KENDALL
Let's hit Frank. Let's offer Frank.

ROMAN
It's bullshit, man. It's fucking nothing.

KENDALL
No, there's something here. There's an angle.

> ROMAN
>
> It's fuck all. Bits of glue and broken shows, and phony news and fucking—
>
> KENDALL
>
> We can do this, man.
>
> ROMAN
>
> It's just nothing. It's nothing, it's fucking nothing.
>
> KENDALL
>
> Nah, man. Nah. I don't believe you.

A deep fear and estimation—

> ROMAN
>
> We're bullshit.

His almost true conviction, and sincere hope—

> KENDALL
>
> We are not bullshit.
>
> ROMAN
>
> You're bullshit, you're fucking bullshit, I'm fucking bullshit, she's fucking bullshit, it's all fucking nothing, I'm telling you because I know – it's fucking nothing, it's nothing, okay?

End of words.

Kendall is defeated.

INT. WAYSTAR – OUTSIDE BOARDROOM – DAY

Kendall walks out. He looks to the boardroom where people look out.

Maybe Shiv is in the boardroom registering her vote.

*He doesn't look or waves it away.**

INT. WAYSTAR – ELEVATOR BANK – DAY

Kendall walks out and around to the elevator bank.

* The additional action as filmed of Kendall going back to the boardroom all shell-shocked was worked out on the day.

He looks at a little embossed metal plate set into the wall – Waystar Royco.

Maybe a mid-level employee arrives from the other direction. Checks Kendall out. The CEO. The big man's son. Nods respectfully.

Kendall looks at him. Nods.

INT. WAYSTAR – OUTSIDE BOARDROOM – DAY

The Waystar GC comes out of the board meeting and tells the lawyers the board has approved the deal.

The lawyers agree to send each other their signature pages and that's the deal signed.

INT. WAYSTAR – BOARDROOM – DAY

Karl and Frank and Karolina and Hugo look at Tom glad-handing.

> FRANK
> The PowerPoint prevails. The odorless gas rises.

> KARL
> He got his dick in, and the rest of that dumb fucking lunk followed.

> FRANK
> So, what you thinking? Golden parachute?

> KARL
> Or one last rodeo? What you think?

> FRANK
> *(considering)*
> I'm thinking we shoulda slit his throat in the cradle.

INT. WAYSTAR – OUTSIDE BOARDROOM – DAY

With Tom. Hugo approaches.

> HUGO
> Hey, man. Great one. The losers never triumph! Always been hoping. Let's talk. I got you.

Tom looks at him. Nope. No sugar for Hugo.

> TOM

Where's Karolina?

Dagger to the heart, Hugo heads off to look.

As Tom catches Greg's eye. Lets him know, with the slightest of nods, he can come over.

Greg arrives, nervous after their last interaction.

> GREG

How – we looking?

> TOM
> (*looking around*)

Uh-huh.

Gerri is arriving with a pair of assistants, looking regal.

> GREG

Plans? Planning?

> TOM

I wanna talk to Gerri.

Greg looks at him.

Yeah. Gerri gets it.

> GREG

Okay. And who else?

Tom looks into the boardroom.

> TOM

Frank dead. Karl dead. I don't need those old cunts on my shoulder.

Greg coughs: And me?

You? You fucked it, Quad Man. Matsson hates you. Wants a clean-out.

> GREG

Uh-huh. Uh-huh. Fuck.

Tom has something in his pocket.

> TOM

You piece of fucking shit.

(*peels off a sticker*)
I got you. I got *just* enough capital.

He places one of his stickers on Greg's forehead.

I got you.

Frank and Karl make it out to shake hands. As Greg goes to Gerri—

FRANK
Thomas! Congratulations. Hearty congratulations.

KARL
Hey, you! Look at you! Hey, big man.

TOM
Hey here we go! My guys, my fucking guys! My rocks!

They hug. Tom inhabits his new role lightly. Breaks off to see Gerri.

GERRI
I'm very grateful for the offer and I'm intrigued. Obviously I'll have a few rather outrageous demands?

TOM
Naturally, Gerri!

INT. WAYSTAR – BIG MEETING ROOM – DAY*

Tom and Matsson do a signing for a corporate photographer.

Roman is there to sign for the other side. Hugo, Karolina, Frank, Karl, Oskar and Ebba watch.

Shiv watches. Through glass.

Quite frozen.

Afterwards, Tom smiles and comes and asks something. She assents. No enthusiasm. The end. But it would be rude not to let the victor close the game out.

---

* The material in the signing room was a collaboration on the day. Kieran really didn't feel Roman would go into the big room to sign, so we used that to work up with him and Fisher a piece at the door. This was the last beat of New York filming on the show and everyone had an extra bit to suggest, cast, director and writers – and every extra bit we did felt great. I don't think any of us of us wanted it to end.

INT. BAR — DAY

Roman arrives.

> ROMAN
>
> Hey hey hey, whatup, motherfucker.

> BARMAN
> *(re his face)*
>
> Are you okay?

> ROMAN
>
> This? Oh yeah. You should see the other guy.
> *(then)*
> Very hot. I paid him to beat me up. Then I had him shot. That's
> my thing.

He looks at the barman.

> Can I get a Martini Big Gulp with an olive the size of a severed
> testicle please?

*We stay on his face for a while. And as he looks at the barman, the
room, he scans himself. Maybe he's okay? Maybe he's numb. But
maybe that's okay?*

INT. WAYSTAR — UNDERGROUND CAR PARK — DAY

Tom is there glad-handing with Karolina, Frank, Karl.

Greg is there, a little way behind.

INT. CAR — DAY

Shiv waits.

Eventually, in his own time. Tom gets in. Chilly.

> TOM
>
> Hey.

> SHIV
>
> Hey. Congratulations.

> TOM
>
> Oh no. No. No.

On the central console he offers an upturned hand. Not eager but available. A little regal.

Shiv puts her dry hand on his – no squeeze. Just contact.

Something steel here. An accommodation, equilibrium, that could last with a certain stability, proxy wars and détentes, for many years to come . . . nothing needy from either side. A queen and a prince. Two bombs being transported with great care.

EXT. BATTERY PARK – DAY

Kendall walks for a while and we might be close on his face.

He breathes. The park. The water there around, the water.

But maybe he lives his life now, a little liberated?

Then, maybe he walks past us – leaves the frame.

And we see with him, a few paces back, the shape of Colin following him.

Maybe we see it from high. A man followed forever by family, protection, insulation, his particular and general history.

APPENDIX

Logan's Dinner

INT. LOGAN'S APARTMENT – NIGHT

It's after dinner a few months back. Logan, Kerry, Frank, Karl, Gerri, Connor and Willa are a few glasses of wine in. Captured on iPhone.

Willa is filming.

> LOGAN
>
> Film it! Are you – sing it, Karl. Con – film him, film this.

> CONNOR
>
> Willa's filming, Pop—

> WILLA
> *(off)*
>
> I'm doing it.

> KARL
>
> You go Loge, the pipes need priming. You go.

> GERRI
>
> Do the losers list. Losers.

Logan considers, thinks. Then—

> LOGAN
>
> . . . Gore, Dole, Bush, Mike D.,
> Mondale, Carter, A. Ford not a Lincoln for me,
> Hippy George, Humphrey, St Barry, Dick the Bad, Stephenson,
> Dewey so saddy,
> Wilkie, Landon, Hoover, Al Smith of the Vatican,
> Davis, Cox, Hughes, Taft, Bryan try that again,
> Parker, Bryan once more, Harrison, Cleveland, Blaine, Hancock,
> and more,
> Tilden, Greeley, Seymour,
> George B. McClellan, in the union's blue,
> Stephen A. Douglas he lost too. Fremont, Scott, Cass and Clay,
> heroes of their day but all went away,
> Martin Van Buren, White, and Old Tippecanoe,

Clay, hey JQA, how many elections you lose today?
Clay, Crawford, Jackson, King, Clinton, the first but not the worst,
Pinckney twice,
Adams, Jefferson, all very nice!

Cheers.

KARL

Gerri? Party piece?

GERRI

My party piece has been keeping you out of jail for twenty
years.

KARL

Do your Sandy. Do your Sandy face?

Gerri, reluctantly.

LOGAN

Not very nice, Gerri, not very nice. Do the – do the limerick!

GERRI

'Far dearer to me than my treasure,'
The heiress declared, 'is my leisure.
For then I can screw,
The whole Harvard crew—
They're slow, but that lengthens the pleasure.'

Laughs.

There was a young girl named Anheuser
Who said that no man could surprise her.
But Pabst took a chance,
Found Schlitz in her pants,
And now she is sadder Budweiser!

Laughs.

Frank, do – do Karl's retirement speech!

Frank considers.

FRANK

What can I say about my dear Karl, retiring shortly. Graduating
from St Dumpster State College he went on to study biology,
or at least venereal diseases, during eight years in the US Navy

where many commanding officers learned that in a crisis Karl
Muller could always be depended upon – to crap his pants
and hide in his bunk. After the Navy he entered the world of
business and quickly earned himself a reputation for being both
a tough negotiator and extremely overpaid. But he never became
pompous or self-satisfied – he was just always like that. He
will be much missed, but leaves behind a set of expense claims
which will be remembered amongst the great works of American
fiction.

Laughs.

> GERRI

Kerry. Do the kids. Have you seen her do the kids? Do—

*Kerry prepares and does some quick impressions, maybe stands and
copies some key gestures.*

> KERRY

I'm Kenny, ever so slick—
And I'm Roman, concerned with my dick,
And I'm Shivvy, married to a hick!

Laughs. But maybe Logan doesn't love seeing Kerry mock the kids.

> LOGAN

Connor?

> CONNOR

I give you, ladies and gentlemen. 'I Am a Little Teapot', in the
manner of, Mr Logan Roy. Ahem!
> (*then*)
I'm a little teapot. (Fuck off!)
Short and stout. (What did you fucking call me?)
Here's my handle.
Here's my fucking spout.
When I get all steamed up, here me shout—
> (*then*)
Frank Vernon is a moron and Karl Muller is a Kraut!

Laughs.

Willa!?

WILLA
(*off; I can*)

Oh no I can't. I can't.

She hands the phone over to Connor. Quite eager to perform.

CONNOR

She has a number of Shakespearean insults and—

WILLA

'You scullion! You rampallian! You fustilarian! I'll tickle your catastrophe!' 'You Banbury cheese!' 'Thou whoreson zed, thou unnecessary letter!'

Not Logan's favorite—

LOGAN

Great stuff. Very good.
(*then, kidding*)
Say, is there a game on?

Chuckles.

WILLA

'I shall comb your noddle with a three-legged stool!'

LOGAN

Karl. Come on. Sing it.
(*then*)
Film him. I want a copy of this. I'd like to have it with me always—
(*then*)
in case I go fucking rat-catching. Go on. Karl! Sing it!

Karl prepares—

KARL

(*sings*)
There's nought but care on ev'ry han',
In every hour that passes,
O What signifies the life o' man,
An' 'twere na for the lasses, O.

Logan is affected. Maybe he holds Kerry's hand.

To cover the emotion—

LOGAN

You're fucking murdering it, man.

KARL

Green grow the rashes,
O Green grow the rashes, O
The sweetest hours that e'er I spend,
Are spent among the lasses, O.

Maybe over him a little, or at the end of phrases—

LOGAN

Kerry! Listen, he's murdering it. He's killing it!

KARL

The warl'y race may riches chase,
An' riches still may fly them, O
An' tho' at last they catch them fast,
Their hearts can ne'er enjoy them, O.

Maybe here or earlier, some or all of them join in a bit.

ALL

Green grow the rashes, O
Green grow the rashes, O
The sweetest hours that e'er I spend,
Are spent among the lasses, O.

Acknowledgements

The story of the show is one of a series of very fortunate collaborations. I can't list them all, but some key thanks I owe include:

Frank Rich – my friend and fellow executive producer, frequent first reader, who originally championed my work at HBO and got me to meet Richard Plepler who was so encouraging of my working there. Meanwhile, Kevin Messick, with a keen eye for a script and a sharp edit, first commissioned me to write about US politics and opened up the path to a relationship with Adam McKay.

These relationships came together for the pilot which Adam shot, and through which he has had such a wide and long-lasting influence on the show – bringing in all the excellent pilot heads of departments – and leading us, in conjunction with the brilliant Francine Maisler, to much of the main cast. Adam has carried on being the most generous executive producer, supporting me in becoming a showrunner when I didn't even really know what one was.

The unbelievably talented and collaborative cast, including: Brian, Hiam, Jeremy, Peter, Rob, Nick, Kieran, Sarah, Matthew, Alan, Scott, Natalie, Swayam & Quentin, Juliana, JSC, David, Dag, Justine, Arian, Ash, Larry, Zack, James, Eric, Caitlin, Harriet, Danny, Jeannie, Patch, Holly, Cherry, Annabelle, Fisher, Zoë, Jihae, Dasha, Sanaa, Hope, Justin, Alexander, Pip. Neither I nor my fellow writers could or would have written what we did without knowing that they would be receptive. Their notes and thoughts and comments, not to say improvisations and freestylings, have enriched the show at every turn.

Adam McKay also brought Nicholas Britell, genius musician and composer, to the *Succession* party. Even if the show is decent, people think it is 58% better than it is because of the brilliance and depth of the work of Nick and his colleagues, Todd Kasow and John Finklea.

Simon Chin encouraged me to write something about Rupert Murdoch. Leanne Klein at Wall to Wall offered unstinting enthusiasm even when it became time to stint. Liza Marshall at Channel 4 was supportive, but we could just never make it happen. Gregory McKnight was the first person who suggested there was perhaps something in a fictional media-family show. He and my UK agent Cathy King and US TV agent Dan Erlij have supported me throughout.

Mark Mylod – the time we've spent! The care he takes! The way he marshals a set! To have seventeen things going on, to be thinking about twenty others, and then, when I appear at his shoulder with my little clutch of thoughts and adjustments, to meet each one – not without ego or a proprietorial pride, but to feel those things and ride them and still listen and adjust.

His fellow directors – Andrij Parekh, Bob Pulcini & Shari Springer Berman, Lorene Scafaria, Adam Arkin, Becky Martin, Kevin Bray, Miguel Arteta, S. J. Clarkson, Matt Shakman, Cathy Yan.

Lisa Molinaro and Holly Unterberger – constant monitor companions and friends and creative advisors. Sharp eyes, warm hearts.

Amy Lauritsen, Christo Morse, John Silvestri, Michelle Flevotomas – assistant directors who kept the train running and the mood up. And coped with changes, late and big beyond the call of duty, with barely a flinch.

Most of the writers who've worked on the show are recorded herein on episode titles: Tony Roche, Jon Brown, Lucy Prebble, Will Tracy, Georgia Pritchett, Susan Soon He Stanton, Ted Cohen, Will Arbery, Mary Laws, Anna Jordan, Jonathan Glatzer. But not all of them. My friend Simon Blackwell had just enough time to write 'alts' for the pilot before disappearing to meatier things. We also got to work in the room with Alice Birch, Miriam Battye, Francesca Gardiner, Cord Jefferson, Lucy Kirkwood, Gary Shteyngart. All brilliant. All good things sprang from the rooms where we all sat together and plotted and laughed.

Tony and Lucy, Jon and Will Tracy I've leant on most heavily to help me write – and to rewrite – when we had an episode that wasn't firing. And Tony and Lucy were most often at hand through the long months of the shoots as good companions and stout hearts. I've leant on them for creative wisdom and valued their kindness and friendship.

Beth Gorman, Ed Cripps, Jamie Carragher, Siobhan James-Elliott kept the notes in our UK rooms. Jamie for the longest stretch. He stayed up many a night transcribing and ordering and filtering, and still found time to chime in and add a thought or a historical or literary reference that left the rest of us agog at his breadth of knowledge.

Callie Hersheway Love, who I met on *Veep* and has been a constant help, guide, aide, friend and protector of my time and concentration, and has been intimately across every nook and cranny of these scripts, lately with the help of Terry McGrath. Also, Nate Elston who at first I thought I didn't need but soon discovered I was unable to function without, it's been the greatest pleasure to have his company and friendship. Ali Reilly and Danny Klain are also amongst the best of the best.

At HBO: Casey Bloys to whom I first pitched the show, Frannie Orsi, Nora Skinner and Max Hollman, Sally Harvey. HBO could not have been a happier or more supportive home, and they are brilliant and subtle executives whose guidance and support has been steadfast and sustaining.

Jane Tranter, who guided me through the US system and reassured my American partners that we were in the writers' room, not in the pub. Ilene Landress, who produced the pilot, and Jonathan Filley, the first season, and Scott Ferguson – indefatigable producer who got us on to yachts and into nations at short notice and kept the show on the road, with Gabrielle Mahon, when we could have come off the rails.

Our DPs – Pat Capone, who once made me cry with his call to arms amidst the myriad problems of shooting through Covid, Andrij, Chris, Kate. And the camera operators – who dance with the actors, Gregor and Ethan. They are the silent scene partners and need emotional intelligence that matches their iron grip and falcon's eye.

Stephen Carter, head of an art department of obsessive attention to detail matched only by his flexibility and good humour. Also my friends George DeTitta Jr., Katrina Whalen, Ben Relf, Andre Azevedo, Monica Jacobs, Alley O'Shea.

Ken Ishii, Pete and Ethan, Billy Sarokin, Andy Kris, Nicholas Renbeck – for keeping us sounding good against the odds. To catch on the fly every beat and every late-added line and improvisation clean enough to use. Extraordinary.

Merissa Marr has been my guide through the business moves from the first season and guided us towards some excellent areas and away from corporate faux pas. Brilliant on technical detail but also attuned to what we might need and what might work. Likewise Jon Klein on media. Jesse Eisinger and Matt Friedrich on legal matters. Tracey Pruzan and Derek Blasberg on society and New York. Faisal A. Quereshi on oddities, curios, cultural updates and sex parties. Eric Schultz and Ben Ginsberg on politics, and Justin Geldzahler on everything all together all at once. All invaluable.

Doug Aibel and Henry Russell Bergstein, and Avy Kaufman, who helped find and land so many remarkable acting talents.

Angel DeAngelis, Nuria Sitja, Michelle Johnson, Patricia Regan, kind, talented and warm bosses of hair and make-up.

Michelle Matland, Jon Schwartz, Midge and Danny. Costume department of dedication and flair and good humour and hard work.

Paul Eskenazi, who has helped us into and out of our many and ever-evolving list of locations.

Ken Eluto, Jane Rizzo, Bill Henry, Anne McCabe, Brian Kates, Ellen Tam and Venya Bruk – editors of subtlety and wisdom. Who made a thousand good choices before we ever started on the ones we got to worry over together. Dara Schnapper who, with Val, James and Genevieve, presided over post-production with such attention to detail and allowed me such room for manoeuvre.

To Alex Bowler at Faber & Faber who was generous enough to think it was worth starting this scriptbook ball rolling, and his colleague Steve King who has edited this volume with care and sensitivity under a ticking clock, and Jodi Gray for setting it with precision.

To the folks at HBO responsible for enabling this book to come together: Michele Caruso, Tara Bonner, Stacey Abiraj, Arielle Mauge and Andrew Kelley.

And to my support network. Sam Bain, my kind and thoughtful compadre, with or from whom I've learnt everything I know about writing film and TV.

To Pat Halpin and Phillip Rossini. For getting me in and out and putting me up.

To everyone at First Touch FC, especially Mikey, Keith, Euan, Case and John C. for keeping me roughly in shape and pretty much sane. Likewise Chelsey Kapuscinski.

To Ju, Jas, Rob, Mark, Will, Andy & Andy Yates. Rock-solid old pals.

Chris (with whom some of the thoughts about satire in the introduction to this fourth volume were discussed (i.e. he said them and I basically wrote them down)), Jo and all the family and friends who sustained my most important people while I was often absent.

And my family. I don't think I had any idea going into this how consuming it would be and how much it would take me away. The pandemic was particularly tough. I couldn't and wouldn't have done it without your love and support. M, A&A, I love you. My mum and dad and sister and her family, too. Thank you.

Jesse Armstrong